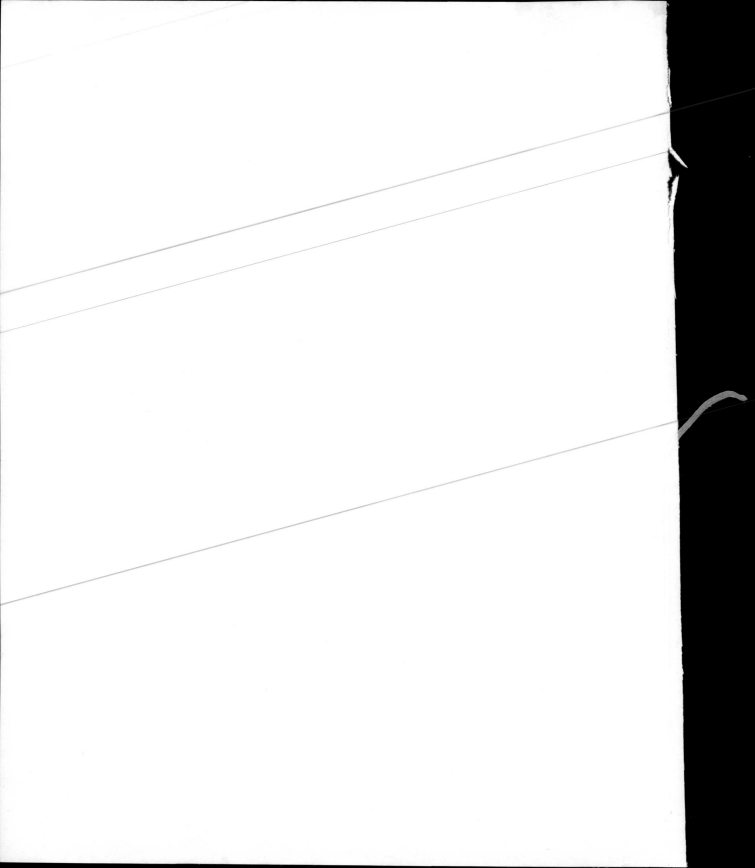

THE RATIONAL BIBLE: GENESIS

THE RATIONAL BIBLE

GENESIS
God, Creation, and Destruction

DENNIS PRAGER

EDITED BY JOSEPH TELUSHKIN

THE ALPERSON EDITION

REGNERY
FAITH

Regnery Faith™ is a trademark of Salem Communications Holding Corporation Regnery® is a registered trademark and its colophon is a trademark of Salem Communications Holding Corporation

All Scripture taken from New JPS Translation, Jewish Publication Society. Philadelphia, PA 1985. Used by permission.

Cataloging-in-Publication data on file with the Library of Congress

ISBN 978-1-62157-898-7
ebook ISBN 978-1-62157-899-4

Published in the United States by
Regnery Faith, an Imprint of
Regnery Publishing
A Division of Salem Media Group
Washington, D.C.
www.Regnery.com

Printed in Italy

10 9 8 7 6 5 4 3

Books are available in quantity for promotional or premium use. For information on discounts and terms, please visit our website: www.Regnery.com.

CONTENTS

To Sue

"It is not good for a man to be alone.
I will make him a helper who is his equal."
—*Genesis 2:18 (literal translation)*

INTRODUCTION

To the reader: This introduction will greatly enhance your understanding and enjoyment of this commentary.

GENESIS IS THE FIRST BOOK OF THE BIBLE. THIS COMMENTARY ON GENESIS, however, is the second volume of my five-volume commentary on the first five books of the Bible (the Torah).

The beginning of Genesis is probably the best-known story in world history, containing, as it does, God's creation of the world, Adam and Eve and the Garden of Eden, Cain and Abel, the Flood and Noah's ark. What is not well-known is how this story changed the world. The first verse, "In the beginning God created the heavens and the Earth," alone changed the world. As I explain, this verse asserted for the first time in history that that there is one God; that this God is universal (as opposed to tribal); and that God is not within nature but is its sole creator—unlike every other god in history.

Genesis also contains the story of the beginning of the Hebrews, the Israelites—the Jews, as they later became known—the people who, through the Hebrew Bible, most influenced the world. From the first Hebrew, Abraham, we are taught that arguing with God is not only acceptable, it is expected. The very name of this people, "Israel," means "struggle with God."

Genesis is filled with human drama that touches and helps every one of us on a personal level. For example, every family in Genesis is what we today would call dysfunctional. I regard this as a divine gift. If your family is dysfunctional, the fact that all the families in Genesis are dysfunctional should provide you with some solace. I think the Bible is telling us that family dysfunction is a normal—though not necessarily inevitable—part of the human condition. Indeed, all of Genesis is a statement of how troubled the human condition is. The rest of the Bible, especially the next four books, provides solutions to the troubled human condition. To put it in medical terms, Genesis describes the patient's (the human being's) pathology, and the books that follow offer the wisdom and moral instruction necessary to cure the patient.

Some of the following appeared in the Introduction to Exodus:

WHY THIS COMMENTARY?

I have been teaching the Torah all of my adult life and have devoted decades to writing this explanation of, and commentary on, the Torah. I have done so because I believe if people properly understand the Torah and attempt to live by its values and precepts, the world will be an infinitely kinder and more just place.

Since childhood, I have been preoccupied—almost obsessed—with the problem of evil: people deliberately hurting other people. At the age of sixteen, I wrote in my diary that I wanted to devote my life "to influencing people to the good." That mission has animated my life. In a nutshell, I love goodness and hate evil. My favorite verse in the Bible is "Those of you who love God— hate evil" (Psalms 97:10).

Because of my (and the Torah's) preoccupation with evil, in this commentary I frequently cite the two most recent examples of mass evil—Nazism and Communism. I assume all readers of this commentary have some acquaintance with Nazi evil. Too few people have much knowledge of Communist evil. So I should note here that Communist regimes murdered about a hundred million people and enslaved and destroyed the lives of more than a billion. If you hate evil, you must confront what Nazis and Communists wrought in the twentieth century (and what others wrought before them and are doing at this time).

I have had one other mission in life: to understand human beings as best as possible. These two missions—promoting goodness and attaining wisdom—

are linked, because it is impossible to do good without wisdom. All the good intentions in the world are likely to be worthless without wisdom. Many of the horrors of the twentieth century were supported by people with good intentions who lacked wisdom.

Here, too, because it has so much wisdom, the Torah—and the rest of the Bible—is indispensable. However, we live in an age that not only has little wisdom, it doesn't even have many people who value it. People greatly value knowledge and intelligence, but not wisdom. And the lack of wisdom—certainly in America and the rest of the West—is directly related to the decline in biblical literacy. In the American past, virtually every home, no matter how poor, owned a Bible. It was the primary vehicle by which parents passed wisdom on to their children.

In the modern period, however, people have increasingly replaced Bible-based homes and Bible-based schools with godless homes and with schools in which no reference to the Bible is ever made. As a result, we are less wise and more morally confused. As I showed in Exodus, in my discussion of secular education as a potential "false god," the best educated people in the West have often both lacked wisdom and been among the greatest supporters of evil ideologies and regimes.

Given the supreme importance of goodness and the indispensability of wisdom to goodness, the Torah, the greatest repository of goodness and wisdom in human history, is the most important book ever written. It gave birth to the rest of the Bible, to Christianity, and to Western civilization. It gave us "Love your neighbor as yourself," the Ten Commandments, a just and loving God, and other bedrocks of humane civilization.

WHO IS THIS TORAH COMMENTARY FOR?

I have written this book for people of every faith, and for people of no faith. Throughout my years teaching the Torah, I would tell my students, "The Torah either has something to say to everyone or it has nothing to say to Jews." The idea that the Torah is only for Jews is as absurd as the idea that Shakespeare is only for the English or Beethoven is only for Germans.

That is why, over time, half the people taking my Torah classes—at a Jewish university, no less—were not Jews.

Nevertheless, I would like to address some groups specifically.

To Jewish Readers:

Because the Torah has formed the basis of Jewish life for three thousand years, there are very many Jewish commentaries, a good number of which have passed the hardest test: the test of time. However, the modern world poses intellectual and moral challenges that did not exist when the classic Jewish commentaries—most dating to the Middle Ages—were written. Therefore, most modern Jews read neither those commentaries nor the Torah. I hope this commentary will address nearly all the intellectual and moral objections of these Jews.

In general, it has not gone well for Jews (or for the world) when Jews ceased believing in the Torah. Belief in the Torah as a divine document has probably been the single most important reason Jews have stayed alive for three thousand years and it has formed the core of Jews' moral values. When Jews abandoned belief in the Torah, they or their offspring almost always ceased being Jews; and, too often, they created or joined social movements with non-Torah, or even anti-Torah, values.

To Jews who already believe in the Torah as a divine document: I hope this commentary gives you *chizuk* (strengthened faith). And I hope it encourages you to go into the world to teach Torah-based values. To all other Jews, I hope this commentary leads you to an intellectual appreciation of the Torah's unique greatness and consequently causes you to at least entertain the possibility that God is its ultimate author.

To Christian Readers:

One cannot be a serious Christian without being familiar with the Hebrew Bible (or Old Testament, as the Christian world named it). Nor can one understand Jesus, a Jew who was not only observant of Torah law, but asserted he came to change not "one jot or one tittle" of it.

For the many Christians who already believe the Torah embodies the word of God, I hope this commentary strengthens your faith in the Torah. As Maimonides, widely considered the greatest Jewish philosopher, wrote nine hundred years ago, his differences with Christian theology notwithstanding, it is Christians who have been primarily responsible for disseminating knowledge of the Torah to so much of the world.

I should also add I have greatly benefitted from reading Christian Bible scholars. In this volume, I frequently cite Victor Hamilton (1941-), Professor of Old Testament and Theology at Asbury University from 1971 to 2007. Hamilton's masterful two-volume commentary on Genesis enormously contributed to my understanding of this great book of the Bible.

At the same time, the Bible scholar who most influenced my understanding of Genesis and Exodus was a Jew, the late Professor Nahum Sarna (1923-2005), Professor of Biblical Studies at Brandeis University from 1967 to 1985. His Jewish Publication Society commentaries on Genesis and Exodus are extraordinary.

To Non-Religious Readers:

I have had you most in mind when writing this commentary. With every passing generation in the West, fewer and fewer people believe in God, let alone in the Bible. This is a catastrophe for the West, and it is a tragedy for you. Having God, religion, a religious community, and a sacred text in one's life enables one to have a far deeper and happier—not to mention wiser—life. If you keep an open mind when reading this commentary, that life will, hopefully, become appealing to you.

To readers outside of the West, the Torah has as much to say to you as to anyone in the West. Just as Beethoven has as much to say to a Japanese as to a German, and Shakespeare has as much to say to an Argentinian as to an Englishman, the Torah as much to say a non-Jew and a non-Christian as to a Jew or a Christian.

I look forward to your reactions. They will surely influence my writing of subsequent volumes.

In writing this commentary, I have no hidden agenda. My agenda is completely open: I want as many people as possible to take the Torah seriously, to entertain the possibility it is God-given, or, at the very least, to understand why many rational people do.

Nor do I have a parochial agenda. I am a believing Jew, but neither God, nor the Torah, nor later Judaism ever obligated Jews to make non-Jews Jewish. Jews have always welcomed—and until prohibited (when the Roman Empire adopted Christianity) from doing so, even sought—converts; but what God and the Torah obligate Jews to do is to bring humanity to the God of the Torah, to His basic moral rules, and to the Torah's values and insights. People can and have lived according to the Torah's moral values as members of other faiths (most obviously Christians), or simply as non-denominational believers in God ("ethical monotheists"—such as the American Founding Father Benjamin Franklin).

THE TORAH IS NOT MAN-MADE

For reasons I develop throughout the commentary, I am convinced the Torah is divine, meaning God, not man, is its ultimate source. The Torah is so utterly different—morally, theologically, and in terms of wisdom—from anything else preceding it and, for that matter, from anything written since—that a reasonable person would have to conclude either moral supermen or God was responsible for it.

To cite just a few examples of what the Torah introduced to the world:

- A universal God (the God of all people): This began the long road to human beings believing that with one "Father in Heaven," all human beings are brothers and sisters.
- An invisible, incorporeal God: Therefore, the physical is not the only reality. Life is infinitely more than the material world in which we live during our brief lifetime on earth.

- A moral God: All gods prior to Torah's God were capricious, not moral. A just and moral God meant, among other things, ultimately justice will prevail (if not in this life, in the next). It also meant human beings, imbued with a sense of justice, can argue with, and question, this just God (the name "Israel" means "wrestle—or struggle—with God.")

- A God beyond nature: God made nature, and is therefore not natural. This led to the end of the universal human belief in nature-gods (such as rain-gods). And sure enough, as belief in the Torah's God declines, nature-worship seems to be returning.

- A God who loves and who wants to be loved: This was another world-changing concept introduced by the Torah to the world.

- Universal human worth: Every human being is "created in God's image." Nothing like this had ever been posited prior to the Torah.

- Universal human rights: Another world-altering consequence of universal human worth.

I do not believe some people made all of that up. In the words of a contemporary Jewish thinker, Rabbi Saul Berman: "The more I study the Torah, the more I am convinced that it is the revealed word of God. The more I study ancient cultures, the more I see the absolutely radical disparity between the values of pagan civilizations and the values which Torah brought into the world. Torah was God's weapon in the war against idolatrous culture; and war it was."

I would only add that the Torah's battle, and sometimes war, with many of the dominant ideas of our time is as great as it was with the cultures of three millennia ago, when the Torah came into the world.

The other major reason I am convinced the Torah is not man-made is it so often depicts the people of the Book, the Jews ("Israelites," "Hebrews") in a negative light. Had Jews made up what is, after all, their book and their story, they would never have portrayed themselves as critically and even negatively as the Torah (and the rest of the Hebrew Bible) often does. There is no parallel to this in any ancient national, or any religious, literature in the world.

MAN-MADE OR GOD-MADE: WHY IT MATTERS

What difference does it make if the Torah is man-made or God-made? I can best answer this question by recounting a personal experience.

Most people, especially in their younger years, pass through a difficult time with one or both of their parents. In my teen years and twenties, I was one of them. But no matter how I felt, there was never a time I did not honor my parents. For example, from the age of twenty-one, when I left my parents' home, I called my parents every week of their lives.

I treated my parents with such respect because I have always believed God commanded me to do so: "Honor your father and mother" (The Fifth of the Ten Commandments). The Torah—as the first five books of the Bible have always been known in Hebrew—commands us to love our neighbor, to love God, and to love the stranger; but we are never commanded to love our parents. We are commanded to honor them (and we are not commanded to honor anyone else).

There is no comparison between "God commanded" and "Moses (or anyone else) commanded." If I believed the Ten Commandments were written by men, I would not have honored my parents as much as I did during periods of emotional ambivalence. Those who believe God is the source of the Torah's commandments are far more likely to obey them than those who believe they are all man-made.

A second difference is that only because I believe the Torah is God-made have I worked to understand and explain difficult passages of the Torah. If you believe the Torah is man-made, when you encounter a morally or intellectually problematic verse or passage, you have an easy explanation: Men wrote it. (Ancient men, at that.) And you are then free to dismiss it. But those of us who believe God is the source of the Torah don't have that option. We need to try to understand the verse or passage morally and intellectually.

Let me offer one of many examples. There is a Torah law that says if you have a particularly bad—a "wayward"—son, you may take him to the elders (the court) of your city; and if they find him guilty, they are to stone him to death. When modern men and women read that, they dismiss it as morally primitive: "What do you expect from something people wrote three thousand years ago?"

But since I don't believe it is "something people wrote," I don't have that option. Consequently, I have had to look for rational explanations for seemingly irrational laws and passages and for moral explanations for seemingly immoral laws and passages.

And I have almost always found them. In this case, for example, I came to understand this law was one of the great moral leaps forward in the history of mankind. In this law, the Torah brilliantly preserved parental authority while permanently depriving parents of the right to kill their child, a commonplace occurrence in the ancient world and even today (such as "honor killings" in parts of the Muslim world). The law permits only a duly established court ("the elders")—not parents—to take the life of their child. And we have no record of a Jewish court executing a "wayward" son.

My belief in the divinity of the Torah led me to seek a moral explanation of what appears to us to be an immoral law and, solely because of that belief, I found one. This has happened repeatedly regarding seemingly immoral or irrational laws, verses, and passages.

A third difference is only those who believe in the text as God-given will continue to live by it, carefully study it, and try to impart its wisdom generation after generation. There will always be a few individuals who believe the Torah is man-made who will nevertheless diligently study it. But it is doubtful their grandchildren will. If Jews long ago believed the Torah was man-made, there would be no Jews today.

I would go further: If you believe in God, but you don't believe in any divinely revealed text, how do you know what your God wants of you? How do you know what God wants of humanity? Of course, you or your society can make up laws and values, including some good ones the Torah would approve of. But if God told us nothing, we become our own gods when it comes to determining moral values.

HOW WAS THE TORAH TRANSMITTED?

I take no position on how God revealed the Torah. What concerns me most is *who* authored the Torah. That is infinitely more important than *how* it was written.

REASON, TORAH, AND GOD

The title of this commentary is "The Rational Bible." There are two reasons for this.

First, my approach to understanding and explaining the Torah is reason-based. I never ask the reader to accept anything I write on faith alone. If something I write does not make rational sense, I have not done my job. On those few—thankfully, very few—occasions I do not have a rational explanation for a Torah verse, I say so.

Second, reason has always been my primary vehicle to God and to religion. My beliefs—in God, the revelation at Sinai, the Torah, etc.—are not rooted in faith alone. *We Have Reason to Believe*, the title of a book written in 1958 by the British Jewish theologian Louis Jacobs, had a deep impact on me.

The title has an important double meaning. The obvious one is there are reasons to have religious faith. The less obvious meaning of the title is the one I cherish: we human beings have the faculty of reason—and are to use it *in order* to believe.

Of course, there is a faith component to my religious life. The primary example is the foundation of this commentary—my belief in the Torah as a divine document. While reason has led me to this belief, I acknowledge there are a few verses or passages that challenge this belief. Whenever I encounter such passages, however, I am not prepared to say, "'Love the stranger' is divine, but this difficult part is man-made." Once one says that, the Torah not only ceases to be divine, it ceases to be authoritative. When you say, "this part is divine, but that one isn't," you become your own Torah. As I put it in a number of public dialogues with a secular Jewish scholar, Professor Alan Dershowitz of Harvard Law School:

"I think I can sum up our basic difference this way: When Professor Dershowitz differs with the Torah, he thinks the Torah is wrong and he is right. When I differ with the Torah, I think the Torah is right and I am wrong." Professor Dershowitz agreed with that summation.

My approach is to abandon neither faith nor reason. I neither abandon the claim of reason because of the dictates of faith, nor abandon the faith claim because of reason. In the Torah, faith and reason nearly always live together in harmony, but when they do not, I do not deny either.

Moreover, there is a faith component to everyone's, including the atheist's, life. Any atheist who believes good and evil really exist, or that life has a purpose beyond one he or she has made up, or that free will exists, or, for that matter, that science alone will explain how the universe came about, or how life arose from non-life, or how intelligence arose from non-intelligence, has taken a leap of faith.

WHY READ THIS COMMENTARY?

Why should people devote time to reading my explanation of the Torah?

Here is my answer: I have devoted more than fifty years to studying and teaching the Torah. That includes a life-long immersion in Torah Hebrew—both its grammar and its vocabulary. I could not have written this commentary without this extensive knowledge of Hebrew. But most importantly, I have sought to make the Torah completely relevant to my life and to the lives of others.

In my case, "others" means millions of others. Every good teacher learns from his or her students, and I am no exception. But I have been blessed to have something very rare among teachers or scholars: millions of "students"—of almost every nationality, ethnicity, religion, and philosophy.

For over three decades, I have been a radio talk show host, broadcasting for more than half of that time on radio stations throughout America and on the internet internationally. This has enabled me to discuss virtually every subject imaginable with a very large number of people—live on the radio and through tens of thousands of emails. It also has enabled me to dialogue about religious matters with many of the leading theologians and scholars—especially Jewish and Christian—of my time; and to debate many contemporary leading atheists. I have been able to bounce ideas off, and learn from, lay people and scholars of every background.

Given this uncommon, if not unique, background, I decided, after much soul-searching, to write this commentary from the first-person perspective where appropriate. I became convinced that showing how the Torah's ideas and values have played themselves out in one individual's life makes the commentary more interesting, more real, and more relevant.

Shortly before finishing the first volume (Exodus), I had the great honor of being invited to speak about my Torah commentary to the Bible faculty and students of Israel's religious university, Bar-Ilan University. They did not invite me because they thought I know more than, or even as much as, any one of them does about the Torah. They invited me because they believed I bring a fresh understanding of the Torah. That is why I wrote this commentary.

A FEW DETAILS

Why Exodus Was Volume 1

The primary reason I began my commentary with the second book of the Torah, Exodus, and not the first, Genesis, is Exodus contains the Ten Commandments, the most important moral code in world history, and the central moral code of the Torah. If people lived by those ten laws alone, the world would be almost devoid of man-made suffering.

In addition, Genesis is almost all narrative, while Exodus is, in equal parts, narrative, laws, and theology.

BC or BCE?

Some readers will wonder why I use the letters "BCE" rather than the more familiar "BC" in dates. I struggled with this issue because I have no problem with "BC." But virtually all academic works and many general works now use "BCE." BCE stands for "Before the Common Era," but any reader who prefers to read the letters as "Before the Christian Era," is certainly welcome to—that is, after all, what "Common Era" denotes.

God as "He"

I refer to God as "He" because that is how the Torah refers to God. I explain why the Torah does so in an essay in chapter 1 of Genesis.

On How to Read This Commentary

The reader can benefit from reading this commentary in any way he or she desires. It can, of course, be read straight through, or be used as a reference work for one's own Bible study. But those are not the only ways to read it. Readers can equally benefit from choosing to read any subject heading that strikes them as interesting. And that is made easier by simply perusing the table of contents to see the subjects covered.

The Use of Post-Biblical Jewish Sources

I often cite non-Jewish sources, but more frequently I cite Jewish sources such as the Talmud. The Jews, after all, had the Torah for more than a thousand years prior to the rise of Christianity. The Talmud is the encyclopedia-sized compendium of Jewish law and philosophy that reflects those thousand-plus years of Jews' studying and living the Torah.

ACKNOWLEDGMENTS

This is the most difficult part of this introduction because so many people have influenced me with their insights into life and the Bible that I am certain to unwittingly omit names that should be included.

I attended yeshivas (all-day religious Jewish schools) from first grade until twelfth; and I continued formal study thereafter as well. That formal education made my Torah teaching possible. Two teachers at the Yeshiva of Flatbush

High School in Brooklyn, New York, who particularly influenced me were the principal, Rabbi David Eliach, and my Torah teacher, Rabbi Amnon Haramati. I also obtained a superb knowledge of Hebrew language and grammar there. All my religious studies teachers were from Israel, so we students spoke Hebrew half the day. Unlike most mortals, I loved studying grammar, and soaked in every grammatical rule these teachers imparted. My Hebrew was also greatly abetted by spending a half-dozen summers at a Hebrew-speaking camp, Camp Massad in Pennsylvania.

In my late twenties and early thirties (1976-83), as the director of the Brandeis-Bardin Institute, a Jewish educational center in California, I had the unique opportunity to meet and have extended dialogues with most of the influential Jewish thinkers of the time—Orthodox, Conservative, Reform, and secular, from North and South America, Europe, and Israel. They included (in alphabetical order) Yehuda Bauer, Eliezer Berkovits, Saul Berman, Eugene Borowitz, Emil Fackenheim, Norman Frimer, Martin Gilbert, Arthur Hertzberg, Louis Jacobs, Norman Lamm, Julius Lester, Hyam Maccoby, Jacob Milgrom, Pinchas Peli, Jakob Petuchowski, Gunther Plaut, Emanuel Rackman, Richard L. Rubenstein, Uriel Simon, David W. Weiss (the Israeli immunologist), and Elie Wiesel.

From 1982 until 1992, I was given another unique opportunity—a true gift—to discuss religion for two hours every Sunday night with clergy and spokesmen of virtually every religion in the world. I was the moderator of a radio show, "Religion on the Line," broadcast on the American Broadcasting Company (ABC) radio station in Los Angeles. This constituted a decade-long immersion in religious conversation with people who devoted their lives to their respective religions—Reform, Conservative, Orthodox, and Reconstructionist rabbis; mainstream and evangelical Protestant ministers; Roman Catholic priests; Eastern Orthodox priests; Mormon bishops; Muslim imams; Seventh Day Adventist ministers, Buddhist priests, and others. It was a life-shaping and life-changing experience.

I not only learned from all these people; I was also able to test my religious beliefs with lucid minds of all faiths. And of no faith: I regularly invited atheist and humanist spokesmen on the show as well. And I ended up speaking in at least a hundred synagogues, in scores of churches, and at the largest mosque in the Western United States.

After 1992, I continued to raise religious issues on my daily radio shows and to discuss religious matters with highly knowledgeable Jewish friends such as Rabbi Shmuley Boteach, Izzy and Rita Eichenstein, Allen and Susie Estrin, Rabbi Leonid Feldman, Rabbi Mordecai Finley, Rabbi Michael and Jill Gotlieb, Drs. Stephen and Ruth Marmer, Rabbi Eyal and Tzippy Ravnoy, Rabbi David Wolpe, and Rabbi David and Beverly Woznica. I would be particularly remiss if I did not mention the role Chabad rabbis around the world have played in my religious life. I would like to mention all of them, but I must at least mention my family's three Chabad rabbis at whose homes I have spent Shabbat evenings talking about God, Torah and just about everything else—Rabbi Moshe Bryski of Agoura Hills, California, Rabbi Simcha Backman of Glendale, California, and Rabbi Yosef Lipsker of Reading, Pennsylvania.

Special mention must be made of a man who combines uncompromising intellectual honesty, Jewish religious faith and practice, and extraordinary biblical scholarship: Professor Leeor Gottlieb of the Department of Bible at Bar-Ilan University. He read every word of this commentary, and his contribution—including more than a few corrections—has been indispensable. We do not agree on everything, which makes his help all the more helpful and admirable.

I also wish to express my gratitude to the distinguished scientist and theologian Gerald Schroeder for his scientific explanations of the early chapters of Genesis.

Knowledgeable and wise Christian friends such as Father Gregory Coiro, Joshua Charles, Gregory Koukl, Dr. Wayne Grudem, Pastor John Hagee, Eric Metaxas, and Msgr. Jorge Mejia, Michael Nocita, and Dr. Hugh Ross (who has written extensively on Genesis and science, and generously given of his time to me), and Ravi Zacharias have helped me form my thoughts on the Bible and religion generally.

I wish to thank Benjamin and Tiferet Telushkin for all their help in preparing this manuscript. May your newborn child and children hopefully yet to come study the fruit of your labor.

Ilana Kurshan, a prominent writer and serious thinker, edited the hundreds of hours of tapes of my eighteen-year teaching of the Torah verse-by-verse. She was instrumental in making this commentary a reality. I cannot thank her enough. She was indeed an editor of this commentary.

I cannot thank Barney Brenner of Tucson, Arizona, enough. He caught so many typos, punctuation mistakes, and stylistic errors that no one else caught, I am embarrassed to think how this book would read were it not for him.

Then there is Joel Alperson. Aside from being a close friend since 1982, when we met at a speech I gave in Kansas City, Kansas, I want to first acknowledge that without Joel there would be no commentary. It was Joel who found a company to transcribe my Torah tapes, resulting in the creation of five thousand pages of text. Debbie Weinberger was one of the transcriptionists who did a magnificent job, and this work is written in her memory. Joel then searched for an editor and ultimately found Ilana Kurshan, whose work he carefully reviewed.

Joel was determined that my Torah commentary be put into print. But I knew, as it stood, even after Ilana's superb editing of my lectures, I had much more to say. So one day, Joel—not one to ever give up—put the question to me directly: "What would it take for you to complete and publish the commentary?"

I told him I would do so if Joseph Telushkin served as editor. He is a fount of biblical, rabbinic/Talmudic, and historical knowledge; no one knows my thinking on the Torah as well as Joseph; and we had already written two books together. If Joseph worked with me, I would put all other writing aside for years to write this commentary.

I did not think that would happen, but Joel makes things happen. He not only brought Joseph on board, he has overseen every detail of the highly complex process of putting this vast commentary together, and has played a critical role in the intellectual input. He has also relentlessly insisted that I always live up to the name of the commentary—the name he came up with—*The Rational Bible*.

Joseph Telushkin and I met in our second year of high school at the Yeshiva of Flatbush. We met one day after school at a nearby bookstore. We both loved books because we loved ideas—we wanted to understand life. That was an immediate bond. And there was one other: Neither of us did almost any school-work. Instead, we read books and magazines (and, in my case, attended classical music concerts and studied orchestral scores).

At the age of twenty-six, we wrote and published our first book, *Eight Questions People Ask about Judaism*, which was soon thereafter expanded and published as *The Nine Questions People Ask about Judaism*. The book became one the most widely read introductions to Judaism and remains in print forty-five years later. Working with him on this commentary was a reminder of the joy we experienced when we wrote our first two books together at the outset of our careers. Joseph constantly contributed information that influenced and deepened my arguments—even on those occasions when we disagreed.

From the earliest days of our friendship, people would often say about Joseph and me: "They're as close as brothers." And we have always responded: "Would that all brothers could be so close."

Finally, a word about the person to whom I have dedicated this book—my wife, Sue. She was the final editor of every word of this book. Not just for grammar and syntax, but primarily for her specialty: logic. She is trained as a lawyer, but her ability to think rigorously is an innate gift—as rare a gift as perfect pitch is to the few musicians who have that innate ability. The number of less than clear assertions she uncovered is so great I am almost embarrassed to think this commentary might have been published without her input. And that is only one of the many reasons everyone who knows Sue knows how blessed I am to have her in my life.

And while on the subject of blessings, I must make mention of my two sons, David and Aaron. Not a day passes without my thinking how lucky I am to be their father. And, for that matter, to be the grandfather of Daniel and Jack

Prager, the father-in-law of Myriam Prager, and the stepfather of my two wonderful stepsons, Brandon and Reed. My cup truly runneth over.

I will end with a thank you to my late parents, Max and Hilda Prager, who raised my brother, Kenneth, and me to take the Torah and God seriously. My love of the Torah is in no small part due to them. And, the aforementioned difficulties notwithstanding, I loved them. I wish I could hand deliver *The Rational Bible* to them.

Dennis Prager

February 2019

PREFACE

Joel Alperson

I'VE ALWAYS TRIED TO FIND THE ANSWERS TO THE BIG QUESTIONS OF LIFE.
When I was all of nine years old, after a close friend showed me some magic tricks, I found the magic book he had read so I could perform the same tricks.

Later, as a college freshman, I discovered Plato, who addressed many of the "big questions" I deeply cared about, with arguments that were linear and well thought through. Later, as a college senior, I studied one-on-one with a professor who told me of a legend which held Plato had written a book on "the good." I was so excited. I thought if I could only read this book, I could learn "the secret" of leading a good life. Unfortunately, the legend also held that this volume had been lost in a great fire. So, my search for "the good" began and ended in the span of that one-hour study session.

Who would have guessed that decades later I would not only find myself reading a brilliant explanation of what I have come to regard as the greatest book ever written, but that I also would have helped to make this work possible? My Sunday school and Hebrew school teachers certainly would not have guessed. Given my awful grades and even worse behavior, they'd be shocked.

My grandfather, who was Orthodox, would also be shocked. He had given me a five-volume set of the Torah when I was a teen, but whenever he would open one of those volumes, he would hear the binding crack. He knew I hadn't even touched the books.

My story is hardly unique. The majority of those living in the West have dismissed the Torah and the rest of the Bible as little more than ancient religious fairy tales. And why not? Ten plagues? The creation of the world by a supernatural God? A giant flood wiping out virtually all of mankind? Ten Commandments from three thousand years ago? Why would people choose to study, let alone think their lives could be transformed by, such stories?

I certainly didn't.

Then, one weekend in 1982, I heard Dennis Prager speak at a retreat outside of Kansas City. I remember arguing with him all weekend. But he had answers. And they stayed with me. So began my long journey of realizing that the Torah had more meaning than I ever imagined.

Eventually, Dennis taught the Torah to a class in Los Angeles, line-by-line, over eighteen years, and I started listening to recordings of those classes in my car as I drove around my hometown of Omaha, Nebraska. Realizing that I couldn't focus on the material and my driving at the same time, I asked him if I could transcribe some of those recordings. That was in 2002. Little did I know at the time, his agreement would start the process of creating this remarkable work. I was able to enlist the help of Ilana Kurshan, a very talented student of the Torah. For one year she took approximately five thousand pages of Dennis's Torah class transcripts and converted them into a first draft of this commentary. Her work was excellent and enormously helpful.

It was also our very good fortune that Rabbi Joseph Telushkin was available to help with this project. For all the reasons Dennis listed in his introduction, no one else could have added to this great work as Rabbi Telushkin has. The finished product, as Dennis is the first to acknowledge, was made possible because of Rabbi Telushkin's passionate involvement.

Helping Dennis Prager author this work has been an honor for me. I helped the wisest man I know comment on the wisest book ever written. Having carefully and repeatedly listened to Dennis's Torah lectures, I expected this book to be an edited version of all the wonderful ideas he offered over the years. But I was surprised by the many new and important insights he added to this project. I think even he was surprised. This work captured him. It was obvious from his tremendous investment of time, thought, and research this was not another book. This is arguably his greatest work, and his legacy.

You have only to read a few essays or a single chapter to see the profundity of his writing.

Dennis has repeatedly said how grateful he is to me for helping to make his, as he likes to put it, "magnum opus" possible. He says it is one of the greatest gifts he's ever received. Ironically, after working so closely with him over so many years, I believe the greatest gift I've given was to myself.

I've come to realize the book on "the good" was not lost in a fire.

It's here for you to read.

Acknowledgments: This remarkable project could never have been completed without the help of so many wonderful and devoted individuals. In addition to Dennis's acknowledgments, I would like to thank some of those individuals with whom I worked. I can't possibly give them all the credit they're due, but these individuals' efforts were indispensable in creating this book:

Talia Gordis, Emily Sirotkin, Helen Lin, and Katrina Chen devoted many hours to reviewing lecture transcripts to identify and organize the essay topics which were used throughout this commentary.

Thanks to Scott Dugan for carefully and accurately accounting for the expenses related to this commentary.

Thanks to Pete Sirotkin, whose great work at our office in Omaha allowed me the freedom to work on this book. I would also like to thank him for his important insights on and intimate understanding of Genesis 38. He is an exemplary human being and exemplary Christian—and he believes this is the greatest Bible commentary he's ever read.

While many people were involved in transcribing hundreds of Dennis's Torah lecture recordings, one transcriptionist stands out. Debbie Weinberger lived in Israel and transcribed much of Dennis's work. Very sadly, this remarkable young woman died of cancer in 2007. Her feelings about being remembered in this work were expressed in the following email:

"When he said it was Dennis Prager on the line, I think my heart stopped for a nanosecond! We had a lovely conversation and we agreed that our biggest prayer is that I get to see or receive a copy of Leviticus personally—in other words, that I stick around…So very touched deep in my soul that Dennis wants to add a note about me and my working on the project/book."

When I was struggling to decide whether to devote the necessary time and expense to this commentary, my dear friend Ron Carson asked how I would feel on my deathbed if this book were never published. Thank you, Ron, for helping me to make the right decision.

To my dear friend Dr. Howard Gendelman (Howie), who constantly amazes me with his tremendous courage, passion, and persistence. His life has been a Kiddush Hashem (a sanctification of God's name).

To my dear friend Dennis Prager: There is no one else on the planet for whom I would have involved myself so deeply in such a project. It is your life-changing ideas and the promise they hold of making so many people better human beings that continue to inspire and excite me. What greater goal could one have and how many others could make such a goal attainable? Thank you for allowing me to share in your remarkable dream.

And finally to Conny—my beautiful wife and the mother of our children. Thank you so much for your encouragement, for listening to me endlessly discuss the details of this work, and for celebrating its many successes with me. As I've told you so often, no one's support and enthusiasm means as much to me. How can I possibly thank you for your endless love, kindness, and devotion? May we spend many happy hours teaching our children, Hannah, Rachel, Aaron, and David, the lessons contained within this great work. And may our children teach them to their children.

JOEL ALPERSON
JANUARY 2019

CHAPTER

I

ESSAY: THE FIRST VERSE—A FIRST IN HUMAN HISTORY

1.1 In the beginning God created the Heavens and the Earth.[1]

The first verse of Genesis is, in some ways, the most important verse in the Bible. While many Torah verses influenced history, Genesis 1:1 changed history in monumental ways.

- First, the verse posits a Creator of the universe. That means, among many other things, there is meaning to existence. If there is no Creator, there is no ultimate purpose to existence, including, of course, human existence. We humans can make up a meaning because we are the one species that cannot live without meaning. But the fact remains that we made it up.

  Of course, atheists argue that believers in God made up God; therefore, God does not really exist. But they don't always apply this rule to the existence of what they acknowledge they made up: meaning. If what we make up (God) doesn't exist, what atheists make up (meaning) doesn't exist.

  If there is no God, we know there is no ultimate meaning or purpose to life: that all existence—including, of course, our own—is the result of random chance. But we do not know there is no Creator. So, unlike those who know they make up meaning, neither we who believe in God nor atheists know we made up God. On the contrary, there are very strong arguments for a Designer of the world, but there are no arguments for an ultimate purpose to life if there is no God.

- Second, the word "created" (*bara*) implies nothing preexisted Genesis 1:1. When *bara* is used in the Torah, it is used only with reference to God—because only God can create from nothing. Human beings cannot create; they can only "make," like making something from something, such as wood and paper from trees.

- Third, everything—with the exception of God—has a beginning. Prior to God's creating, there was nothing. That includes time. Thanks to Einstein, we know that time, too, had a beginning. God, therefore, also created time, which means God exists not only outside of nature but outside of time. God precedes time and will outlive time.

- Fourth, for the first time, a creation story has but one Creator. The moral and intellectual consequences of the Torah's monotheism have changed the world. They are listed in detail in the commentary to Exodus 8:6 (and summarized in the commentary to Genesis 35:2).

- Fifth, unlike pre-Bible creation stories, there is complete silence regarding a birth of the deity. The God of Genesis 1:1, the God of the Bible, is not born.

- Sixth, for the first time in history, we are presented with a god who is completely separate from nature—because God created nature. God, for the first time, is not part of nature.

- Seventh, for the first time in history, the Creator and the act of creation are completely desexualized.

All of that is contained in this opening verse of the Bible.

ON THE QUESTION "WHO CREATED GOD?"

As noted above, Genesis 1:1 is completely silent with regard to God's origins. All prior creation stories contained descriptions of how the gods came into existence (these are called "theogonies"). Therefore, Genesis 1:1 begins not with God's origins—because He has none—but with God acting (creating the world).

For this reason, the question "Who created God?" while meaningful regarding pagan religion, is meaningless with regard to the God of the Bible. If God were created, God wouldn't be God. God's creator—we'll call him God's Dad—would be God. But the same people who ask "Who created God?" would then ask "Who created God's Dad?" And after that, they would ask "Who created God's Dad's dad?" *Ad infinitum*. People who ask this question would feel intellectually at home in the pagan world where this question was meaningful.

> *If God were created, God wouldn't be God. God's creator would be God. But the same people who ask "Who created God?" would then ask "Who created God's Dad?"*

The question is akin to asking, "What is the highest number?" and after being told "googolplex," asking, "What about googolplex plus one?" It is playing with words, not serious thought. The God of Genesis—the God the Western world came to affirm—is the First Cause, Who always was and always will be. That cannot be said about any other ancient god.

Skeptics will respond that just as the theist posits God always existed, the atheist posits the universe always existed. But this is untenable on both scientific and logical grounds.

Regarding science, the predominant view at this time is the universe did indeed have a beginning, what is popularly known as the Big Bang. This has disturbed scientists committed to atheism. Some have therefore posited an infinite number of Big Bangs and/or the existence of the "multiverse," an infinite number of universes. But this is truly a statement of faith because there is no possible way of finding another universe. Nor is there evidence for an infinite number of Big Bangs.

The logical argument is this: How does the atheist explain existence? *Why is there anything?* To that, the atheist has no answer. The theist has a plausible—not provable, but easily the most logically compelling—answer: A Creator. God.

ESSAY: GOD'S EXISTENCE

Given the supreme importance of Genesis 1:1—that is, of God's existence—to life, to meaning, and to morality; and given the Bible rests on this verse and its premise of God's existence, a brief review of the rational arguments for God's existence is necessary.

The most compelling rational argument is, as noted, the question "Why is there anything?" Science and atheism have no answer to this question. Nor will either ever have an answer. It is outside the purview of science. Science explains what is. But it cannot explain why what is came about—why something, rather than nothing, exists. Only a Creator of that something can explain why there is something rather than nothing.

> *Science cannot explain why something, rather than nothing, exists.*

It is true that the existence of a Creator cannot be scientifically proved. Given that a Creator is outside of nature and that science can prove only that which is within nature, the fact that science cannot prove God's existence is not meaningful.

Moreover, a Creator remains the only rational explanation for existence. And if only one thing can explain something, it is overwhelmingly likely that one thing is the explanation. The only alternatives are a) creation created itself from nothing or b) creation always existed. But each of these propositions is considerably less rational than a Creator, and neither can ever be proved.

Nor can science explain the emergence of life on earth. It is as mystified by the emergence of life from non-life as it is by the emergence of non-life from nothing. Again, only a Creator can explain that.

And science cannot explain consciousness. Why are human beings (and perhaps, to a much lesser degree, some animals) self-aware? To the best of our knowledge, nothing else in all the universe is self-aware. How did self-aware creatures emerge in a universe of non-awareness?

To be an atheist is to believe the universe came about by itself, life came from non-life by itself, and consciousness came about by itself.

On purely rational grounds—the grounds on which I believe in God—the argument for a God who created the world is far more intellectually compelling than atheism.

It is not belief in the existence of a Creator God that most troubles intellectually honest people; it is the existence of unjust suffering—both natural (diseases, earthquakes) and man-made (murder, torture). In other words, the intellectually honest atheist should acknowledge that the existence of the universe, of life, and of consciousness argue for God; and the intellectually honest believer should acknowledge that the amount of unjust suffering challenges faith in a good God.

However, I have never met a believer in God who has not acknowledged this challenge, whereas atheists, by definition, do not acknowledge the overwhelming evidence for a Creator. If they did, they would no longer be atheists; they would be believers or agnostics. To paraphrase the American rabbi and theologian Milton Steinberg (1903-1950), the believer has to account for the existence of unjust suffering; the atheist has to account for the existence of everything else—for the world, life, consciousness, beauty, love, art, music. It would seem the believer has the upper hand.

So, then, how do believers in the good God of the Bible rationally affirm their faith?

The primary rational arguments are these:

It does not make rational sense that the Creator wouldn't care about His creations.

It does not seem likely that the Creator of beings who care about good and evil does not Himself care about good and evil.

It does not seem likely caring beings were created by an uncaring Creator.

I believe the most intellectually honest response to all the unjust suffering in the world is not to deny God exists, but to be occasionally angry with God.

That is, in fact, one of the reasons I believe in the God of the Bible—because the name of God's People is "Israel," which means "Struggle with God" (see the commentary to Genesis 32:29). The very Book that introduced God to humanity invites us to fight with and even get angry with that God.

Finally, I believe God is good because this Book—the Bible—makes such a compelling case for God's goodness. If after reading this commentary, the reader is not persuaded the world is governed by a just and good God, I will have failed my primary task in writing this commentary.

If Genesis described exactly how the world was created, it would be unintelligible to us, let alone to all those who preceded us over the past three thousand years.

ESSAY: DO SCIENCE AND GENESIS CONFLICT?

A major barrier to many modern men and women taking the Bible seriously is the belief that science and Genesis conflict and, consequently, that religion and science conflict.

Therefore, this subject needs to be addressed.

First, the notion that the Genesis Creation story must agree with science is itself untenable. If Genesis described exactly how the world was created, it would be unintelligible to us, let alone to all those who preceded us over the past three thousand years. It might not even be in intelligible language but in yet-to-be-discovered mathematical or physics equations.

The Torah must speak in language that is intelligible to human beings—in every past generation as well as in every future generation. Clearly, then, it cannot speak in scientific terms. At the same time, it should not violate essential scientific truths (for example, it accurately depicts human beings as the last creation).

Moreover, we have no idea what science will say about cosmology (the beginning of the universe) in a hundred years. In my lifetime alone, science went from positing a universe that always existed to positing a universe that had a beginning (the Big Bang). So, in just one generation, the Torah, in describing a beginning to the universe, went from conflicting with science to agreeing with science. But this is not necessarily a comment on the Torah because science—to its credit, I might add—is always changing.

> *The believer has to account for the existence of unjust suffering; the atheist has to account for the existence of everything else.*

Second, while Genesis 1 must accord with what is true, the purpose of Genesis 1 is not to teach science. It is to teach about God, man, and nature. That is why the Torah is eternal—and why few scientific claims are.

Among other things, Genesis 1 teaches:

- God is beyond nature (all previous gods were gods of nature or part of nature).
- Therefore, there is a reality outside of nature. And that has incomparably important ramifications for us humans. It means this physical world is not all there is.
- God is not a sexual being (all previous gods engaged in sex—with other gods and/or mortals).
- There is only one God of humanity (all pre-existing gods were attached to one tribe, religion, or nation—there was no god of all humanity).

- God represents order versus the forces of disorder and chaos, which are the norm—both in nature and in human society.
- God has a special role for the human being.
- God is moral and has a moral will.
- Because of all of this, there is a transcendent purpose to life.

Science, on the other hand, teaches none of that. Science teaches science, which is no small thing—a vast number of people, myself included, are alive thanks to science. But science doesn't teach right from wrong—or even that there *is* a right and wrong. Nor does it provide ultimate purpose: Science is the study of the physical universe, which, without God and religion, is bereft of ultimate purpose. If there is no God, we humans spend an infinitesimally tiny period of time between oblivion (before we are born) and extinction (after we die).

Genesis 1 does not seek to teach science. It seeks to teach wisdom. While the present generation knows more science than any generation in history, I believe it possesses less wisdom than many preceding generations. And the biggest single reason is that it has decided God, the Bible, and religion are not necessary and that only science is.

Finally, it is worth noting many scientists believe in God and the Bible.[2] In 2010, Oxford University published a book titled *Science vs. Religion: What Scientists Really Think* by Elaine Howard Ecklund, a Rice University professor of sociology. This was her finding: "After four years of research, at least one thing became clear: Much of what we believe about the faith lives of elite scientists is wrong. The 'insurmountable hostility' between science and religion is a caricature, a thought-cliché, perhaps useful as a satire on groupthink, but hardly representative of reality."

> *Science doesn't teach right from wrong—or even that there is a right and wrong.*

ESSAY: WHY GOD IS DEPICTED IN MALE TERMS

The complete desexualization of God and of religion was a radical innovation of the Torah. In religions before the Torah and in its own time, gods were depicted as celestial men and women, and those gods engaged in sexual activity—with human beings and with other gods. In the Torah, God is never depicted either as a man or as a woman and is completely removed from any sexuality.

Before the Torah, religion had never before been wholly removed from the sexual realm.

However, the Torah does depict God in the masculine. Hebrew is one of the few languages in the world in which verbs are masculine and feminine. They must, therefore, agree with the noun to which they refer in gender and in number. For example, the verb "created" in the first verse of the Torah is in the masculine and in the singular. So, we immediately know there is not more than one God and there is no goddess.

Gender-wise, the Torah had three choices in depicting God:

> *The purpose of Genesis 1 is not to teach science. It is to teach about God, man, and nature.*

a) Masculine

b) Feminine

c) Neuter

We can readily rule out the third choice. First, a neutered depiction of God is simply impossible in Hebrew. Unlike English and most other languages, there are no neuter verbs or nouns in Hebrew.

Second, the biblical God is a personal God to whom we can and must relate. We cannot relate to, let alone obey or love, an "It."

Moreover, if one wants to depict a genderless God, "he" is closer than "she." When people hear the word "she," they immediately imagine a female. But that is not always the case with "he," which is often used to cover an entire population. For example, when people kill a fly, they say "I killed him," because they have no idea—or interest in—whether the fly was male or female.

Any discomfort one feels with a masculine depiction of God is not comparable to the pain one will feel if boys are not civilized into good men.

And no one who heard "I killed him" would think about the fly's gender. But if a person said, "I killed her," everyone would immediately think of gender.

Nevertheless, it would be disingenuous to argue the Torah uses the masculine solely because using neuter was not possible. The depiction of God in masculine terms is deliberate because it is essential to the Torah's fundamental moral purposes.

To understand why, we have to acknowledge three premises:

1. The Hebrew Bible's primary concern is a good world.
2. A good world can be achieved only by making good people.
3. The primary perpetrators of evil (of a violent nature) are males.

Given these premises, it is in both men's and women's best interests to depict God in the masculine.

BOYS TAKE RULES FROM MEN

When males are young, they need to feel accountable to a male authority figure. Without a father or some other male rule-giver, young men are likely to do great harm. If there is no male authority figure to give a growing boy rules, it is very difficult to control his wilder impulses.

In 2008, then-U.S. Senator Barack Obama told an audience, "Children who grow up without a father are five times more likely to live in poverty and commit crime; nine times more likely to drop out of schools, and twenty times more likely to end up in prison." Commenting on that speech, Dr. Alvin Poussaint, a psychiatrist with Harvard Medical School, confirmed Obama's statistics: "The absence of fathers corresponds with a host of social ills, including dropping out of school and serving time in jail."[3]

The data are overwhelming:[4]

A report released by the Minnesota Psychological Association, concluded:[5]

"The more opportunities a child has to interact with his or her biological [or adoptive] father, the less likely he or she is to commit a crime or have contact with the juvenile justice system.[6]

"In a study of female inmates, more than half came from a father-absent home.[7]

"Youths who never had a father living with them have the highest incarceration rates.[8]

"*Youths in father-only households display no difference in the rate of incarceration from that of children coming from two-parent households.*" (Italics added.)[9]

In other words, if one's primary goal is a good world—specifically, a world with far less murder, child abuse, theft, rape, and torture—a God depicted in masculine terms (a Father in Heaven), not a goddess (a Mother in Heaven), must be the source of moral and ethical commandments such as "Do not murder" and "Do not steal."

> *If one's primary goal is a good world—specifically, a world with far less murder, child abuse, theft, rape, and torture—a God depicted in masculine terms, not a goddess, must be the source of moral commandments.*

If the father figure/rule-giver that boys need is not on Earth, a morally authoritative Father in Heaven can often serve as an effective substitute.

Any discomfort one feels with a masculine depiction of God is not comparable to the pain one will feel if boys are not civilized into good men.

MALES NEED MALE ROLE MODELS

To transform a wild boy into a good man, a male role model is as necessary as a male rule-giver. When the Bible depicts God as merciful, compassionate, and caring for the poor and the widow, it is not so much interested in describing God as in providing a model for humans, especially males, to emulate. If God were depicted as female, young men would deem traits such as compassion, mercy, and care for the downtrodden as feminine and would not identify with them. But if God, their Father in Heaven, who is strong—on occasion even a warrior—cares for the poor and loves justice, mercy, and kindness, these traits are also masculine and to be emulated. The argument that girls equally need female role models to avoid violence is not true—because the problem of mayhem and violence is overwhelmingly a male one. Of course, girls need female role models, but not to avoid violence. Like boys, girls are also more likely to obey a male authority figure.

> *It is ironic that any women are attempting to render the God of Western religious morality less masculine. If their goal is achieved, it is women who will suffer most from lawless males.*

THE MALE IS MORE RULE-ORIENTED

A third reason for depicting God in masculine terms is the indispensability of law to a just and humane society. "Law and order" can be code words for repression, but they are in fact the building blocks of a decent society. That is why the Torah identifies God with the gender that is more naturally disposed to rules and order—the male. Females are more naturally inclined toward feelings and compassion, which are also essential qualities for a decent life. But a male depiction of God helps make a law-based society possible. And the Torah is nothing if not law-based. It is ironic that any women are attempting to render the God of Western religious morality less masculine. If their goal is achieved, it is women who will suffer most from lawless males.

We have too many absent fathers on Earth to begin to even entertain the thought of having no Father in Heaven.

GOD IS NOT WITHIN NATURE. GOD CREATED NATURE.

Another completely new innovation of Genesis 1:1 is that, because the world was created by God, God exists independently of the world. God is therefore

not part of nature. We do not worship trees—because trees are
creators. We worship the Creator of trees. Unlike the other rel
ancient world, biblical religion never worshipped nature.

Another reason not to worship nature—if another is necessary—is that
nature, unlike God and human beings, is amoral. That is why we think of
a human being who commits murder as evil, but we don't think of an earthquake or a hurricane, which may inflict far more suffering and destruction,
as evil.

God is good. Man can be good and/or evil. Nature is neither good
nor evil.

God's Name

The word used here for "God" is *Elohim*. It is a plural noun. But the word used
for "created," *bara*, is in the singular. The Torah says "Elohim created" using
the singular of the Hebrew verb "create." If Elohim were plural, it would utilize
the plural of the verb. The verb therefore tells us God is a singular entity. English provides an example—the word "fish." It can be used in both the singular
and plural—and only the verb tells us whether "fish" is in the singular or
plural: "The fish swim" means "fish" is plural; "the fish swims" means "fish"
is in the singular.

Any number of theories have been offered to explain why God's name is
in the plural. The one that make the most sense to me is that "God" (Elohim)
encompasses all gods.

The Bible Begins with the God of All the World, Not the Story of the Jews

The Torah doesn't begin with Jews, and God didn't begin with Jews. Jews make
no appearance in the Torah until Abraham, whose birth is related at the end of
chapter 11 (verse 27). The Torah and God are preoccupied with all of humanity,

not just Jews. No other ancient national history began with the creation of the world (and I do not know of a modern national history that does so either).

DISORDER—THE NATURAL STATE OF THE WORLD WITHOUT GOD

1.2 The earth being unformed and void,

Genesis describes the original state of the earth as *tohu* and *vohu*, translated here as "unformed and void." Robert Alter, professor of Hebrew and comparative literature at the University of California, Berkeley, writes in his commentary on Genesis, "*Tohu* by itself means emptiness or futility, and in some contexts is associated with the trackless vacancy of the desert." The King James Version translates the terms as "without form and void." University of Georgia Professor Richard Elliott Friedman, who has translated the Torah into English, uses "shapeless and formless."

One may infer from this description that God's work was not only creating and making, but composing order out of chaos. Genesis 1 is about Divine Order as much as it is about Creation. God is the Maker of Order and Distinctions. Order and distinctions are fundamental characteristics of the Torah's worldview. As we shall see in Genesis 1, God distinguishes between light and dark, day and night, land and water, and humans and animals; and, as we will see elsewhere in the Torah, God distinguishes between man and God, good and evil, man and woman, the holy and the profane, parent and child, the beautiful and the ugly, and life and death.

> *Genesis 1 is about Divine Order as much as it is about Creation. God is the Maker of Order and Distinctions.*

Preserving God's order and distinctions is one of man's primary tasks. But, like the unformed chaos of this verse, undoing God's order and distinctions is the natural state of man. The battle for higher civilization may be characterized as the battle between biblical distinctions and the human desire to undo many of those distinctions. As Western society abandons the Bible and the God of the Bible, it is also abandoning these distinctions. I fear for its future because Western civilization rests on these distinctions.

1.2 (cont.) with darkness over the surface of the deep

Theories about the earth's earliest atmosphere are in flux. Some scientists conjecture that earth's early atmosphere was much thicker than our present-day atmosphere; other scientists have theorized it was much thinner than today's.[10] But there is a consensus that the young earth was bombarded by collisions with other celestial bodies; a dense mixture of gases, dust, and debris enveloped the early earth; and the sun was a considerably dimmer star than it is today. All that rendered the earth's atmosphere essentially opaque—the "darkness" described in this verse. "You would not have been able to see much, just clouds covering everything," is how the early earth was described by Dave Stevenson, a Caltech professor of planetary science.[11]

It is also generally believed the earth was nearly or completely covered with water from a very early point. "Early earth was covered in a global ocean and had no mountains" reads a headline from the British science magazine *New Scientist*.[12] This is the "surface of the deep" described in this verse. And that raises an interesting question: how did Genesis know, more than three thousand years ago, that the nascent planet was submerged in darkness and water?

1.2 (cont.) and a wind from God sweeping over the water.

With these words, a subtle—so subtle almost all readers miss it (including me until writing this commentary)—but extremely significant transition occurs: The perspective has shifted from outside the world—the level of the cosmos or God's perspective, as it were—to Earth's surface. Why this is important will be made clear in the commentary on the next verse.

The Hebrew word translated here as "wind" (*ruach*) is the same word as "spirit," which is the word most other translations use. The King James Version and, among modern translations, the previous JPS translation (1917) and Richard Elliott Friedman use "spirit." The more common translation therefore reads, "and the spirit of God hovered over the face of the waters."

Many scholars, including Leeor Gottlieb, professor of Bible at Bar-Ilan University in Israel, understand *elohim* here as meaning "powerful" or "mighty." This accords with the present translation—"a mighty wind." In the Hebrew Bible, *Elohim* almost always refers to God. But on occasion, it means "mighty" or "great" (see, for example, Genesis 30:8 and Jonah 3:3).

GOD SPEAKS AND HIS WILL IS DONE

1.3 God said, "Let there be light" and there was light.

This verse is another radical innovation in history: God's will alone is all that is needed for something to happen. There are no cosmic battles, no mating with humans, no consultation with other deities.

Throughout history, people have understood "Let there be light" to mean "God created light." And that is an entirely legitimate translation—"Let there be" (*yihee*) can mean "Come into being." But there is no verb here meaning "create," "make," or "form." And that may strongly suggest another meaning. There are scientists who believe in the Bible who understand "Let there be light" to mean that God did not create or make light in this verse; *He made light appear.* These scientists focus on the shift in perspective from God's view at the level of the cosmos in verse 1 to the *view from the surface of the earth* in verse 2 (as noted, many translations render the last part of verse 2: "and the Spirit of God hovered over the surface of the waters").

No light had yet appeared on earth because in earth's earliest period, the earth's atmosphere was opaque, either from clouds or cosmological dust and debris, or both. In the words of former MIT physicist and member of the United States Atomic Energy Commission Gerald Schroeder: "There was light, but no sources of light were visible from the earth due to the cloud cover over the still-warm earth. Warm earth = high vapor pressure = clouds."[13] Now, as God hovered over the waters, with His words "let there be light," the atmosphere began to clear, and the light of the sun (but not the sun itself) became visible from the surface of the earth—just as it is visible to us when the skies are overcast: we see the light, but not its source. Thus, in the opinion of Schroeder, Ross

and other scientists who reconcile science with Genesis, the s
(but is not seen until Day Four).

WHY DOES GOD DECLARE HIS CREATION "GOOD"?

1.4 God saw it was good

This is the first of seven occasions in the opening chapter of Genesis that states God saw what He created was good (the others are verses 10, 12, 18, 21, 25, and 31). Such repetition of this phrase "God saw that it was good" can only mean the Torah considers it very important.

It means the world God created was good. In addition to meaning Creation and Order are good, it may be expressing an inherent optimism to life and existence. That the world God created is good gives all of us who believe in the Bible a reason for optimism, even when our life is troubled. Ultimately, this world is good, and good will eventually prevail (here or in an afterlife).

God took pleasure in seeing how well His work had turned out. This is also a human teaching moment. God's expressing admiration for, and taking pleasure in, His work teaches the meaning of humility. If you do good work— meaning the work was good and it was done to achieve good—you are allowed to say you have done good. We are not to be falsely humble by minimizing, let alone denying, our good accomplishments. Humility means knowing your strengths but not allowing them to make you arrogant.[14]

1.4 (cont.) and God separated the light from the darkness.

As explained above, in verse 2, distinctions are central to the biblical worldview. Separating is the first thing God does after creating the world. God is now in the process of shaping *tohu* and *vohu*—chaos—into order.

1.5 God called the light Day, and the darkness he called Night. And there was evening and there was morning, a first day.

Evening precedes morning for the simple and even obvious reason that darkness preceded light. Prior to the universe, all was dark. Light needed to be created, not darkness. Darkness is the absence of light. Light is not the absence of darkness. The description of each day—"there was evening and there was morning"—is why days in the Hebrew calendar begin at sunset (not midnight). The weekly Sabbath, for example, commences on Friday evening.

In Professor Gottlieb's view, there is another important meaning to "darkness" and "light" and to "night" and "day." God works during the day, not at night. This is so significant because there will be only one "day" when God does not work: the Sabbath. *The Sabbath is central to creation.* It is so important, it is the only ritual commandment in the Ten Commandments.

ESSAY: WHAT DOES "DAY" MEAN IN GENESIS 1?

Nothing in Genesis appears to present as irreconcilable a conflict between science and the Bible as the claim in Genesis that the world was created in six days and the scientific claim that the universe is 13.8 billion years old.

This seems to present those of us who believe in both the Bible and science with this dilemma: If "day" in Genesis 1 is a twenty-four-hour period, six days of creation cannot be reconciled with science.

Can one reconcile science, which dates the universe at about fourteen billion years, with six twenty-four-hour days? Dr. Gerald Schroeder, who taught physics at MIT and the Weizmann Institute in Israel, reconciles science and "day" in Genesis 1 in this way:

"We look back and measure fourteen billion years from today back to the creation. The Bible looks forward and sees six days from the beginning looking forward to Adam.... Two views of one reality and both are true: six days and fourteen billion years. In an expanding universe they both are mathematically true."[15]

I respect the views of religious scientists such as Schroeder and Hugh Ross (Ph.D. in astrophysics and a postdoctoral research fellow at Caltech), and I also recognize most readers throughout history understood these days as literal days and that a substantial number of believers today continue to do so. I will explain why "day" in the Hebrew Bible does not necessarily mean a twenty-four-hour period, but I do not disparage those who do believe it means a twenty-four-hour period. Despite their rejection of science regarding creation, these people should not be dismissed as "anti-science." I know some of these people, and they are highly respectful of science; some of them study science (and all of them go to doctors). People who truly reject science would forego modern medicine. I know no one who does. They go to doctors when ill, they vaccinate themselves and their children, esteem physicians and other scientists, and build hospitals.

Nevertheless, "day" (*yom*) does not always mean "twenty-four hours." In the very next chapter of Genesis, the Torah states: "These are the generations of the heavens and the earth when they were created, *on the day* God made the earth and the heavens" (Genesis 2:4—italics added). Clearly "day" in that verse alludes to the entirety of God's creating the world, so in that verse *yom* cannot mean one twenty-four-hour period. "Day" in the Bible can mean an indefinite period of time just as it can when we use the word in English: "In that day and age...." "in our day...." etc. And the Bible itself later asserts, "A thousand years in your sight are like a day that has just gone by, or like a watch in the night" (Psalm 90:4).

I find those examples persuasive. But I do not ascribe great importance to this particular debate for another reason: What matters is not *how long* it took God to create the world; what matters is *that* God created it. What matters is that, if there were no God, there would be no world. All existence, not to mention all life, and intelligent life in particular, is a miracle. When I look at the world and recite the words of Psalm 92:5—"How great are your works, Lord, how profound your thoughts"—it does not occur to me think how long it took God to make His great works. Genesis 1 teaches God created the world, not chance. That is what matters.

1.6 God said, "Let there be expanse in the midst of the water that it may separate water from water."

The Hebrew word *rakiya*—translated here as "expanse"—is found only here in the Bible. Whatever *rakiya* literally means, it is the "expanse" between the waters on earth and the waters above—such as cloud cover. The waters below are *mayim* (the Hebrew word for "water"), and waters above are *sham-mayim*—which some, but by no means all, scholars believe means "water there" (*sham* is Hebrew for "there"). It is ultimately referred to—as verse 8 states—as the "sky."

1.7 God made the expanse, and it separated the water which was below the expanse from the water which was above the expanse. And it was so.

Genesis 1 teaches God created the world, not chance. That is what matters.

1.8 God called the expanse Sky. And there was evening and there was morning, a second day.

On the second day, God engaged in separating—the waters above from the waters below, making order—and life on earth possible. Separations and distinctions are essential elements in Genesis 1, the building blocks of the divine order.

1.9 God said, "Let the water below the sky be gathered into one area, that the dry land may appear." And it was so.

According to Schroeder, this coincides with the scientific record: "When the molten earth formed, as it cooled from its initial molten state, it was relatively smooth, not like a billiard ball, but also without the deep ocean trenches of today. The water was distributed over the entire earth. The amount of water in the oceans today would cover such a 'smooth' earth by one and half miles. Only as the earth cooled and the continents formed did dry land appear."

When the earth's tectonic plates moved, the trenches of the ocean were formed, enabling the waters that had covered the earth to recede—thereby enabling land to appear.

1.10 God called the dry land Earth, and the gathering of waters He called Seas. And God saw that this was good.

1.11 God said, "Let the earth sprout vegetation: seed-bearing plants, fruit trees of every kind on earth that bear fruit with the seed in it." And it was so.

PLANTS BEFORE THE SUN?

1.12 The earth brought forth vegetation: seed-bearing plants of every kind, and trees of every kind on earth that bear fruit with the seed in it." And God saw that it was good.

Schroeder says this: "People constantly ask me, 'How can we have plants when the sun doesn't appear until the next day?' There were the sun, moon, and stars—but they were not visible from the earth's surface. The earth was still hot at this time and therefore high vapor pressure enveloped it in thick clouds.

"I have personally measured photosynthesis, the growth of plants and the production of oxygen from that photosynthesis on days when the overcast was so heavy no sun or even hints of a sun could be seen through the clouds, but there was plenty of light and the plants were doing fine with their photosynthesis. By the time of Day Four, the earth had cooled; the clouds were opened and the sun, moon, and stars could be visible from the earth. Obviously there were no humans, but the Bible's view is from the earth: We know this because the sun and moon are called 'great bodies' (verse 16), and the only location in the universe where the sun and moon seem the same size is earth. That is because the sun's diameter is 400 times greater than the moon's diameter but the moon is 400 times closer to the earth than the sun. Parallax gives the visual impression of equal sizes."

To summarize Professor Schroeder's response to the question "How can there be vegetation before there was a sun?"—there was a sun (plausibly the light referred to in verse 3), but it was not visible from Earth until Day Four. And vegetation can take place when the sun is covered (by clouds, for example). Again, the narrative's perspective is from earth, not from above, as most people understandably assume. And verse 16 will make this earth-perspective clear: It calls both the sun and the moon "great bodies" even though the sun is four hundred times larger than the moon—because *from the earth* they appear of equal size.

1.13 And there was evening, and there was morning, a third day.

1.14 God said, "Let there be lights in the expanse of the sky to divide the day from the night and to be signs for seasons, for days and years.

1.15 and they shall serve as lights in the expanse of the sky to shine upon the earth." And it was so.

The Hebrew word for "lights" here is not the same as the word for *light* on Day One (verse 3). There, the word is *ohr*; here it is *mi-ohrot*, meaning illuminators, "bodies that give light." According to scientists who believe in the biblical narrative, this does not mean new celestial bodies were made in this verse; what was new was the clearing of the earth's formerly opaque atmosphere enabling the bodies giving light—the sun, moon, and stars, which had been previously created—to be visible from earth.

THE SUN AND THE MOON DETHRONED AS GODS

1.16 God made the two great lights, the greater light to dominate the day and the lesser light to dominate the night, and the stars.

This verse does not describe the making of something new; it offers further details regarding verse 14. More important, it provides a superb illustration of the primary purposes of Genesis 1—to teach humanity about God and man. Regarding God, the purpose of verse 16 is *to teach humanity that the sun and moon are not deities*. The sun and the moon, which were worshipped throughout the ancient world, are not even mentioned here by name. This served to dethrone these two gods while reemphasizing God is the only god. In fact, the sun is not even mentioned by name until Genesis 15:12; and Deuteronomy 4:19 explicitly forbids the Israelites from worshipping the sun, moon, and stars.

The other purpose of the verse is to explain *why* the two luminaries were made; not *that* they were made. They were made for man—"the greater light to dominate the day and the lesser light to dominate the night." The world was made for the human being.

Changing the way humanity saw the universe is what Genesis 1 is about. It succeeded.

1.17 And God set them in the expanse of the sky to shine upon the earth,

1.18 to dominate the day and the night, and to separate light from darkness. And God saw that this was good.

The purpose of verse 16 is to teach humanity that the sun and moon are not deities. The sun and the moon, which were worshipped throughout the ancient world, are not even mentioned here by name.

This is another debunking of all beliefs contemporaneous with the Torah. The pagan worldview regarded the lights in the sky as astrological signs governing the fate of the world. In contrast, the Torah describes these lights as celestial bodies that separate night from day (and delineate time cycles—verse 14). In other words, *God made them*—to serve His (and man's) purposes.

1.19 And there was evening and there was morning, a fourth day.

1.20 God said, "Let the waters bring forth swarms of living creatures, and birds that fly above the earth across the expanse of the sky."

WHY "SEA MONSTERS" ARE MENTIONED

1.21 God created the great sea monsters and all the living creatures of every kind that creep, which the waters brought forth in swarms, and all the winged birds of every kind.

The Hebrew *taninim*, translated here as "great sea monsters," refers to a sea creature worshipped by other nations in biblical times. The Torah singles out this creature to emphasize that these animals, which were worshipped as gods, are not gods but were created by the One True God. As biblical scholar Nahum Sarna puts it, "By emphasizing that 'God created the great sea monsters'...the narrative at once strips them of divinity."[16]

This verse contains the second use of the word "created" (*bara*). Something new was created—the animals, the "living *nephesh*" ("soul") creatures. Again, there are three things created in this chapter: The world, the animals, the human being.

1.21 (cont.) And God saw that this was good.

1.22 God blessed them, saying, "Be fertile and increase, fill the waters in the seas, and let the birds increase on the earth."

1.23 And there was evening, and there was morning, a fifth day.

1.24 God said, "Let the earth bring forth every kind of living creature: cattle, creeping things, and wild beasts of every kind." And it was so.

1.25 God made wild beasts of every kind and cattle of every kind, and all kinds of creeping things of the earth. And God saw that this was good.

THE CREATION OF "MAN"

1.26 Then God said, "Let us make man in Our image, according to Our likeness.

Genesis 1 describes the human being—*Adam*—in two ways: *Adam* and *Ha-Adam*, "man" and "the man."

In this verse, the word is *man* (*Adam*). In the next verse it is *the man* (*ha-Adam*). *Man* may be understood to denote man-like creatures that lacked a human soul. This *man* is physiologically both animal-like and man-like. But it is not necessarily *Ha-Adam*, *The Man*, the human being with a human soul, which is a different creation, as we shall see in the next verse.

Regarding the question "To whom is the verse referring when it says 'Let us…in Our image'?" there are Jewish and Christian faith answers, but there is no definitive one. It may be the "royal we" that has been used historically by kings in referring to themselves (and by popes to this day). Indeed, one doesn't have to be royalty; I have used this term for decades on my radio show: "We'll be back right after this break." It may connote celestial bodies such as angels. And it may refer to the animals—an explanation that comports with the creature "man" referred to here—as opposed to "the man" referred to in the next verse.

"For some medieval commentators," writes Orthodox Jewish writer Scott A. Shay, "[man] is both a creature descended from animals and different from them.... Rambam and Abarbanel explain that man originally resembled an animal and was created along with the rest of creation before the sixth day."[17]

Whether or not one accepts this last explanation—which I first heard from an Orthodox rabbi—the human being could indeed be regarded as part animal and part divine because human life is a constant battle between the animal and the divine.

1.26 (cont.) They shall rule the fish of the sea, the birds of the sky, the cattle, the whole earth, and all the creeping things that creep on earth."

THE CREATION OF "THE MAN"

1.27 And God created man in His image, in the image of God He created him;

This verse seems to describe precisely what the previous verse described—the creation of man in God's image. But it does not.

There are four differences—each of which is highly significant:

1. In the previous verse, God "makes." In this verse, God "creates." "Makes" implies something preexisting; "creates" implies something new is made.
2. In the previous verse, God makes *man (Adam).* In this verse, God creates *the man (ha-Adam).* (This translation does not note this.)
3. In the previous verse, *man* is made in "Our image." In this verse, *the man* is created only in "God's image."

4. In the previous verse, no mention is made of the creation of male and female. This verse says, "male and female He created them."

THE MALE-FEMALE DISTINCTION IS PART OF GOD'S ORDER

1.27 (cont.) male and female He created them.

"The man" is described as having been "created" as "male and female." This is an example of the Divine Order in Creation. *The male-female distinction is part of God's order.* It is that important. (This is discussed in detail in the commentary to Deuteronomy 22:5.)

There are ancient and modern readers who believe this statement suggests the human being (Adam) was created androgynous (both male and female). Such a reading cannot be reconciled with the plain text. If Adam were created as a male and female being, the last word of the verse would not be the plural "them"—"male and female He created *them*." It would read "him" or "it."

1.28 God blessed them and God said to them, "Be fertile and increase, fill the earth and master it,

To have children is the first commandment in the Torah. One obvious reason is the world's continuity depends on people having children. Today, young people in many European countries and Japan are having so few children that the continued existence of some of those nations is at risk. This phenomenon is almost exclusive to highly secular societies. See the essay "On Having Many Children" at Genesis 9:1.

EITHER MAN WILL RULE OVER NATURE, OR NATURE WILL RULE OVER MAN

1.28 (cont.) and rule the fish of the sea and the birds of the sky, and all the living things that creep on earth."

God grants man dominion over the animals and all of nature ("the whole earth") because man is a higher being. He alone is created in God's image; and, though obviously a physical being, he is, like God, outside of nature. Nature is not sacred; human life is.

God intended for man to dominate the natural world ("they shall rule"). This does not mean humans have the right to abuse nature—or to inflict unnecessary suffering on animals—but it does mean the world was created for human use.[18]

That man is depicted as ruler over the animal kingdom and the "whole earth" means he is to rule over nature, which is in stark contrast to the pagan worldview, according to which nature ruled over man and man worshipped nature. All the pagans could do in the face of nature's great power was offer sacrifices and perform incantations.

This biblical instruction to rule over nature has profoundly influenced those societies touched by the Bible. Among other things, it opened the way to finding cures for diseases. It is no coincidence that the Western world essentially developed modern medicine. In order to develop medicine, the first requirement is to understand human beings must learn how to conquer nature—*conquer*, not pray to natural forces (like rain gods) or try to propitiate them.

That is one reason diseases like smallpox and polio were eliminated in those parts of the world influenced by the Bible.

Human progress is not possible unless humans rule over nature. Many secular people in our time romanticize nature, perhaps not realizing—or not wanting to

> *Nature is not sacred; human life is.*

realize—that either humans rule over nature or nature will destroy humans. Either we conquer natural diseases, or they conquer us. Either we rule over (not abuse) the animal kingdom, or it rules over us. Until the very modern age, people everywhere feared being eaten by animals. Most of us no longer give this a moment's thought because most of the human race has come to successfully rule over the animal kingdom.

1.29 God said, "See, I give you every seed-bearing plant that is upon all the earth, and every tree that has seed-bearing fruit; they shall be yours for food,

God's original intention was for both human beings and, as the next verse makes clear, animals, too, to be vegetarian. The theme of universal vegetarianism is returned to again by the prophet Isaiah: "The wolf and the lamb shall graze together, and the lion shall eat straw like the ox, and the serpent's food shall be earth. In all My sacred mount nothing evil or vile shall be done, said the Lord" (Isaiah 65:25; see also Isaiah 11:6-9). For reasons explained in the commentary to Genesis 9:3, human beings were subsequently permitted to eat meat.

For a much fuller discussion of this subject, see the essay "Does the Torah Advocate Vegetarianism?" in Genesis 2:16.

1.30 And to all the animals on land, to all the birds of the sky, and to everything that creeps on earth, in which there is the breath of life, [I give] all the green plants for food." And it was so.

1.31 And God saw all that He had made, and found it very good. And there was evening and there was morning, the sixth day.

CHAPTER

2

2.1 The heavens and the earth were finished in all their array.

FROM CREATING TO MAKING

2.2 On the seventh day God finished the work that He had been doing. He ceased on the seventh day from all the work that He had done.

The Hebrew, as well as the English, is complicated. The last words, "that He had done," seem to be superfluous. The verse should have read, "He ceased on the seventh day from all His work." Why are the words "that He had done" appended?

To understand why, it is necessary to understand the literal Hebrew. It is not "that He had done" but "to make." The end of the verse reads: "…because He ceased from all His work to make."

This sounds awkward in English, but it is equally awkward in the Hebrew, which is why it is usually translated "that He had done."

What then does "that God created to make" mean? The most likely meaning is that creation in and of itself is not necessarily meaningful. Something must be "made" of what God created.

To put it another way, creation was only the beginning. "To make" something of creation is our task as human beings. This is in fact the normative Jewish view: Human beings are "partners" with God in "making" the world. We live in the "Eighth Day," the post-Creation world, which is ours to make of what God created in the first Six Days.

HOLY TIME—UNIQUE TO THE TORAH

2.3 God blessed the seventh day and made it holy

Of all the days, only the Sabbath is called "holy."

In making the seventh day holy, God announced time could be sanctified. This was another unique Torah innovation. Throughout the ancient world, physical things—people, animals, buildings—were deemed holy. Never time. As Nahum Sarna writes, "This first use of the key biblical concept of holiness relates to time. This is in striking contrast to the Babylonian cosmology, which culminates in the erection of a temple to Marduk by the gods, thereby asserting the sanctification of space."

In creating the Sabbath, God, in the words of theologian Abraham Joshua Heschel, made the seventh day into a "cathedral in time."

Anyone who has experienced Yom Kippur, "the Sabbath of Sabbaths" (Leviticus 16:31), in Israel, with its almost complete suspension of technology—there is almost no traffic; theaters, restaurants, and stores close; radio and television stations do not broadcast—can appreciate what it means to have society experience sacred time.

2.3 (cont.) because He ceased from all the work

The Hebrew word for "ceased" is *shavat*, spelled with the same three letters that spell *Shabbat*, the Hebrew word for Sabbath. The Sabbath thus has both its etymological and religious origin in God ceasing work on the seventh day of Creation. Every Friday night to Saturday night for more than three thousand years, Jews have attested to God's creation of the world by observing the Sabbath.

TWO WORDS FOR "WORK"

This verse uses the Hebrew word *milacha* to refer to work instead of the more common word *avoda*. *Milacha* is not truly translatable; it is best understood as creative work—work that produces something.

On the Sabbath, we are prohibited from *milacha*, to affirm there is more to our life than work: human beings have value even when not producing. Even if one engages in the work voluntarily, working seven days a week violates this principle. Most important, it violates the primary reason for Shabbat—to imitate God and thereby affirm there is a Creator. (For more on the Sabbath—the only ritual commanded in the Ten Commandments—and the central place it plays in the biblical worldview, see the commentary on Exodus 20:8-11.)

God worked for six days to create the world and then stopped to reflect on what He had done. The Sabbath induces us to ask: "What am I alive for? "What did I produce all of these things for?" And, most importantly, "What am I doing of value the other six days of the week?"

2.3 (cont.) that He had done.

As explained above, the Hebrew is literally "to make."

A SECOND DESCRIPTION OF CREATION— DETAILS ABOUT MAN'S CREATION

2.4 Such is the story of heaven and earth when they were created. When the Lord God made earth and heaven.

The second half of the verse does not say "when" but "*on the day* the Lord God made earth and heaven." This is another example (see commentary to Genesis 1:5) of the Creation story using the word "day" (*yom*) to signify more than a 24-hour period. Since creation took six "days," the word *yom* here cannot mean a 24-hour day or any other specific period of time, but rather an indeterminate period of time.

Many modern Bible scholars regard this verse as the beginning of "the second creation story," which they believe often contradicts the "first" creation story in Genesis 1. But there are contradictions only if one views this is as a "second creation story," rather than as something else entirely—providing further insights into creation and most importantly, to offer a much more detailed description of the creation of the human being.

THE ONLY TIME (BUT ONE) THE TORAH CONJOINS BOTH OF GOD'S NAMES

This story contains the first and only times (except for one instance in Exodus) the Torah conjoins both names of God—*YHVH* and *Elohim* ("Lord God"). *YHVH* is frequently pronounced "Jehovah" or "Yahweh" (we do not know exactly how it was pronounced). Sarna explains:

"This combination of the personal divine name YHVH with the general term *elohim* appears twenty times in the present literary unit, but only once again in the Torah, in Exodus 9:30. It is also exceedingly rare in the rest of the Bible. The repeated use here establishes that the absolutely transcendent God of the Creation (*elohim*) is the same immanent, personal God (YHVH) who shows concern for the needs of human beings."

THE WORLD NEEDS BOTH MERCY AND JUSTICE

The ancient Rabbis associated the names *Adonai* and *Elohim* with two characteristics: mercy (*Adonai*) and justice (*Elohim*). Their reasoning was that both are necessary for the world to function. If the world were ruled solely by justice, it would be destroyed, as it almost was during the time of Noah (Genesis 6:11-22)—where only Elohim is used to describe God. However, if the world were ruled solely by mercy, there would be no room for justice, and such a world, too, would cease to function. An overabundance of mercy means an increase in injustice. If, for example, mercy were extended to all murderers, their victims and the victims' loved ones would suffer a terrible injustice (hence the Midrashic teaching, "those who show mercy to the cruel end up being cruel to those who deserve mercy"). And, of course, if everyone knew they would receive only mercy, not justice, no matter what crime they committed, the amount of crime in society would increase exponentially.

An ancient proverb teaches, "To spare the ravening leopard is an act of injustice to the sheep." That is why the Rabbis spoke of mercy and justice as the two necessary attributes of God—and therefore of a decent society.

As described above, this is not a "second creation story." It is another way of expressing what occurred—like looking at a sporting event filmed with a camera from another vantage point. Robert Alter, professor of Hebrew and comparative literature at the University of California, Berkeley, describes the two accounts as one account: "[First] is a harmonious cosmic overview of creation and then a plunge into the technological nitty-gritty and moral ambiguities of human origins."[1]

This is most likely another reason the term "Lord God" is, with one exception in the Torah, used only here: to make clear that the two creation stories—the first using the universal Elohim and this one using both of God's names—comprise one story.

2.5 When no shrub of the field was yet on earth, and no grasses of the field had yet sprouted, because the Lord God had not sent rain upon the earth. And there was no man to till the soil.

According to some scholars, this verse and verse 7 constitute one of the "contradictions" that seem to exist between the "first" and "second" creation accounts. This verse says there were no shrubs or grasses—because there was no rain, and there was no rain because there was no man—and then verse 7 describes the creation of man. Yet, Genesis 1 tells us vegetation preexisted man, and there is no mention here of the creation of vegetation before man's creation in verse 7.

But this second creation narrative gives very few of the details contained in Genesis 1. The Torah sees no need to restate when God created vegetation— because this second narrative is ultimately about the creation of man (and woman), not about vegetation or anything else.

The point here is to explain that rain was created for man. With no human beings—and therefore no need for crop cultivation—there was no need for rain. Even the ancient Jewish commentators saw this verse as indicating rain is a gift to man. It cannot be emphasized too often that the Torah regards nature—that is, the world—as having been created for man. Nature does not have intrinsic worth beyond man's use. The Torah is first and foremost theocentric (God-centered); beyond that, it is anthropocentric (man-centered). This contrasts with widespread contemporary secular views of nature as inherently purposeful. In the words of a well-known Midrash: "When God created Adam, He led him around the Garden of Eden and said to him: 'Behold My works! See how beautiful they are, how excellent! All that I have created, for your sake did I create it. See to it that you do not spoil and destroy my world; for if you do, there will be no one to repair it after you.'"[2]

Physicist Gerald Schroeder writes, "The sequence in Chapter 2 is correct: world created; no plant life yet; mist goes up from the earth as the earth cools; rain comes—water being the prerequisite for plant life; then Adam and Eve."

2.6 but a flow would well up from the ground and water the whole surface of the earth.

This verse answers an obvious problem raised in the previous verse. Though rain was not yet provided, water necessary for nature's sustenance was provided. Schroeder says, "The mist going up from the earth is literally true. The current theory is that water was brought to the earth by rocks and comets that combined to form the earth approximately 4.6 billion years ago. The forces of the formation caused the earth to melt. Water, as disassociated molecules, dissolves in molten rock (magma, lava) by about 3% by weight. As the earth cooled and the lava solidified, the water that was dissolved in it was forced out and indeed a mist would have gone up from the earth as the earth cooled and returned as rain to water the earth."

2.7 And the Lord God formed man from the dust of the earth

We have already read an account of the creation of Adam in 1:27. This second account does not contradict the first; instead, it offers additional insight into the human being.

The literal meaning of *Adam* is earthling. *Adam* derives from the word for earth, *adama*. The similarities between the name *Adam* and *adama* reflect our origins, rooted in the earth from which we were formed ("for dust you are and to dust you shall return"—Genesis 3:19).

2.7 (cont.) and He blew into his nostrils the breath of life and man became a living being

The Hebrew words translated here as "the breath of life" (*nishmat chayyim*) can also mean "soul of life." This term is used only for human beings, not animals. When the animals are created, they are called a living being, *nefesh chaya,* but they are not given what God breathes into Adam—the "soul of life," *nishmat chayyim* (Genesis 7:22 does describe all land creatures as having something similar, but not the same: *nishmat* ruach *chayyim*). The human-animal distinction is one of the many distinctions the Torah makes and upon which higher civilization is based. The contemporary age, in its rejection of the Bible and its values, is undoing distinctions. Examples, as noted in Genesis 1:2, include good and evil, male and female, God and man, holy and profane.

> *The contemporary age, in its rejection of the Bible and its values, is undoing distinctions.*

2.8 The Lord God planted a garden in Eden, in the east, and placed there the man whom He had formed.

2.9 And from the ground the Lord God caused to grow every tree that was pleasing to the sight and good for food, with the tree of life in the middle of the garden, and the tree of knowledge of good and bad.

This does not describe the creation of trees, only the specific trees of the Garden of Eden.

The Torah explicitly states that all the trees of the garden were both beautiful to look at and good to eat. God did not make the Tree of Knowledge of Good and Evil uniquely tempting. (Unlike this translation, I use the more frequently used term for this tree—"Good and Evil"—because "evil" is the opposite of good more so than "bad." Unlike English, Hebrew has only one word to describe what is not good.)

The Tree of Life represents the innocence that preceded mortality (and, with it, sexuality as we know it). So long as Adam and Eve kept eating from the Tree of Life and not from the other tree, they understood they would live forever.

2.10 A river issues from Eden to water the garden, and it then divides and becomes four branches.

2.11 The name of the first is Pishon, the one that winds through the whole land of Havilah, where the gold is.

2.12 The gold of that land is good; bdellium is there, and lapis lazuli.

2.13 The name of the second river is Gihon, the one that winds through the whole land of Cush.

2.14 The name of the third river is Tigris, the one that flows east of Asshur. And the fourth river is the Euphrates.

2.15 The Lord God took the man and placed him in the Garden of Eden, to till it and to tend it.

ESSAY: DOES THE TORAH ADVOCATE VEGETARIANISM?

2.16 And the Lord God commanded the man, saying, "Of every tree of the garden, you are free to eat.
Both Adam and the animals were created vegetarian. After the flood, God permits humans to eat animals—but prohibits eating animal blood (Genesis 9:3-5). Later, in laws specific to Jews, the Torah curtails, but does not completely prohibit, meat eating: certain animals under certain conditions may be eaten. Many years later, the prophet Isaiah prophesied of the future Kingdom of God on earth in which all creatures would again be vegetarians ("the wolf shall dwell with the lamb... and the lion, like the ox, shall eat straw"—Isaiah 11:6-9).

Does the vegetarianism of the Garden of Eden and Isaiah's end-of-days prophecy mean that that the Torah regards vegetarianism as the human ideal?

Many argue it does.

Vegetarianism for moral reasons is certainly praiseworthy. But using the Garden of Eden as the reason to be vegetarian is not necessarily valid. The

Garden did not represent life as we know it, and the Torah's aim is to teach us how to live in this—the post-Garden of Eden—world. (As to why God permitted meat-eating after the flood, see commentary to Genesis 9:3.) Therefore, it is concerned not with vegetarianism but with humane treatment of animals. It repeatedly legislates kind treatment of animals—another first for the Torah. Indeed, proper treatment of animals is legislated in the central moral document of the Torah—the Ten Commandments—which mandates that animals rest one day a week. The Torah also prohibits muzzling an animal (which would prevent it from eating or drinking) when it labors in the fields (Deuteronomy 25:4) and yoking two animals of different sizes to the same plow (Deuteronomy 22:10). And, according to Jewish teaching, the ban on blood consumption specifically banned tearing off the limb of a live animal. This practice was used in the ancient world to avoid killing an animal and losing some of its meat to decay. This practice kept the animal alive—and its meat fresh—for a few more days, but it resulted in terrible suffering to the animal. As this ban is written before Jews existed, it is considered a universal ban—one of the "Seven Noahide Laws" incumbent upon all of humanity.

In a nutshell, the Torah is not preoccupied with preventing animal death; it is preoccupied with limiting animal suffering.

With regard to human beings, however, the Torah is preoccupied with both preventing death (unjust death, to be precise) and suffering.

Thus, for example, the Torah would allow experimenting on animals (providing animal suffering is, to the extent possible, avoided) to discover cures to human diseases and to directly save human life (as in killing a pig to use its heart valves in a human being).

Moreover, as praiseworthy as vegetarianism is, I have not been able to find a direct link between vegetarianism and moral behavior. While cruelty to animals almost always leads to cruelty to human beings, kindness to animals does not necessarily lead to kindness to human beings. (See the commentary on treatment of animals in Genesis 6:21.) Indeed, the most sadistic regime in history, the Nazi regime, banned animal experimentation (and allowed hideous experiments on non-sedated human beings).

ruelty to animals almost always leads to cruelty to human beings, kindness to animals does not necessarily lead to kindness to human beings.

2.17 but as for the tree of knowledge of good and bad, you must not eat of it,

Ian Pear, an American-Israeli rabbi, has noted that if you ask people, including those familiar with the Bible, what the first biblical injunction related to eating is, they will generally answer, "Not to eat from the Tree of Knowledge." But that is incorrect. The first directive regarding food is the commandment in the preceding verse to eat from all the other trees in the garden. Pear makes the point that the vast majority of people remember the negative command rather than its predecessor, the positive command; that is like a parent taking a child to a supermarket and telling the child to take anything he or she wants... but then adding that one item, and *only* one item, is off limits. Human nature is such that most children—and adults as well—would focus on the negative prohibition. But God wants us to partake of the world's pleasures. The Talmud is quite emphatic about this: "In the future world, a man will be required to give an accounting for every permitted pleasure he could have experienced but refused to."[3]

In permitting Adam to eat from the Tree of Life but prohibiting him from eating from the Tree of Knowledge of Good and Evil, God gives man a choice between two mutually exclusive ways of living. Either he can eat from the Tree of Life and live forever without knowing good and evil or he can eat from the Tree of Knowledge, know the difference between right and wrong—and be mortal.

As we will see, the point of the Adam and Eve story is that, if given the choice, we humans want a life of knowledge and choice more than a life of innocence.

2.17 (cont.) for as soon as you eat of it, you shall die.

God does not say that He will "punish" Adam if he eats from the Tree of Knowledge of Good and Bad. God simply states the consequence that will ensue.

The Hebrew says, *"on the day you eat from it, you will die."*

Once again, the word *yom*, "day," does not mean a twenty-four-hour day (see comment on 2:4), since Adam and Eve did not die on the day they ate the fruit. The late twentieth-century Etz Hayim commentary explains it this way: "You will have to live with the knowledge that one day you will die, a burden of awareness that no other creature bears."

Essay: It Is Not Good for Man to Be Alone

2.18 The Lord God said, "It is not good for man to be alone.

Until this verse, the only adjective God used to describe what He created was "good." Now, for the first time, God declares something "not good." In the words of the great seventeenth-century writer John Milton (*Paradise Lost*): "Loneliness is the first thing which God's eye named not good."

It is important to note that it is not Adam who said this; it was God who made this observation. Men do not independently know that it is not good for them to be alone. They know they need sex, but sex alone does not end loneliness.

As this verse is followed by the creation of a woman, with whom Adam is to bond (i.e., marry—see verse 24), it is clear God wants men to marry. Marriage is a prescription, a moral and social value, more than it is a male instinct. The dramatic decrease in marriage rates at this time attests to this (with regard to women as well), as does the fact that more people in the West and other developed societies are living by themselves than at any time in recorded history. So, while more and more men and women choose not to marry, loneliness has become a major social pathology. In the words of the National Institutes of Health, "Loneliness is a painful universal phenomenon."[4]

God wants us to partake of the world's pleasures.

Such reports are legion. Here's one other example:

"Researchers say loneliness is now a major public health issue and represents a greater health risk than obesity and is as destructive to your health

rds of the great
*   ...th-century writer*
John Milton (Paradise
Lost): "Loneliness is the
first thing which God's
eye named not good."

as smoking 15 cigarettes a day. The study, published in the journal 'Perspectives on Psychological Science', was a meta-analysis that looked at 70 studies covering over 3 million people. The results: social isolation, loneliness and living alone can increase mortality risk by 29%, 26%, and 32% respectively, after adjusting for age, gender, socio-economic status and pre-existing health conditions."[5]

Of course, no one should be so naïve as to assume marriage always solves the problem of loneliness. There are lonely married people. But, by ending Adam's alone-state by making one woman—not more than one woman, not another man, not children, and not a community of people—God is declaring the human ideal is that a single man bond with a single woman.

Because the statement "it is not good for man to be alone" occurs just before the creation of woman, people understand this verse as primarily referring to a man's need for a woman. But even independent of the male-female relationship, it is not good for a person to be alone—people need friends, children, and communities to assuage loneliness.

In Harvard professor Robert Putnam's 2000 book *Bowling Alone*, the author famously noted that in recent years fewer Americans were joining bowling leagues; more were "bowling alone" and leading lives unconnected to others. A decade later, Putnam revised his thesis, pointing out that what sociologists designate as "social capital" (the network of personal relationships that enable a society to function effectively) were still to be found—in churches and synagogues. And such people not only benefitted personally, they did more good for society. In other words, it is not good—*for society as well as for the individual*—that man be alone.

Jonathan Sacks, Jewish theologian and former chief rabbi of the United Kingdom, summarized this aspect of Putnam's findings:

"Regular attendees at a place of worship were more likely than others to give money to charity, engage in volunteer work, donate blood, spend time with someone who is depressed, offer a seat to a stranger, help someone find a job…*Regular attendance at a house of worship is the most accurate predictor of altruism,* more so than any other factor, including gender, education, income, race, region, marital status, ideology and age. Most fascinating of his [Putnam's] findings is that the key factor is *being part of a religious community*…an atheist who goes regularly to a house of worship (perhaps to accompany a spouse or a child) is more likely to volunteer in a soup kitchen than a fervent believer who prays alone. The key factor again is community."[6]

A Protestant pastor whose name I unfortunately do not recall made another telling point regarding this verse. God, the pastor pointed out, declared Adam "alone" despite the fact that Adam had a relationship with God. The lesson? God declares that even He, God, does not fully assuage our aloneness. God is essential, but we also need people.

"It is not good for man to be alone" even if the individual devotes himself to spiritual or intellectual pursuits. In a memoir entitled *Meetings*, the philosopher Martin Buber (*I and Thou*) wrote:

> *Marriage is a prescription, a moral and social value, more than it is a male instinct. The dramatic decrease in marriage rates at this time attests to this (with regard to women as well).*

"Imagine yourself in a situation where you are alone, wholly alone on earth, and you are offered one of the two, books or men. I often hear men prizing their solitude but that is only because there are still men somewhere on earth, even though in the far distance. I knew nothing of books when I came forth from the womb of my mother, and I shall die without books, with another human hand in my own. I do, indeed close my door at times and surrender myself to a book, but only because I can open the door again and see a human being looking at me."[7]

2.18 (cont.) I will make a fitting helper for him."

A literal translation is "a helper who is his equal."

There is a brilliant tension in this description of the woman's relationship to her man: She is both his helper and his equal. The Hebrew is clear, since *k'negdo*—even in modern Hebrew—means "equal to him."

This description flies in the face of many traditional as well as modern views of a woman's relationship to a man. The former reject the equality and the latter reject the helper aspect. But this is the Torah's view of the ideal husband-wife relationship. She is both his equal and his helper (assuming, of course, he is a man worthy of her help).

Furthermore, if we dissect the word literally, *k'negdo* means "as opposed to him." This implies that the woman helps her man in part by challenging him (to be better). Every man in a good marriage knows how true that is. As my longtime friend, former presidential speech writer Bruce Herschensohn, once put it to me, "In the beginning God created man and critic."

Finally, the word "helper" (*ezer*) in no way implies an inferior role. God Himself is called an *ezer* more than a dozen times in the Hebrew Bible (see, for example, Deuteronomy 33:29, Psalms 121:1-2, and Psalms 33:20).

ANIMALS CANNOT REPLACE HUMANS

2.19 And the Lord God formed out of the earth all the wild beasts and all the birds of the sky, and brought them to the man to see what he would call them; and whatever the man called each living creature, that would be its name.

This is another alleged contradiction some scholars and others find in this second creation narrative. To be fair, it does sounds like God made animals after making man. But, again, the purpose of mentioning the animals here, like the vegetation in verse 5, is to teach something significant about man. *This verse is not necessarily a chronological account about when animals were created—explaining chronology is not the purpose of the second creation narrative.* These verses concern man's inability to find a suitable companion among animals—not when all animals were created.

Sarna writes: "The dominant theme of this section, to which all else is subordinated, is man and the human condition. The narrative now focuses on humankind's mastery over the animals. Mention of their creation is therefore made incidentally, not for its own sake, and is no indication of sequential order in regard to the creation of man."

Also, it is possible to translate "the Lord God formed" as "the Lord God *had* formed," because the past tense of a Hebrew verb can be perfect ("formed") or pluperfect ("had formed"). Only context can explain which form of the past tense it is.

2.20 And the man gave names to all the cattle and to the birds of the sky and to all the wild beasts, but for Adam no fitting helper was found.

In a certain sense, this end of this verse seems to be a non-sequitur since we just read that God was going to create a helper who is man's equal. Perhaps God wants Adam to first attempt to find a partner from among the animals and to come to his own understanding about why he can't achieve such a relationship with an animal. This is not farfetched. More and more people in our time regard an animal as their best friend. A friend of mine told me he heard a father say he was getting a dog for his young son to guarantee the boy "would always have a best friend." While it surely is a blessing to have a loving animal in one's life, the ideal closest relationship is with another human being.

The Torah does not say Adam couldn't find a helper; animals could be and are helpers. It says Adam could not find a helper "who is his equal." But an animal cannot be any person's equal. And any companion that is not a true equal, even a human being, cannot fully alleviate loneliness.

That is why, when God finally makes the helper who is Adam's equal, it is a peer, not, for example, a child. Children are a unique blessing, and love for one's children is a unique love. But children are not our peers and therefore cannot alleviate loneliness in the way an adult companion can.

My parents had an extraordinarily close relationship of seventy-three years' duration. When my mother died shortly before her ninetieth birthday, my father, Max Prager, was devastated. Before he died at the age of ninety-six, he opened up to me on this subject. "I have been truly blessed," he said, "with two wonderful sons and extremely loving grandchildren and great-grandchildren, all of whom I deeply love. But no one can replace your mother. No child, grand-child, or great-grandchild can fill that hole."

2.21 So the Lord God cast a deep sleep upon the man; and while he slept, He took one of his ribs and closed up the flesh at that spot.

Most contemporary scholars agree that the Hebrew *tzela* does not mean, as it is often translated, "rib." Therefore, this might be better translated "and God took from one of Adam's sides and then he closed the skin over it."

2.22 And the Lord God fashioned the rib that He had taken from the man into a woman, and He brought her to the man.

Since creation in Genesis develops progressively, with each creation on a higher level than the creation preceding it (for example, fish are created on the fifth day, while land animals, followed by mankind, are created on the sixth), woman may be considered to be the culmination of creation.

"We have no other example in the ancient Near East of a creation story of a woman."

Also, whereas man was created in just one verse, it takes six verses (2:18-2:23) to describe the creation of a woman, suggesting that God took more care, time, and effort to bring her into existence (Sarna).

"We have no other example in the ancient Near East of a creation story of a woman" (Sarna). The creation story is one of many examples of the high value placed on women in the Torah.

2.23 Then the man said, "This one at last is bone of my bones and flesh of my flesh. This one shall be called Woman for from man was she taken."

Adam awakened and realized he needed a woman. Most men who, in their youth, think it is good to be alone and carefree eventually come to a similar conclusion. We humans often do not know what is best for us.

ESSAY: MARRY AND BECOME A MAN

2.24 Hence a man leaves his father and mother and clings to his wife, so that they become one flesh.

If we read these words descriptively, they are a natural con the previous verses. Since woman was originally a part of ma man leaves his parents to marry, he can rejoin her so they ag.... ...... one flesh.

But we should read these words prescriptively. The biblical narrative is interrupted to present a vital psychological and moral insight: In order to grow up and become a man, a man must leave his parents and bond with a wife. Only after abandoning dependence on his parents is he ready to marry. And he should marry.

This is a good example of the continuing relevance of the Torah (and the rest of the Bible). At the time of this writing, the percentage of single adult men in their twenties and thirties in Europe, America, Japan, and elsewhere living in their parents' home is unprecedentedly high. One reason, according to British professor Frank Furedi of the University of Kent, is "young adults are being 'treated childishly...parents are allowing young people to remain in extended adolescence' instead of forcing them to make their own way in life."[8]

Ask any man whether marriage matured him, and in virtually every instance—including when his marriage ended in divorce—a man will say it did. Of course, there are some exceptions, but exceptions do not invalidate rules. Occasionally, wearing a seat belt in a car crash causes a person to die. But that in no way invalidates the rule that seat belts save lives. So, too, the existence of mature and responsible men who have never married in no way invalidates the rule that marriage makes men.

Of course, this matters only in a society in which males wish to grow up and become men.

> *In order to grow up and become a man, a man must leave his parents and bond with a wife.*

This is also an important verse for parents to internalize. When their son becomes involved in a serious relationship with a woman (or vice versa), parents should not feel that the child is in some way deserting or rejecting them. Rather, this is the way of the world as God made it; and this is what God wants to see happen.

Although the Bible, in keeping with the mores of the time in which it was written, permitted polygamy, the very phrasing of this verse makes it clear monogamy is the ideal because it alone allows for relationships of equality and reciprocity. God ordains here that one husband should cleave to one wife, suggesting that loneliness is best assuaged by a monogamous union of two people who can give their all to each other. Polygamous marriages in the Torah and later books of the Hebrew Bible are almost always described as unhappy.

Rabbi Nahum Rabinovich, the former dean of the London-based rabbinical school, Jews College, and the holder of a Ph.D. in statistics and probability, notes that God arranged the world so that the population in all societies is approximately half male and half female. This makes it clear "the desirable state is the permanent pairing of one man with one woman and that such pairing is divinely intended."[9]

2.25 The two of them were naked, the man and his wife, yet they felt no shame.

Adam and Eve were as innocent as children who are not aware of their nudity and therefore not embarrassed by it. One might even say they were similar to animals in this way—they, too, have no shame regarding their lack of clothing.

CHAPTER
3

IS THE GARDEN OF EDEN LITERALLY TRUE?

One of the most common objections to taking the Torah seriously, let alone as a divine text, is the seeming impossibility of taking some of its stories literally. Aside from creation in six days, probably the most frequently cited example is the Garden of Eden story. Only religious fundamentalists, the argument goes, could possibly believe there was an actual Garden of Eden, actual people named Adam and Eve, and a snake that spoke.

I have never been troubled by this issue.

If there is a God who created the universe, He could surely create a serpent that could communicate. Therefore, for those who accept the God of Genesis 1, there should be no issue here. And for those who reject the Creator of Genesis 1, there is also no issue here: Since there is no God, there was no Garden of Eden, no revelation at Sinai, and none of the other non-provable events described in the Torah.

Having said that, I was taught by my Orthodox Torah teacher, Rabbi Amnon Haramati of the Yeshiva of Flatbush High School, that one need not take the Garden of Eden literally; even an Orthodox Jew could regard the story as a divinely conceived parable intended to teach about the nature of the human soul. Nor was this a singular view. A well-regarded Orthodox scholar, Rabbi Moshe Shamah, in *Recalling the Covenant,* a commentary on the Torah, introduces his discussion of the Garden of Eden by saying, "In the early chapters of Genesis, set in the primeval era of human existence, the Torah provides metaphorical and symbolic expositions of some of the most profound religious and psychological insights into the human condition."

So, the question of whether this story is literal history or divine parable has never vexed me. In either case, I believe the Torah to be a divine text. What matters is what God wants us to learn from the story.

3.1 Now the serpent was the shrewdest of all the wild beasts that the Lord God had made. He said to the woman, "Did God really say: You shall not eat of any tree of the garden?"

3.2 The woman replied to the serpent, "We may eat of the fruit of the other trees of the garden.

3.3 It is only about fruit of the tree in the middle of the garden that God said, 'You shall not eat of it, or touch it, lest you die.'"

Victor Hamilton writes: "Regarding the serpent's origin, we are clearly told that he was an animal made by God. This information immediately removes any possibility that the serpent is to be viewed as some kind of supernatural, divine force. There is no room here for any dualistic ideas about the origins of good and evil."

The serpent did not go to Adam; it went to the woman. One might conclude the serpent thought the woman would be more persuadable; however, she actually proved harder to convince than Adam. The serpent used cunning and logic to sway her; the woman merely handed Adam the fruit and said, "Eat" (verse 6). The likely reason the serpent went to the woman is that it assumed Adam, having heard the prohibition directly from God, would be the more difficult party to convince. The woman learned about the prohibition secondhand.

MISQUOTING GOD OR MAN CAN LEAD TO CATASTROPHIC CONSEQUENCES

In posing the question, "Did God really say: You shall not eat of any tree of the garden?" the serpent deliberately distorted God's words, claiming that God prohibited eating from all the trees in the garden, when in fact God prohibited eating only from one.

The woman, too, misrepresented what God actually said. God did not prohibit touching the Tree of Knowledge of Good and Evil; He prohibited eating from it.

Why did she misquote God? One possible explanation is she repeated what Adam had told her. Adam, in order to ensure Eve not eat from the forbidden tree, may have told her just touching it would be fatal. This is an ancient understanding as well.[1]

The Talmud comments on Eve's incorrect citing of God's instructions: "One who adds to God's words actually detracts from them."[2] For this reason, the Torah legislates (Deuteronomy 4:2, 13:1) that we should not only not subtract from God's commands, we should not add to them either. This also applies to the words of human beings. Misquoting someone or adding to their words to reinforce what the person said—even when done with good intentions—is not only immoral,[3] it can easily lead to catastrophic results, as it did in this case.

3.4 And the serpent said to the woman, "You are not going to die,

3.5 but God knows that as soon as you eat of it, your eyes will be opened

The serpent tried to persuade the woman the prohibition was given for God's sake—to protect God from Adam and Eve becoming like Him—and becoming His competitors.

3.5 (cont.) and you will be like divine beings who know good and bad."

This is the third step of the process by which the serpent led the woman astray.

First, it overstated the prohibition ("Did God really say: You shall not eat of any tree of the garden?") so that God's command seems both absurd and oppressive.

Second, it attacked God's motive: God does not want mankind to become as knowledgeable as He.

Third, the serpent convinced the woman she will not only not suffer if she violates the prohibition, she will greatly benefit ("you will be like God").

These three steps offer a classic presentation of the way people are often led to do wrong: Exaggerate, then denigrate the other side's motive, then promise a reward.

One obvious, but rarely asked, question is this: Why is the serpent necessary to the story?

I think one answer suggests itself. The serpent represents the root of human evil—attempting to displace God as moral authority. The serpent is the voice in human beings telling them they are—or should be—God-like, meaning they can rely solely on themselves to determine what is right and wrong. This is what is happening in the secular West. People increasingly rely on their feelings to determine right and wrong. They do not rely on God; they do not rely on a religion; they do not rely on a Bible. Morally speaking, they are their own gods.

> *The serpent represents the root of human evil—attempting to displace God as moral authority.*

THE UNIQUE POWER OF THE EYE

3.6 When the woman saw that the tree was good for eating and a delight to the eyes, and that the tree was desirable as a source of wisdom,

The tree tempted the woman's appetite ("good for eating"), eyes ("delight to the eyes"), and mind ("a source of wisdom"). By emphasizing that the tree offered these great rewards to the woman, the Torah may be eliciting some sympathy for, and certainly an understanding of, Eve's decision to disobey God and eat from the tree.

One clear lesson is how much trouble our eyes get us into ("the woman *saw* that the tree was...a *delight to the eyes*"). The ear is ultimately more trustworthy than the eye. It is generally less superficial and emotional. In America, the expression "eye candy" describes television programs, movies, and advertisements that are intellectually empty but enticing visually (usually depicting attractive women). There is no comparable expression "ear candy."

3.6 (cont.) she took of its fruit and ate. She also gave some to her husband,

> God had warned Adam and, by implication, Eve, that if they ate from the Tree of Knowledge, they would die. To her credit, the woman did not use Adam as a guinea pig. Once she decided to listen to the serpent, she sampled the fruit herself. And when she remained alive, the woman concluded the serpent was right and shared the fruit with her husband.

3.6 (cont.) and he ate.

> Seeing that Eve did not die, Adam ate without hesitation.

3.7 Then the eyes of both of them were opened, and they perceived that they were naked;

> Adam and Eve looked at their bodies and discovered sexuality. They already knew about procreative sex (2:24), but such sex was what we would call "innocent." Only after they ate from the Tree of Knowledge of Good and Evil did they become aware of the non-innocent erotic aspects of human sexuality. Adam and Eve grew up, in much the same way young people do when they become sexually aware.
>
> The word for "naked" here is subtly different from the word for "naked" in Genesis 2:25, where the Torah describes Adam and Eve as "naked" but not embarrassed by their nakedness. There the word is *a-rumim*, here the word is *ay-rumim*—to underscore this is a different "naked" than before.

WE ARE ALL ADAM AND EVE

The Adam and Eve story is the story of all of us.

> Human beings are rarely satisfied with what they have. Even in the Garden of Eden, where every human need was met—there was no illness, no hunger, no disease, and not even death—Adam and Eve wanted more.
>
> Moreover, humans prefer knowing and experiencing all of life—even with the inevitability of suffering and the certitude of death—to a more childlike existence with no suffering or death.

In other words, one lesson of the Garden of Eden story is that the full experience of this life means we will suffer and die.

The dominant Christian understanding of the story is that it represents "The Fall" of man. That is certainly true. But I see it more as the "The Choice" of man.

3.7 (cont.) and they sewed together fig leaves and made themselves loincloths.

Presumably these were leaves that covered their genitals.

3.8 They heard the sound of the Lord God moving about in the garden at the breezy time of day; and the man and his wife hid from the Lord God among the trees of the garden.

3.9 The Lord God called out to the man

God addressed Adam and not the woman because it was Adam to whom He delivered the prohibition against eating from the tree.

3.9 (cont.) and said to him, "Where are you?"

Of course, God knew where Adam was. This question was posed not for God's sake but to elicit a response from Adam—which is what then occurred:

3.10 He replied, "I heard the sound of You in the garden, and I was afraid because I was naked, so I hid."

3.11 Then He asked, "Who told you that you were naked? Did you eat of the tree from which I had forbidden you to eat?"

God's question forced Adam to admit the truth.

3.12 The man said, "The woman you put at my side—she gave me of the tree, and I ate."

Adam not only shifted blame to the woman, he also blamed God. By referring to his wife as "the woman You gave me," he clearly implied he never asked God to create the woman; and if God had not made her, he would never have eaten from the tree.

Blaming others for wrongs we have done is literally as old as humanity. Adam blamed Eve (and implicitly God); and Eve, as we shall now see, blamed the snake. Neither took personal responsibility. As psychiatrist Dr. Abraham Twerski puts it, "Human beings need four things: air, food, drink, and someone to blame."

Blaming others for the wrongs we do is not only morally wrong; it makes emotional and moral growth impossible. Yet, it remains a universal epidemic. To cite just a few examples, many adults blame their parents for all their serious problems; many regimes blame imperialism for their country's corruption; and many murderers blame poverty or a difficult childhood for their criminality.

> As psychiatrist Dr. Abraham Twerski puts it, "Human beings need four things: air, food, drink, and someone to blame."

3.13 And the Lord God said to the woman, "What is this you have done?" The woman replied, "The serpent duped me and I ate."

Victor Hamilton favorably compares the woman's response to the man's: "She does not say 'the serpent whom *you* made' "—unlike Adam, who said, "the woman whom you made." Nonetheless, she, like Adam, blamed someone other than herself.

3.14 Then the Lord God said to the serpent, "Because you did this,

God did not interrogate the serpent as He interrogated Adam and Eve because there is nothing the serpent could say in its defense. There was no one left for the serpent to blame.

3.14 (cont.) more cursed shall you be than all cattle and all the wild beasts; On your belly shall you crawl, and dirt shall you eat all the days of your life.

Among other things, God's curse de-deified the serpent, which was worshipped in many pagan societies, including the Egyptian, Sumerian, Hittite, and Canaanite. Throughout the Torah, the Torah seeks to undermine polytheism by dethroning the gods of the ancient world. Thus, for example, nine of the Ten Plagues of the Exodus were directed against Egyptian gods (see a list of those gods in the commentary to Exodus 7:5).

3.15 I will put enmity between you and the woman, and between your offspring and hers; They shall strike at your head, and you shall strike at their heel."

3.16 And to the woman He said, "I will make most severe your pangs in childbearing; in pain shall you bear children.

Unlike the words He addressed to Adam and the serpent, God did not use the word "curse" in addressing the woman. While the woman is punished, she was not cursed.

Also, God did not say He will create pain in childbirth, but rather that He will *multiply* it (the translation here is "make most severe"), suggesting that some pain would have accompanied birth even in the Garden of Eden.

Essentially, God was telling the man and the woman He was no longer going to protect human beings from the harshness of nature. But this does not prevent people from trying to conquer the harshness of nature on their own. Human progress depends on doing so.

THE WOMAN'S DESIRE FOR A MAN

3.16 (cont.) Yet your urge shall be for your husband,

This is a verse that understandably disturbs many moderns. The modern ideal is that a woman never depend on, let alone have an "urge" for, a man, a husband. A well-known feminist slogan of the 1960s put it this way: "A woman without a man is like a fish without a bicycle." And, to be sure, a certain percentage of women do not yearn for a man. But most women's "urge" for a man to love and be loved by is a reality—even though much contemporary thinking denies it: "You don't need a man," "Never be dependent."

What we have here is another statement of the reality that accompanies leaving Eden. God is saying in the real world in which Adam and Eve will now live is now the reality. It is not necessarily either a curse or a punishment. And it is certainly not a command. It is a description of what will ensue in the real world.

Only time will tell whether this denial of a woman's yearning for a man—and its replacement with a yearning for a career, for example—will produce happier women and a healthier society. If it does, this verse will no longer describe reality. On the other hand, if denying this verse does not lead to happier women and a healthier society, perhaps one day more people will look at the Garden of Eden story with renewed respect.

ESSAY: WOMAN'S DESIRE FOR A DOMINANT MAN

3.16 (cont.) and he shall rule over you."

The second, and considerably greater, problem for many people is this second part of the verse. At the very least, it contradicts egalitarian thinking.

The reality is most women do seek a man stronger than they are. It is why, for example, most women seek a man who earns more money than they do. Even very wealthy women generally seek a man at least as wealthy as they are (whereas wealthy men generally do not seek a wealthy, let alone a wealthier, woman). And they seek professional ambition in men more than most men seek this trait in a woman. If you ask most single men seeking a wife, "Are you interested in meeting a woman who is beautiful, very kind, and very smart, but not professionally ambitious?" most men would respond in the affirmative. But if you ask most single women seeking a husband, "Are you interested in meeting a man who is very handsome, very kind and very smart, but not professionally ambitious?" most women would respond in the negative.

This is true not only regarding ambition and wealth. No matter how smart a woman is, most women are more attracted to a smarter man; no matter how tall, most women are more attracted to a taller man; no matter how successful, most women are more attracted to a more successful man.

Even a completely secular, evolutionary understanding of male and female natures argues for female attraction to dominant males:

"Evolutionary psychologists claim that women prefer dominant partners because such men have superior genes. Evidence has shown that women prefer more dominant men when they themselves are at the most fertile point of their menstrual cycle, whereas most men do not similarly seek out dominant women."[4]

To deny this female desire is to deny reality. Even in our time, when men and women are raised on "gender equality" and most university-educated men and women strongly affirm a desire to make a home that is egalitarian, few marriages are egalitarian. Scores of studies in many countries conclude no matter how much both a husband and wife affirm equality, even if both spouses earn roughly the same amount of money, wives do more housework than their husbands.[5]

Again, my understanding of the Garden of Eden story is that it reflects the choice we humans make to be fully human: awareness over immortality. This verse seems to suggest that part of the sexual awakening resulting from eating of the Tree of Knowledge was a woman's urge for a more dominant partner. For most women, a man whom she can dominate is not alluring while a dominant man is alluring—assuming, of course, he treats her with love and respect. This is in no way a defense of any form of male abuse of a woman—whether physical, sexual, verbal, psychological, or economic. Abuse is evil. But in the complex interaction of male and female, a dominant male is sexually alluring for most women.

Of course, many will argue that most modern women want neither a dominant nor a dominated man—just an equal. But the Torah has already stated that the sexes are equal. That a woman will be more attracted to a dominant man does not negate that equality.[6]

This seeking of a dominant man is the unhappy reason many young women are drawn to "bad boys," males who will mistreat them and who mistreat others. But a dominant man is not necessarily a bad man. A dominant man can be and must also be loving and kind. The man who embodies all three traits, for most women, is the best man.

Finally, this consequence of eating from the Tree of Knowledge is descriptive, not prescriptive. Women are entirely free to choose a non-dominant man.

3.17 To Adam He said, "Because you did as your wife said and ate of the tree about which I commanded you, 'You shall not eat of it,'

Adam faced harsh consequences not because "you did as your wife said" but because he listened to his wife rather than God. In a later instance, when Abraham did not listen to his wife, Sarah, God specifically instructed him to listen to her (Genesis 21:12).

3.17 (cont.) cursed be the ground because of you; By toil shall you eat of it all the days of your life:

Unlike the serpent, Adam was not cursed directly; the ground was cursed, and as a result, he will have to toil all the days of his life.

The consequences the man must face are macro and broad, pertaining to the earth and to work; the consequences to the woman are micro and personal, pertaining to feelings, pain, and desire. This also reflects the natures of men and women. Men tend to be more preoccupied with the macro and women with the micro. That is why women are more likely than men to enter fields that deal with children (from teacher to pediatrician to child therapist); more likely to vote for candidates who advocate policies that expand the state's role in taking care of its citizens; and more likely, when witnessing a car accident, to notice the pain and suffering of those hurt than to notice the make and color of the car.

The micro and macro are of equal importance, but the two must balance one another. Too much focus on either leads to a dysfunctional society. That is one reason why men need a woman; women need a man; and society needs both (ideally, according to the Torah, when they are married).

3.18 Thorns and thistles shall it sprout for you. But your food shall be the grasses of the field;

3.19 By the sweat of your brow shall you get bread to eat, until you return to the ground—

The woman will suffer in bringing forth life; the man will suffer in bringing forth bread.

3.19 (cont.) For from it you were taken. For dust you are and to dust you shall return."

This was God telling Adam that humans beings will be the opposite of what the serpent promised they would be—not "like gods"—but mere dust.

But, of course, because we are created in God's image, we are not merely dust. It is good for us to be constantly aware of both—when we get too arrogant, to remember we are dust; and when we feel low and unworthy, to remember we are created in God's image.

3.20 The man named his wife Eve because she was the mother of all the living.

"Eve" means "life" in the same way "Adam" means "earth." These names, "earth" and "life," suggest Adam and Eve are prototypes for all of humanity.

3.21 And the Lord God made garments of skins for Adam and his wife, and clothed them.

The first thing God did for Adam and Eve is make them clothing.

God does not want human beings walking around naked. The obvious reason is sexual modesty. But there is an equally important, though much less obvious, reason: Clothing distinguished the human being from, and elevates the human being above, animals. Animals are naked, human beings are to be clothed. As delineated in the Torah, the divine order is composed of distinctions:

Human-God
Human-Animal
Man-Woman
Parent-Child
Life-Death
Good-Evil
Holy-Profane

WHAT DOES IT MEAN WHEN MAN BECOMES LIKE GOD?

3.22 And the Lord God said, "Now that the man has become like one of us, knowing good and bad,

In the Torah, the phrase "good and evil" ("good and bad" in this translation) can mean "everything." It can also mean moral free will—animals do not have moral free will because they do not know the difference between good and evil. And, as the serpent correctly noted, "knowing good and evil" can also mean being the one who determines what is good and what is evil. That is what is meant in this verse by "man has become like one of us, knowing good and evil."

The moral message of the Torah—ethical monotheism—is God determines good and evil. *When man determines good and evil, man becomes god*, which is precisely what God says in this verse. And it is precisely what has happened in the West since the French Enlightenment. Man has displaced God as the source of right and wrong. As Karl Marx wrote,

> *Clothing distinguished the human being from, and elevates the human being above, animals. Animals are naked, human beings are to be clothed.*

"Man is God." And as Lenin, the father of modern totalitarianism, said, "We repudiate all morality derived from non-human (i.e., God) and non-class concepts." Lenin, his Communist Party, and his successor, Josef Stalin, did indeed become gods.

3.22 (cont.) what if he should stretch out his hand and take also from the tree of life and eat, and live forever."

This sounds almost as if God is afraid of man. But, of course, that is impossible. Even if man had free will and lived forever, he could not threaten God. What God "feared" was man, being both immortal (having eaten from the Tree of Life) and replacing God as the arbiter of good and evil (by eating from the Tree of Knowledge of Good and Evil). The world would then be populated by immortal beings doing evil—the very opposite of what God envisioned in making the world and making man.

Why Didn't Adam and Eve Protest Their Expulsion from Eden?

3.23 So the Lord God banished him from the garden of Eden to till the soil from which he was taken.
We might have expected Adam and Eve to protest God's decrees and/or the expulsion from Eden. We might also have expected Adam to get angry at his wife for having given him the fruit. And yet the Torah gives no indication of any protest or anger. Perhaps they were simply relieved that God had not killed them. Perhaps they didn't really understand what life was going to be like. Perhaps they believed that they deserved their fates.

The Jewish educator Dr. Shlomo Bardin offered a parable on this story with an utterly original explanation as to why Eve might have actually engineered the expulsion from Eden. "Imagine," Bardin taught, "a young woman marries a young man whose father is president of a large company. After the marriage, the father makes the son a vice-president and gives him a large salary, but because he has no work experience, the father gives him no responsibilities. Every week, the young man draws a large check, but he has nothing to do. His wife soon realizes she is not married to a man but to a boy, and as long as her husband stays in his father's firm, he will always be a boy. So she forces him to quit his job, give up his security, go to another city, and start out on his own. That," Bardin concluded, "is the reason Eve ate from the tree."

The Bardin explanation accords with my own belief that the Garden of Eden story describes the human situation. When given the choice between Eden-like innocence, with its lack of challenges to overcome, lack of sexual awareness, etc., and a world in which one must grow up, overcome challenges, experience adult sexuality—and, yes, suffer and die—human beings will choose the latter.

Both Judaism and Christianity use this story to explain human suffering. For Christianity, sin (and therefore suffering) entered the world through the

Original Sin of Adam and Eve. And while Judaism does not use the term "Original Sin," it explains the introduction of suffering in essentially the same way. A difference between Christian and Jewish teachings on this issue is that Christian theology teaches that because of Adam and Eve's sin, all people are born in a state of sin while the Jewish belief is people are born innocent (though prone to do bad). Or, as Joseph Telushkin puts it, "The prevailing attitude among Jewish scholars is that people sin *as* Adam and Eve sinned, not *because* they sinned."

3.24 He drove the man out, and stationed east of the garden of Eden the cherubim and the fiery ever-turning sword, to guard the way to the tree of life.

CHAPTER

4

4.1 Now the man knew his wife Eve,

The biblical word used here for sexual intercourse, "knew" (*yada*), is from the same root as the word used for "knowledge" (*da'at*) in the Tree of Knowledge of Good and Evil. Use of the word "knew" is appropriate given that sexual intercourse is a unique form of knowing someone.

4.1 (cont.) and she conceived and bore Cain, saying "I have gained a male child with the help of the Lord."

The Hebrew name for Cain, *Kayin*, comes from the Hebrew word *kana*, which can mean "acquire," which is the word most scholars have used to explain Cain's name. However, Professor Gottlieb of Bar-Ilan University makes a persuasive case that the other meaning of *kana*—to "create" or "make"—is the likely meaning of Cain's name. (For examples of *kana* meaning "create" or "make," see Genesis 14:19 and 22, Deuteronomy 32:6, Psalms 139:13, and Proverbs 8:22.) In Gottlieb's words, "the woman calls her baby Cain because she realizes she was partner to God in its creation."

4.2 She then bore his brother Abel. Abel became a keeper of sheep, and Cain became a tiller of the soil.

The Hebrew name for Abel, *Havel*, is usually translated as "nothingness," "vanity," or "futility," as in the verse in Ecclesiastes that reads "vanity of vanities, all is vanity" (*havel havelim, hakol havel*—Ecclesiastes 1:2). Bible Professor Leeor Gottlieb explains that its original meaning is "vapor, the warm breath that comes out of our mouths, something that is seen, but cannot be held, something that disappears after a short time (hence, evaporates) and leaves no real mark on the world."[1]

And, indeed, Abel did "disappear" at a young age. The Torah thus named him "Vapor," not his mother.

4.3 In the course of time, Cain brought an offering to the Lord from the fruit of the soil.

The Torah states matter-of-factly that Cain and Abel brought offerings to God, suggesting the universality of sacrifice, prayer, and belief in a deity. We know of no pre-modern society that was atheistic and of no ancient society that did not have sacrifices to its god(s).

The widespread extent of atheism and secularism in our time is unique in human history. Whether modern godless societies can long survive is an open question.

WHEN DO INTENTIONS MATTER?

4.4 And Abel, for his part, brought the choicest of the firstlings of his flock. The Lord paid heed to Abel and his offering.

We know of no pre-modern society that was atheistic. Whether modern godless societies can long survive is an open question.

4.5 but to Cain and to his offering, He paid no heed.

The Torah never tells us how Cain knew that God preferred Abel's offering to his own. The implication of the biblical text is Abel's offering was more heartfelt than Cain's: "Cain brought an offering to the Lord from the fruit of his soil, and Abel…brought the *choicest* of the firstlings of his flock" (emphasis added). Perhaps Cain, seeing the devotion and generosity with which his brother offered his sacrifice, realized his sacrifice was comparatively lacking. Or perhaps there was some reaction from God the Torah does not record. In any case, Abel's greater commitment, epitomized by his bringing "the choicest" of his flock is what mattered.

This brings us to the important issue of intention.

When it comes to ethical behavior, actions matter muc intentions or sincerity. What matters is that we help our fellow human beings. If a man's primary—even his sole— motivation for building a hospital is to have his name on the building, it makes no difference to any of the people whose lives will be saved by that hospital. But when it comes to religious ritual—what is referred to in Jewish sources as "laws between man and God"—intentions do matter. For example, if a person acts piously, carrying out rituals or making declarations of faith solely to impress others, that motive makes a mockery of his piety.

> *When it comes to ethical behavior, actions matter much more than intentions or sincerity. But when it comes to religious ritual—"laws between man and God"—intentions do matter.*

DO WE ENVY OR EMULATE THOSE WHO SURPASS US?

4.5 (cont.) Cain was much distressed and his face fell.

When others achieve more than we do, we can have two possible reactions. We can admire what they have accomplished and strive to emulate or even surpass them, or we can grow jealous and wish them harm—as Cain did.

How people react to individuals or groups that have succeeded more than they or their group is a test of character and a predictor of behavior. The noted economist and intellectual George Gilder wrote about this in his book *The Israel Test*. By "Israel Test," Gilder (a non-Jew) discerned a way to determine whether an individual or group will succeed or fail. Those who resent Israel's outsized achievements are likely to fail morally, economically, and socially. Conversely, those who admire Israel and seek to emulate its achievements will likely create their own free and prosperous societies. A significant cause of Jew-hatred throughout history has been a resentment of Jews' achievements.[2]

After seeing his brother's superior sacrifice and God's preference for it, Cain could have simply resolved to bring a more generous offering next time. Instead, his "face fell," and he grew angry—but not at himself. At Abel.

When to get angry and when and how to express it are among the most important lessons humans can learn. Cain's rage at Abel is a classic example of misplaced rage.

4.6 And the Lord said to Cain, "Why are you distressed and why is your face fallen?

GOODNESS AND HAPPINESS

4.7 Surely, if you do right, there is uplift.

In one sentence, God expresses one of life's truisms: doing good uplifts us—not only morally, but in terms of happiness. That raises an obvious question: Given most people want to be happy, why don't more people do good? One major reason is most good actions are not fun, and people pursue fun, which provides immediate pleasure, over happiness, which usually comes as a result of doing things that are not fun. Visiting the sick is not fun; but just about everyone who visits and brings comfort to the sick is happier after doing so. On the other hand, watching television is fun, but few people are happier as a result of having watched a lot of television.[3]

4.7 (cont.) But if you do not do right, sin couches at the door,

We have here another essential truism about a moral life. The less we engage in good behavior ("do not do right") the more bad behavior becomes tempting and even inevitable ("sin couches at the door"—or, as in most other translations, "crouches at the door"). The reason is that life largely consists of habits—doing good leads to doing more good; doing bad leads to doing more bad.

Aristotle states this idea emphatically in his *Nicomachean Ethics:* "We become just by doing just acts, temperate by doing temperate acts, brave by doing brave acts.... It makes no small difference, then, whether we form habits

of one kind or another from our very youth; it makes a very gre
or rather all the difference."

4.7 (cont.) its urge is toward you,

Human nature inclines toward sin (see Genesis 8:21); therefore, it is always tempting.

ESSAY: THE MOST EMPOWERING IDEA IN LIFE

4.7 (cont.) yet you can be its master."

The statement "yet you can be its master" is one of the Torah's most important statements. It means we have moral free will. That we can rule over our desire to do wrong is the most empowering idea in life. The only way we can end bad behavior—actions that are either destructive to others or to ourselves—is to first recognize that we "can be its master." If we regard ourselves as incapable of controlling ourselves (e.g., "When I get angry, I just can't control my temper"), we never will. One might say self-control is the most important achievement we can attain. That many parents work harder to instill self-esteem than self-control in their children is a moral tragedy. And, ironically, no self-esteem can equal the self-esteem that derives from self-control.

> *That we can rule over our desire to do wrong is the most empowering idea in life.*

The power of the words "you can rule over it" is the subject of one of the most remarkable and unexpected passages in modern literature. It takes place in the middle of John Steinbeck's *East of Eden*, the novel which the Nobel-prize winning Steinbeck regarded as his greatest literary achievement.

Set in California in the early twentieth century, *East of Eden* tells the story of two families whose generations unwittingly reenact the story of Adam and Eve's fall and the rivalry of Cain and Abel. A central character in the novel is

Lee, a Chinese-American man who learned the biblical story of Cain and Abel from a Christian friend and became obsessed with it. What exactly, he wanted to know, did God say to Cain about his ability to overcome his evil desires?

Not knowing Hebrew, Lee consulted the King James Version of the Bible: "If thou doest not well, sin lieth at the door. And unto thee shall be his desire, *and thou shalt rule over him.*"

Lee understood that God promised Cain that he would conquer sin. But then Lee consulted the American Standard Bible, which renders the last words differently: "*but do thou rule over it.*" According to this translation, these words are not a promise from God but an order from God to rule over sin.

Wanting to know which of these translations was correct, Lee went to the wisest Chinese elders in San Francisco, who then, along with Lee, spent two years studying Hebrew, hiring a rabbi to teach them so they could properly understand this story that they regarded as containing so much wisdom and truth.

"After two years," Lee explains, "we felt that we could approach the sixteen verses of the fourth chapter of Genesis."

They concluded that the word God said to Cain, *timshol*, means "*may* rule": "Thou *mayest* rule over sin."

When a listener asked Lee, "Why is this word (*timshol*) so important?" he responded that whereas the King James Version promises that man will triumph over sin and the American Standard translation *orders* man to triumph over sin, the Hebrew text says, "Thou *mayest.*"

In other words, the Bible is teaching that human beings have a choice; and this choice is, in Steinbeck's words (put in Lee's mouth), "What makes a man [what distinguishes man from animals]: A cat has no choice, a bee must make honey…these sixteen verses are a history of humankind in any age or culture or race."

This one word and its meaning were so significant to Steinbeck that the final word spoken in this six-hundred-page novel is the Hebrew word *timshol.*

4.8 Cain said to his brother Abel . . . and when they were in the field, Cain set upon hi and killed him.

> The Torah does not tell us what Cain said to Abel. The reader is left to imagine the words. Perhaps this broken verse suggests that Cain in his fury just couldn't speak coherently. Perhaps the Torah doesn't think what Cain said is significant enough to record. But whatever he said, Cain killed Abel. That is what the Torah deems significant.

4.9 The Lord said to Cain, "Where is your brother Abel?"

> God interrogated Cain just as He interrogated Adam in Eden.

4.9 (cont.) And he said, "I do not know.

> Cain could have responded, "I killed him. What's the problem?" After all, God had not yet told people not to murder, so why did Cain feel he had to lie about what he had done?

> The implication of Cain's response is that he knew that what he did was wrong. And that, in turn, implies the existence of a conscience. In other words, even without divine revelation, the human being has an inner voice—the conscience—that can perceive the difference between right and wrong.

> *Conscience works in some exceptionally moral human beings, but for the vast majority of human beings, conscience alone is not enough.*

> Clearly, however, conscience is not enough for good to prevail in the world. It didn't work with Cain, the son of the first human couple, and it hasn't worked much since. Conscience works in some exceptionally moral human beings, but for the vast majority of human beings, conscience alone is not enough.

> The most obvious reason is it is very easy to do evil with a clear conscience. Murderers and other criminals, communists and Nazis, slave owners

throughout history, and so many other people engaged in evil have carried out horrible acts with clear consciences. That is why divine revelation is necessary: If we could rely solely on our conscience to do good, we wouldn't need the Bible or even the Ten Commandments.

4.9 (cont.) Am I my brother's keeper?"

There are at least two different ways to interpret Cain's response:

1. "I don't know. Am I my brother's keeper?"

This is what we may refer to as the "snide" response, basically conveying the thought, "I don't know and I don't care."

2. "I don't know. Am *I* my brother's keeper?"

This is the "shifting responsibility" response. Cain shifts responsibility for what happened to God: "I'm not responsible for my brother. You, God, are."

The rest of the Bible can be read as an answer to Cain's question, "Am I my brother's keeper?" The answer to that question is "Yes."

4.10 Then He said, "What have you done? Hark, your brother's blood

The Hebrew actually says "bloods," not "blood." The Talmud interpreted "bloods" as referring not just to Abel's blood but to the blood of all his potential descendants who will now never be born.[4] When one person kills another, he has not only killed that person but also all those who would have descended from him.

Furthermore—and ironically—even the descendants of the killers (or murderers, as the case may be) may end up suffering for their ancestor's crime. Some years ago, Harvard law professor Alan Dershowitz was giving a talk to lawyers in Hamburg and asked the audience members, "How many of you have suffered from the Holocaust?" A few hands of several elderly lawyers were raised. Dershowitz then asked, "How many of you or your family members have had cancer, coronary problems, diabetes, or a stroke?" This time, nearly every hand was raised. Dershowitz paused, and then asked, "How can you be sure that the cures for those diseases did not go up in the smoke of Auschwitz or Treblinka?" There was a stunned silence. Following my talk," Dershowitz recalled, "dozens of these German lawyers came up to me and said, 'We too have suffered from the Holocaust.' "[5]

4.10 (cont.) cries out to Me from the ground!

God, repelled by Cain's annoyed response, "Am I my brother's keeper?" informs Cain that it is Abel, whose voice is screaming at Him, who is, justifiably, furious.

4.11 Therefore you shall be more cursed than the ground, which opened its mouth to receive your brother's blood from your hand.

God says "bloods" here as well.

God curses Cain but does not kill him, which some find surprising, given that capital punishment for murder is one of the only laws in the Book of Genesis. It is a fundamental moral precept of the Torah that if you premeditatedly murder someone, you are to be put to death (see commentary to Genesis 9:6). In fact, some religious opponents of the death penalty for murder use God's response to Cain as a biblical basis for opposition to the death penalty. But the reason God does not impose the death penalty here is not that God opposes the death penalty. How could God oppose what He demands—capital punishment for murder—in every book of the Torah? (See Genesis 9:6; Exodus 21:12; Leviticus 24:17; Numbers 35:16ff.; Deuteronomy 19:11-13).

The reason is that, according to Torah law, the death penalty is imposed only on those who engage in premeditated murder; and we have no reason to assume Cain planned to murder Abel. The way the story is told, Cain's attack was more likely what we would call today a "crime of passion," an impulsive act committed in the heat of a moment of fury.

Furthermore, there is good reason to believe Cain did not even realize hit-
ng his brother would lead to Abel's death—no human being had yet died.

4.12 If you till the soil, it shall no longer yield its strength to you. You shall become a ceaseless wanderer on earth."

Ironically, this part of the punishment—ceaseless wandering—seems to
have later been remitted, as Cain became the founder of the first city (see
verse 17).

4.13 Cain said to the Lord, "My punishment is too great to bear!

The Hebrew word translated here as "my punishment" (*avoni*) may also be
translated as "my sin," suggesting that Cain was unable to bear the guilt he felt
for killing his brother. The two—equally valid—translations give diametrically
opposed meanings to Cain's statement. When the Torah, as in this case, introduces ambiguity in its choice of words, it is quite possible it intends both meanings. Cain might therefore be saying both his punishment and his guilt are too
great to bear.[6]

4.14 Since you have banished me this day from the soil and I must avoid your presence and become a restless wanderer on earth, anyone who meets me may kill me."

Cain realizes now that he has sinned, and sinned grievously, he can no longer
expect God's providential care. People who deliberately hurt others do not want
to experience the pain they inflicted on their victims.

4.15 The Lord said to him, "I promise, if anyone kills Cain, sevenfold vengeance shall be taken on him." And the Lord put a mark on Cain, lest anyone who met him should kill him.

This mark is God's way of protecting Cain from avengers or from anyone else
who might want to kill him. Although people often think of the mark of Cain
as a blemish or a curse, it was in fact a lifesaver.

4.16 Cain left the presence of the Lord and settled in the land of Nod, east of Eden.

4.17 Cain knew his wife, and she conceived and gave birth to Enoch.

Whom does Cain marry? So far, the Torah has mentioned only four people: Adam, Eve, Cain, and Abel. Cain likely married a sister—we are told in Genesis 5:4 that "Adam begat sons and daughters." Of course, the Torah later condemns in the strongest terms and prohibits sexual relations between close relatives (see Leviticus, chapter 18). But at this point in human history, there was no way for Adam and Eve's children to procreate except with siblings.

4.17 (cont.) And he then founded a city and named the city after his son Enoch.

This verse begins a chronicle of the key stages in the development of civilization.

4.18 To Enoch was born Irad, and Irad begot Mehujael, and Mehujael begot Methusael, and Methusael begot Lamech.

4.19 Lamech took to himself two wives: the name of the one was Adah, and the name of the other was Zillah.

4.20 Adah bore Jabal; he was the ancestor of those who dwell in tents and amidst herds.

Tent-dwelling and animal husbandry are the next two historical developments chronicled here.

4.21 And the name of his brother was Juval. He was the ancestor of all who play the lyre and the pipe organ.

The Torah includes the origin of music among the basic stages in the development of civilization, suggesting that music is primeval and foundational.

I have long believed music is an argument—an argument, not a proof—for God's existence. Specifically, I regard it as a gift from God. It has absolutely no intrinsic value; it is only pure joy for the great majority of humanity. Even people committed to finding an evolutionary explanation for everything have been mystified by music. As one pro-evolution writer put it: "From an evolutionary perspective, it makes no sense whatsoever that music makes us feel emotions."[7] And the father of evolution, Charles Darwin himself, wrote, "Man's faculties for enjoying and producing music must be ranked among the most mysterious with which he is endowed."[8]

4.22 As for Zillah, she bore Tubal-cain, who forged all implements of copper and iron.

This is the final stage of the development of artistic and technical civilization chronicled here.

4.22 (cont.) And the sister of Tubal-cain was Naamah.

4.23 And Lamech said to his wives, "Ada and Zillah, hear my voice. Oh wives of Lamech, give ear to my speech. I have slain a man for wounding me, and a lad for bruising me.

In this, the first instance of poetry in the Torah, Lamech bragged about committing revenge and gloried in his love of violence. He was also the descendent of the founder of the first city, as well as the father of the first lyre-player and the copper instrument-forger. There may be a lesson here (as my high school principal Rabbi David Eliach often noted): the development of morality and the development of civilization do not go hand-in-hand. This was certainly the case in modern times in Germany: the most well-educated and cultured society in the world unleashed World War II and the Holocaust.

4.24 If Cain is avenged seven-fold, then Lamech seventy-seven fold."

Lamech boasts that if any man touches him, he will kill seventy-seven of his opponent's men in retaliation. This type of unbalanced retribution was the norm in all societies. That is why the Torah's "an eye for an eye, a tooth for a tooth" must be understood as a moral triumph—even if taken literally (which it never was). It limited retaliation to one-for-one (see the commentary on Exodus 21:24). The Torah outlawed the indiscriminate violence celebrated by Lamech and replaced it with retributive justice, one in which the punishment may not exceed the crime ("an eye for an eye," not "two eyes for an eye," or "a life for an eye").

The Torah recognizes that like often begets like; a violent man
likely to have a violent descendant like Lamech (children raised
households are far more likely to commit violence). Following this verse, the
Torah returns to Adam and Eve with no further mention of the descendants of
Cain. Cain's family line seems to end suddenly, perhaps in the sort of clan
violence reflected in Lamech's boasting.

4.25 Adam knew his wife again, and she bore a son and named him Seth, meaning "God has provided me with another offspring in place of Abel," for Cain had killed him.

The Hebrew name *Shet* means given; Seth was the additional offspring given
to Eve. The birth of Seth and the apparent end of Cain's family line free humankind from the burden of believing they are all descendants of a killer.

4.26 And to Seth in turn, a son was born, and he named him Enosh. It was then that men began to invoke the Lord by name.

The Torah posits here that the first people to have a relationship with the divine
believed in the one God. Accordingly, monotheism was not a specifically Jewish revolution because it predated Abraham by several generations. The Jewish
revolution was *ethical* monotheism (see "The uniqueness of the Torah's flood
story" in the commentary to Genesis 6:9 and the commentaries on Genesis
35:2 and Exodus 8:6)—specifically, the Ten Commandments, the Torah, and
the Hebrew Bible.

CHAPTER 5

5.1 This is the record of Adam's line. When God created man, He made him in the likeness of God;

This verse figured in a Talmudic debate between Rabbi Akiva, who argued the most important principle in the Torah is "Love your neighbor as yourself" (Leviticus 19:18) and Rabbi Ben Azzai, who argued that this verse, Genesis 5:1, is the most important. Ben-Azzai's reasoning was that people are far more likely to love their neighbor as themselves when they recognize that they and their neighbor come from the same parent (Adam), and therefore all people are brothers and sisters. Add the belief that concludes the verse—all human beings are created in God's image—and one has a second reason to regard all human beings as equal in worth and infinite in value.[1]

The Hebrew word translated here as "record" is actually the Hebrew word "generations" (*toldot*). Used here to describe the creation of individual human beings, it is the same word used in Genesis 2:4 to describe the creation of the world, suggesting that every individual constitutes a whole world: "Therefore was Adam created singly to teach us that he who saves one life it is as if he saved an entire world, and he who destroys one life it is as if he destroyed an entire world."[2]

MALE AND FEMALE ARE EQUAL—AND CONSTITUTE A DIVINE DISTINCTION

5.2 male and female He created them.

The Torah restates God's creation of human beings into two distinct groups—male and female. This is the only distinction the Torah makes in describing the creation of the human being.

One reason is to remind us that men and women are equally important. Historically, many, if not most, men have had trouble accepting this principle, which the Torah emphasizes repeatedly—such as in the Fifth of the Ten Commandments, which commands us to honor our father and mother.

The other reason is to emphasize there are two types of human beings—male and female. Not one and not more than two. The male-female distinction is the only built-in human distinction that matters. Race doesn't matter, nor does ethnicity or nationality. Only the sex distinction does. Attempts to undo this division of human beings fundamentally tamper with the divine order as presented in the Torah. (This is discussed at length in the commentary to Deuteronomy 22:5.)

> *There are two types of human beings—male and female. Not one and not more than two. The male-female distinction is the only built-in human distinction that matters.*

5.2 (cont.) And when they were created, He blessed them and called them Man.

5.3 When Adam had lived 130 years, he begot a son in his likeness after his image, and he named him Seth.

5.4 After the birth of Seth, Adam lived 800 years and begot sons and daughters.

5.5 All the days that Adam lived came to 930 years; then he died.

5.6 When Seth had lived 105 years, he begot Enosh.

5.7 After the birth of Enosh, Seth lived 807 years and begot sons and daughters.

5.8 All the days of Seth came to 912 years; then he died.

5.9 When Enosh had lived 90 years, he begot Kenan.

5.10 After the birth of Kenan, Enosh lived 815 years and begot sons and daughter:

5.11 All the days of Enosh came to 905 years; then he died.

5.12 When Kenan had lived 70 years, he begot Mahalalel.

5.13 After the birth of Mahalalel, Kenan lived 840 years and begot sons and daughters.

5.14 All the days of Kenan came to 910 years; then he died.

5.15 When Mahalalel had lived 65 years, he begot Jared.

5.16 After the birth of Jared, Mahalalel lived 830 years and begot sons and daughters.

5.17 All the days of Mahalalel came to 895 years; then he died.

5.18 When Jared had lived 162 years, he begot Enoch.

5.19 After the birth of Enoch, Jared lived 800 years and begot sons and daughters.

5.20 All the days of Jared came to 962 years; then he died.

5.21 When Enoch had lived 65 years, he begot Methuselah.

5.22 After the birth of Methuselah, Enoch walked with God 300 years; and he begot sons and daughters.

5.23 All the days of Enoch came to 365 years.

Two reasons stand out for the genealogies. Both contrast the Torah with its contemporaneous pagan societies. First, other ancient Near-Eastern genealogies depicted man-gods. But there are no man-gods in the Torah—all the genealogies from Adam forward are of human beings. Second, the other genealogies list kings; the Torah's genealogies do not. It is the Torah's way of saying every individual human being matters, not just royalty.

The Torah cannot be appreciated without first understanding how utterly different it was morally and theologically from the values of its time. It is one of the reasons the Torah should be regarded, like creation, as *ex nihilo*—from nothing. Nothing existed before creation; and nothing like the Torah existed before the Torah.

5.24 Enoch walked with God; then he was no more, for God took him.

We are given no details about Enoch's life. But he was clearly special. Like Noah, Enoch is described as having "walked with God." The term is used only three times in the Bible. And, along with Elijah the Prophet, Enoch is the one person of whom it is not said that he "died," but that *God took him.*

5.25 When Methuselah had lived 187 years, he begot Lamech.

5.26 After the birth of Lamech, Methuselah lived 782 years and begot sons and daughters.

5.27 All the days of Methuselah came to 969 years; then he died.

Methuselah is widely known as the Bible's longest-living character. The Bible records no other achievement of Methuselah, even though he lived almost a thousand years. There is a lesson here. As much as all of us would like to live long lives, in the final analysis, it is the quality, not the quantity, of our lives that most matters. Moses lived one-eighth as long as Methuselah.

5.28 When Lamech had lived 182 years, he begot a son.

5.29 And he named him Noah, saying, "This one will provide us relief from our work and from the toil of our hands, out of the very soil which the Lord placed under a curse."

5.30 After the birth of Noah, Lamech lived 595 years and begot sons and daughters.

5.31 All the days of Lamech came to 777 years; then he died.

There was a man named "Lamech" in the preceding chapter. Was this particularly vicious and violent man (see 4:18-24) the father of the righteous Noah? A close reading of the text reveals the Lamech of chapter 4 to be a different man from the Lamech in this verse. The earlier Lamech was a sixth-generation descendant of Cain, but the Lamech described here, Noah's father, was an eighth-generation descendant of Adam through his son, Seth.

ESSAY: THE PROBLEM OF THE LONG LIVES

How are we to explain the length of time—the hundreds of years—the individuals listed here lived?

Here are the three most possible explanations:

1. The ages at which these individuals died are literally true, and we just cannot explain them.
2. The numbers mean something other than, or in addition to, a literal number of years. This is common in the Torah. For example, the number forty signifies a significant period of time and one in which God is involved: the forty days of the Flood, the forty years the Israelites wandered in the desert, the forty days and nights Moses was on Mount Sinai receiving the Ten Commandments, the four hundred years the Israelites were in Egypt (Genesis 15:13), etc.
3. Astrophysicist and theologian Hugh Ross maintains the key to understanding these long ages is *when* God limited how long human beings could live. He did so *immediately after the Flood* (Genesis 6:3). God's preoccupation throughout the Torah is with goodness. That was the reason He destroyed the world—the

world was engulfed in evil. Obviously, the longer people live, the more time they have to commit evil and to spread evil ideas. While God originally intended man to live many years, God's concern with the triumph of good over evil meant the years people could live had to be drastically reduced.

Of course, one might argue the good can also live a long time and counter all that evil. But given how often evil people slaughter good people, long-living evil individuals will prevail. So, then, by limiting the number of years the evil can live, the amount of evil on earth can be contained.[3]

In other words, what is important here, as in all the stories of Genesis—from Creation to the Garden of Eden to the ages listed before the Flood and on to the patriarchs and Joseph—is what moral lessons are to be learned and what God wants from us.

This does not answer the scientific challenge to people living hundreds of years. But, as pointed out in the Creation story, the Torah was not written to teach science. It was written to teach wisdom and how to live according to the will of a moral God. That is precisely what the Torah and the Bible have done.

5.32 When Noah had lived 500 years, Noah begot Shem, Ham, and Japheth.

CHAPTER

6

6.1 When men began to increase on earth and daughters were born to them,

6.2 the divine beings saw how beautiful the daughters of men were and took wives from among those that pleased them.

The words translated here as "divine beings" are the Hebrew words *b'nei ha-elohim,* literally "sons of the gods." We do not know exactly what the Torah is referring to here. We do know the Torah is adamant that God is the one true deity.

The strange happenings described here are probably a polemic against the popular ancient belief that gods and human women could mate to produce semi-divine beings. It is essential to recall that the Torah had to be relevant to people living three thousand years ago, and they understood parts of it better than we do today, just as we understand parts of the Torah better than people in the Late Bronze Age did.

This story is recounted right before the flood, suggesting that the polytheistic idea that gods and people could have sexual relations was so inimical to God's moral design for the world it was one reason He decided it was time to start the world anew. The distinction between man and God is one of the distinctions that serve as pillars of the civilization the Torah seeks to create. We have here an intermingling of divine and human that God deems unacceptable. That is what the serpent promised Eve: Eat from the Tree of Knowledge of Good and Evil "and you will be like God" (Genesis 3:5).

The blurring of the distinction between man and God—a defining characteristic of pre-Torah religions—leads to a wicked world, as described in verse 5.

6.3 The Lord said, "My breath shall not abide in man forever, since he too is flesh; let the days allowed him be one hundred and twenty years."

6.4 It was then, and later too, that the Nephilim appeared on earth—when the divine beings cohabited with the daughters of men who bore them offspring. They were the heroes of old, the men of renown.

We do not know what the Torah had in mind in this opaque verse. Jews thousands of years ago most likely understood this reference and the point the Torah wished to make better than we do. Other than being giants (see Numbers 13:33), we cannot even be sure who the Nephilim were. Were they the products of the union of "divine beings" and earthly women? Or were they the "*b'nei elohim,*" the "divine beings" themselves?

Richard Elliott Friedman, a Bible scholar who has both translated the Torah and written a commentary on it, offered this understanding of the role of the Nephilim in the Hebrew Bible:

"Some Bible stories are virtually self-contained. Even though they may have implications elsewhere in the *Tanakh* [Hebrew Bible], we can still read them as sensible, comprehensible individual units. But this account of the giants is an example of another type of story: those whose elements are widely separated, distributed across great stretches of the narrative. These stories provide the connections that make the *Tanakh* a united work, telling a continuous story, rather than a patchwork of little tales.

"The issue is that there are giants: uncommonly big, powerful persons, who are frightening.... This does not come up again in the story until thousands of years later. When Moses sends men to scout the promised land, they see the giants: "the Nephilim" (Numbers 13:33). That is what scares the scouts, and their fear infects the Israelites, changing the destiny of the wilderness generation. A generation later, Joshua eliminates all the giants from the land except from the Philistine cities, particularly the city of Gath (Joshua 11:21–22). And later still,

the most famous Philistine giant, Goliath, comes from Gath (1 Sa
And David defeats him.

"We can read each of these stories without noticing that they are a connected account, building to a climactic scene, but obviously we miss something
that way. Such widely distributed stories are there because the Bible is not a
loose collection of stories. It is an intricate, elegant, exquisite, long work with
continuity and coherence. When we know our Bible well, we read this story
about the giants in creation, and we are aware that they will play a part in the
tragedy of the wilderness generation, that Joshua will defeat them, and that
David will face the most famous (and last?) of them. This episode...is a
reminder that one cannot really learn the Torah without learning the rest of
the Tanakh as well."

The following verse makes clear that though these men are referred to as
"men of renown," it has nothing to do with moral greatness (in modern English, the word "renown" has a positive connotation). In a wicked society,
those who are renowned are rarely renowned for being good; more likely,
they are renowned for being physically powerful.

WE NEED BOTH THE GOOD URGE AND THE BAD URGE

6.5 The Lord saw how great was man's wickedness on earth, and how every plan devised by his mind was nothing but evil all the time.

The Hebrew word *yetzer* (translated here as "plan") is the noun of the biblical
verb "to form" or "make." It is therefore often translated as the creative "urge"
or "impulse." One may understand it as what Freud called the "Id"—the human
being's primal drives and impulses that need to be reined in by the conscience.
Yetzer has been central to Jewish thought from the earliest times to the present.
The human being, Judaism teaches, has a good yetzer (*yetzer hatov*; often
translated as "the good inclination") and a bad yetzer (*yetzer harah*, "the evil
inclination"), and they are in permanent conflict. However, Judaism has also
long held that we need both *yetzers*. This is an enormously important insight.

"Were it not for the evil inclination," the Midrash teaches, "men would not build homes, take wives, have children, or engage in business."[1] In other words, we do a variety of good things for very mixed, sometimes purely selfish, motives.

At the same time—and this point is less commonly noted—the *yetzer hatov* also must be reined in. Much of the evil of the twentieth century was caused by ideologies that appealed to the *yetzer hatov*. Communism—in its insistence on "equality" and that the state should own all the means of production and use that ownership to eliminate poverty—is the best example. It resulted in about 100 million dead innocents (non-combatants) and more than a billion people deprived of elementary human rights. (The other great twentieth-century evil, Nazism, was rooted in racism, and therefore primarily appealed to the *yetzer harah*.)

PEOPLE ARE GUILTY FOR THEIR BAD ACTIONS, NOT THEIR BAD THOUGHTS

The Torah acknowledges this baser component of the human psyche and therefore does not demand that people feel guilty over their bad thoughts. It is only bad actions—the "wickedness" mentioned in the first half of this verse—that are punished. (The one seeming exception, the tenth of the Ten Commandments, not to covet what belongs to our neighbor, is explained in the commentary to Exodus 20:14).

Concerning the goodness or badness of human nature, see the essay in Genesis 8:21: "Why the Belief that People are Basically Good is Both Wrong and Dangerous").

DOES GOD KNOW THE FUTURE?

6.6 And the Lord regretted that he had made man on the earth

God regretting something He had done seems to be incompatible with omniscience. If God knows everything, how could He "regret" anything—let alone anything He Himself had done? Doesn't omniscience mean God knows what will happen? The traditional Jewish solution to this apparent contradiction was to assert "everything is foreseen, yet permission [free will] is given" (*ha-kol tzafuey v'hareshut nituna*).[2] This means God gives us freedom of choice, but He knows what we will choose.

This explanation assumes, of course, God knows the future. And how could God know the future? Because He exists outside of time. Since Einstein, we have known time is relative. Therefore, the notion of existence outside of time is both scientifically and theologically tenable.

However, there is another way to explain God regretting something He had done: When it comes to what human beings will do, God may in fact not know the future. While God knows the future behavior of everything else in nature—animals, trees, stars—it is possible God does not know what human beings will do. Unlike everything else in the universe, humans were endowed with the ability to go against God's will. So, yes, God knows everything that humans do—but not necessarily everything humans *will* do.

GOD: "THE MOST TRAGIC FIGURE IN THE BIBLE"

6.6 (cont.) and His heart was saddened.

Based on this verse, Rabbi David Hartman described God as the most tragic figure in the Bible. His reasoning? God is repeatedly disappointed by His favorite creature—the human being. The beginning of Genesis is a series of successive frustrations on the part of God, who sets about creating a world that will be good for human beings, only to find that they thwart his plans for the world to such an extent that He ultimately destroys it.

Consistent with this tragic sensibility, Nahum Sarna notes that God destroys the world out of sadness rather than anger. Although there are other points in the Torah where God is angry, this time He is simply sad.

One more point concerns God having an emotion—in this case, sadness. Does God have emotions? Given how we humans regard emotions—as something purely human (but experienced to a lesser extent by higher animals)—we tend not to identify God with emotions. Indeed, given that we are made in His image, why would we humans possess an ability God does not possess?

ESSAY: WHY WOULD A GOOD GOD DESTROY THE WORLD?

6.7 The Lord said, "I will blot out from the earth the men whom I created

Critics of the Bible frequently point to this story as an example of a mean-spirited God. In my view, this story shows the opposite: a God preoccupied with goodness.

After God created man—and only then—did God announce that what He created was "very good." After the other days' creations, He saw what He created and announced they were "good," but never "very good" (see Genesis 1:26-31). The reason God now says "very good" is God had such high aspirations for humanity.

But, to God's immense sadness ("His heart was saddened"), God saw how much human beings engaged in cruelty to other human beings. And given how widespread this cruelty was, God decided to start over again. God wanted a good world, meaning a world in which people treated others decently, or at the very least, were not cruel to others. Therefore, if evil dominates and there is virtually no good in the world, there is no longer any purpose to human existence. Indeed, if God were to allow humanity to continue, that would mean only more and more gratuitous suffering on earth. God was not prepared to allow that.

> *If God were to allow humanity to continue, that would mean only more and more gratuitous suffering on earth.*

I admire such a God. I admire a God who, more than anything else, wants us humans to be good to one another—just like most parents want more than anything else for their children to be good to each other.

Man's evil to other people was the reason God decided to destroy the world. Unlike other flood stories the world over, in the Torah, the reason for the flood is human cruelty—one obvious proof being the one person God saved was saved because he was "righteous."

In fact, in light of that, one can ask an even more troubling question than why God destroyed the world—why didn't He destroy humanity entirely? Why did He save even one family—for it was from this one family that all the world's later evil people descended. Given how much cruelty humans have inflicted upon other humans since the Flood (the staggering amount of torture, murder, rape, slavery and sheer sadism that so many people have suffered), one might ask why God saved Noah and his family. Think about those hundreds of millions of horrifically suffering people and consider how *they* might have answered the question: "Do you wish that God had destroyed the entire world?" In other words, was saving humanity worth all the terrible suffering to come?

Whatever their response might be, what is abundantly clear from the Flood story that is about to follow is God so loathes human cruelty He decided to destroy the world and preserve only the most righteous person (and his immediate family)—in the hope a better humanity would issue from him.

ESSAY: WHY WERE ANIMALS DESTROYED IN THE FLOOD?

6.7 (cont.) —men together with beasts, creeping things and birds of the sky, for I regret that I made them."

Many readers naturally ask, "What did the animals do wrong that they deserved to die?" Since animals do not have free will, they obviously could not be guilty of any wrongdoing. Clearly, then, the animals weren't killed as punishment.

Since we humans cannot know the mind of God, we cannot know the definitive reason animals were destroyed. But we can surmise some explanations.

The most obvious answer to the animal question is that the only way God could have saved all the animals was to have them removed from the earth during the flood. While God can presumably do anything, such an act would have stretched the reader's credulity. Having all the animals hover in midair for forty days—and somehow either eat food or not need to eat any food while doing so—would have made the story, whose lesson is entirely one of morality, sound distinctly absurd.

Of course, one may respond that God could have killed all the human beings in some other way—one which had no effect on animals. That brings us to a second explanation.

Another possible reason for the death of the animals is this: Without man, there is no intrinsic purpose to the world. The biblical view is everything—the entire world, and, indeed, the entire universe—was created for man. Stated plainly, if there are no human beings to appreciate animals and rivers and mountains, there is no point to them. This is, of course, an anthropocentric view of the world. The only other possible view of the world would be nature-centric. But nature has no self-awareness—no ability to know good and evil, to love, to relate to God, to compose a symphony, to think about life. The notion that the world absent the human being has significance is meaningless. Only human beings give nature significance.

Why else would God create nature—including animals—if not for man to appreciate and (humanely) use? Moreover, unlike human beings, animals do not consciously seek immortality. Only humans do. The death of animals—unlike the infliction of gratuitous suffering on animals, which the Torah repeatedly prohibits (see, for example, Deuteronomy 22:10 and 25:4)—is not an inherently moral problem.

But, one might ask, if the world was created for man, why did animals preexist man for so many years? The Torah's view would be they were created to prepare the world for the coming of man. Certainly, secular people would argue that animals made the natural world as we know it possible. And they made modern civilization possible. From the beginning of the Industrial Revolution, all our energy came from fossil fuel. Without fossils and the fuel they provided, we would still be living as people did in the Middle Ages, burning candles for light and riding on horses rather than in cars. Whatever energy sources (e.g., wind, sun) mankind ultimately uses, it was fuel from animal remains—fossils—that made all technological progress possible. And that has enormous moral implications. The modern lifesaver, the hospital, for example, cannot function without electricity.

To those moderns who place the same value on animal life as ～
life, no explanation for the death of the animals in the Flood is a ～
But the Bible does not value human and animal life equally. The Bible
is anthropocentric.

6.8 But Noah found favor with the Lord.

6.9 This is the line of Noah.

ESSAY: PEOPLE ARE TO BE JUDGED BY THE STANDARDS OF THEIR TIME, NOT OF OURS

6.9 (cont.) Noah was a righteous man; he was blameless in his age; Noah walked with God.

Noah is called a *tzaddik* (translated as "righteous man"), the highest moral appellation in later Judaism. Literally, the word would be translated as "just," and it also means "innocent."

The phrase "in his age" (literally, "in his generations") raises one of the most interesting questions in religious and moral thought: Why was that phrase included? The verse could simply have stated, "Noah was a righteous man." Why did it add "in his age"?

According to one rabbinic opinion, this phrase is intended to suggest that Noah was good only in comparison to his depraved contemporaries; had he lived in an essentially decent society, he would have been regarded as nothing special. But others hold the opposite opinion—that "in his age" reflects well upon Noah, given that he managed to be a good person even though he was raised and lived among evil people.

Jewish tradition has tended to favor the first interpretation, that Noah was not particularly outstanding. As an example, unlike Abraham, who argued strenuously with God not to destroy Sodom (Genesis 18:16-33), when God told Noah of His intention to destroy the world, Noah did not argue with God but concerned himself solely with building an ark to save himself and his family.

The minority view, as expressed by Rabbi Resh Lakish, was that Noah's remaining a good man while living among evil people demonstrated how good a man he was. Resh Lakish's background, as recorded in the Talmud, may have influenced his opinion. In one report, he was raised in a circus; in another, he was raised among a band of thieves.[3] In contrast to the large majority of rabbinic sages, who grew up among very decent people, Resh Lakish was therefore aware from personal experience how difficult it is to overcome a bad environment.[4]

> *By stating Noah was righteous "in his age," the Torah makes it clear we are to judge people by the standards of their age, not the standards of our age.*

These contrasting opinions raise a fundamental question about judging human beings: Is it easier, and therefore less of an accomplishment, to be good when you are surrounded by essentially good people; or is it easier to be relatively good in comparison to an evil society?

In my view, both opinions are valid. But I side with the minority. It is extremely difficult to be decent when living among indecent people. Few people have the moral courage to reject their environment.

That is one reason I believe the words "in his age" were appended—to emphasize Noah's virtue, not to minimize it.

But there is another, perhaps even more important, reason. By stating Noah was righteous "in his age," the Torah makes it clear we are to judge people by the standards of their age, not the standards of our age. There is a great temptation to judge people who lived before us by the moral standards of our time. This is wrong. By doing this, we end up concluding virtually no one who lived before us was a good person, an obviously absurd proposition. For this reason, the Torah states Noah was righteous in his age. That is the only age that counts in assessing the morality of people.

That God entrusted the future of humanity in Noah reinforces this view. God Himself judged Noah within "his age."[5]

This issue is quite relevant to our time. In America, for example, students are taught from the youngest age that many of America's founders owned slaves, and that America itself allowed slavery (in the South). Therefore, the these were bad men and America was a bad place.

This provides a superb example of the overriding thesis of this commentary—ignorance of the Bible in the Western world has led to an abandonment of wisdom in the Western world. People familiar with the Noah story have the wisdom to know that a person must be judged as God judged Noah: "in his age." At the time of America's founding, virtually every society in the world—including non-Western Asian, African, and Muslim societies—practiced slavery, often in far greater numbers than America did. Moreover, it was America and the Western, Bible-based ("Judeo-Christian") civilization that abolished slavery before any other civilization did. And ultimately, the American founders' values created a nation that provided more non-whites with more liberty and more prosperity than any other society. That is how George Washington and Thomas Jefferson should be judged: the way God judged Noah—"in his age"—and by the freedom-loving and freedom-spreading society they ultimately created.

THE UNIQUENESS OF THE TORAH'S FLOOD STORY

The biblical Flood story was unprecedented in that it was based on the concept of ethical monotheism.

Ethical monotheism is the overriding idea, the supreme ideal, and the primary innovation of the Torah idea: that God is moral, that God demands moral behavior from all human beings, and that God will judge them according to His universal moral law.

Other ancient Near Eastern cultures had their own flood stories in which the gods destroyed the world—for reasons having little or nothing to do with human evil. They often saved a single person—but it was because the person was handsome or wealthy or was a half-god, not because he was more moral than other people.

For example, in the ancient Sumerian Epic of Gilgamesh, the gods destroyed mankind except for a man named Utnapishtim. Why? Because human beings were making too much noise, making it impossible for the gods to sleep. Likewise, in other Near Eastern flood stories, the gods simply made a capricious decision to destroy mankind.

This is a good place to explain the importance of the Torah even if one doesn't believe all the stories in it. Whether there was an enormous flood that destroyed much or nearly all of humanity cannot be proved. I believe there was such a flood because I believe the Torah stories and because virtually every culture in the world had a flood story. But what matters more than whether there was a great flood are the lessons one derives from the story. That the Torah was alone in making the Flood story entirely a moral story is what matters. And it is, therefore, one of the many reasons I believe the Torah is divine in origin: mere mortals would not have made it up. No mortals anywhere else did.

NOAH WAS NOT A JEW

One of the primary reasons I believe both in the divine authorship and truthfulness of the Torah is its portrayal of Jews and non-Jews. Jews (called the "Children of Israel" in the Torah) are regularly depicted as morally flawed, and non-Jews are often depicted as morally heroic. I know of no parallel in world literature before the modern period to such a critical description of one's own people and the heroic description of members of other nations.

Noah, the good man who walked with God, the man from whom all human beings descend, is not an Israelite.

6.10 Noah begot three sons: Shem, Ham and Japheth.

6.11 The earth became corrupt before God; the earth was filled with lawlessness.

6.12 When God saw how corrupt the earth was,

Unlike the national gods of other Near Eastern cultures, who concerned themselves only with their people, the God of the Torah is concerned with the entire world.

6.12 (cont.) for all flesh had corrupted its way on earth.

6.13 God said to Noah, "I have decided to put an end to all flesh, for the earth is filled with lawlessness because of them: I am about to destroy them with the earth.

> That God told this to Noah is yet another distinguishing aspect of the Torah story. "In contrast to the gods of the Babylonian flood account, who keep their decisions secret from any person so that all will be killed, God takes Noah into his confidence."[6]
>
> As noted above, there was no purpose to human life when humanity was evil. Therefore, God destroyed the world and resolved to start again with someone who is good and to whom He would entrust a basic moral code. This is yet another argument on behalf of Noah's exceptional goodness.

6.14 Make yourself an ark of gopher wood; make it an ark with compartments, and cover it inside and out with pitch.

> The Hebrew word for ark, *tevah*, is also used to describe the basin that Moses's mother builds for her baby son (Exodus 2:3). In both stories, God navigates the ark, directing it in accordance with His divine plan. An ark, therefore, differs from other vessels in that it is steered by God.
>
> The Hebrew word *gopher* is not mentioned anywhere else in the Torah. Nor is it found in other ancient Semitic languages. For this reason, we do not know what kind of wood it is.

6.15 This is how you shall make it: the length of the ark shall be three hundred cubits, its width fifty cubits, and its height thirty cubits.

> The dimensions of the vessel are given explicitly and, according to scholars, correspond roughly to a length of 450 feet (135 meters) a width of seventy-five feet (twenty-three meters), and a height of forty-five feet (fourteen meters) with a displacement of forty-three thousand tons.

6.16 Make an opening for daylight in the ark, and terminate it within a cubit of the top. Put the entrance to the ark in its side; make it with bottom, second, and third decks.

6.17 For My part, I am about to bring the Flood—waters upon the earth—to destroy all flesh under the sky in which there is breath of life; everything on earth shall perish.

6.18 But I will establish My covenant with you, and you shall enter the ark, with your sons, your wife, and your sons' wives.

> Noah is instructed to take only his family with him on the ark. Clearly God mistrusts the moral character of other people.

6.19 And of all that lives, of all flesh, you shall take two of each into the ark to keep alive with you; they shall be male and female.

6.20 From birds of every kind, cattle of every kind, every kind of creeping thing on earth, two of each shall come to you to stay alive.

> The categories of creatures needing refuge on the ark include only land-based species. Water-dwelling creatures are absent from this part of the story because, as implied in Genesis 7:22, they weren't imperiled by flood waters.

IS THERE A RELATIONSHIP BETWEEN HOW PEOPLE TREAT ANIMALS AND HOW THEY TREAT PEOPLE?

6.21 For your part, take of everything that is eaten and store it away, to serve as food for you and for them."

> Noah and his family were responsible for feeding the animals on the ark. Rabbi Zalman Sorotzkin, a twentieth-century Orthodox rabbi known by the title of his Torah commentary, *Oznayim l'Torah* (*"Ears to the Torah"*), speculates that since Noah and his family would have been required to spend much of their time tending to the animals, they had to be consistently kind. The ark, therefore, might have served to train them to function in a new world where people would act kindly—at least toward animals.
>
> However, this raises the interesting question of the relationship between kindness to animals and kindness to humans.

Most people today assume that kindness to animals leads people to act kindly to people. Though it sounds intuitively correct, there is little evidence to support this notion. It is undeniably true that cruelty to animals usually leads to cruelty to people. Children who act sadistically toward animals often become violent adults. But the converse is not true. There is no relationship between kind treatment of animals and kind treatment of people. The Nazis provided perhaps the clearest example. The Nazi regime was so pro-animal it outlawed medical experiments on animals (vivisection). Yet the very same regime performed grotesque medical experiments on live, non-anaesthetized Jews and other prisoners in Nazi concentration camps. The Nazi love for animals was such that Stanford University historian Robert Proctor, in his book, *The Nazi War on Cancer*, includes a Nazi newspaper cartoon depicting animals giving a Heil-Hitler salute to the Nazi leader Hermann Goering.[7]

> *It is undeniably true that cruelty to animals usually leads to cruelty to people. But the converse is not true. There is no relationship between kind treatment of animals and kind treatment of people.*

Having said that, and as will be noted elsewhere in the commentary, the Torah repeatedly demands the kind treatment of animals. To cite two examples, both unique to Torah legislation, Exodus 20:10, the Fourth Commandment, legislates a weekly day of rest for animals, while Deuteronomy 25:4 forbids the muzzling of an ox while it is working in the field.

WHY DIDN'T NOAH ARGUE WITH GOD?

6.22 Noah did so; just as God commanded him, so he did.

Many people have criticized Noah for not uttering a word in protest. They negatively compare his complete silence on being told God will destroy all of humanity with Abraham's long argument with God when God told him He would destroy the cities of Sodom and Gomorrah (see Genesis 18:16-33).

I find this criticism of Noah unpersuasive. If the world was as evil as the Torah states and if Noah knew it, why would he argue for sparing humanity rather than trust God's judgment that the only way to make a kinder world necessitated eradication of all evil people?

Moreover, once Abraham was assured by God there weren't even ten good people in Sodom, he, like Noah, kept silent.

CHAPTER

7

7.1 The Lord said to Noah, "Go into the ark, with all your household, for you alone have I found righteous before Me in this generation.

7.2 Of every clean animal,

"Clean animals" refers to animals fit for sacrifice. As we will see in the following chapter (Genesis 8:20), these are the animals—and birds—Noah sacrificed to God.

7.2 (cont.) you shall take seven pairs; males and their mates,

The extra pairs of the clean animals would be used for sacrifice. Richard Elliott Friedman makes the point very clear: "Noah takes seven pairs of the 'pure' animals and only one pair of the 'not pure,' because he will offer sacrifices after the flood. If he were to have only two sheep, then his sacrifice would wipe out the species."

According to some scholars, "You shall take seven pairs," contradicts Genesis 6.19, where God told Noah to take one pair of every animal. But there is only a contradiction if one insists on seeing one. In this instance, God specified extra pairs of "clean animals" for sacrifice.

7.2 (cont.) and of every animal that is not clean, two, a male and its mate.

7.3 of the birds of the sky also, seven pairs, male and female, to keep seed alive upon all the earth.

7.4 For in seven days' time I will make it rain upon the earth, forty days and forty nights, and I will blot out from the earth all existence that I created."

7.5 And Noah did just as the Lord commanded him.

7.6 Noah was six hundred years old when the Flood came, waters upon the earth.

7.7 Noah, with his sons, his wife, and his sons' wives, went into the ark because of the waters of the Flood.

7.8 Of the clean animals, of the animals that are not clean, of the birds, and of everything that creeps on the ground,

7.9 two of each, male and female, came to Noah into the ark, as God had commanded Noah.

7.10 And on the seventh day the waters of the Flood came upon the earth.

7.11 In the six hundredth year of Noah's life, in the second month, on the seventeenth day of the month, on that day, All the fountains of the great deep burst apart, And the floodgates of the sky broke open.

7.12 The rain fell on the earth forty days and forty nights.

As noted in other cases of "forty," this number usually signifies a divinely ordained period of time. Otherwise one would have to argue it is pure coincidence the Israelites wandered in the desert forty years, Moses was on Mount Sinai forty days and nights, and the rain of the Flood "fell on the earth forty days and forty nights."

7.13 That same day Noah and Noah's sons, Shem, Ham, and Japheth, went into the ark, with Noah's wife and the three wives of his sons—

7.14 they and all beasts of every kind, all cattle of every kind, all creatures of every kind, every bird, every winged thing.

7.15 They came to Noah into the ark, two each of all flesh in which there was breath of life.

7.16 Thus they that entered comprised male and female of all flesh as God had commanded him. And the Lord shut him in.

> God shut the hatch on the ark, in contrast to the Mesopotamian flood stories in which the hero shut himself in. In the Bible, God is in control.

7.17 The Flood continued forty days on the earth, and the waters increased and raised the ark so that it rose above the earth.

7.18 The waters swelled and increased greatly upon the earth, and the ark drifted upon the waters.

7.19 When the waters had swelled much more upon the earth, all the highest mountains everywhere under the sky were covered.

7.20 Fifteen cubits higher did the waters swell, as the mountains were covered.

7.21 And all flesh that stirred on earth perished—birds, cattle, beasts, and all the things that swarmed upon the earth, and all mankind.

7.22 All in whose nostrils was the merest breath of life, all that was on dry land, died.

7.23 All existence on earth was blotted out—man, cattle, creeping things, and birds of the sky; they were blotted out from the earth. Only Noah was left, and those with him in the ark.

7.24 And when the waters had swelled on the earth one hundred and fifty days,

> From verse 13 until this verse, we are given a repeat of the events concerning the boarding of the ark and the flood—another example of non-linear

repetition of an event (with added details) that characterizes many Torah stories. Advocates of the Documentary Hypothesis (the widespread academic belief that the Torah consists of at least four documents that were edited many years after the events depicted in the Torah) would see this as an example of two separate documents.

CHAPTER 8

8.1 God remembered Noah and all the beasts and all the cattle that were with him in the ark,

As elsewhere, "God remembered" does not mean God had previously forgotten and now remembered; it means "God decided to act."

GOD MADE NATURE FOR MAN

8.1 (cont.) and God caused a wind to blow across the earth and the waters subsided.

God, the Creator of nature, is fully in command of the forces He created. Unlike the gods in other ancient flood narratives, He is able to stop the flood as soon as He wishes. By contrast, the gods of the Mesopotamian flood story could not stop the waters they had unleashed, and they themselves became scared of what they had unleashed. The Torah narrative demonstrates yet again a central point of the early stories of Genesis: Nature, whose manifestations (the sun, the moon, rivers, springs, and so on) pagans worshipped as gods, was created by, and subservient to, God. Because the whole world worshipped nature, the Torah makes this point again and again.

The people we call pagans were not stupid. They were simply untouched by biblical ideas. In the West, we are now living in a largely post-biblical world, which means much of mankind might well revert to many pre-biblical pagan values and beliefs. One such example is

> *The people we call pagans were not stupid. They were simply untouched by biblical ideas.*

the elevation of nature to a god-like status. If there is no God higher than nature, and if man is not more important than nature, nothing is higher than nature.

But there are serious moral prices paid for elevating nature. Chief among them is that human beings cease to have the special value posited by the Bible. The Bible has a theocentric (God-centered) and anthropocentric (man-centered) view of the world. *As the theocentric view collapses, so does the anthropocentric.* As counterintuitive as it may seem, human worth is dependent on there being a God (specifically, the God of the Bible).

The belief human beings are sacrosanct comes from the Bible—specifically, from the belief that man is created in the image of God. If there is no God, in whose image is man created? The answer is no one's. Man is nothing more than stellar dust. If there is no God, humans are no more than one part of the ecological system—and a destructive part of it at that.

The notion that the world was created for man's sake is Bible-based. Therefore, with the decline of the Bible's influence, this anthropocentric view has not only been rejected, it has become the object of ridicule. No sophisticated person is supposed to think of man as the center of the universe. As Carl Sagan, the best-known astronomer of his generation, said to me (I paraphrase), "When I look into space, I am overwhelmed by the realization of how insignificant we human beings are."

Or, as another eminent scientist, the great British physicist (and atheist) Stephen Hawking put it, "We humans [are] mere collections of fundamental particles of nature."

As counterintuitive as it may seem, human worth is dependent on there being a God (specifically, the God of the Bible).

There is a great difference between being created in God's image and being a collection of particles.

As nature is elevated, human worth is reduced. And humans are reduced to the status of animals. What inevitably follows is the equation of humans with animals. Humans are increasingly described as "other animals," as in the commonly used expression, "humans and other animal...."

8.2 The fountains of the deep and the floodgates of the sky were stopped up, and the rain from the sky was held back;

8.3 the waters then receded steadily from the earth. At the end of one hundred and fifty days the waters diminished,

8.4 so that in the seventh month, on the seventeenth day of the month, the ark came to rest on the mountain of Ararat.

8.5 The waters went on diminishing until the tenth month; in the tenth month, on the first of the month, the tops of the mountains became visible.

These last two verses seem to contradict one another. Verse 4 states the ark came to rest in the seventh month, and verse 5 states the tops of the mountains became visible only in the tenth month. If no mountain top was visible until the tenth month, how could the ark come to rest on a mountain top in the seventh month—when all mountains were still under water?

There is a great difference between being created in God's image and being a collection of particles.

The ark was a very high structure; God instructed Noah to build it forty-five feet high (Genesis 6:15). That means thirty feet or more were under the water line. So it is quite possible the bottom of the vessel could have come to rest on a mountain—run aground, so to speak—while the mountains were still under twenty-five to thirty feet of water. And it took another couple of months for the water to recede enough for the mountaintops to emerge.

8.6 At the end of forty days, Noah opened the window of the ark that he had made

Robert Alter clarifies the timing: forty days "after the ark comes to rest, not the forty days of deluge."

8.7 and sent out the raven; it went to and fro until the waters had dried up from the earth.

8.8 Then he sent out the dove to see whether the waters had decreased from the surface of the ground.

8.9 But the dove could not find a resting place for his foot, and returned to him into the ark, for there was water over all the earth. So putting out his hand, he took it into the ark with him.

8.10 He waited another seven days, and again sent out the dove from the ark.

8.11 The dove came back to him toward evening, and there in its bill was a plucked-off olive leaf! Then Noah knew that the waters had decreased on the earth.

8.12 He waited still another seven days and sent the dove forth; and it did not return to him anymore.

8.13 In the six hundred and first year, in the first month, on the first of the month, the waters began to dry from the earth; and when Noah removed the covering of the ark, he saw that the surface of the ground was drying.

8.14 And in the second month, on the twenty-seventh day of the month, the earth was dry.

8.15 God spoke to Noah, saying,

8.16 "Come out of the ark; together with your wife, your sons, and your sons' wives.

8.17 Bring out with you every living thing of all flesh that is with you: birds, animals, and everything that creeps on earth; and let them swarm on the earth and be fertile and increase on earth."

8.18 So Noah came out, together with his sons, his wife, and his sons' wives.

8.19 Every animal, every creeping thing, and every bird, everything that stirs on the earth came out of the ark by families.

8.20 Then Noah built an altar to the Lord and, taking of every clean animal and every clean bird, he offered burnt offerings on the altar.

UNLIKE PAGAN GODS, GOD DOESN'T NEED FOOD

8.21 The Lord smelled the pleasing odor

In the ancient world, it was commonly believed the gods ate the sacrifices offered by human beings. By noting that God smelled Noah's offering, the Torah debunks the idea God needs physical sustenance. As Robert Alter puts it, "What is rigorously excluded from the monotheistic version of the story is any suggestion that God eats the sacrifice—in the Mesopotamian traditions, the gods are thought to be dependent on the food men provide them through the sacrifices, and they swoop down on the postdiluvian [post-flood] offering 'like flies.' "

In other words, God "smelled the pleasing odor" means God recognized the sacrifice as the act of gratitude it was. In the name of theological sophistication, would we prefer a god who was incapable of knowing an odor was pleasing?

The pagan gods (the gods with which the first Israelites were familiar) needed food from human beings. God does not need food or pleasing odors. The point was thereby made to ancient man that God is thoroughly different from everything you thought about gods: man needs God; God doesn't need anything from man and certainly doesn't sustain Himself by eating.

We need to remember the Torah had to be understood by primitives living in the Late Bronze Age, three thousand years ago, as well as by us today and by our descendants generations from now.

Finally, as the Talmud put it, "The Torah speaks in the language of human beings." We need to remember the Torah had to be understood by primitives living in the Late Bronze Age, three thousand years ago, as well as by us today and by our descendants generations from now. That it has succeeded in this regard is one of its many achievements.

8.21 (cont.) and the Lord said to Himself, "Never again will I doom the earth because of man,

God vowed not to curse the earth again (the word translated as "doom" [*arur*] means "curse"). But there is no implication God regretted what He had done.

Jonathan Sacks notes one thing God did not consider doing was taking back the gift of free will. That would certainly have ended evil on earth. But that was not God's design: we humans are to choose to be good freely. Free will is what most distinguishes us from animals.

If God is not going to destroy the world again and yet continue to allow humans free will, He was going to have to do something to prevent mankind from relapsing into evil. That something was moral revelation.

GOD'S THREE ATTEMPTS TO HAVE MAN DO GOOD

One might say that in the Hebrew Bible, God tried three times to have man do good. The first attempt was implanting a conscience in human beings. The second was revealing moral laws to Noah and his descendants. The third was revealing the Ten Commandments and the large body of laws in the Torah to a specific (or "chosen") group.

The first attempt—endowing human beings with a conscience—obviously failed.

Why isn't the conscience enough to ensure goodness?

- Because the conscience can be easily manipulated into thinking it is doing good while doing evil. Most of those who commit evil in the name of their god or some secular ideology are at peace with their conscience.
- Because the conscience can be easily dulled. The more bad a person does, the more inured they become, and the quieter the voice of the conscience becomes.

- Because the conscience is usually not nearly as powerful as the natural drives. Greed, envy, sex, alcohol—any of these often overpower the conscience.

- Because without explicit moral laws, the conscience alone is often a poor guide to doing what is right. In instances in which only one can be saved, do you save your beloved dog or a stranger? The conscience, without an external value system, can just as easily argue for either choice.

ESSAY: THE BELIEF PEOPLE ARE BASICALLY GOOD IS FOOLISH AND DANGEROUS

8.21 (cont.) since the devisings of man's mind are evil from his youth;

Why the Belief is Foolish

The Torah, as this verse makes apparent, does not hold that people are basically good. The idea that human beings are born good and corrupted by society is a relatively new one—largely associated with philosophers of the French Enlightenment such as Jean-Jacques Rousseau (1712-1778).

It is difficult to overstate how wrong and how morally destructive this idea has been. It is another example of the damage caused—and the foolishness generated—by Western society's abandonment of the Bible. To believe people are basically good after all the horrors committed by human beings against other human beings throughout history is to engage in a level of irrational thinking that has few parallels.

How can a rational person believe people are basically good?

- Are there any parents who haven't had to teach their children to be good people? How many times has the average parent told his or her child, "Say, 'Thank you' "? If people were basically good, wouldn't telling a child once or twice suffice? Why would all of us need to be told thousands of times to express gratitude to someone who has done us a kindness?

To believe people are basically good after all the horrors committed by human beings against other human beings throughout history is to engage in a level of irrational thinking that has few parallels.

- Haven't most children been bullied—physically hurt or sadistically taunted—by other children?
- What percentage of children have been physically, verbally, or sexually abused by adults?
- If people are basically good, how does one account for all the Roman citizens who paid to watch and laugh at people eaten alive by wild animals, men fighting each other to the death, and women raped by animals in the Roman coliseum? Were all these people aberrations?
- What about all the wars, few of which were morally justified, with their mass killing, barbarity, torture, and rape?
- If people are basically good, why did virtually every society in history practice slavery, which, in addition to its inherent cruelty, was so frequently accompanied by sadism?

And then there is the twentieth century, the century in which more people were murdered than in any other recorded century. It included:

- the Holocaust—the Nazi genocide of the Jews of Europe—and Nazi mass murder and sadism throughout German-occupied Europe;

- the Soviet Union, which murdered between twenty and thirty million innocents during Stalin's regime;
- Cambodia, where the communist Khmer Rouge murdered nearly a third of the Cambodian population;
- Ukraine, where four to six million people were starved to death by the Soviet Communists;
- and China, where the Communist regime under Mao Zedong starved at least sixty million people by sending food abroad to pay for weapons;
- the Japanese massacres of Chinese and Korean civilians, use of hundreds of thousands Chinese and Korean women as "comfort women" for their soldiers, and the Nazi-like medical experiments without anesthesia on Chinese civilians.
- the Hutu mass murder—in a one hundred-day period—of between five hundred thousand and one million Tutsis in Rwanda; and
- the Turks' mass murder of Armenians.

Why, in light of all the evidence, have some people chosen to believe man is basically good? One reason is many people who don't believe in God and religion have to believe in man or they will have nothing to believe in—and that would lead to complete despair. Another reason is the rejection of the Bible as people's primary source of wisdom. Bible-based Jews and Christians do not believe people are basically good because the Bible says they're not. A third is naivete resulting from living in a good society. During a debate I had with two students with left-wing views at the University of California, Berkeley, I asked the students if they believe people are basically good. They said yes. I replied the reason they believe that is they live in America, a very decent country, largely populated by decent people.[1] And America's decency is largely the legacy of its adherence to a biblical worldview throughout most of its history.

> *Parents and teachers who believe people are basically good do not feel the need to teach children how to be good. Why teach what comes naturally?*

Why the Belief is Dangerous

Why is the belief that people are basically good dangerous?

1. Children are not taught to be good.

   Parents and teachers who believe people are basically good do not feel the need to teach children how to be good. Why teach what comes naturally? Only when people realize how difficult it is to be a good person do they realize how important it is to teach goodness. In our time, there is virtually no character education in schools, and parents are more likely to be concerned with their children's self-esteem than with their self-control, and more concerned with their children's grades than their goodness.

2. God and religion become morally unnecessary.

   If we are basically good, who needs a transcendent source of morality—a good God or a Bible? In the West and elsewhere, the more people have come to believe people are basically good, the less religious and the less Bible-centered they have become. And the less religious and less Bible-centered they have become, the more they have come to believe people are basically good.

3. Society, not the individual, is blamed for evil.

   Another dangerous conclusion drawn by people who believe people are basically good is outside forces rather than the individual are to blame for human evil. If people are basically good, the reasoning goes, the evil that people do must be caused by something outside of them. Why else would a basically good creature commit evil? This is why the most widespread modern explanation for violent crime has been poverty. "Poverty causes crime," the argument goes.

But this is just not so. For one thing, the great majority of poor people do not commit violent crimes. They don't because they have a moral value system that tells them criminal violence is wrong. And what could possibly link poverty to, let us say, rape? If one argues poor people steal because of poverty, at least there is a plausible link between the two. But what has poverty to do with rape?

The Carter Center, named for its founder, former U.S. President Jimmy Carter, issued a statement, one of whose subjects was "Poverty and Terrorism."

Under that heading, it wrote:

"Effectively addressing poverty can make an important contribution to avoiding conflict and combating terror."[2]

Likewise, when he was the U.S. Secretary of State, John Kerry, also a one-time presidential candidate, said, "We have a huge common interest in dealing with this issue of poverty, which in many cases is the root cause of terrorism."[3]

Those who link terrorism to poverty might consider, for example, the economic backgrounds of the Islamic terrorists who killed 2,977 people on September 11, 2001 in the United States. The terrorists came from middle- and upper-class families. And the architect of the attack, Osama bin Laden, was a multi-millionaire.

Since people who believe in evil ideologies are as likely to be wealthy as poor, ending poverty does virtually nothing to

If escaping poverty made people better, the rich would be the kindest and most honest people in the world.

end ideological evil. It also does nothing to end non-ideological crime. If escaping poverty made people better, the rich would be the kindest and most honest people in the world.

Another outside force frequently blamed for violent criminality—when the criminal is a member of a minority race or ethnicity—is racism. Yet the same arguments against attributing violent crime to poverty apply to attributing violent crime to racism. The great majority of individuals who are members of a racial minority—such as blacks in America—do not commit violent crimes—and did not do so even when they were subjected to systemic racially based persecution. And the reason is clear: their moral values did not permit them to do so.

Values and moral self-control matter far more than outside forces. Nearly all people who commit violent crimes do so because they possess a malfunctioning conscience, a morally defective value system, and/or lack impulse control. The best way to make good people is through the combination of good values, good laws, and a God who commands goodness—such as that of the Bible. If people lived by the Ten Commandments alone, the world would be a beautiful place (see the commentary on the Ten Commandments, Exodus Chapter 21).

The biblical view of human nature was perfectly described in secular terms by Professor James Q. Wilson, a Harvard and UCLA political scientist:

"The forces that may easily drive people to break the law, a desire for food, sex, wealth, and self-preservation, seem to be instinctive, not learned, while those that restrain our appetites, self-control, sympathy, and a sense of fairness, seem to be learned and not instinctive."[4]

Those who blame evil on outside forces—i.e., "society"—rather than on the individual will encourage people to battle society rather than battle their nature. Indeed, the need to change society rather than have people control their nature has become the dominant outlook in the Western world.

The Torah teaches that, especially in a free society, the battle for a good world is not between the individual and society but between the individual and his or her nature.

The Torah teaches that, especially in a free society, the battle for a good world is not between the individual and society but between the individual and his or her nature. There are times, of course, when the battle for a better world must concentrate on evil emanating from outside the individual. This is always true in a tyranny and is sometimes true in democracies. But even then, in free societies, the battle for a moral world is waged primarily through the inner battle that each of us must wage against our nature: against weakness, addiction, selfishness, ingratitude, laziness, and evil.

The most important question a society that wishes to survive can ask is this: How do we make good people? But societies that believe people are basically good will never ask that question.

> *The most imp... question a so... wishes to sur... is this: How do we make good people? But societies that believe people are basically good will never ask that question.*

8.21 (cont.) nor will I ever again destroy every living being, as I have done.

8.22 So long as the earth endures, seedtime and harvest, cold and heat, summer and winter, day and night, shall not cease."

God guarantees that He will never again be responsible for ending the world. If the world is destroyed, it will be because human beings did it, not God.

CHAPTER

9

9.1 God blessed Noah and his sons and said to them, "Be fertile and increase and fill the earth.

These are the exact words that God said to Adam and Eve in Genesis 1:28, indicating that with Noah's family, the world is starting all over again. Therefore, just as we are all descendants of Adam and Eve, we are now all descendants of Noah, who is described as a *tzaddik,* a "just" (or "innocent") person—the only individual so described in the Torah—and his wife. Because Noah descended from Adam and Eve's son, Seth, we are not descendants of Cain, a killer, whose descendants perished in the flood.

ESSAY: ON HAVING MANY CHILDREN

Having destroyed mankind except for Noah and his family, God's first desire and commandment is that man repopulate the earth. This is the very opposite of the gods' desires in the other major Near Eastern flood story, the Gilgamesh Epic. In Vicroi Hamilton's words: "[The Gilgamesh Epic] concludes on a note exactly the opposite of the biblical story. It says overpopulation is the earth's primary problem, hence the need for population control, which can be accomplished either by nature or by the gods. Viewed in this light, Genesis 9:1 looks like a conscious rejection of the Gilgamesh Epic."

This universal law will be followed five verses later by another universal law: to put murderers to death. They are related: the first is a command to increase human life, and the second is a law to eliminate those who intentionally decrease human life (see the essay on capital punishment on verse 6).

To many of those who regard the Bible as binding, this blessing and command to "fill the earth" means one should strive to have as many children as possible. ("As possible" should be rationally understood as the number of children parents can adequately provide for.)

Others, however, argue this injunction was issued when the world was essentially empty and needed to be populated. In our time, they argue, we should not regard this commandment as applicable. Indeed, many people actively oppose large families on the grounds that the earth cannot sustain an ever-increasing number of people. Beginning shortly after World War II and accelerating in the 1960s, doctrines such as Zero Population Growth (ZPG) arose in the West. As it has turned out, the earth has not only been able to sustain a vast increase in human population, a dramatically smaller percentage of people than ever died of hunger. In other words, while the number of humans grew dramatically, the large majority have been adequately fed. Generally speaking, the only people who have died of hunger in the contemporary world did so either because of war, an oppressive government, and/or a corrupt society—not because there was not enough food on earth to feed them.

Nevertheless, the ZPG message took hold in the popular consciousness. Consequently, in the West at the present time, with rare exceptions, the people who have large families (four or more children) are religious—devout Roman Catholics, Orthodox Jews, evangelical Christians, and faithful Mormons. Meanwhile, the irreligious (with the exception of some of those relying on state assistance) increasingly have few or no children. The same holds true for marriage: the religious are more likely to marry. These are two examples of how differently people who base their lives on the Bible live from those who do not.

The most widely accepted explanations for people having fewer children are affluence and the greater independence of women. But this does not account for why affluent religious people continue to have many children. Therefore, one must add what is one of the most—and perhaps *the* most—important explanations for low birth rates in the modern world: secularism with its concomitant abandonment of the Bible.

And why do secular people have so few children? The primary reason is that without God and religion, people are understandably determined to enjoy the only world they believe exists: the material world. Without God, only matter is real. Such people, consciously or unconsciously, reason that one should therefore enjoy this world as much as possible in the short amount of time one exists. And children are regarded—not without reason—as depriving parents of the ability to enjoy many of life's pleasures. In addition to the great financial expenses associated with raising children, it is much more difficult to eat out, go to the movies, and travel abroad as often as one would like when one has to take care of children.

9.2 The fear and dread of you shall be upon all the beasts of the earth and upon all the birds of the sky—everything with which the earth is astir—and upon all the fish of the sea; they are given into your hand.

MAN MAY EAT ANIMALS

9.3 Every creature that lives shall be yours to eat; as with the green grasses. I give you all these.

Why does God allow meat-eating?

The traditional explanation is that it was a concession to man's desire for meat. Of course, that implies vegetarianism is the biblical ideal, in which case, as progress is made in making a vegetarian diet more protein-based, human beings should strive to eat less meat or eliminate it altogether from their diet. The fifteenth-century Spanish-Jewish philosopher Joseph Albo hoped this would be the direction in which humankind would evolve: "In the killing of animals [even in the best of circumstances] there is cruelty...."[1]

For a fuller discussion about morality and vegetarianism, see the essay on "Does the Torah Advocate Vegetarianism?" at Genesis 2:16.

HUMANE TREATMENT OF ANIMALS IS UNIVERSALLY BINDING

9.4 You must not, however, eat flesh with its life-blood in it.

Asserting that the Bible's ultimate ideal is vegetarianism is speculative. But what can be said with certainty is God and the Bible are greatly concerned with preventing animal suffering. While God does not ban meat eating, He does demand humane treatment of animals. Treating animals humanely is legislated or ordained ten times in the Torah. For example, the Torah prohibits muzzling an ox while it is working in the field (Deuteronomy 25:4); it obligates us to help an animal overwhelmed by a burden (Exodus 23:5); and we are commanded to give animals a day of rest (and that is in the Ten Commandments).

Here, however, is the Torah's first law: God commanding humane treatment of animals. Moreover, it is considered binding on all people, not only on Jews.

This verse has been understood in Jewish sources from earliest times as prohibiting eating the limb of a living animal—because tearing the limb off a living animal induces great pain.

THE BAN ON CONSUMING BLOOD

There is a second law contained in this injunction: we are not allowed to consume the blood of an animal; it must be drained prior to eating the flesh.

This law has no parallel in the ancient Near East. At one time, there was speculation among some Bible scholars that this blood prohibition reflected an ancient taboo. But the eminent Bible scholar Jacob Milgrom, longtime professor and chair of the department of Near Eastern Studies at the University of California at Berkeley, discovered that "none of Israel's neighbors possessed this absolute and universally-binding blood prohibition. Blood is everywhere [else] partaken of as food.... [But in the Bible's view] man has a right to nourishment, not to life. Hence the blood, which is the symbol of life, must be drained, returned to the universe, to God."[2]

9.5 But for your own lifeblood, I will require a reckoning. I will require it of every beast; of man, too, will I require a reckoning of human life, of every man for that of his fellow man.

In this Noahide Law—a law that is binding on the children of Noah (meaning all mankind)—God outlaws murder. As noted, until this point, God relied on conscience to induce human beings to behave righteously. However, as the story of Cain's killing of Abel and the world's being consumed by violence demonstrated, conscience alone was not enough to prevent man from acting violently. With the Noahide Laws, God makes a second effort to teach humanity how to be good. Morality is now revealed, though only a few rules are conveyed.

(This, too, as we will see, will not be sufficient. God will therefore try a third time to make a good world—with the revelation known as the Ten Commandments.)

Even animals that kill a human being are to be put to death. This is not a statement about animal free will and moral culpability but about the seriousness of taking a human life.

That murder is the first act prohibited by God after the Flood likely implies murder was rampant in the world when God decided to destroy it.

ESSAY: THE DEATH PENALTY FOR MURDER IS A MORAL CORNERSTONE OF SOCIETY

9.6 Whoever sheds the blood of man, by man shall his blood be shed; for in his image did God make man.

Taking the life of a murderer is another Noahide Law—a law binding on all humanity. Indeed, the Torah considers the death penalty for (premeditated) murder so essential to creating a civilized society, it is one of the first three commandments God gives to mankind.[3]

In the Torah's view, God deems taking the life of premeditated murderers fundamental to the moral order of society—every society, not just Jewish society. Very few commandments in the Torah are demanded of all people, but the death penalty for murderers is one of those few; it is listed here *prior* to the existence of the Israelites.

The Torah considers the death penalty for (premeditated) murder so essential to creating a civilized society, it is one of the first three commandments God gives to mankind.

The verse also makes it clear God expects human beings to take the murderer's life, providing a direct rejoinder to those who believe that only God is allowed to take human life. But that is obviously not true. Not only are people commanded to execute murderers, but human beings are permitted to kill others in self-defense and when fighting in a just war. The notion that only God can take human life is nowhere stated in the Bible. What is clear is that human beings can kill, but only in morally justifiable circumstances.

In addition, this is one of very few commandments in the Torah accompanied by an explanation: a murderer's life is to be taken because "in His image did God make man." We are to take a murderer's life precisely because human life is uniquely precious. Unlike all other creatures, human beings are created in God's image.

Opponents of the death penalty argue the very opposite: precisely because human life is uniquely precious, we should not take even the life of a murderer. But both in the view of the Torah and in terms of simple logic having nothing to do with God or theology, allowing every murderer to keep his life *reduces* the worth of human life—because it belittles murder.

This is easily demonstrated. Imagine the punishment for murder were the same as the punishment for shoplifting. Everyone would acknowledge this would belittle the seriousness of murder. And when murder is belittled, the worth of human life is cheapened. Society teaches how bad an action is by the punishment it metes out. Only when a society takes the life of a murderer is it announcing in the clearest way possible that murder is the ultimate sin. Keeping every murderer alive makes no such announcement—even if it involves life imprisonment. Life in prison is a harsh punishment—but the murderer, while not free to leave prison, is allowed to keep his life. I have talked to murderers in prison for life; every one of them far prefers imprisonment to death. It is also worth noting, however, that at the largest maximum security state prison in

America—the State Penitentiary in Angola, Louisiana—I asked ab
men convicted of murder if they believed some murderers shou... .. ...
death. The majority raised their hands.

Why did Israel, which banned capital punishment, make an exception and
execute Adolf Eichmann, the architect of the Holocaust?

It did so because the Israeli government, judiciary, and the overwhelming
majority of Israelis—and, one would hope, the overwhelming majority of
mankind—believed that allowing Eichmann to keep his life after having organized the murder of millions of innocent men, women, and children would
constitute an injustice of cosmic proportions. They believed, in short, that
Eichmann had forfeited his right to life.

But if a person forfeits his right to keep his life after murdering millions, why
does he not forfeit the right to keep his life after murdering a hundred people—
or, for that matter, one person? Every human is, after all, infinitely precious.

The Torah is preoccupied with justice. And allowing every murderer to
keep his life is a cosmic injustice.

Perhaps the following will illustrate this point better than any argument:

On the afternoon of July 23, 2007, in the American town of Cheshire,
Connecticut, two men entered the home of a physician, Dr. William Petit. They
beat Dr. Petit severely with a baseball bat, tied him up, and dumped him in the
family basement. Then one of the men raped the doctor's wife, Jennifer, and
the other sexually assaulted their eleven-year-old daughter, Michaela—an
assault he photographed with his cell phone. While the men were preoccupied
with the females, Dr. Petit managed to escape, but the two men strangled Mrs.
Petit to death, tied the two daughters to their beds, doused them with gasoline,
and while the girls were still alive, the murderers set fire to the house.

Those opposed to capital punishment believe that those two men have a
right to keep their lives. These people believe there is nothing a person can do
to deserve to be put to death.

And what about the loved ones of those who are murdered? For the great
majority of such people, their suffering is immeasurably increased knowing

that the person who murdered their son, daughter, husband, wife, parent, close friend—and who often inflicted unspeakable suffering and unimaginable terror on that person—is alive and being cared for. Putting their loved one's murderer to death doesn't bring their loved one back to life, but it does provide some sense of justice.

That is why Dr. Petit, whose life was devoted to saving lives, publicly announced that he wanted the murderers of his wife and daughters put to death. In words addressed to those who oppose capital punishment, he said, "My family got the death penalty, and you want to give murderers life. That is not justice."

The doctor's position is the same as the Torah's.

While it is true there are a number of laws in the Torah whose violation calls for the death penalty, I believe in almost every case, aside from murder, the death penalty is listed in order to show how serious the Torah deems the particular sin, not in order to actually be carried out. In the case of murder, however, the Torah repeatedly emphasizes putting murderers to death is a fundamental moral building block of a decent society. The death penalty for murder is understood as necessary to preserve the sanctity of human life. Precisely because human beings are created in God's image, anyone who intentionally takes the life of an innocent person loses his or her own right to life. Any lesser penalty means that the taking of a life is not considered the horrible offense that it is.

Genesis explicitly adds another critical element: It is human beings, not God, who are to execute murderers. It is as if Genesis foresaw the argument that capital punishment should be abolished because "only God can take life." Genesis makes it as clear as possible that this is not the Torah's view: "By *man* shall his [the murderer's] blood be shed."

So important is the death penalty for murder that it the only law in the Torah repeated in each of its five books:

Genesis 9:6 (this verse).

Exodus 21:12: "He who fatally strikes a man shall be put to death." That the Bible intended this punishment only for premeditated murderers is made clear in the following verse: "If he [the killer] did not do it by design...I will assign to you a place to which he can flee" (Exodus 21:13).

Leviticus 24:17: "If anyone slays a human being, he shall be put to death."

So important is th
penalty for murde
it is the only law in the
Torah repeated in each of
its five books.

Numbers 35:16: "Anyone, however, who strikes another with an iron object so that death results is a murderer; the murderer must be put to death."

Modern opponents of the death sentence view the death penalty as an ancient and morally primitive punishment for murder. They therefore regard lesser punishments for murder as reflecting a more morally advanced society and culture. However, the premise is not true.

The societies that surrounded the ancient Hebrews, some of whose legislation is older than that of the Torah, offered murderers alternatives to capital punishment. For example, the family of the victim could accept money from the murderer in return for absolution. It was in direct repudiation of this practice the Torah legislated "And you shall not take reparation for the soul of a murderer who deserves to die, but he shall be put to death" (Numbers 35:31). Allowing murderers to pay a bribe to the family of the victim granted a great advantage to wealthy murderers. To this day, highly affluent murderers—being able to hire the finest defense attorneys—almost always avoid execution.

Deuteronomy, the Torah's fifth and final book, rules that if a premeditated murderer tries to claim asylum in one of the cities of refuge (set aside for those who had killed someone unintentionally), he should be expelled from the city of refuge and executed: "Do not look on him with pity. Thus you will purge Israel of the blood of the innocent" (Deuteronomy 19:11-13).

Deuteronomy 19:20 adds the commonsensical notion that the death penalty is necessary "so that people shall hear and be afraid." Relying on common sense, the Bible argues the threat of being put to death will deter at least some people from committing murder. One of the reasons for all societal punishments is to deter crime. To deny the death penalty would ever deter murder is to argue murder is the only crime that can never be deterred.

> *To deny the death penalty would ever deter murder is to argue murder is the only crime that can never be deterred.*

The Bible is so emphatic about the death sentence it also decrees that "You shall take a murderer from My very altar to die" (Exodus 21:14). Murderers cannot claim sanctuary in a temple, as was and has been permitted in many societies throughout history, because allowing a murderer to seek safe haven in God's sanctuary makes a mockery of the God who hates murder.

Within the context of the time at which it was written, the Torah had the equivalent to the American criterion for conviction: guilt must be established beyond a reasonable doubt. In the case of the Torah, this was accomplished by mandating a minimum of two eyewitnesses (Numbers 35:30). I would argue that DNA evidence today, for example, would constitute "two eyewitnesses" to help ensure an innocent person not be executed.

In Judaism, the Bible is not the only source of law: Talmudic law often carries almost equal weight, and Jewish opponents of the death penalty frequently cite the famous Talmudic statement that a Jewish court that sentenced one person to death every seven years (one rabbi said every *seventy* years) was known as a "killer court."[4]

Yet within the very same paragraph, Rabbi Simeon ben Gamliel, the head (*nasi*) of the Sanhedrin (the Jewish High Court) dismissed this view: "They [the rabbis opposed to capital punishment] would have increased bloodshed...."[5]

Moreover, the "killer court" statement was made at a time when Jews had neither a state nor the political power to put these views into practice. The statement was purely theoretical. As the authoritative *Encyclopedia Judaica* notes, when "the Sanhedrin had power to inflict the death sentence...they exercised it."

To their credit, the Rabbis made it difficult to administer capital punishment. For example, aware that confessions were often obtained through torture, Jewish law forbade admitting confessions—no matter how non-violently obtained—as evidence in capital cases. But the Talmud also ruled that

in times of great violence, the death sentence could and shou
wider use.

Much of rabbinic opposition to capital punishment was r
tion to practices among the Romans who controlled Judea; the , ... vast
numbers of innocent people and used torture to extract confessions.

It would appear, therefore, the Rabbis who made the death sentence very
difficult to administer were thinking either in terms of a state in which murder
was extremely rare and/or an unjust state. Their thinking was not intended to
apply to a state in which murder was common.

Because every human being is created in God's image, murder is the ultimate crime. Hence, the Bible insists it deserves the ultimate punishment.

9.7 Be fertile, then, and increase; abound on the earth and increase on it."

9.8 And God said to Noah and to his sons with him,

9.9 "I now establish my covenant with you and your offspring to come,

9.10 and with every living thing that is with you—birds, cattle, and every wild beast as well—all that have come out of the ark, every living thing on earth.

9.11 I will maintain My covenant with you; never again shall all flesh be cut off by the waters of a flood, and never again shall there be a flood to destroy the earth."

9.12 God further said, "This is the sign that I set for the covenant between Me and you, and every living creature with you, for all ages to come.

9.13 I have set My bow in the clouds, and it shall serve as a sign of the covenant between Me and the earth.

9.14 When I bring clouds over the earth, and the bow appears in the clouds,

9.15 I will remember My covenant between Me and you and every living creature among all flesh, so that the waters shall never again become a flood to destroy all flesh.

> In the aftermath of the Flood and the fear of God this occasioned, the covenant now offered by God is unilateral: a promise that He will never again destroy mankind—at least not by flood. Of course, it is possible *man* will destroy life on earth—via nuclear weapons, the unleashing of a deadly virus, etc. Picking up on this theme, the late African-American writer James Baldwin titled what was perhaps his most famous book, *The Fire Next Time*, with words drawn from a black spiritual: "God gave Noah the rainbow sign, 'No more water, the fire next time.' "

9.16 When the bow is in the cloud, I will see it and remember the everlasting covenant between God and all living creatures, all flesh that is on earth.

9.17 That," God said to Noah, "shall be the sign of the covenant that I have established between Me and all flesh that is on earth."

9.18 The sons of Noah who came out of the ark were Shem, Ham, and Japheth—Ham being the father of Canaan.

> Canaan is the name of the land that the Israelites entered after the Exodus. The Israelites were repeatedly instructed not to be like the Canaanites, who were associated with polytheism, and most horrifically, according to the Torah, child sacrifice. To provide further confirmation for the odiousness of the Canaanites' behavior, the Torah states that Ham, the villain of the story that follows, was the father of Canaan.

9.19 These three were the sons of Noah, and from these the whole world branched out.

9.20 Noah, the tiller of the soil, was the first to plant a vineyard.

> The Torah traces the history of alcohol consumption back to Noah, thereby reminding us both of the dangers that can ensue from drunkenness and that

drunkenness has been a problem since the beginnings of mankin

often morally confused world, much more emphasis has been pl

dangers of cigarette smoking (which does indeed cause many poin~~~~~~~~

than on the dangers of alcohol, even though far more human evil—such as

spousal and child abuse, rape, and homicide—is directly related to alcohol,

while tobacco plays no role in such evils.

9.21 He drank of the wine and became drunk and he uncovered himself within his tent.

ESSAY: WHEN GOOD PEOPLE HAVE BAD CHILDREN

9.22 Ham, the father of Canaan, saw his father's nakedness and told his two brothers outside.

In the Torah to "uncover nakedness" (see Leviticus 18:7-16) or to "see naked-ness" (see Leviticus 20:17) implies sexual activity. However, even if Ham did nothing sexual with his father, this act alone—telling his two brothers about their father's naked state—was wrong. Ham publicly humiliated a human being, and not just any human being, his father.

Ham, who either sexually violated his father or humiliated him, is the son of Noah, the most righteous man of his time.

How does the finest man in the world produce an awful son?

We have here another universally applicable lesson: Parents can and often do have a great deal of influence on the children they raise. But not always.

Virtually every adult reader of this commentary knows good people who have raised children whose values are the opposite of their parents'. There are good, fine, and kind parents who have an awful child; and there are awful parents who have extraordinarily kind and upstanding children. Regarding the latter, I know a man well whose childhood was filled with sexual, physical, and verbal abuse and who was raised in foster homes where he was abused again. Had he turned out to be a murderer, people would say, "It makes sense— just look at his childhood."

But this man did not turn out to be a murderer; he turned out to be one of the finest and most honest people I have had the honor to know. And he in turn raised magnificent children.

How does one explain this man?

When I have asked him to explain how he turned out, he always speaks about an inexplicable bond with God he had from his earliest memories. But that, of course, only prompts the obvious question: where did that bond come from?

Likewise, I was riveted by a book, *A Mother's Reckoning* by Sue Klebold. Her seventeen-year-old son Dylan was one of the two boys who murdered twelve students and one teacher and wounded more than twenty others at Columbine High School outside of Denver, Colorado, in 1999.

As described in a *New York Times* review of her book, Dylan Klebold experienced "a home life that was, if not perfect, better than ordinary. Dylan grew up with happily married parents: a work-from-home dad who shared a snack and the sports pages with his teenage son every day after school, and a mom who worked with disabled college students, setting a moral example at the office before coming home at night to make the 'gloppy, layered Mexican casseroles' her two sons loved."

Having read her book, I fully agree with this reviewer: "Politely, methodically, she eviscerates in the reader the dearly held conviction that had he or she been in Sue Klebold's place, all could have been prevented."

In other words, the Klebolds no more produced a mass murderer than my friend's pathologic parents produced a superb human being.

> We who have good children may be partially or even very responsible for that fact. But we are also very lucky.

Nothing in life is as humbling as being a parent. We learn sooner or later we are not only not gods, we are only people who can do our best in raising our children. What ultimately ensues is simply not in our hands. (The same can be said about our Father in Heaven, who is not fully responsible for how all His children—human beings—have turned out.)

I recall once after a speech I gave, overhearing a conversat
who had been in attendance, had with a man who approache
record, my father did not see where I was and had no idea I c̲o̲ ̲ ̲ ̲
was said. The man said to my father: "What a son you have. You must have
been a great father."

My father, a man not known for his modesty, thought for a moment, and responded. "Actually, I was just very lucky."

It does not detract from my father's contribution in making me the man I became to note my father's admirable response was correct. We who have good children may be partially or even very responsible for that fact. But we are also very lucky.

> *The relationship between being a good person and being a good parent is almost as small as the relationship between being a good musician, doctor, or plumber and being a good parent.*

One reason I not only revere the Torah but love it is its honesty. About everything. Thus, every family described in the book of Genesis is what we would today call "dysfunctional." This is the Torah's gift to every human being who has dysfunctional relatives. The Torah is telling us, "This is—unfortunately—normal."

Next time you are filled with guilt about one (or more) of your children, remember the most righteous man in the world produced a bad son.

There is, however, another lesson to be drawn from Noah, the most righteous man, having a bad child: being a good person is not the same as being a good parent. There are very many good people who do not know how to raise a good child. The relationship between being a good person and being a good parent is almost as small as the relationship between being a good musician, doctor, or plumber and being a good parent.

Too many parents think their being a good person—a "good model" in modern parlance—suffices to produce good children. If that were the case,

Noah would have had the finest children in the world. And nearly all good people would have good children.

But while providing a good model to one's child is very important, it is not sufficient. To offer an analogy, if a parent wishes to raise a child who will be a good pianist, it means little if the parent is a good pianist. The parent needs to give the child piano lessons. The same holds true for goodness. Parents need to give their children goodness lessons; otherwise, their being models of goodness will likely mean little.

> Parents need to give their children goodness lessons; otherwise, their being models of goodness will likely mean little.

In our time, many parents, including the best-educated, think love is all a child needs. But if all a child receives is love and nothing in turn is demanded from the child, he or she will probably become a narcissist.

How does one give a child "goodness lessons"?

First, by emphasizing character above all other qualities. For many years, I have asked parents to ask their child—whether their child is five or fifty years-old—this question: "What do you think I most want you to be—happy, successful, smart, or good?"

In most cases, the child answers something other than "good."

For good reason. Most parents do not make it clear that they care much more about their son or daughter's character than about their school grades, or what university they go to, or how financially successful they are, or even how happy they are at any given moment.

Indeed, what they do make clear when speaking to others—often in the presence of the child—is they are most proud of their child's academic, athletic, and cultural attainments and—particularly in the case of girls—their looks. Joseph Telushkin has been advocating for years that parents reserve their highest praise of their children for when their children do kind acts.

Second, parents need to constantly emphasize goodness, integrity, and honesty. To cite a few examples, parents should make clear how disappointed they would be if their child cheated on an exam; they should vigilantly monitor how their child treats other people, whether those people are friends or adults; and they should vigilantly monitor the decency of their children's friends.

Third, children need moral discipline—and the earlier it begins, the more likely it will work. When children do something wrong, it is very tempting to ignore it or to dismiss it. For example, parents might say "He's only five," and say nothing, assuming he or she will outgrow the bad behavior. Likewise, when children are disciplined in school, parents must reinforce the school's decision (assuming it is a fair one), not rush to defend their child.

And fourth, grounding their moral teachings in the Bible can only help. The moral wisdom of the Bible is unparalleled (making that clear is the primary reason for this Bible commentary). Having children recognize that there is a God who expects them to be decent is a particularly powerful impetus to good behavior. And, of course, it is very inspiring for children to see that their parents feel bound by the same rules they are asking them to observe.

Making good people is the single most important thing society and parents must do. Whether because of bad luck or lack of parental guidance, in the case of Ham, the most righteous man, Noah, failed.

9.23 But Shem and Japheth took a cloth, placed it against both their backs and, walking backward, they covered their father's nakedness; their faces were turned the other way, so that they did not see their father's nakedness.

Shem and Japheth, understanding that Ham has humiliated their father, covered their father's nakedness and turned their faces.

9.24 When Noah woke up from his wine and learned what his youngest son had done to him,

The Torah does not explicitly state what Ham did to his father. Nor do we know how Noah learned what happened while he was sleeping (was he informed by his two other sons?).

There are two likely possibilities about what occurred:

1. Ham did something far worse than gaze at—and perhaps mock—his father's nakedness. The term used in the Torah, that Ham looked upon his father's nakedness (*ervah*), is reminiscent of Leviticus 18, which lists a variety of sexual offenses, among them uncovering the *ervah* of close relatives (verses 7-18). This term has therefore been understood as a euphemism for sexual relations. For that reason, this verse might suggest that Ham had some form of sexual contact with his father. But, again, the Torah—perhaps to safeguard Noah's dignity—does not explicitly tell us. (Similarly, in Numbers 12:1, the Torah relates that Miriam and Aaron, Moses's sister and brother, angered God by engaging in mean-spirited gossip about Moses, but it does not tell us what they said.)

2. Ham did nothing more than look at his naked father and tell his brothers about it. When Noah awoke to find himself covered, he questioned his other two sons, who told him what Ham said to them and that they covered him without looking. This is closest to a literal reading of the story.

This may seem a relatively trivial sin. But it isn't. Protecting parental dignity is a fundamental value in the Torah.

What is clear is it didn't take long for at least some human beings to resume their bad ways. If God thought bringing the Flood would teach the few surviving humans a moral lesson, He was to be disappointed again by His favorite creation.

9.25 he said, "Cursed be Canaan. The lowest of slaves shall he be to his brothers."

Noah's curse of Ham's son, Canaan, is clearly undeserved and u
violates the Torah principle that children shall not be punished for
sins (see Deuteronomy 24:16).

9.26 And he said, "Blessed be the Lord, the God of Shem; Let Canaan be a slave to them,

Much later, some Christians and Jews justified black slavery based on these
two verses. They argued that Ham was the father of the black race and that
therefore the black race was cursed to be enslaved.

There are at least three responses to this belief that was as baseless as it was
vile. The first is the Torah in no way hints Ham was black or that the Canaanites' lineage was African. The second is Ham is not cursed, Canaan is. The third
is God in no way participates in this curse. The curse is from Noah alone.

**9.27 May God enlarge Japheth, and let him dwell in the tents of Shem; and let Canaan be a slave
to them."**

9.28 Noah lived after the flood 350 years.

The story of the uncovering of Noah's nakedness is the only incident from the
last 350 years of Noah's life that is chronicled in the Torah; it is likely, therefore,
this story is, among other things, meant to underscore the dangers of excessive
drinking, a danger emphasized a few chapters later in Genesis when the inebriated and oblivious Lot sleeps with his daughters (Genesis 19:32-35). The place-
ment of these two episodes in the Torah, incidents that Jews read in synagogue
every year, may have played a role in the historically low rates of excessive
drinking and alcoholism among Jews.

9.29 And all the days of Noah came to 950 years; then he died.

CHAPTER

10

The God of the Torah Is the God of All Nations

This chapter of Genesis is known as the Table of Nations because it contains the genealogical tables of Noah's descendants and the nations that came from them. The Torah divided the world of the time into seventy nations. The number seventy has its own significance, as do all recurring numbers in the Torah, the most prominent examples being seven (including multiples of seven) and forty.[1]

This chapter is another example of a Torah text that seems irrelevant but is in fact not only significant but revolutionary. This chapter affirms God is the God of all nations and is interested in all nations. There is nothing like this in any other contemporaneous religious literature. From the first chapter of Genesis until now, the Torah has had nothing to say about Israelites, Hebrews, or Jews. The God of the Torah is the God of the world, not just of the Jews. And the Jews are chosen to be a blessing to the nations of the world.

> *God is the God of all nations and is interested in all nations. There is nothing like this in any other contemporaneous religious literature.*

In the words of Robert Alter:

"In keeping with the universalist perspective of Genesis, the Table of Nations is a serious attempt, *unprecedented in the ancient Near East*, to sketch a panorama of all known human cultures—from Greece and Crete in the west through Asia Minor and Iran and down through Mesopotamia and the Arabian Peninsula to northwestern Africa. This chapter has been a happy hunting ground for scholars armed with the tools of archeology, and in fact an impressive proportion of these names have analogues in inscriptions and tablets in other ancient Near Eastern cultures."[2]

And Bruce K. Waltke writes:

"The Table of Nations" represents the nations as of one blood, multiplying under God's blessing as distinct tribes and nations. *The Table represents God's broad concern for all peoples, not just the Israelites, which is understood by the omission of Israel from this Table.* The narrator presents a symbolic seventy nations based on ethnic, geographic, linguistic, and political factors.

"Seventy nations are given: fourteen from Japheth, thirty from Ham, and twenty-six from Shem. Seventy, a multiple of seven and ten (both connoting completeness), represents a large (see Judges 8:30; 2 Kings 10:1) and complete number. This number compares with the number of Abraham's seed at the end of the book. By the time of their descent into Egypt, they, too, have reached the symbolic, complete, and full number.

"Thus, the sovereign God has laid a firm foundation for making this microcosm of the nations [Abraham's seed] into a nation [Israel] able to bless the earth (cf. Gen. 46:27; Ex. 1:5)."

SEVEN SONS OF JAPHETH

10.1 These are the lines of Shem, Ham, and Japheth, the sons of Noah: sons were born to them after the Flood.

10.2 The descendants of Japheth: Gomer, Magog, Madai, Javan, Tubal, Meshech, and Tiras.

SEVEN GRANDSONS OF JAPHETH

10.3 The descendants of Gomer: Ashkenaz, Riphath, and Togarmah.

10.4 The descendants of Javan: Elishah and Tarshish, the Kittim and the Dodanim.

10.5 From these the maritime nations branched out. These are the descendants of Japheth by their lands—each with its language—their clans and their nations.

FOUR SONS OF HAM

10.6 The descendants of Ham: Cush, Mizraim, Put, and Canaan.

SEVEN GRANDSONS OF HAM

10.7 The descendants of Cush: Seba, Havilah, Sabtah, Raamah, and Sabteca. The descendants of Raamah: Sheba and Dedan.

AND THE MIGHTY NIMROD

10.8 Cush also begat Nimrod, who was the first man of might on earth.

10.9 He was a mighty hunter by the grace of the Lord; hence the saying, "Like Nimrod a mighty hunter by the grace of the Lord."

10.10 The mainstays of his kingdom were Babylon, Erech, Accad, and Calneh in the land of Shinar.

10.11 From that land Asshur went forth and built Nineveh, Rehoboth-ir, Calah,

10.12 and Resen between Nineveh and Calah, that is the great city.

SEVEN SONS OF MIZRAIM (EGYPT)

10.13 And Mizraim begot the Ludim, the Anamim, the Lehabim, the Naphtuhim,

10.14 the Pathrusim, the Casluhim, and the Caphtorim, whence the Philistines came forth.

ELEVEN DESCENDANTS OF CANAAN AND THEIR LAND

10.15 Canaan begot Sidon, his first-born, and Heth;

10.16 and the Jebusites, the Amorites, the Girgashites,

10.17 the Hivites, the Arkites, the Sinites,

10.18 the Arvadites, the Zemarites, and the Hamathites. Afterward the clans of the Canaanites spread out.

10.19 The [original] Canaanite territory extended from Sidon as far as Gerar, near Gaza, and as far as Sodom, Gomorrah, Admah, and Zeboiim, near Lasha.

10.20 These are the descendants of Ham, according to their clans and languages, by their lands and nations.

DESCENDANTS OF SHEM

10.21 Sons were also born to Shem, ancestor of all the descendants of Eber and older brother of Japheth.

10.22 The descendants of Shem: Elam, Asshur, Arpachshad, Lud, and Aram.

10.23 The descendants of Aram: Uz, Hul, Gether, and Mash.

10.24 Arpachshad begot Shelah, and Shelah begot Eber.

10.25 Two sons were born to Eber: the name of the first was Peleg, for in his days the earth was divided; and the name of his brother was Joktan.

10.26 Joktan begot Almodad, Sheleph, Hazarmaveth, Jerah,

10.27 Hadoram, Uzal, Diklah,

10.28 Obal, Abimael, Sheba,

10.29 Ophir, Havilah, and Jobab; all these were descendants of Joktan.

10.30 Their settlements extended from Mesha as far as Sephar, the hill country to the east.

10.31 These are the descendants of Shem according to their clans and languages, by their lands, according to their nations.

> The genealogical line that will continue to play a significant role in this story is that of Shem, the ancestor of Abraham.

10.32 These are the groupings of Noah's descendants, according to their origins, by their nations; and from these the nations branched out over the earth after the Flood.

CHAPTER

11

11.1 Everyone on earth had the same language and the same words.

> Given that the Torah traces all human beings to a single couple, it traces all languages to a single language. This may well be so, but linguists will probably never be able to either prove or disprove it.

11.2 And as they migrated from the east, they came upon a valley in the land of Shinar and settled there.

11.3 They said to one another, "Come, let us make bricks and burn them hard."—Brick served them as stone, and bitumen served them as mortar.

> This verse is another example of the Torah's antiquity. Sarna writes that the Torah here "displays an accurate and detailed knowledge of Mesopotamian construction techniques," further evidence for its origins in the period described.

11.4 And they said, "Come, let us build us a city,

> We tend to remember only the Tower of Babel, but every time the Torah mentions the tower, it also mentions the city that was built with it.

11.4 (cont.) and a tower with its top in the sky,

> To this day, people identify—or more precisely, confuse—"big" with "important."

ESSAY: THE SELF-DESTRUCTIVE PURSUIT OF FAME

11.4 (cont.) to make a name for ourselves;

Nothing has changed regarding human nature. To this day, countries vie with one another to build the tallest building in the world for no other reason than to become the country that built the tallest building in the world—"To make a name for ourselves." But having the tallest building in the world says nothing about a country other than it has the tallest building in the world.

The Torah does not necessarily oppose making a name for oneself. In the very next chapter, God tells Abraham that He will make Abraham's name great (12:2). The sin of the builders of Babel—and of most people wanting to make a name for themselves—is wanting to do so solely to make a name for themselves, to bring glory to themselves. As God is completely absent, they recognize nothing higher than themselves to bring glory to.

As explained in the commentary on the Ten Commandments' prohibition against having false gods, this "nothing higher" issue is at the core of the problem of contemporary art, most of which is meaningless, and much of which is degrading. There is a whole genre of contemporary art that is scatological in nature—see the essay on false gods in the commentary to Exodus 20:3 and the footnote for examples of scatological art.[1] By contrast, nearly all great Western art was produced by artists whose art and/or whose societies affirmed God.

As I note in the commentary to Exodus, I asked John Eliot Gardiner, one of the greatest Bach conductors and the author of a major biography of Bach, if he thought there was a decline in the quality of classical music in the modern period—and if so, whether he would ascribe that decline in large measure to secularism, with its absence of faith in God. To my surprise, he fully agreed.

When there is nothing higher than man, most art is simply self-referential: "Look at me." That's what the builders of the Tower of Babel cared about.

The Babel story has been pertinent to every age. But it is particularly relevant today when so many people yearn, perhaps more than anything else, to be famous, to—in the Torah's words here—"make a name" for themselves. This yearning often starts at a very young age. I have asked young people for decades what they want to be when they get older, and over the years I have found increasing numbers respond, "Famous."

And it is not only young people. Many adults in the country I know best, America, ache to be famous. To appear on any public media, make even a non-speaking appearance in a movie, or see one's name in print or on screen is to stand out, to validate one's worth.

Before explaining why the pursuit of fame is a bad idea, it is important to acknowledge once more the desire to make a name for oneself is not necessarily a bad thing. If a person wants to become known for achieving a worthwhile goal, that can be a spur to pursuing that goal. Also, as long as a person is focused on the worthwhile end, the fame that comes as a byproduct is well-earned and will not distort the values or emotional stability of a balanced person.

But if a person's primary goal is to be famous, fame becomes a false god. And like all false gods, it can be dangerous—because one of the characteristics of a false god is something that becomes higher than morality. Therefore, a person might do anything to become famous. For example, many experts believe a primary goal of young people who shoot their schoolmates is to have their "fifteen minutes of fame."

Aside from theology and morality, there are other reasons why the pursuit of fame is pointless and often self-destructive:

First, in almost every case, whatever fame a person achieves will die with him—if his fame even lasts that long.

A medieval Jewish text, *The Ways of the Righteous*, puts it this way: "Think about how many proud men have vanished from the world and have been forgotten as if they never existed." There were many people who lived in, say, the sixth century who thought they were very important. How many of them can you name?

One doesn't have to go back to the sixth century. Take, for example, presidents of the United States. To the vast majority of Americans, let alone non-Americans, the names of many of these men—Franklin Pierce, Rutherford Hayes, and Chester Arthur to cite just three—mean nothing. Yet to Americans living in those presidents' lifetimes, those individuals were the most famous people alive. Today, the large majority of even those familiar with these presidents' names probably cannot specify a single accomplishment by any of them.

This is true even in our own lifetimes. As we get older, we all come to the often unexpected, and always sobering, realization that almost every person who was a "household name" when we were younger is unknown to the next generation.

As a Persian proverb puts it, "After the game is over, the pawn and the king go into the same box."

Second, fame is fleeting for the vast majority of those who attain it—that is, it doesn't even last until their death. Only a small minority of those who are famous at thirty will be famous at sixty.

Third, when people who pursue fame lose it, they often end up emotionally and psychologically depressed. The more you value fame, the more you lose your purpose for living when you lose that fame.

Fourth, even if you do stay famous, if you value fame, you will devote your life to keeping it. And little is more pathetic than watching a person devote their life to trying to stay famous.

The famous are rarely significant, and the significant are rarely famous. Very few of us can or will be famous. But all of us can be significant.

Fifth, unlike other things people desire, fame is available only to an extremely small number of people. Theoretically, very many people can be rich, healthy, or happy. But how many people can be famous? By definition, only an infinitesimally small number. There are, after all, only a limited number of names people can keep in their heads. In pursuing the goal of fame, one is almost inevitably pursuing an unattainable goal.

Sixth, few things distort a person's thinking, values, and even personality as much as fame. The greater the fame, the greater the inclination to think one is better than others. The percentage of young people

who become very famous and then become almost entirely differen
quite high.

Given the powerful appeal of fame, is there an antidote?

In addition to realizing how pointless, fleeting, and self-destructive the
pursuit of fame is, the most effective antidote is to take religious faith seriously.
The more important God becomes, the less important fame becomes. A genu-
ine and humble faith in God puts things into perspective like nothing else.

Finally, and most important, we all need to remember this rule of life: *The
famous are rarely* significant, *and the* significant *are rarely famous.* The care-
taker of an invalid is the most significant person in the world to that invalid—but
hardly famous. On the other hand, many movie stars are extremely famous—but
hardly significant—and the people who personally know them, love them, and
regard them as significant do not do so because of their fame.

Very few of us can or will be famous. But all of us can be significant.

11.4 (cont.) else we shall be scattered all over the world."

The builders' fear of being scattered—wittingly or unwittingly—defied God's
plan for the world. God's first commandment to Adam and Eve, and then again
to Noah's family, was to be fruitful, multiply, and *fill the earth.* But "man did
not perceive this to be a blessing and so devised means to thwart its fulfillment"
(Sarna). The tower builders want to stay in one place.

We cannot grow up unless we leave what is most comfortable and venture
out into the world. And God and the Torah, as we shall repeatedly see, want
us humans to grow up. Growing up begins with leaving our mother and father
and bonding with a spouse (Genesis 2:24). It also may include leaving the place
in which one has grown up (see the commentary to Genesis 3:23). The next
chapter begins with God telling Abram to leave his home and go to a new land.

11.5 The Lord came down to look at the city and tower that man had built,

Biblical scholar Moshe David Cassuto writes: "It is difficult to miss the irony
in this verse. The builders' intention is to erect a tower whose top will be 'in

the heavens,' that is, among the gods. But even though they build the tower, it is so far from the heavens that God must come down to see it."

ESSAY: IS WORLD UNITY A GOOD IDEA?

11.6 and the Lord said, "If, as one people with one language for all, this is how they have begun to act,

Speaking one language, the builders want a united world. God declares this is not a good idea.

Here is Hamilton's summary: "God comes down not to inspect the scenario, as in verse 5, but to thwart it. His method is perhaps surprising: he will confuse their language. Why not simply topple the tower? Because that would solve the problem only temporarily. Towers are replaceable.... The solution must go deeper than that. It is not the tower that must be done away with, but what makes possible the building of that tower—an international language that provides communication among linguistic groups. If this ability to communicate is removed, it is unlikely that the individuals will continue with their work."

Needless to say, knowing more than one's own language is a virtue. But the Torah is making a rather audacious point: the world would not be better if people abandoned all languages but one.

It is very tempting to seek a united world—one language and one governing authority, with no divisive national identities. But God declares such a world dangerous. For one thing, it inevitably concentrates power in the hands of the few who run that united world—and power corrupts. For another, diverse national identities and cultures are a good thing.

The united world the Torah seeks is a world of nations united in acknowledging the one God and living by His moral code. Beyond that, diversity in national identity, language, and even religion is welcome. Regarding the latter, the Torah and later Judaism are unique among monotheistic faiths in not seeking a world in which all people are members of their religion. Rather, the Torah wants all people to be ethical monotheists—people who acknowledge the one God of the Torah and live by His moral demands. As Rabbi Jonathan Sacks, the former British Chief Rabbi and scholar, put it, "God is God of all hu[man]

between Babel and the end of days no single faith is the faith of all [

Virtually every call for "unity" is disingenuous. People who call for ideo-logical unity do so on the presumption that it will be based on *their* values. When a Christian calls for Christian unity, he is calling for a unity based on *his* understanding of Christianity. Protestants who call for Christian unity are hardly willing to accept the Catholic pope or Sacraments; and Catholics who call for Christian unity are hardly willing to give up the papacy or the Sacraments. Likewise, Orthodox Jews who call for Jewish unity assume it means all Jews embracing *Halacha* (Jewish law); and few non-Orthodox Jews who call for Jewish unity are willing to embrace most, let alone all, of *Halacha*.

The founders of the United States, the freest country ever to exist, understood the limitations of unity (perhaps because their values were so deeply rooted in the Bible). That is why they gave the states of the United States so much power. According to the U.S. Constitution (Tenth Amendment), unless a power is specifically given to the federal government, all powers belong to the states: "The powers not delegated to the United States by the Constitution, nor prohibited by it to the States, are reserved to the States respectively, or to the people." So, too, the Constitution gave the United States Senate much more power than it gave the nation's population: states with very small populations have as many senators (two) as states with enormous populations.

And the Torah never calls for all the world's people to unite as Jews—only as followers of the Torah's God.

> *The Torah never calls for all the world's people to unite as Jews—only as followers of the Torah's God.*

11.6 (cont.) then nothing that they may propose to do will be out of their reach.

God warns against technological advancement for its own sake—or worse, for the sake of human ego. Technology without God can be dangerous. When people who are not guided by the Bible have access to advanced technology, we get such things as cloned human beings. And only God knows where Artificial

Intelligence unconstrained by God-centered values will lead us. Already, at the time of this writing, some people (men in particular) are beginning to relate more to human-like robots than to human beings.

11.7 Let us, then, go down and confound their speech there, so that they shall not understand one another's speech."

Once again, we are confronted with the rare divine usage of "us" (as in Genesis 1:26: "Let us make man in our image"). Who is included in the "us" to whom God is speaking? Here I believe it is God mocking the tower makers, who had said in verse 4, "Come, let us build us a city, and a tower with its top in the sky…" In effect, they said, "Let us go up," and God responded, "Let us go down."

11.8 Thus the Lord scattered them from there over the face of the whole earth;

Jonathan Sacks comments, "The results of human behavior are often the opposite of what was intended. The builders wanted to concentrate humanity in one place—'Let us build a city…else we shall be scattered all over the world.' The result was that they were dispersed—'the Lord scattered them from there over the face of the whole earth.' They wanted to 'make a name' for themselves, and they did, but the name they made—Babel—became an eternal symbol of confusion."

To this day, and based on this biblical episode, the word in English for speaking incoherently is "babble." Some years ago, Dore Gold, the former Israeli ambassador to the United Nations, titled his memoir about the U.N.—an institution where truth and moral coherence are rare (how could it be otherwise, given how many of the member states of the United Nations are corrupt and/ or dictatorships?)—*Tower of Babble*.

THE TORAH MISTRUSTS CITIES

11.8 (cont.) and they stopped building the city.

Rabbi Gunther Plaut (1912-2012), author of *The Torah: A Modern Commentary*, notes the tower is not mentioned here because the tower is the embodiment of the city; and it is the building of the city that is the primary sin. Another biblical scholar, Patrick D. Miller, Professor Emeritus of Old Tʁ ogy at Princeton Theological Seminary, suggests the story shouⁱ be captioned "The City of Babel," not "The Tower of Babeˡ Alter writes: "The polemic thrust of the story is against urbanism and overweening confidence of humanity in the feats of technology."

The Torah presents the story of Babel as a warning against human hubris and also as a warning against the often-immoral nature of cities.

The Torah warns us about cities for moral and religious reasons.

City dwellers are far more capable of anonymity than people who live in small towns and in rural areas. And when people are anonymous, they feel less moral obligation to their neighbors—who are also likely to be anonymous. When both the individual and his neighbors are anonymous, people inevitably feel much less connected to one another. And they often act worse—just look at the difference between anonymous comments on the internet and comments whose authors are identified.

A study by the University of Indiana Center on Philanthropy concluded, "[American] rural donors donated a statistically significant higher percentage of their income to charity than urban donors did."[3]

It is not surprising that so many of Israel's great prophets were shepherds, the most rural of folk. Moses, too, was a shepherd. And nearly all of the terrible ideas of the modern period were thought up in cities: Marx in London, Hitler in Vienna, Lenin in a host of European cities, etc.

Of course, there are fine people who live in cities, and there are bad people who live in rural areas. Moreover, even more than whether one is a city or rural resident, affiliation with a church or synagogue is the greatest predictor of how much a person will be involved in neighbors' lives (see the essay, "It Is not Good for Man to Be Alone" in Genesis 2:18). But given their role as incubators of bad ideas and the anonymity they afford, cities are a moral problem.[4]

Cities have enriched civilizations culturally, artistically, scientifically, and medically. But morally—the Torah's preoccupation—has often been another matter.

11.9 That is why it was called Babel, because there the Lord confounded the speech of the whole earth; and from there the Lord scattered them over the face of the whole earth.

> The Hebrew name *Bavel* is a play on words; it sounds like *balal,* the Hebrew word for "confound" or "mix up." In addition, *Bavel* is the Hebrew name for Babylon; thus, according to the Torah, Babylon means "mixed up."

11.10 This is the line of Shem. Shem was 100 years old when he begot Arpachshad, two years after the Flood.

11.11 After the birth of Arpachshad, Shem lived 500 years and begot sons and daughters.

11.12 When Arpachshad had lived 35 years, he begot Shelah.

11.13 After the birth of Shelah, Arpachshad lived 403 years and begot sons and daughters.

11.14 When Shelah had lived 30 years, he begot Eber.

11.15 After the birth of Eber, Shelah lived 403 years and begot sons and daughters.

11.16 When Eber had lived 34 years, he begot Peleg.

11.17 After the birth of Peleg, Eber lived 430 years and begot sons and daughters.

11.18 When Peleg had lived 30 years, he begot Reu.

11.19 After the birth of Reu, Peleg lived 209 years and begot sons and daughters.

11.20 When Reu had lived 32 years, he begot Serug.

11.21 After the birth of Serug, Reu lived 207 years and begot sons and daughters.

11.22 When Serug had lived 30 years, he begot Nahor.

11.23 After the birth of Nahor, Serug lived 200 years and begot sons and daughters.

11.24 When Nahor had lived 29 years, he begot Terah.

11.25 After the birth of Terah, Nahor lived 119 years and begot sons and daughters.

11.26 When Terah had lived 70 years, he begot Abram, Nahor, and Haran.

There are ten generations from Adam to Noah and there are another ten generations from Shem to Abraham.

This is the first mention of Abraham, the patriarch of the Jewish people, whose original name is Abram. The Torah has now moved from universal history to the history of one specific people: the Chosen People, known later as Jews. But, in keeping with the Torah's—and God's—overriding concern for all nations, the purpose of this Chosen People is to be a blessing to all the nations. Its mission will be to bring the other nations to God and His moral Law.

11.27 Now this is the line of Terah: Terah begot Abram, Nahor, and Haran; and Haran begot Lot.

11.28 Haran died in the lifetime of his father Terah, in his native land, Ur of the Chaldeans.

11.29 Abram and Nahor took to themselves wives, the name of Abram's wife being Sarai and that of Nahor's wife Milcah, the daughter of Haran, the father of Milcah and Iscah.

11.30 Now Sarai was barren, she had no child.

The theme of women who give birth after long years of infertility is a recurring one in Genesis, and it is likely meant to underscore that the people of Israel came into existence through repeated divine intervention. The first detail we learn about Sarai is she is barren, and she remained so for many years.

We know it was Sarai and not Abram who was infertile because Abram, at Sarai's urging, has a child with Sarai's maid, Hagar (Genesis 16:1-4).

A generation later, Isaac and Rebecca did not have a child for twenty years, and in the following generation, Rachel, Jacob's beloved wife, was so upset with her barrenness (Jacob has already had four children with her sister Leah), she wanted to die (Genesis 30:1). The lesson is clear: Had nature taken its course, the Jewish people would not have come into existence. But God intervened and the barren matriarchs—Sarai, Rebecca, and Rachel—all gave birth to children.

11.31 Terah took his son Abram, his grandson Lot the son of Haran, and his daughter-in-law Sarai, the wife of his son Abram, and they set out together from Ur of the Chaldeans for the land of Canaan; but when they had come as far as Haran, they settled there.

11.32 The days of Terah came to 205 years; and Terah died in Haran.

Note to reader: Abram's name is later changed to Abraham and Sarai is changed to Sarah, the names by which they are known today (see Genesis 17:5 and 17:15). In conformity with the biblical text, they are referred to as Abram and Sarai until their names are changed.

WHY DID GOD CHOOSE ABRAM?

12.1 The Lord said to Abram,

The Torah does not explain why God chose Abram. Noah was chosen because of his righteousness (Genesis 6:9). And Moses' nobility of character is revealed before God chooses him: We learn he killed an Egyptian overseer who was beating a Hebrew slave, he tried to resolve a fight between two feuding Hebrews, and he stood up on behalf of Midianite women who were being mistreated (Exodus 2:11-17). But Abram's selection seems completely arbitrary. Unlike Moses and Noah, we come to understand Abram's greatness only later.

There are two possible reasons for the choosing of Abram. One is he himself "discovered" the one God. And God responded accordingly. A second is God recognized Abram as a particularly great man worthy of being the father of the monotheistic nation of Israel, but there is no reason we can discern why Abram was chosen.

The truth is it really doesn't matter. What matters is what happens once God chooses this individual named Abram. All of history will change.

ABRAM'S FIRST TEST

12.1 (cont.) "Go forth from your native land and from your father's house to the land that I will show you.

This is the first of several instances in which God tests Abram's faith. Here, Abram is told to leave everything that is familiar to him and move to a place that is completely unknown. It is virtually identical to God's later command (Genesis 22)—the ultimate test—that Abram sacrifice his son Isaac. As Rashi, the preeminent medieval biblical Jewish commentator (France, 1040-1105), noted, God told Abram to sacrifice his son on one of the mountains that "I will tell you," virtually the same words used here ("I will show you"). Rashi also notes the connection between the triplet here—the Hebrew reads *"your land and your birthplace and your father's house"* (for some reason, the present translation does not include "birthplace") and the triplet in chapter 22—"your son, your only one, whom you love."

ALL NATIONS WILL BE BLESSED THROUGH ONE NATION

12.2 I will make of you a great nation and I will bless you; I will make your name great, and you shall be a blessing.

A blessing to whom? The answer is in the next verse: All the families of the earth.

To say nothing like this existed prior to the Torah is to understate the case. The idea that one nation will be a blessing for all other nations has no parallel.

In the course of Jewish history, many Jews have lost sight of this purpose of the Jewish people. One reason is antisemitism—Jews have often been so preoccupied with simply surviving, they forgot their mission to humanity. Another reason is Judaism's dual nature: it is both universal—as this verse makes clear—and particularistic. And the particular has often overwhelmed the universal. Likewise, and more commonly in the contemporary world, the universal has often overwhelmed the particular (see the essay on universalism and particularism at Genesis 19:5). Many Jews have abandoned Judaism to embrace universal doctrines. But the universal doesn't work without the particular. This is a major contemporary issue for non-Jews as much as for Jews: Do we work for a world without particular national identities, or do we make a better world through our particular national identities? The Torah's answer was already given in the Tower of Babel story.

THOSE WHO BLESS AND THOSE WHO CURSE THE JEWS . . .

12.3 I will bless those who bless you and curse him that curses you;

One does not have to be a religious believer in order to acknowledge that this promise has held true. Nations that have treated the Jews favorably, the United States being the most obvious modern example, have been blessed with prosperity and freedom.

The reverse applies as well.

In the medieval world, Spain went into an economic and cultural decline after the 1492 expulsion of the Jews. In the modern era, Germany, the country that cursed the Jews of Germany and Europe with the Holocaust, then endured its own curse: During World War II, approximately seven and a half million Germans were killed (German Red Cross estimate, 2005), about two million German women were raped (generally by Russian troops), almost a quarter of a million of whom died as a result, and Germany was divided for forty-four years. Nor is Germany's future even now secure given the massive immigration of people, many of whom do not share Germany's Western values, and the very low birth rate of native Germans.

After World War II, another group arose that has cursed the Jews—many of the countries in the Arab and fundamentalist Islamist worlds; and they are among the most benighted of societies.

12.3 (cont.) And all the families of the earth shall bless themselves by you."

God does not tell Abram that *his* family will be blessed through him but that *all* the world's families will be blessed through him. That this theme is mentioned only three verses after introducing us to Abram makes it clear the mission of

Abram and the Jewish people is universal. On four subsequent occasions in Genesis, the theme of universal blessings through the Jews is stated and tied to Abram and his descendants (see Genesis 18:17-18; 22:16-18, 26:2-4, and 28:10-14).

The present translation is literal: The Hebrew says, the world's families "will bless themselves by you," not "be blessed by you." And how will people "bless themselves by you"? When the families of the earth learn how to act toward one another through living by the moral laws and values God will reveal to Abraham and his descendants. The road to a good world is through this Torah and the rest of the Bible. The world ignores the Torah and the Bible at its peril.

12.4 Abram went forth as the Lord had commanded him, and Lot went with him. Abram was seventy-five years old when he left Haran.

Abram was already an old man when he was sent on his world-changing mission. One lesson here is no one should ever think of himself as too old to change or to do something meaningful. Later, in Exodus 7:7 Moses is described as eighty when he confronted Pharaoh. Both of these verses are particularly significant today when human lifespans have increased dramatically and people are remaining active and vital until much older ages.

The road to a good world is through this Torah and the rest of the Bible. The world ignores the Torah and the Bible at its peril.

THE TORAH'S VIEW OF WEALTH

12.5 Abram took his wife Sarai and his brother's son Lot, and all the wealth that they had amassed,

It is not an insignificant detail that Abram was a wealthy man. Few great thinkers have been poor. Great thinkers think about the purpose of existence. For the poor, the purpose of life is quite clear: to provide food and shelter for themselves and for their family. Only when people do not have to worry where their next meal is coming from do they have the time to think about great issues such as the purpose of life. This may also help to account for the fact that centuries later it was not a Hebrew slave who led the revolt against Pharaoh; it was Moses, the one Hebrew who had been raised in wealth.

Also, the Torah has no problem with wealth. Abram, the man through whom all the nations and families of the earth will be blessed, was wealthy. There are good and bad rich people and good and bad poor people. The Torah judges people by their character, not their wealth.

There are good and bad rich people and good and bad poor people. The Torah judges people by their character.

12.5 (cont.) and the persons that they had acquired in Haran; and they set out for the land of Canaan. When they arrived in the land of Canaan,

12.6 Abram passed through the land as far as the site of Shechem, at the terebinth of Moreh. The Canaanites were then in the land.

These seemingly innocuous words—"the Canaanites were then in the land"—have created controversy among Bible scholars. That the words are phrased in the past tense suggests that they were written at a time when the Canaanites were no longer in the land. But at the time of Moses, which tradition dictates as the time when the Torah was written, the Canaanites were still very present in the land. Therefore, some scholars cite these words to argue that there are verses in the Torah written after the age of Moses (see commentary to Deuteronomy 1:1).

However, even Robert Alter, who believes in later authorship and editing of the Torah, writes that such a reading is unnecessary: "The point of the notation, as Gerhard von Rad has seen, is to introduce a certain tension with the immediately following promise that the land will be given to Abram's offspring."

12.7 The Lord appeared to Abram and said, "I will assign this land to your offspring." And he built an altar there to the Lord who had appeared to him.

here he moved on to the hill country east of Bethel and pitched his tent, with Bethel on
Ai on the east; and he built there an altar to the Lord and invoked the Lord by name.

12.9 Then Abram journeyed by stages toward the Negev.

12.10 There was a famine in the land, and Abram went down to Egypt to sojourn there, for the famine was severe in the land.

> "Egyptian texts substantiate the possibility of such an itinerary in the 2nd millennium B.C."[1]

12.11 As he was about to enter Egypt, he said to his wife Sarai, "I know what a beautiful woman you are.

IT IS OK FOR BELIEVERS TO HAVE DOUBTS—EVEN ABRAM DID

12.12 If the Egyptians see you, and think, 'She is his wife,' they will kill me and let you live.

Abram's statement "they will kill me" raises an interesting question. God has already promised Abram many descendants, so why would Abram believe he might be killed? His fear reminds us that even great people of faith sometimes have doubts. Doubts are part of faith. We should not feel overly concerned and certainly not demoralized when we have doubts. Doubts do not mean we are non-believers; rather, we are, in the words of the American writer Louis Auchincloss, "a believer who is having doubts."

I have rarely met a believing Jew who never experienced doubts. I have met a few Christians who say they never have doubts, and I suspect more believing Muslims than either Jews or Christians would say they never have doubts. But, by and large, the only group as a whole that I have encountered whose members say they never have doubts has been atheists. When I debated the head of American Atheists at their annual convention in Minneapolis, Minnesota, I asked the audience if any of them ever doubted their atheism and thought God might actually exist. Among the many hundreds of people present, not one hand was raised (apparently, and despite the common folk wisdom, these people would remain atheists in foxholes).

The great American rabbi Emanuel Rackman, president of Bar-Ilan University, wrote: "Doubt is good for the human soul, its humility.... God may have had His own reasons for denying us certainty with regard to His existence and nature. One apparent reason is that man's certainty with regard to anything is poison to his soul. Who knows this better than moderns who have had to cope with dogmatic fascists, communists, and even scientists?"[2]

> *Doubts do not mean we are non-believers; rather, we are "a believer who is having doubts."*

With regard to Abram's fear of Egyptian violence, the Egyptians were deemed quite capable of killing strangers and taking their wives. Perhaps this story is included in order to show just how revolutionary was the new system of ethical monotheism that God was trying to institute. In contrast to the normative behavior toward strangers in Egypt, God commands the Jews to love the stranger (Leviticus 19:34, Deuteronomy 10:19, Exodus 22:21). In the words of the German Jewish philosopher Hermann Cohen: "The stranger was to be protected, although he was not a member of one's family, clan, religion, community, or people, simply because he was a human being. In the stranger, therefore, man discovered the idea of humanity."

This was not the case anywhere else (see, for example, Genesis 19). I have not found any other civilization that demanded love of the stranger.

ESSAY: ABRAM TELLS SARAI TO LIE: WAS THAT MORAL?

12.13 Please say that you are my sister, that it may go well with me because of you, and that I may remain alive thanks to you."

Throughout history, more than a few Bible readers have criticized Abram for having Sarai tell the Egyptians she is his sister. He was criticized on two grounds: asking his wife to lie and putting her in a situation in which adultery would almost certainly take place.

For example, the eminent thirteenth-century Bible commentator Nachman-es (Ramban) wrote: "Know that our father Abram inadvertently committed great sin by placing his wife in a compromising situation because of his fear f being killed. He should have trusted in God to save him."

More recently, Rabbi W. Gunther Plaut, author of a widely read commentary on the Torah, expressed agreement with Nachmanides and concluded that, on balance, Abram's behavior was sinful.

I respectfully disagree. When making moral decisions, the most important question is often this: What are my choices? If Abram and Sarai had decided she should tell Pharaoh the truth, they had every reason to believe Abram would have been killed. Would that have been the right choice? Would Sarai have preferred that choice? Would *any* wife who loved her husband? Moreover, how would that have guaranteed Sarai's safety? With her husband dead, Sarai would still have ended up in Pharaoh's harem.

It would seem that those who argue that Abram should have told Sarai to speak truthfully believe they are choosing morality over immorality, but what they are really choosing is chivalry and avoiding a one-time life-saving lie over morality, common sense, and the preservation of life. Those were the real choices confronting Abram.

While the Torah neither praises nor condemns Abram for asking Sarai to lie, the Bible does strongly suggest elsewhere that lying sometimes is justified. This is illustrated by an incident in the Book of Samuel when God instructs the prophet Samuel to lie. This took place during the reign of King Saul. The king had been appointed by God and anointed by the prophet Samuel. Yet when Saul disobeys a divine order, God instructs the prophet to go and anoint the young and valiant shepherd David as king. Samuel fears doing so: "If Saul hears of it, he will kill me." God then instructs Samuel, "Take a heifer with you and say, 'I have come to sacrifice to the Lord'" (I Samuel 16:1-3).

Instead of assuring Samuel He will protect him, God tells Samuel to lie, thereby teaching him, and by implication all future Bible readers, one does not owe would-be murderers the truth (the prophet Jeremiah similarly lies to save his life, and the flow of the biblical text makes it clear he was not regarded as wrong for doing so; see Jeremiah 38:14-28).

As regards adultery, although it seems Abram is asking Sarai to commit adultery, in fact Sarai would not have been considered an adulterer if Pharaoh had taken her against her will. A woman who submits to a forced sexual act (whether she herself is married or whether the man forcing her is married) is not an adulteress.

During World War II, a Polish woman, Irene Gut Opdyke, hid twelve Jews in the villa of a Nazi major, Eduard Rugemer, for whom she was working as a housekeeper. When Rugemer discovered the Jews, he told Opdyke that he would have them all murdered unless she agreed to become his mistress. The arrangement between Opdyke and the married Rugemer continued for several months, until Opdyke and the twelve Jews were able to flee to the forest. In 1982, Opdyke was honored at Israel's Holocaust Memorial, Yad Vashem, where she planted a tree on the "Avenue of the Righteous." In 1995, she was also honored with a papal blessing from Pope John Paul II. Both Jews and Catholics recognized that Irene Opdyke was a saintly religious model.

We, of course, have no way of being certain about what Sarai thought of her husband's plan. However, given the openness of the Torah and the fact that Sarai does not hesitate to express her opinion on later occasions (see, for example, Genesis 21:9-10), her silence was likely agreement.

12.14 When Abram entered Egypt, the Egyptians saw how very beautiful the woman was.

12.15 Pharaoh's courtiers saw her and praised her to Pharaoh, and the woman was taken into Pharaoh's palace.

12.16 And because of her, it went well with Abram; he acquired sheep, oxen, asses, male and female slaves, she-asses, and camels.

Cynics might argue that Abram asked Sarai to sleep with Pharaoh not just to save his life but to acquire more wealth as well. However, based on Abram's future behavior, this explanation is not tenable. Abram refused wealth on two separate occasions: in the very next chapter, when he offered Lot superior land to what he took for himself (13:9-11) and again when he declined the spoils of war offered by the King of Sodom (14:21-24).

12.17 But the Lord afflicted Pharaoh and his household with mighty plagues on account of Sarai, the wife of Abram.

12.18 Pharaoh sent for Abram and said, "What is this you have done to me! Why did you not tell me that she was your wife?

12.19 Why did you say, 'She is my sister,' so that I took her as my wife? Now, here is your wife; take her and begone!"

It turns out that Abram's belief that Pharaoh would kill him if the king knew Sarai was his wife was probably right. Would Pharaoh have returned Sarai to Abram absent the plagues that struck his household? There is ample reason to believe Abram and Sarai knew the nature of the people they were going to be dealing with in Egypt. Nor did they have reason to assume God would use a miracle to save them from Pharaoh.

12.20 And Pharaoh put men in charge of him, and they sent him off with his wife and all that he possessed.

13.1 From Egypt, Abram went up into the Negeb, with his wife and all that he possessed, together with Lot.

13.2 Now Abram was very rich in cattle, silver, and gold.

13.3 And he proceeded by stages from the Negeb as far as Bethel, to the place where his tent had been formerly, between Bethel and Ai,

13.4 the sight of the altar that he had built there at first; and there Abram invoked the Lord by name.

13.5 Lot, who went with Abram, also had flocks and herds and tents,

13.6 so that the land could not support them staying together; for their possessions were so great that they could not remain together.

> Sheep and cattle require extensive grazing area, so those who had great holdings could not live close to one another.

13.7 And there was quarreling between the herdsmen of Abram's cattle and those of Lot's cattle. The Canaanites and Perizzites were then dwelling in the land.

ABRAM WAS A MAN OF PEACE, NOT A PACIFIST

13.8 Abram said to Lot, "Let there be no strife between you and me, between my herdsmen and yours, for we are kinsmen.

Pacifism, the belief ethat killing is never moral, decreases peace in the world

Abram was a man of peace who, as shown here, went to great lengths to avoid unnecessary conflict. As Sarna writes: "Abram displays great nobility of character. Although the older man, the uncle, and apparently the erstwhile guardian, he does not insist on seniority or priority of rights. Peace-loving and magnanimous, he selflessly offers his nephew first choice of grazing land and watering places."

However, it should be noted that loving peace and pursuing peace—two biblical ideals—have little in common with pacifism. Indeed, in the very next chapter, Abram goes to war to save his nephew. Pacifism, the belief that killing is never moral, decreases peace in the world—for the obvious reason that often the only way to stop the murder of innocent people is to kill the murderer(s). Peace is beautiful—but not at the expense of justice or goodness. In formulating a plan of action, the paramount question individuals and governments must ask is not "Will it lead to peace?" but "Will it lead to good or evil?" If one does not resist evil, temporary "peace" is easily obtained. But such peace is mere delusion; all it does is ensure more violence.

13.9 Is not the whole land before you? Let us separate: if you go north, I will go south; and if you go south, I will go north."

Abram, eager both to steer clear of strife—and very possibly, to separate from Lot—gave his nephew his choice of land—no questions asked.

In addition to acting generously and maturely, there may have been another reason Abram did not regret the need to separate from his nephew. Several chapters later, it becomes apparent that although Lot was morally superior to the awful citizens of Sodom, he had a far from impressive character (see Genesis 19:8 and 30-38).

13.10 Lot looked about him and saw how well watered was the whole plain of the Jordan, all of it—this was before the Lord had destroyed Sodom and Gomorrah—

> By the time the Israelite reader would have encountered this story, Sodom and Gomorrah would already have been destroyed and therefore appeared desolate. This statement is therefore inserted here to explain that the destruction of these cities had not yet taken place.

13.10 (cont.) all the way to Zoar, like the garden of the Lord, like the land of Egypt.

13.11 So Lot chose for himself the whole plain of the Jordan, and Lot journeyed eastward. Thus they parted from each other;

13.12 Abram remained in the land of Canaan while Lot settled in the cities of the Plain, pitching his tents near Sodom.

> Ironically, although Abram allowed Lot to choose the land he wanted, Abram, as we shall see in chapter 19, wound up with the better end of the deal.

13.13 Now the inhabitants of Sodom were very wicked sinners against the Lord.

> According to archeological evidence, Sodom and Gomorrah were once fertile and well-watered—another argument for the antiquity and accuracy of the Torah, since writers living later would not have known about Sodom and Gomorrah's earlier fertility.
>
> Lot chose this land because he believed it would make him wealthy, ignoring the fact—or, at the very least, not interested in learning—that its inhabitants were deeply immoral. He was like a man who had the choice in the 1930s to live anywhere he wanted in Europe and chose Berlin because he heard the Nazis were offering investors lucrative business opportunities. Abram, who had different values, let his nephew have wealthy Sodom.
>
> How many people have made moral compromises in the hope they would financially prosper?

13.14 And the Lord said to Abram, after Lot had parted from him,

Rashi comments that the whole time the "wicked one"—as Rashi refers to Lot—was with Abram, God barely spoke to Abram (just a few words in Genesis 12:7). But now, "after Lot had parted," God speaks to Abram more often and at greater length.

13.14 (cont.) "Raise your eyes and look out from where you are, to the north and south, to the east and west,

GOD GIVES THE LAND OF ISRAEL TO THE JEWS FOREVER

13.15 for I give all the land that you see to you and your offspring forever.

The land is given by God to Israel unconditionally and in perpetuity. As Radak [Rabbi David Kimchi, 1160-1235] said, "Even though Israel will go into exile, it is destined to return." Henceforth, there exists an inextricable bond between Israel and the land, a bond powerful enough to defy thousands of years of exile.

There is nothing analogous in the world to the Jews' attachment to Israel. Nor is there anything analogous to the Jews' return to Israel after almost two thousand years of exile. For many Christians as well as Jews, it is the most obvious and dramatic example of a divine promise fulfilled. It could be likewise for Muslims, given that the Jews' attachment to the land of Israel is affirmed in the Koran (5:21): "O my people, enter the Holy Land which God has prescribed for you" (this statement is clearly directed to the Jews). But, for reasons beyond the scope of this commentary, at the present time, few Muslims regard the return of the Jews to their land as positive, let alone a manifestation of divine promise.

Even those who have no belief in God, let alone in an alleged promise God made three thousand years ago, must acknowledge the historical fact that the Jewish people—and only the Jewish people—have been attached to the Land of Israel for three thousand years. They must also acknowledge that the only sovereign states to have ever existed on that land have been Jewish: the first Jewish state, 1010 (the reign of King David) to 586 BCE; the second Jewish state, 530 BCE to 70 CE (AD); and the third Jewish state, 1948 to the present. No other sovereign state ever existed in the land of Israel.

Putting aside contemporary Middle East politics, how could anyone, even an atheist, not marvel at the return of the Jews to their homeland after two thousand years? (In addition, Hebrew is the only "dead" language to have ever been revived.)

As there is nothing comparable in all of human history, how is it to be explained?

THE TORAH IS EARTH-BOUND (AS WELL AS HEAVEN-BOUND)

Both biblical and later Judaism are deeply grounded in the material world. God gave the Torah to material beings living in a material world. One major example is the Land of Israel.

From ancient times, Jews have described Judaism as consisting of three components: God, Torah, and Israel ("Israel" refers both to the Jewish people and to the Land of Israel). Many of the Torah's commandments are therefore preoccupied with ways of sanctifying the physical world, whether it be the land (such as letting the land lie fallow every seventh year—Leviticus 25:1-7) or the body (such as the laws regarding sex, eating, cleanliness, and purity).

Many religious people of every faith deem the material world corrupted and therefore identify separating from it with true spirituality and religiosity. Not the Torah. God made the material world and "saw that it was good." Of course, God is non-material. But God placed us in a material world where we are to lead good and holy lives.

13.16 I will make your offspring as the dust of the earth, so that if one can count the dust of the earth, then your offspring too can be counted.

God promised Abram that he would have many descendants, yet his wife was barren. He will later challenge God about his and Sarai's childlessness (Genesis 15:2-3). At this point, he was probably torn between bafflement and excitement by God's promise.

13.17 [Get] up, walk about the land, through its length and its breadth, for I give it to you."

If we live in a fully secular place, it is difficult to become God-centered. At the same time, the religiosity of people who have lived only in a religious world can easily become more of an unthinking habit than a thought-through conviction.

13.18 And Abram moved his tent, and came to dwell at the terebinths of Mamre, which are in Hebron; and he built an altar there to the Lord.

Just as Abram had to leave his pagan environment to connect with God, modern men and women need to leave their secular environment, at least for a brief time, to have a chance to connect with God. We are all profoundly affected by our environment. If we live in a fully secular place—most Western cities and universities, for example—it is difficult to become God-centered. At the same time, the religiosity of people who have lived only in a religious world can easily become more of an unthinking habit than a thought-through conviction.

Neither a secular ghetto nor a religious ghetto fosters personal or intellectual growth.

CHAPTER

14

14.1 Now, when King Amraphel of Shinar, King Arioch of Ellasar, King Chedorlaomer of Elam, and King Tidal of Goiim

14.2 made war on King Bera of Sodom, King Birsha of Gomorrah, King Shinab of Admah, King Shemeber of Zeboiim, and the king of Bela, which is Zoar,

14.3 all the latter joined forces at the Valley of Siddim, now the Dead Sea.

14.4 Twelve years they served Chedorlaomer, and in the thirteenth year they rebelled.

14.5 In the fourteenth year Chedorlaomer and the kings who were with him came and defeated the Rephaim at Ashteroth-karnaim, the Zuzim at Ham, the Emim at Shaveh-kiriathaim,

14.6 and the Horites in their hill country of Seir as far as El-paran, which is by the wilderness.

14.7 On their way back they came to En-mishpat, which is Kadesh, and subdued all the territory of the Amalekites, and also the Amorites who dwelt in Hazazon-tamar.

14.8 Then the king of Sodom, the king of Gomorrah, the king of Admah, the king of Zeboiim, and the king of Bela, which is Zoar, went forth and engaged them in battle in the Valley of Siddim:

14.9 King Chedorlaomer of Elam, King Tidal of Goiim, King Amraphel of Shinar, and King Arioch of Ellasar—four kings against those five.

14.10 Now the Valley of Siddim was dotted with bitumen pits; and the kings of Sodom and Gomorrah, in their flight, threw themselves into them, while the rest escaped to the hill country.

14.11 [The invaders] seized all the wealth of Sodom and Gomorrah and all their provisions, and went their way.

14.12 They also took Lot, the son of Abram's brother, and his possessions, and departed; for he had settled in Sodom.

> "Lot has greedily picked the best of the country, but now his choice turns out to have been disastrous…" (Sarna).

THE TERM "HEBREW"

14.13 A fugitive brought the news to Abram the Hebrew, who was dwelling at the terebinths of Mamre the Amorite, kinsman of Eshkol and Aner, these being Abram's allies.

The term "Hebrew" (*ivri*) is used here for the first time in the Torah. No one knows exactly what it means. But there is certainly no lack of attempts to explain it.

Some scholars link it to "Habiru," the name of a nomadic people living in biblical times.

Others link *ivri* to the Hebrew verb *avar*, "pass," or, more loosely, "wander," since Abram (from the moment God chose him) and his descendants, the Jews, have been wanderers through so much of their history. The writer Chaim Potok titled his history of the Jews *Wanderings*.

Jon Levenson, professor of Jewish Studies at the Harvard Divinity School, notes that the most that can be said with confidence is that it "seems to refer to an ethnic group" consisting of those descended from Abraham (see Genesis 39:14; Exodus 1:19, and Jonah 1:9).

Sarna cites three possibilities offered in the Midrash on Genesis: "One connects it with Eber, grandson of Noah, who is mentioned in 10:24 and 11:14; another derives from Hebrew *ever*, 'beyond,' that is, 'the one from

beyond [the river Euphrates]'; the third is homiletical and allud
religious nonconformism: 'All the world was on one side (*ever*)
other side.'"

A Man Who Loves Peace Goes to War

14.14 When Abram heard that his kinsman had been taken captive, he mustered his retainers, born into his household, numbering three hundred and eighteen, and went in pursuit as far as Dan.

Though he pursued peace, Abram knew how and when to wage war. As the Bible later put it: "God will grant his people strength, God will bless His people with peace" (Psalms 29:11). The moral of that verse is understood to be: To live in peace, a nation first has to be strong. That explains the 318 "retainers" (long-time servants and their offspring) in Abram's entourage.

One of history's enduring lessons is that weakness provokes aggression. The modern Jewish thinker Irving Yitz Greenberg commented that one of the lessons Jews learned from the Holocaust is to never again be so weak that their very weakness invites aggression.

> As the Bible later put it: "God will grant his people strength, God will bless His people with peace" (Psalms 29:11). To live in peace, a nation first has to be strong.

Good people must be stronger than bad people, and good nations must be stronger than bad nations—or they will be attacked by the bad. To put it in terms of peace, peace is maintained only as long as the decent are stronger than the indecent.

Abram pursued peace, but he was prepared for war and went to war. His behavior and the verse in Psalms are examples of biblical wisdom that run contrary to much modern thought. In today's non-Bible-based age, many people believe in pacifism and many free nations do not believe in keeping a strong military. Biblically based people do not share these naïve views about how to confront evil and preserve peace. Indeed, the Bible is an antidote to naïveté.

Peace is maintained only as long as the decent are stronger than the indecent.

14.15 At night, he and his servants deployed against them and defeated them; and he pursued them as far as Hobah, which is north of Damascus.

14.16 He brought back all the possessions; he also brought back his kinsman Lot and his possessions, and the women and the rest of the people.

Though Abram seems to have had mixed feelings towards his nephew Lot, he is, nonetheless, a devoted uncle, willing to travel a considerable distance to fight Lot's enemies in order to liberate him and his people from captivity.

14.17 When he returned from defeating Chedorlaomer and the kings with him, the king of Sodom came out to meet him in the Valley of Shaveh, which is the Valley of the King.

14.18 And King Melchizedek of Salem brought out bread and wine; he was a priest of God Most High.

King Melchizedek of Salem was a non-Hebrew, but he was a monotheist, "one of the few select non-Israelite individuals who, in the scriptural view, preserved the original monotheism of the human race in the face of otherwise universal degeneration into paganism" (Sarna). Abram, therefore, was not the only monotheist of his day, but he was the one entrusted by God with the mission of bringing the world to ethical monotheism.

14.19 He blessed him, saying, "Blessed be Abram of God Most High, Creator of heaven and earth.

14.20 And blessed be God Most High, who has delivered your foes into your hand." And [Abram] gave him a tenth of everything.

14.21 Then the king of Sodom said to Abram, "Give me the persons, and take the possessions for yourself."

14.22 But Abram said to the king of Sodom, "I swear to the Lord, God Most High, Creator of heaven and earth:

14.23 I will not take so much as a thread or a sandal strap of what is yours; you shall not say, 'It is I who made Abram rich.'

Abram refused everything he was offered, demonstrating, once again, he was not preoccupied with wealth. He also did not want to be beholden to Sodom and have its king take credit for making him wealthy.

Abram's willingness to join forces with the king of Sodom, a city which the Bible has already described as evil (Genesis 13:13), is another example of biblical moral wisdom. In waging war against evil, we cannot always choose whom we would most like as our allies. Sometimes we are morally bound to fight alongside bad people in order to defeat worse people. There are those who reject this assertion, arguing that "the lesser of two evils is still evil." But no one denies that the lesser evil is evil.

The biblical and moral argument is that between a greater and a lesser evil, good is achieved by first defeating the greater evil for the obvious reason that less evil is always better than more evil. After Hitler invaded the Soviet Union, Winston Churchill, one of the staunchest anti-Communists, joined forces with the Communist Soviet Union and its murderous dictator, Josef Stalin, in order to defeat Hitler and Nazism. As Churchill put it to the British Parliament: "If Hitler invaded hell, I would make at least a favorable reference to the Devil in the House of Commons."

> *Sometimes we are morally bound to fight alongside bad people in order to defeat worse people.*

14.24 For me, nothing but what my servants have used up; as for the share of the men who went with me—Aner, Eshkol, and Mamre—let them take their share."

CHAPTER

15

15.1 Some time later, the word of the Lord came to Abram in a vision.

God did not speak to Abram directly but through a vision or, in other instances, a dream. In the Torah, there are several levels of divine revelation. Only Moses communicated with God "face-to-face" (as to the meaning of this expression, given that God has no physical form [Deuteronomy 4:12], see the commentary to Exodus 33:11).

THE ONLY ANTIDOTE TO FEAR

15.1 (cont.) He said, "Fear not, Abram, I am a shield to you;

What is God telling Abram not to fear?

One source of fear is God. Who wouldn't fear God when in His presence? Adam did (Genesis 3:10), as will others who directly encounter God—Jacob (Genesis 28:17) and Moses (Exodus 3:6). God is aware His presence is awe-inspiring and terrifying; therefore, He reassured Abram that not only is He not a threat, but He is Abram's protector.

Rabbi Harold Kushner has pointed out the most frequent statement of God to man in the Hebrew Bible is "Do not fear."

The other, often greater, source of fear is people. We fear being hurt by others.

God is, therefore, telling Abram not to fear other people. And the greatest antidote to fear is faith in God. Even an atheist would acknowledge that anyone

> *The most frequent statement of God to man in the Hebrew Bible is "Do not fear."*
>
> who has faith in God (not merely believes there is a God) will have little reason to fear. Those who have faith in God are the only people who can believe that whatever happens to them, things will ultimately turn out for the good—if not in this world, in the afterlife.

15.1 (cont.) Your reward shall be very great."

Reward for what? According to Sarna, it is for "Abram's refusal to have any part in the spoils of war mentioned in 14:22ff. The material reward, so disdainfully spurned, is to be vastly exceeded by a recompense of a different kind."

Also likely is that God is reassuring Abram His promises will in fact materialize. For example, despite Sarai's advanced age, God's promise of a nation of descendants is still in place.

15.2 But Abram said, "O Lord God, what can You give me, seeing that I shall die childless, and the one in charge of my household is Dammesek Eliezer!"

Abram's profound fear of dying childless is made clear.

15.3 Abram said further, "Since You have granted me no offspring, my steward will be my heir."

Unlike Noah, who never questioned God, Abram did. The first Hebrew spoken to by God exhibited a trait that is characteristically, almost uniquely, Jewish: he talked back to God. It is little wonder that Abram's grandson is later named "Israel," a Hebrew word meaning "wrestle/struggle with God" (Genesis 32:29).

15.4 The word of the Lord came to him in reply, "That one shall not be your heir; none but your very own issue shall be your heir."

15.5 He took him outside and said, "Look toward heaven and count the stars, if you are able to count them." And He added, "So shall your offspring be."

ESSAY: THE IMPORTANCE OF BOTH FAITH

15.6 And because he put his trust in the Lord, He reckoned it to his merit.

God's response to Abram's questioning Him apparently suffices.

The Torah credits Abram for *trusting in* God, not for believing that God exists. The Torah takes God's existence as a given. The Bible views atheism as simply foolish—see, for example, Psalm 92:5-6: "How great are your works, Lord, how profound your thoughts! Senseless people do not know, fools do not understand."

In the modern world, people have generally defined "faith" as belief in God's existence. But in the Torah's view, this type of faith is meaningless. It is like believing in the existence of one's neighbor: the issue is not whether the neighbor exists but whether the neighbor can be trusted. So, too, with God. Trust in, not belief in, is the issue (as in the expression, "I believe in you"). That is what Abram exhibited.

This verse has often been cited by Christians as evidence the Hebrew Bible teaches that faith alone ("he put his trust in the Lord"), not good works, is required for salvation. The Christian emphasis on faith has led innumerable Christians to devote their lives to doing good works—think, for example, of all the hospitals and charities Christians have established or of all the Christians who have devoted their lives to serving the poor in their own countries and in the world's poorest countries.

However, this verse teaches God considers faithfulness meritorious, not that faith is the only thing that God considers meritorious or the only thing God requires of men. Moreover, even while acknowledging that in Christian theology faith is the source of salvation, the New Testament repeatedly declares the necessity of good works in addition to, and as a manifestation of, faith.

For example, James declares: "What good is it, my brothers and sisters, if you say you have faith but do not have works? Can faith save you? If a brother or sister is naked and lacks daily food, and one of you says to them, 'Go in peace; keep warm and eat your fill,' and yet you do not supply their bodily needs, what is the good of that? So faith by itself, if it has not works, is dead" (James 2:14-17).

Elsewhere the New Testament states:

"[God] will render to every man according to his deeds. He will give eternal life to those who keep on doing good...." (Romans 2:6-7).

"I will give unto every one of you according to your works." (Revelation 2:23)

See also 2 Corinthians 5:10; Matthew 5:16, 12:36-37; John 14:12; and Revelation 20:13, 22:12.

As regards the Hebrew Bible, God demands good works more than anything else. The prophet Micah says, "He [God] has told you, O man, what is good and what the Lord requires of you: Only to do justice, and to love goodness, and to walk humbly with your God" (Micah 6:8).

This is an affirmation of both faith and works. While faith without works is dead, works without faith also ultimately die. Virtually every mass genocide in the twentieth century was committed by secular, anti-religious regimes. This does not mean there are no good atheists or bad religious people. There are good people who do not believe in God and bad people who do. But individuals and societies that believe in the morally demanding God of the Bible—at the very least, the Ten Commandments—will generally behave better and have clearer moral judgments. Perhaps the most morally confused institution in the West at this time is also the least religious one—the university.[1]

> *While faith without works is dead, works without faith also ultimately die.*

The most important way to exhibit trust in God is to live by God's will. And that means, first and foremost, acting morally toward fellow human beings.

15.7 Then He said to him, "I am the Lord who brought you out from Ur of the Chaldeans to assign this land to you as a possession."

This is almost precisely the same language with which God begins the Ten Commandments: "I am the Lord your God who brought you out of the land of

Egypt...." (Exodus 20:2). It is one of the myriad hints at a unity of authorship of the Torah.

15.8 And he said, "O Lord God, how shall I know that I am to possess it?"

Abram's question is an expression of curiosity, not skepticism. He is simply asking how God plans to bring about His promise.

15.9 He answered, "Bring Me a three-year-old heifer, a three-year-old she-goat, a three-year-old ram, a turtledove, and a young bird."

To the modern reader, God's answer to Abram appears to be a complete non-sequitur. But in the ancient world, these kinds of signs were often part of important legal pacts. That is obviously how Abram understood it. His immediate and unquestioning obedience strongly implies he was familiar with what was about to happen.

15.10 He brought Him all these and cut them in two, placing each half opposite the other; but he did not cut up the bird.

15.11 Birds of prey came down upon the carcasses, and Abram drove them away.

15.12 As the sun was about to set, a deep sleep fell upon Abram, and a great dark dread descended upon him.

Despite the fact that God had just told him not to fear His presence, Abram experiences dread. However, he did not do so while awake but while in a "deep sleep." The Hebrew word for "deep sleep" (*tardema*) is the same word used to describe the deep sleep of Adam when the woman was made from his side.

15.13 And He said to Abram, "Know well that your offspring shall be strangers in a land not theirs,

That land is, of course, Egypt.

A Torah Inconsistency?

they shall be enslaved and oppressed four hundred years;

ιose who look for inconsistencies in the Torah point to this number as an example. Here the Israelites' time in Egypt is given as four hundred years, but Exodus records the time as 430 years (Exodus 12:40-41). But as the British scholar Kenneth Kitchen, professor of Egyptology at the University of Liverpool, wrote, "the 400 years is a round figure in prospect, while the 430 years is more precise in retrospect."[2]

Kitchen's point simply makes sense. Moreover, wouldn't any competent human author or editor have seen such an apparently glaring discrepancy and presumably made the two time periods the same? The very fact that the two numbers are left unedited argues for their compatibility and for the authenticity of the text: God was giving Abram a general idea of the time the Israelites would serve in Egypt; and after it took place, the Torah provided the precise number of years.

15.14 but I will execute judgment on the nation they shall serve, and in the end they shall go free with great wealth.

Why does God deem it necessary to tell Abram what will happen to his descendants in Egypt? Of what use is this knowledge to Abram? I can only conclude this is told for the benefit of the Torah reader—God knows what will happen to the Israelites and, most important, plays a role in its happening. From a Torah perspective, whether God knows everything men will do is an open question. God knows everything men do—but not necessarily what they *will* do because human beings have free will. That is why, for example, the Torah says that after seeing how bad men turned out, "God regretted He had made man on earth" (Genesis 6:6). If God knew how men would turn out, why would He regret how they turned out? He would have known. And why would He have made man to begin with?

I take no position on this question. I only wish to emphasize that a possible reason God told Abram his descendants would be enslaved is that, for some reason, this was God's plan.

THE TORAH IMPLIES AN AFTERLIFE

15.15 As for you, You shall go to your fathers

Often, in describing death, the Torah and the rest of the Hebrew Bible use the phrase "gathered to one's kin." Here, the Torah describes Abram's eventual death as Abram going "to your fathers." For reasons I will explain at length, the Torah never directly declares there is an afterlife. But throughout the Torah, an afterlife is clearly implied. Sarna notes, "In whatever form, the phrase certainly originates from the belief in an afterlife in which one is reunited with one's ancestors irrespective of where they are buried."

ONLY ABRAHAM DIES IN PEACE

15.15 (cont.) in peace; You shall be buried at a ripe old age.

God promises Abram he will die in peace. In the Torah, only Abraham and Isaac (Genesis 35:29) are described as dying "in peace" and at a "ripe old age." To die in peace is a blessing few people experience. When the renowned short story writer and poet Dorothy Parker (1893-1967) expressed her disappointment to movie mogul Samuel Goldwyn that he hadn't made a movie out of any of her stories, Goldwyn told her: "People want happy endings. All your stories have unhappy endings." Parker responded: "Mr. Goldwyn, since the world was created, billions and billions of people have lived, and not one has had a happy ending."

15.16 And they shall return here in the fourth generation,

According to the biblical scholar and archaeologist William F. Albright (1891-1971), editor of the *Bulletin of the American Schools of Oriental Research* (1931 to 1968), the Hebrew word for "generation" (*dor*) originally meant "lifetime," not "generation." "The early Hebrews," he explained, "dated long periods by lifetimes, not by generations."[3] Accordingly, this verse refers to a period of four lifetimes—about four hundred years (the patriarchs all lived more than one hundred years)—not four generations.

THE MORAL BASIS FOR THE EXPULSION OF THE CANAANITES

15.16 (cont.) for the iniquity of the Amorites is not yet complete."

The Amorites were one of the nations living in Canaan in Abram's time. God informed Abram that He would not dispossess the Amorites until these people had become so evil that they deserved exile (see Leviticus 18:24-30). Only then, four lifespans later, would Abram's descendants be able to return to Canaan.

Even though God assigned the Land of Israel to the People of Israel, He would permit them to enter the land only if and when its previous inhabitants had been sufficiently immoral as to warrant their expulsion. That God felt it necessary to explain the morality of the Israelite conquering of Canaan is one more illustration of the centrality of morality to the Torah.

15.17 When the sun set and it was very dark, there appeared a smoking oven, and a flaming torch which passed between those pieces.

15.18 On that day the Lord made a covenant with Abram,

This covenant, known as *brit bein habetarim*, "the Covenant of the Pieces," (referring to the animals severed in two at God's command in verses 9-10) is the second covenant God made with humanity (the first was the covenant with Noah—Genesis 9:8-17). It is also the first covenant God made with the Israelites who, of course, become the Jews. Unlike later covenants, these first two covenants are unconditional on God's part: they demand nothing of human beings.

The notion of a covenant between God and man was revolutionary because all other cultures and religions believed that the gods acted capriciously and that the world was therefore completely erratic and unpredictable. When God covenanted with Noah and Abram, He pledged to be dependable and trustworthy, thereby creating for the first time immutable spiritual and moral laws.

15.18 (cont.) saying, "To your offspring I assign this land, from the river of Egypt to the great river, the river Euphrates:

15.19 the Kenites, the Kenizzites, the Kadmonites,

15.20 the Hittites, the Perizzites, the Rephaim,

15.21 the Amorites, the Canaanites, the Girgashites, and the Jebusites."

CHAPTER
16

16.1 Sarai, Abram's wife, had borne him no children.

The Torah repeats that Sarai has not been able to conceive a child to add perspective to the drama that is to follow.

In the ancient world—and in much of the world to this day—it was common for men to divorce their wives when the wife did not bear children. Given how accepted and common that practice was, it is a testament to Abram's commitment to Sarai and their marriage that he did not divorce her.

16.1 (cont.) She had an Egyptian maidservant whose name was Hagar.

16.2 And Sarai said to Abram, "Look, the Lord has kept me from bearing. Consort with my maid;

While the Torah mentions Hagar's name, Sarai does not. To Sarai, Hagar is merely "my maid." Her resentment and belittling of Hagar has begun.

SARAI'S WELL-INTENTIONED, BUT BAD, IDEA

16.2 (cont.) perhaps I shall have a son through her." And Abram heeded Sarai's request.

According to the Laws of Hammurabi and other ancient Near Eastern legal documents, it was common for an infertile wife to provide her husband with a concubine in order to bear children for the couple. Those children were considered the wife's children as much as biological children would be.

The concubine was entirely Sarai's idea. We cannot be certain whether Abram was enthusiastic about it; but based on his lack of reaction—he said nothing—one suspects he was not. All we are told is, "And Abram heeded Sarai's request."

16.3 So Sarai, Abram's wife, took her maid, Hagar the Egyptian—after Abram had dwelt in the land of Canaan ten years—

As noted, Sarai's suggestion is understandable given that ten years went by without the fulfillment of God's promise.

16.3 (cont.) and gave her to her husband Abram as concubine.

The Hebrew word translated here as "concubine" is actually the Hebrew word for "wife" (*isha*). Why this translation uses the word "concubine" is difficult to explain. Nearly all other translations—including the previous JPS translation (1917), the King James Version, and the NIV—translate the word as "wife." This, of course, renders the relationship among the three—Sarai, Abram, and Hagar—far more emotionally complicated than if Hagar were only a concubine.

16.4 He cohabited with Hagar and she conceived; and when she saw that she had conceived, her mistress was lowered in her esteem.

Hagar suddenly felt superior to Sarai because in the ancient world—and, sadly, much of the world through the modern period—a wife's worth declined if she could not give birth. Ancient Near East documents reveal that even a slave woman who gave birth to her master's child felt superior to a mistress who had not given birth.

16.5 And Sarai said to Abram, "The wrong done to me is your fault! I myself put my maid in your bosom; now that she sees that she is pregnant, I am lowered in her esteem. The Lord decide between you and me!"

Amazingly, Sarai became angry at her husband, even though all he had done was heed her wish. Apparently, she regretted her suggestion, and she was now angry at Abram for acting on it.

16.6 Abram said to Sarai, "Your maid is in your hands. Deal with her as you think right."

THE TORAH DOES NOT HIDE THE FLAWS OF ITS HEROES

16.6 (cont.) Then Sarai treated her harshly,

Abram's response was not impressive. But it was certainly understandable. Most men will do almost anything to end a wife's anger and try to make her happy. That's where we get the motto "Happy wife, happy life." And, of course, the converse is equally true: "Unhappy wife, unhappy life." Abram allowed his wife to take control of the situation, hoping that would end her anger.

The Torah is ethic-centric, not ethnic-centric.

A more precise translation than "treated her harshly" is "tormented her." The Torah uses the same word to describe the Egyptians' mistreatment of the Israelites (Genesis 15:13 and Exodus 1:12). In other words, while, of course, not morally comparable to slavery, the Torah uses the same word to describe an Israelite mistreating an Egyptian as it does to describe the Egyptian mistreatment of the Israelites. *The Torah is ethic-centric, not ethnic-centric.*

The Torah doesn't shy away from describing biblical heroes, including the patriarchs and matriarchs, as flawed people. The same holds true for the traditional Jewish commentators. Two major medieval Jewish commentators, Ramban (Nachmanides—Moses ben Nachman, 1194-1270) and Radak (David Kimchi, 1160-1235), wrote that Sarai sinned in dealing cruelly with her Egyptian maid and that Abram sinned in allowing her to do so.

The female Torah scholar Nehama Leibowitz (1905-1997) argued that while it was noble of Sarai to offer her handmaid to her husband, she should have thought in advance about how she would react to seeing another woman carrying his child. Leibowitz wisely cautioned that before people undertake a mission that requires moral and spiritual discipline, they should first make sure they possess moral and spiritual discipline. Otherwise, they are likely to descend from the "pinnacle of altruism" to selfishness, as is evidenced by Sarai's torment of Hagar.

It is not enough to have good intentions.

16.6 (cont.) and she ran away from her.

Sarai treated Hagar so harshly that Hagar's only recourse was to flee to the desert.

GOD CARES ABOUT EVERYONE—NON-JEW AS WELL AS JEW

16.7 An angel of the Lord found her by a spring of water in the wilderness, the spring on the road to Shur,

The Hebrew word translated here as "angel" (*malach*) refers to a messenger of God. (Interestingly, the Greek word "angel" also means "messenger.")

As in the earlier story of Noah—as well as in later stories—the Torah teaches that God cares about non-Jews just as he cares about Jews. Later in the Hebrew Bible, the prophet Amos proclaimed: "To Me, O Israelites, you are just like the Ethiopians, declares the Lord. True, I brought Israel up from the Land of Egypt, but also the Philistines from Caphtor and the Arameans from Kir" (Amos 9:7). And the Prophet Isaiah declared: "for the Lord of Hosts will bless them, saying, 'Blessed be My People Egypt, My handiwork Assyria, and My very own Israel '" (Isaiah 19:25).

It is very rare, perhaps unique, among the texts of the world's religions that other religious and national groups are depicted as equal in God's (or the gods') eyes.

16.8 and said, "Hagar, slave of Sarai, where have you come from, and where are you going?" And she said, "I am running away from my mistress Sarai."

16.9 And the angel of the Lord said to her, "Go back to your mistress, and submit to her harsh treatment."

HAGAR, AN EGYPTIAN, RECEIVES A UNIQUE GIFT FROM GOD

16.10 And the angel of the Lord said to her, "I will greatly increase your offspring, And they shall be too many to count."

Hamilton makes an important point: "There are many instances in the patriarchal stories where the man is promised a child(ren)/descendants…but Hagar is the only woman in Genesis who is honored with such a revelation. This sets her apart from the matriarchs of Israel." Such is the moral greatness of the Torah and the God of the Torah that a non-Israelite woman received a divine revelation no Israelite woman received.

16.11 The angel of the Lord said to her further, "Behold, you are with child and shall bear a son; You shall call him Ishmael, for the Lord has paid heed to your suffering.

The name "Ishmael"—from the Hebrew words *shma* (hear) and *el* (God)—means "God hears."

16.12 He shall be a wild ass of a man; His hand against everyone, And everyone's hand against him; He shall dwell alongside of all his kinsmen."

In spite of God's troubling characterization of Ishmael, Hagar was probably pleased to learn that she, a lowly concubine, would give birth to a strong, virile man who would fight others and emerge victorious enough to father many descendants.

16.13 And she called the Lord who spoke to her, "You Are El-roi," by which she meant, "Have I not gone on seeing after He saw me!"

The Hebrew *El-Roi* is generally translated as "God sees me." That is in fact what the Hebrew says.

Hamilton again points out the uniqueness of Hagar in the Torah: "Hagar actually confers on the deity a name. No other character in the Old Testament, male or female, does that. It is not unusual for mortals to give names to family members, to animals, to sacred sites, but never to one's God, with the exception of Hagar."

16.14 Therefore the well was called Beer-lahai-roi; it is between Kadesh and Bered.

16.15 Hagar bore a son to Abram, and Abram gave the son that Hagar bore him the name Ishmael.

16.16 Abram was eighty-six years old when Hagar bore Ishmael to Abram.

CHAPTER
17

17.1 When Abram was ninety-nine years old, the Lord appeared to Abram and said to him, "I am El Shaddai.

> This is the one time in Chapter 17 God is referred to as "the Lord" (YHVH). It makes clear that the name "El Shaddai"—a name for God whose definition no one knows—is the same God as YHVH.
>
> In the modern period, some believe this name for God—Shaddai—appears to be related to the Hebrew word *shaddayim* (breasts), and may refer to a feminine aspect of God. Given that half of the human race is female, it would be surprising if God had no feminine aspect. However, the notion that Shaddai comes from *shaddayim* is not borne out in the scholarly literature. In the end-note, six possible explanations for this name of God are listed. The one I find most persuasive is a midrash that divides the word Shaddai into *sheh-dai*, meaning "it is enough/sufficient." That is, "God (El) is the Sufficient One."[1]

17.1 (cont.) Walk in My ways and be blameless.

> The term "blameless" (*tamim*) is the same term the Torah used to describe Noah (Genesis 6:9). Its most accurate translation is "without blemish" (Leviticus 1:3 and 1:10).

17.2 I will establish My covenant between Me and you, and I will make you exceedingly numerous."

17.3 Abram threw himself on his face; and God spoke to him further,

17.4 "As for Me, this is My covenant with you: You shall be the father of a multitude of nations.

Every few years, God returns to Abram and makes the same promise. God, it seems, delays the fulfillment of His promise as a test of Abram's faith, specifically as part of what will constitute the final and greatest test of Abram's faith. By making him wait so long for a son with Sarai, it will be all the more difficult for Abram (Abraham, as he will then be known) to offer up this long-awaited child on an altar to God (chapter 22).

What "multitude of nations" will Abram be the father of? At a minimum, Abram will be the father of the Israelite nation through Isaac, nations that emanate from Ishmael, and nations descending from his second wife, Keturah (Genesis 25:1-4).

17.5 And you shall no longer be called Abram, but your name shall be Abraham, for I make you the father of a multitude of nations.

In the ancient world, a change of name signified an event of great import. It still does. A Roman Catholic cardinal, for example, takes a new name when elected pope. Similarly, when a non-Jew becomes a Jew, he or she receives a new name.

In this verse, when nothing seems to be working out according to the covenantal promise, God changes Abram's name to serve as a sign that something major is about to happen. His new name in Hebrew is Avraham. The "ham" may be related to the Hebrew word for "many" (*hamon*). His new name would then be "Father (*av*) of many."

17.6 I will make you exceedingly fertile, and make nations of you; and kings shall come forth from you.

THE COVENANT: JEWS ARE TO KEEP GOD ALIVE IN THE WORLD AND GOD IS TO KEEP THE JEWS ALIVE

17.7 I will maintain My covenant between Me and you, and your offspring to come,

The covenant between God and the people who ultimately came to be known as Jews stipulates that it is God's task to keep the Jews alive in the world; and it is the Jews' task to keep knowledge of God alive in the world witnesses, declares the Lord" (Isaiah 43:10).

It must be admitted that neither party has done a particularly effective job. God has kept the Jews alive—but just barely, given how many Jews have been slaughtered throughout their history.[2] And for the last two thousand years, the Jews have not done a particularly good job at spreading awareness of God and the Torah's values.

Some readers will be surprised, perhaps scandalized, when reading the above assessment of God. But it should be neither surprising nor scandalizing. A Jew is more than allowed to express his feelings toward God—from love to anger to adulation and disappointment. As Dr. Michael Milgraum, an Orthodox Jewish psychologist, wrote:

> "Some people think the 'if you don't have anything nice to say' maxim also applies to their relationship with God. They believe that it is inappropriate to say to God that they are disappointed or angry with Him.... As a therapist, I know that anyone in a love relationship will experience anger, at least now and then. Why should it be any different in our relationship with God? In addition, anger is a common response to suffering. After all we Jews have suffered, especially during the twentieth century, it is not surprising that many Jews are angry.... God wants us to offer Him our wounded souls with all of their 'ugly' realities, including our anger. That is a real relationship, and it is the only path to real healing, spiritual or otherwise."[3]

The covenant between God and the Jews stipulates that it is God's task to keep the Jews alive in the world; and it is the Jews' task to keep knowledge of God alive in the world.

Judaism's acceptance of arguing with God and allowing intellectual and emotional honesty alongside deep faith has enabled this Jew to be a believing Jew.

Regarding the Jews' side of the covenant, to be fair, it is quite difficult to spread ideas when one is preoccupied with surviving, as has been the case for much of the Jews' history. Nevertheless, even in the contemporary era, in places where Jews have not been preoccupied with survival—specifically, the United States and some other Western countries—with few exceptions, Jews have not been preoccupied with spreading awareness of God and Torah.

The Jews who talk to the world have overwhelmingly been secular, and religious Jews (with the exception of some individuals and the Jewish group, Chabad) have overwhelmingly avoided talking to the world (other than through necessary contact such as in business relations).

> *The Jews' survival and the Jews' mission are inextricably linked. Only when Jews bring the world to God and His moral code will the world become decent. And only in a decent world will Jew-hatred and the killing of Jews (and others) end.*

Regarding Chabad, Joseph Telushkin cited the Chabad leader Menachem Schneerson ("the Rebbe"):

"Making God and his moral demands of human beings known to non-Jews was regarded by the Rebbe as equal in significance to promoting knowledge and practice of the commandments among Jews, a universalist position that one does not find, to say the least, echoed widely in traditional Jewish circles" (this position is cited in Menachem M. Schneerson, *The Letter and the Spirit*, 2:21).

The fact is, however, the Jews' survival and the Jews' mission are inextricably linked. Only when Jews bring the world to God and His moral code—beginning with the Ten Commandments and/or the Seven Noahide Laws—will the world become decent. And only in a decent world will Jew-hatred and the killing of Jews (and others) end.

17.1 (cont.) as an everlasting covenant throughout the ages, to be God to you and to your offspring to come.

This covenant is made visible in the text of the Jewish credo, the *Shma* ("Hear, O Israel! The Lord is our God, the Lord is one"—Deuteronomy 6:4). In the Torah scroll, it is written with the final letters of the first and last words enlarged. These two letters (*ayin* and *dalet*) spell out the Hebrew word *ayd*, "witness."

The promise of an "everlasting covenant throughout the a[g]
from our modern-day vantage point, has been quite accurate. [
only intact people/culture/language/religion from the ancient world. There
remain a number of ancient peoples, but none speak the same language and
practice the same religion as they did in ancient times. As Abba Eban, Israel's
Foreign Minister from 1966 to 1974, expressed it: "Israel is the only nation
whose citizens live on the same land, speak the same language and practice the
same religion as their ancestors did 3,000 years ago."

17.8 I assign the land you sojourn in to you and your offspring to come, all the land of Canaan, as an everlasting holding. I will be their God."

Although in this verse God pledges to be the God of Abraham's descendants,
He is also the God of the entire world. The God of the Torah has always been
universal. That is why the Torah begins with the creation of the world, not with
the creation of the Jews. In addition, God revealed himself to Adam and to
Noah before there were any Jews; God promised Abraham to bless all the
nations of the world through him; and God appeared in the form of an angel
to an Egyptian slave woman in the desert (Genesis 16:7-13). The Jews introduced the God of all the world, not the God of the Jews alone, to the world.
Therefore, no one need become a Jew to accept the God, wisdom, or values of
the Torah.

There are those who mock Jews and
Christians who believe God promised
the Land of Israel to the Jewish people.
But, as noted, even an atheist would

*No one need become a Jew
to accept the God, wisdom,
or values of the Torah.*

have to acknowledge no other people ever established a state there—as
Jews have three times—or have claimed it as their own dating back three
thousand years.

17.9 God further said to Abraham, "As for you, you and your offspring to come throughout the ages shall keep My covenant.

ESSAY: THE CASE FOR—AND MEANING OF—
JEWISH CIRCUMCISION

17.10 Such shall be the covenant between Me and you and your offspring to follow which you shall keep: every male among you shall be circumcised.

Many ancient cultures had rites of circumcision. What rendered the Torah's rite completely different was it did not constitute a rite of passage—the nature of circumcision in all other cultures—but a physical expression of a covenant between God and His people.

The commandment of circumcision applies only to males. It thereby implicitly bans female circumcision, a horror still practiced in parts of the world, known medically as "clitoridectomy" but more popularly referred to as "female genital mutilation."

In modern times, the Torah and Judaism have been accused of sexism for not legislating a comparable physical ritual for baby girls. But what could that physical ritual possibly be? What part of the female body could be permanently removed or marked with as negligible a consequence as the removal of a male baby's foreskin?

Moreover, let us say there was a physical ritual that left a comparably permanent mark on a female Jew's body—and no physically permanent ritual for the baby boy. Wouldn't critics object that the Torah and Judaism were sexist for marking only the female?

There is simply no way to have an equivalent ritual permanently marking a girl's body. Meanwhile, the Jews have survived for almost four thousand years thanks in part to male circumcision.

But sexism is not the only contemporary objection to circumcision. Jews and non-Jews who oppose Jewish circumcision offer four other arguments:

1. Circumcision, whether for religious or medical reasons, is unnecessary.

2. Circumcision is a form of mutilation.
3. Circumcision inflicts serious pain on the eight-day-old for no legitimate reason.
4. Men who are circumcised experience less sexual pleasure than uncircumcised men.

Here, then, are some responses:

1. Circumcision is both medically beneficial and Jewishly necessary, whether performed by a *mohel* (Jewish ritual circumciser) or a physician.

    Regarding the medical benefits:

    Pediatrics, the flagship journal of the American Academy of Pediatrics, published a study of circumcision that concluded: "…now there is much stronger evidence about protective medical benefits associated with circumcision…."[4]

    In 2014, Dr. Jonathan Mermin of the United States Centers for Disease Control and Prevention wrote, "The scientific evidence is clear that the benefits [of male circumcision] outweigh the risks."

    And Dr. Aaron Tobian, a Johns Hopkins University researcher, added, "The benefits of male circumcision have become more and more clear over the last 10 years."

    Among the medical benefits are a lower risk of urinary tract infections, a reduced risk of some sexually transmitted diseases in men, protection against penile cancer, and a reduced risk of cervical cancer in female partners.

Regarding sexually transmitted diseases, in 2013, the United States National Institutes of Health published the following:

"Three randomized trials in Africa demonstrated that adult male circumcision decreases human immunodeficiency virus (HIV) acquisition in men by 51% to 60%....

"Two trials demonstrated that male circumcision reduces the risk of acquiring genital herpes by 28% to 34%, and the risk of developing genital ulceration by 47%....

"Using mathematical models and cost-effectiveness analyses, the Joint United Nations Programme on HIV/AIDS (UNAIDS) and the World Health Organization adopted a policy advocating male circumcision in countries and regions with heterosexual HIV epidemics...."

Many African countries demand that their male citizens get circumcised. Other than sexual abstention, circumcision is the best way to reduce the risk of contracting AIDS.

However, the case for Jewish circumcision in no way rests on its having medical benefits. Even if there were no medical benefits, the case for a Jew continuing the oldest practice of the Jewish religion, practiced for nearly four thousand years, sometimes under threat of arrest and even death, is profound. (That case is made below.)

2. As for "mutilation," that is a misuse of the term. The term properly describes what is done in some Muslim

societies to the genitalia of young girls: "female genital mutilation." Its destructive purpose is to deprive girls and women of the ability to enjoy sexual intercourse. And its effects are prolonged excruciating pain and permanent physical disfigurement. To compare that to the removal of the foreskin trivializes the horror of female genital mutilation.

3. With regard to pain, yes, the baby experiences pain. But what most matters is how much pain, whether there is any lasting trauma, and whether the pain can be eliminated.

    The amount of pain is essentially impossible to judge for a number of reasons. One is that we cannot ask the baby. Another is some babies barely whimper during the *brit milah* ("covenant of circumcision"); indeed, many babies cry more loudly and longer when they have gas or are hungry—and neither condition is regarded as abnormally painful, let alone traumatic.

    Nevertheless, the request of any parent for the use of a numbing medication such as lidocaine prior to the procedure should be honored. Certainly, if it enables the parent(s) to welcome performance of the ritual, it should be done. After all, adult males who undergo circumcision when they convert to Judaism use a local anesthetic.

4. Regarding sexual pleasure, *The New York Times* reported a study in the *Journal of Urology:*[5]

    "Circumcision, many contend, reduces the sensitivity of the penis. But a controlled experiment has found no evidence for the belief....Canadian researchers studied 62 generally healthy men ages 18 to 37, 30 of whom had been circumcised as infants, and 32 who remained uncircumcised. The researchers controlled for age, education, occupation and religious affiliation, and concluded that sexual functioning did not differ between the groups...."

"Neonatal circumcision doesn't make the penis less sensitive," said a co-author of the study, Caroline F. Pukall, a professor of psychology at Queen's University in Ontario. "We can conclude that there are no significant differences in sensitivity between the circumcised and uncircumcised groups."

So, too, the previously cited National Institutes of Health study cited the conclusions of another study: "The male circumcision trials evaluated sexual satisfaction in adult men and their female partners before and after the procedure and compared men randomized to male circumcision with uncircumcised controls. There were no significant differences in male sexual satisfaction or dysfunction among trial participants...."[6]

All these alleged objections pale in comparison to the benefits of giving one's son a "bris"—or *brit milah*, "covenant of circumcision," to give it its full name.

I found the circumcisions of my two sons and two grandsons more emotionally and spiritually moving than any other religious ritual in my life. I cried at the *brit* of both my sons. Here I was, in as dramatic a way as one could imagine, bringing my sons and grandsons into the Jewish people and into the Jewish covenant with God. I thought about how my father had done this with me, how his father had done this with him—going all the way back to Abraham, almost four thousand years ago. I thought about all the Jews who, at the risk of their lives, brought their sons into the covenant during the many antisemitic periods in Jewish history.

To assess whether one wants one's son to undergo a *brit milah*, one has to recognize one of the most important laws of life: everything has a price. There is a price paid for having a *brit*, and there is a price paid for not having one.

The price for having one is momentary pain in an infant (and even that is avoidable). The idea that a man pays some lasting price for not having his foreskin is refuted by the experience of virtually every circumcised male who has ever lived.

As opposed to the small and short-lived price paid for having a *brit*, there is an enormous price paid for a Jew not having a *brit*. The advantages profoundly outweigh the momentary pain. The *brit* uniquely strengthens a Jew's religious identification, and the ceremony instills in the family and in the community present at the ceremony a profound identification with the nearly four millennia of the Jews' unparalleled history.

17.11 You shall circumcise the flesh of your foreskin,

Abraham was probably distressed to learn that, at the age of ninety-nine, he would have to circumcise himself in order to enter into God's covenant. Nonetheless, the ancient rabbis drew a valuable lesson from this: "If a man wishes to convert to Judaism, but says, 'I am too old to convert,' let him learn from Abraham who, when he was ninety-nine years old, entered God's covenant."[7]

17.11 (cont.) and that shall be the sign of the covenant between Me and you.

Just as the physical Land of Israel is a sign of the covenant between God and the Jews, so is the physical act of circumcision. "The ineradicable nature of circumcision symbolized the enduring, irrevocable nature of the covenant" (Sarna).

As noted previously, the Torah is as concerned with the physical as it is with the spiritual. Since we live in a physical world, the physical can and does have a profound impact on the spiritual.

17.12 And throughout the generations, every male among you shall be circumcised at the age of eight days.

An infant boy is circumcised at an age when he is too young to remember the experience, as opposed to other cultures and religions (most famously, Islam), in which circumcision is performed at or in the years preceding puberty. In Judaism, circumcision is not a rite of manhood for the individual who is circumcised. It is a permanent reminder to the Jewish male (and his wife) that he and she are members of a covenantal people. And it is a communal event for everyone who celebrates the entrance of a male Jewish infant into the covenant.

By being performed on the eighth day, circumcision comes to symbolize man's part in creation. God created for six days and rested on the seventh; on the eighth day, we humans take over.

17.12 (cont.)As for the homeborn slave and the one bought from an outsider who is not of your offspring,

17.13 they must be circumcised, homeborn and purchased alike. Thus shall My covenant be marked in your flesh as an everlasting pact.

Even the non-Jew who became a slave or indentured servant was to be circumcised. While this did not render him fully a Jew, it elevated his status—he, too, was to be regarded as a participant in the covenant. For example, he was given the Sabbath day for rest—a law that did not apply to any other slave until modern times—and participated in sharing the Passover sacrifice.

17.14 And if any male who is uncircumcised fails to circumcise the flesh of his foreskin, that person shall be cut off from his kin; he has broken My covenant."

The failure to perform circumcision on a Jewish boy has always been regarded by Jews as a statement that one does not wish to be part of the covenant. That is why innumerable adult Jewish men who were not circumcised—for example, tens of thousands of adult Jews from the Soviet Union, where those practicing ritual circumcision were persecuted—later chose to have themselves circumcised.

Circumcision is one of only two positive commandments for which the Torah ordains the punishment of *karet*, being "cut off" from one's kin. The other is failure to bring the Passover sacrifice (Numbers 9:13), which is today symbolically reenacted by participating in the Passover Seder. It is perhaps not coincidental that circumcision and participation in a Seder remain the two most widely observed Jewish rituals.

We are not sure what the punishment of *karet*, "cut off," precisely entailed. We know it is not the death penalty. But the Torah never explains it. Is it excommunication? Is it being cut off from the afterlife? Is it God cutting off years from the person's life? All of these have been suggested. My belief is the Torah intends it to be a statement as much as, or even more than, a punishment. That perfectly applies here: A Jew who chooses not to circumcise his or her son has, deliberately or not, "cut off" that child from the Jewish people.

17.15 And God said to Abraham, "As for your wife Sarai, you shall not call her Sarai, but her name shall be Sarah.

As Sarai, along with Abraham, played a critical role in the process of creating the Jewish people, she, too, merited a change of name. Her importance was so great, she was the only woman in the Torah to have her name changed.

17.16 I will bless her; indeed, I will give you a son by her. I will bless her so that she shall give rise to nations; rulers of peoples shall issue from her."

Now, finally, God names Sarah as the mother of the Israelite people. Had God done this earlier, would Sarah have come up with the idea of Abraham having a child through Hagar? Perhaps not.

17.17 Abraham threw himself on his face and laughed,

> Abraham was so intimate with God that he was able to laugh in response to God's pronouncement. When God is real to us, we should be able to laugh with Him, get angry at Him (see, for example, Psalm 44:12, "You hand us over like sheep to be devoured"), and challenge Him (Genesis 18:25: "Shall not the judge of all the earth deal justly?").
>
> Sarah, too, will laugh when she hears the news that they are to have a child together (Genesis 18:12).

WHAT IS A MIRACLE?

17.17 (cont.) as he said to himself, "Can a child be born to a man a hundred years old, or can Sarah bear a child at ninety?"

> Under normal circumstances, Abraham and Sarah would be far too old to have a child. The Jews became a nation through divine intervention—a miracle.
>
> Many moderns do not believe in miracles. But a miracle is nothing more than a suspension of a natural law. Now, if one denies the existence of the Creator—the Creator of natural laws—clearly, those laws can never be suspended. But that person has no explanation for how nature and its laws ever came about. That the world created itself from nothing hardly seems more rationally tenable than the existence of a Creator. And if there is a Creator of nature, this Being presumably has the power to manipulate it. That is all a miracle is.

17.18 And Abraham said to God, "O that Ishmael might live by Your favor!"

> Even though Abraham is told that he is going to have a different child with Sarah, he still cares about Ishmael. He does not forget his first son, just as God did not forget Hagar in the wilderness.

17.19 God said, "Nevertheless, Sarah your wife shall bear you a son,

> When Abraham brings up Ishmael's name, God reiterates this is not the son through whom the covenant will be maintained.

For reasons not made clear, Abraham did not share this prophecy with Sarah (Genesis 18:10-12). Similarly, down the road, the wife of this very son, Rebecca, will not share her prophetic vision about the destinies of their twin sons, Jacob and Esau, with her husband (Genesis 25:23).

17.19 (cont.) and you shall name him Isaac;

In Hebrew, the name is Yitzchak, which means "laugh" in both biblical and modern Hebrew. God apparently has a sense of humor. Given that Abraham laughed when told he and Sarah would conceive at their late age, God decided to name their child "Laugh." In effect, God is saying, "You and Sarah may laugh, but I will have the last laugh."

17.19 (cont.) and I will maintain My covenant with him as an everlasting covenant for his offspring to come.

The covenant will be through Isaac, not Ishmael.

17.20 As for Ishmael, I have heeded you. I hereby bless him. I will make him fertile and exceedingly numerous. He shall be the father of twelve chieftains, and I will make of him a great nation.

17.21 But My covenant I will maintain with Isaac, whom Sarah shall bear to you at this season next year."

In case 17:19 wasn't clear, God made it explicit: the covenant is solely through Isaac.

17.22 And when He was done speaking with him, God was gone from Abraham.

17.23 Then Abraham took his son Ishmael, and all his homeborn slaves and all those he had bought, every male in Abraham's household, and he circumcised the flesh of their foreskins on that very day, as God had spoken to him.

Even though the covenant is through Isaac, Abraham circumcised Ishmael. The reason is not that Ishmael was to be a member of the covenantal people. God has just made it clear that he was not. But he was part of Abraham's household, all of whom—verse 27—were to be circumcised in keeping with God's instruction in verses 12-13.

17.24 Abraham was ninety-nine years old when he circumcised the flesh of his foreskin,

17.25 and his son Ishmael was thirteen years old when he was circumcised in the flesh of his foreskin.

17.26 Thus Abraham and his son Ishmael were circumcised on that very day;

17.27 and all his household, his homeborn slaves and those that had been bought from outsiders, were circumcised with him.

CHAPTER
18

18.1 The Lord appeared to him

> This is not an easy verse to understand. In other contexts, when the Hebrew Bible uses the words "the Lord appeared to," God then says something to the person (see, for example, the preceding chapter, verse 1). But nothing was said here by God. The likeliest explanation is God was speaking through the three strangers.

18.1 (cont.) by the terebinths of Mamre;

> Terebinths are trees native to the Mediterranean region.

ABRAHAM'S CHARACTER

18.1 (cont.) he was sitting at the entrance of the tent as the day grew hot.

> This chapter shows Abraham at his greatest. First, we witness his kindness to strangers and his humility, and then we see this very same man of humility argue with God Himself on behalf of justice.

> Although the Torah tells us nothing about Abraham when God first calls out to him, gradually we learn about the extraordinary qualities of the father of God's Chosen People.

18.2 Looking up, he saw three men standing near him. As soon as he saw them, he ran from the entrance of the tent to greet them and, bowing to the ground,

iving in the Western world, Abraham's reaction seems exaggerated. ny non-Western cultures, bowing to people as a sign of greeting is lace.

f it please you, do not go on past your servant.

18.4 Let a little water be brought; bathe your feet and recline under the tree.

18.5 And let me fetch a morsel of bread that you may refresh yourselves;

Abraham did everything in his power to make the visitors comfortable—including bathing their feet, providing shade and rest, and offering to feed them.

A good host delivers more than he promises: "I will bring a morsel of bread" is what Abraham initially said, but he provided his guests with cream and milk, followed by a sumptuous feast of a tender calf and cakes. The Talmud derived a lesson from Abraham's behavior: "The righteous say little and do much."

18.5 (cont.) then go on—seeing that you have come your servant's way." They replied, "Do as you have said."

18.6 Abraham hastened into the tent to Sarah, and said, "Quick, three *seahs* of choice flour! Knead and make cakes!"

18.7 Then Abraham ran to the herd, took a calf, tender and choice, and gave it to a servant-boy, who hastened to prepare it.

Abraham did not ask Sarah to do all the work. While she was making flour cakes, he fetched bread, chose a calf, arranged with the servant to prepare it, and then served it.

THE PATRIARCHS AND LATER JEWISH LAW

18.8 He took curds and milk and the calf that had been prepared and set these before them; and he waited on them under the tree as they ate.

The description of this meal is notable for its contents. Abraham served the visitors milk and meat, a violation of the later Jewish laws of *kashrut*, which prohibit consuming meat and milk together or at the same meal (see the explanation in the commentary on Exodus 23:19). Traditional Jews such as Rabbi Joseph Hertz, in his classic commentary on the Torah, explained Abraham's conduct from an Orthodox perspective: Abraham gave them milk first to slake their thirst and, after some time elapsed, served them meat, in accordance with traditional Jewish dietary regulations (which generally allow meat to be eaten shortly after eating dairy, but mandate that hours must pass before eating dairy after meat).

However, given that Abraham lived many hundreds of years before Jewish ritual law was legislated, it seems unnecessary to justify Abraham's choice of offerings to his guests—just, as noted later, it is unnecessary to justify Amram, Moses's father, marrying his aunt (Exodus 6:20), a violation of Leviticus 18:12; or Jacob marrying two sisters, a violation of Leviticus 18:18.

The irony is that, from a traditional Jewish perspective, the Torah's repeated recounting of Jews engaged in practices that violate later Jewish law actually confirms traditional beliefs about the veracity and the age of the Torah. Had the Torah been written much later—after Jewish law was established—such violations of Jewish law by key Jewish figures likely would never have been recorded.

> *The Torah's repeated recounting of Jews engaged in practices that violate later Jewish law actually confirms traditional beliefs about the veracity and the age of the Torah.*

THE DIVINE MESSENGERS HINT WHO THEY ARE

18.9 They said to him, "Where is your wife Sarah?" And he replied, "There, in the tent."

Given that Abraham does not ask these strangers the obvious question, "How do you know my wife's name?" we may infer Abraham had begun to suspect that these visitors were not ordinary men but messengers from God (angels).

The angels do not talk to Sarah directly because in ancient Middle Eastern society (as in some Middle Eastern societies to this day), men did not normally converse with other men's wives. But they asked her whereabouts because they wanted to ensure she would overhear their announcement to Abraham.

18.10 Then one said, "I will return to you next year, and your wife Sarah shall have a son!" Sarah was listening at the entrance of the tent, which was behind him.

In the preceding chapter, God informed Abraham that Sarah would soon be giving birth (17:16), and for reasons that are not clear, Abraham did not share this divine prophecy with her. Abraham's silence is particularly striking given how significant this issue was to Sarah and how much joy such knowledge would have brought her. As regards Abraham's silence, there are two likely possibilities.

Perhaps he felt God's words were directed to him and not to be shared with others (except if God so commanded). Thus, a few chapters later, the matriarch Rebecca is informed that she will give birth to twins, Jacob and Esau, and Jacob will be the dominant child (Genesis 25:23). However, Rebecca did not share this information with her husband, Isaac, even when she saw Isaac preparing to bless Esau with the leadership role for the following generation (Genesis 27:5).

Alternatively, perhaps having himself been skeptical when God made this promise to him (Genesis 17:17), Abraham felt uncertain about this prophecy. Consequently, he did not want to raise the hopes of Sarah who had long since despaired of having a child (which is, of course, why she arranged for Abraham to have a child with her servant, Hagar).

18.11 Now Abraham and Sarah were old, advanced in years;

Abraham was ninety-nine years old when he was circumcised, so he must have been at least that old at this point; Sarah was ten years younger.

18.11 (cont.) Sarah had stopped having the periods of women.

The Torah explicitly states that Sarah could no longer have children by ordinary means in order to emphasize, yet again, that the birth of the Jewish people was through divine intervention.

18.12 And Sarah laughed to herself, saying, "Now that I am withered, am I to have enjoyment—with my husband so old?"

WHY GOD CHANGES SARAH'S WORDS

18.13 Then the Lord said to Abraham, "Why did Sarah laugh, saying, 'Shall I in truth bear a child, old as I am?'

This may be a continuation of verse 1—"The Lord appeared to him..."—or it may be God speaking through one of the strangers.

Sarah was highly skeptical. A child seemed out of the question because of her advanced age and because her husband was "so old." Interestingly, when God reported Sarah's words to Abraham, He omitted her reference to Abraham as an old man. The ancient Rabbis considered this an example of permissible deviation from the truth: it is allowable when done in order to spare a person gratuitous hurt or to keep peace in the house (*shalom bayit*). They cited God here as the source for this teaching.[1]

The great seventeenth-century French philosopher Blaise Pascal wrote, "if all men knew what others say of them, there would not be four friends in the world."

The biblical text and the rabbinic explanation of it are every bit as relevant for readers today as in the past. Unless there is a pressing reason, it is almost always best not to repeat things one person said about another if it might hurt the other's feelings. "I lay it down as a fact," the great seventeenth-century French philosopher Blaise Pascal wrote, "if all men knew what others say of them, there would not be four friends in the world."

ything too wondrous for the Lord? I will return to you at the same season next year, and have a son."

18.15 Sarah lied,

Once again, the Torah does not shrink from portraying its heroic figures as flawed. In the Hebrew Bible, only God is perfect.

18.15 (cont.) saying, "I did not laugh," for she was frightened. But He replied, "You did laugh."

"He" here refers to God, who is the only one who could know that Sarah laughed to herself. God neither punishes her for laughing nor for lying. He merely set her straight, telling her she did in fact laugh. In addition to the wrongness of lying, this verse also suggests Sarah had an inadequate understanding of God—not realizing that while there are many things you can get away with in this world (as is often the case when you lie to another), lying to God is not one of them.

The Torah does not shrink from portraying its heroic figures as flawed. In the Hebrew Bible, only God is perfect.

18.16 The men set out from there and looked down toward Sodom, Abraham walking with them to see them off.

18.17 Now the Lord had said, "Shall I hide from Abraham what I am about to do,

This may at least partially answer the question raised earlier as to why God would inform Abraham his descendants would be enslaved for four hundred years (Genesis 15:13): God did not hide from Abraham what He was going to do. And if this is a valid answer, it would strongly imply that God, for reasons knowable only to Him, planned the Israelites' enslavement in Egypt.

THE PURPOSE OF JEWISH CHOSENNESS

18.18 since Abraham is to become a great and populous nation and all the nations of the earth are to bless themselves by him?

18.19 For I have singled him out, that he may instruct his children and his posterity to keep the way of the Lord by doing what is just and right,

God Himself explains here what exactly "the way of the Lord" is: doing what is right and just. For the first time, the Torah explicitly states God's purpose for Abraham and his descendants: to do what is just and right and, implicitly, to teach it to the world.

The Torah revealed ethical monotheism, and this is the verse that summarizes what it means. God chose the Jews to bring the world to ethical monotheism, the greatest of all the Torah's teachings. (See essay in Genesis 35:2 on how the concepts of monotheism and ethical monotheism have changed—and still challenge—the world.) In brief, ethical monotheism, as explained in the commentary to Genesis 6:9, means God is moral, God demands moral behavior from all human beings, and God will judge them according to His universal moral law.

18.19 (cont.) in order that the Lord may bring about for Abraham what He has promised him."

18.20 Then the Lord said, "The outrage of Sodom and Gomorrah is so great, and their sin so grave!

THE GREAT TORAH INNOVATION: A MORAL GOD

18.21 I will go down to see whether they have acted altogether according to the outcry that has reached Me; if not, I will take note."

God took a final look at Sodom before casting judgment, just in case the people mended their ways.

One lesson taught here is the need to establish facts before passing judgment; even God does so. One should not condemn, let alone punish, on the basis of hearsay. However, this is the exception, not the rule. Most of us rarely hear the whole story before reaching conclusions.

A second lesson is that God judges all people—and does so according to one set of moral rules. This was an utterly new idea in human history. Unlike pagan gods, who acted according to irrational and amoral whims, God is morally predictable.

A third lesson is that, because God is a moral being, He cares most about how we treat other people, not about how we "treat" Him. This was another enormous difference between the Torah's God and the other gods of the world.

From the outset, this morally judging God, completely new to humanity, has been a cause of Jew-hatred. In the words of the great social thinker Ernest van den Haag, "[The Jews'] invisible God...developed into a moral God....The Jews have suffered from their own invention ever since...."[2] A Roman Catholic scholar, Father Edward Flannery, drew the same conclusion: "It was Judaism that brought the concept of a God-given universal moral law into the world...and willingly or not...the Jew carries the burden of God in history and for this has never been forgiven."[3]

> *Roman Catholic scholar Father Edward Flannery: "It was Judaism that brought the concept of a God-given universal moral law into the world...and willingly or not...the Jew carries the burden of God in history and for this has never been forgiven."*

18.22 The men went on from there to Sodom, while Abraham remained standing before the Lord.

WHY DIDN'T GOD CALL ON THE PEOPLE OF SODOM TO REPENT?

18.23 Abraham came forward and said, "Will You sweep away the innocent along with the guilty?

Abraham does not make a case that the guilty people of Sodom and Gomorrah be allowed to repent. Why not? Perhaps because repentance is possible only in a society where the evil know what they are doing is evil. But in Sodom, the people, as we will see in Genesis 19:4-11—where it says "all" the townspeople participated in attempted rapes—had no cognizance of good and evil. Therefore, they could not consider themselves sinners and therefore would not even understand a call to repentance.

They were like modern-day Islamist terrorists—people who believe that they are doing good when they murder innocent people. Such people would not understand a call to repentance. Concerning such people, the p

warned: "Woe to those who call evil good, and good evil, who pre

as light, and light as darkness" (Isaiah 5:20).

GOD IS MORALLY CHALLENGED—A FIRST IN HUMAN HISTORY

18.24 What if there should be fifty innocent within the city; will You then wipe out the place and not forgive it for the sake of the innocent fifty who are in it?

Abraham argues for sparing the entire city of Sodom if fifty innocent people live there.

18.25 Far be it from You to do such a thing, to bring death upon the innocent as well as the guilty, so that innocent and guilty fare alike. Far be it from You!

Abraham not only argues with God, he *declares* God wrong—"Far be it from You"—if God should kill the innocent along with the guilty. The Hebrew words *chalila l'cha* may also be translated, "Don't you dare do such a thing…"

It is astonishing that anyone would feel he could speak to a deity in this way. Such a statement is unique among all bibles and perhaps all holy literature. But it is the essence of the Torah and of later Judaism that humans may have so real a relationship with God that we can actually speak this way to Him.

This negotiation between Abraham and God led Harvard law professor Alan Dershowitz to title his book on Abraham and the history of Jewish lawyers *Abraham: The World's First (But Certainly Not Last) Jewish Lawyer.*

18.25 (cont.) Shall not the Judge of all the earth deal justly?"

Abraham was arguing a principle made famous thousands of years later by the English jurist William Blackstone. Known as "Blackstone's Formulation" and still adhered to today in Western legal thought, it postulated "It is better that ten guilty persons escape than that one innocent suffer."[4]

What is as incredible as Abraham's arguing with God is his assumption that God is just. It is incredible because we know of no other people at that time or before who made such an assumption about their god(s).

This assumption changed history. Never had a human being challenged a god or gods on moral grounds. This is one of many reasons the Torah is as different from pre-Torah thought as life is from non-life, and it is therefore one of the many reasons the Torah—like the emergence of life from non-life—can best be explained by attributing it to God.

> *What is as incredible as Abraham's arguing with God was his assumption that God is just.*

18.26 And the Lord answered, "If I find within the city of Sodom fifty innocent ones, I will forgive the whole place for their sake."

Equally amazing, God was in no way upset with Abraham for arguing with Him, or even for the manner (verse 25) in which Abraham spoke to Him.

God responded to Abraham's moral argument by agreeing with him. He would spare the entire city if fifty good people live in it.

18.27 Abraham spoke up, saying, "Here I venture to speak to my Lord, I who am but dust and ashes:

Having just won an enormous concession, yet planning to ask for more, Abraham abandoned the aggressive, confrontational stance he took in verse 25 ("Don't You dare..."). He prefaced his next request with a statement of humility.

18.28 What if the fifty innocent should lack five? Will You destroy the whole city for want of the five?"

As a bargaining technique, Abraham did not say "forty-five." He wanted to emphasize the number "five" hoping a compassionate God would not destroy an entire city because just five fewer good people resided there.

18.28 (cont.) And He answered, "I will not destroy if I find forty-five there."

18.29 But he spoke to Him again, and said, "What if forty should be found there?" And He answered, "I will not do it, for the sake of the forty."

Abraham kept lowering the number of innocent people. And God kept agreeing.

18.30 And he said, "Let not my Lord be angry if I go on: What if thirty should be fo
He answered, "I will not do it if I find thirty there."

18.31 And he said, "I venture again to speak to my Lord: What if twenty should be round there?"
And He answered, "I will not destroy, for the sake of the twenty."

IT TAKES MORE THAN ONE TO DO GREAT GOOD; BUT A SINGLE PERSON CAN DO IMMENSE EVIL

18.32 And he said, "Let not my Lord be angry if I speak out this last time: What if ten should be found there?" And He answered, "I will not destroy, for the sake of the ten."

Abraham, in arguing for the entire city to be saved because of the merit of a few, stopped at ten because there has to be some minimum number of good people—arguably, a quorum of ten—in order to change a bad place. Every individual must do as much good as he or she can to improve society. But in reality, one person alone cannot change an evil society.

The way the world works, one individual can do far more evil than good.

Many Americans believe Lee Harvey Oswald, the assassin of President John F. Kennedy, did not act alone but had accomplices. Though the evidence is overwhelming that Oswald did act alone, it is emotionally and even rationally very difficult for people to accept the fact that one person could do so much harm.

Yet, it is true—even on an immeasurably larger plane: It is unlikely, to the point of near-impossibility, there would have been a Holocaust without Adolf Hitler, that the genocidal totalitarian state of the Soviet Union would have come about without Vladimir Lenin, that tens of millions of Soviet citizens would have been murdered were it not for Josef Stalin, that sixty million Chinese would have been killed without Mao Tse-Tung, or that the Cambodian genocide would have happened without Pol Pot.

Nevertheless, a small group, as Abraham's appeal suggests, can make a moral impact. In fact, most of the good that has ever even achieved has been initiated by small groups. Examples include the extraordinary group of founders of

America, the handful of Christians who brought about the abolition of slavery, the dissidents in the Soviet Union and other tyrannies who helped bring down evil regimes, and the moral impact of the tiny group of people known as Jews.

18.33 When the Lord had finished speaking to Abraham, He departed; and Abraham returned to his place.

Abraham's argument with God for justice is another example of his greatness. We had no way of knowing why God chose Abraham when God first did. But we do now. In addition to a preoccupation with justice, Abraham demonstrated a concern for humanity in general (starting with the extraordinary hospitality he exhibited at the chapter's opening). The people of Sodom are not his family, his people, his ethnicity, or his religion, yet their fate weighed on him.

19.1 The two angels arrived in Sodom in the evening, as Lot was sitting in the gate of Sodom. When Lot saw them, he rose to greet them and bowing low with his face to the ground,

> When these men came to Abraham in the previous chapter, they were referred to as "men" (*anashim*). Now they are referred to as "angels" or "messengers" (*malachim*). Modern readers usually think of angels as celestial beings with wings (as depicted, for example, in Exodus 25:2). But "angels" in the Torah and the rest of the Hebrew Bible almost always means God-sent "messengers."
>
> Did Lot perceive them as ordinary people or as something more? We cannot know for certain. On the one hand, given that he was not nearly as decent a person as his uncle Abraham, it is unlikely he would have treated the visitors as cordially as he did unless he perceived them as special. On the other hand, having lived for many years with his uncle, he came from an environment which—completely unlike Sodom's—insisted on hospitality to strangers.

19.2 he said, "Please, my lords, turn aside to your servant's house to spend the night, and bathe your feet; then you may be on your way early."

> Lot's suggestion the visitors leave early may have been due to his fear of what the citizens of Sodom might do to the visitors once they saw them. That could argue in favor of his not having perceived them to be angels—if they were angels, they would presumably have had supernatural protection.

19.2 (cont.) But, they said, "No, we will spend the night in the square."

19.3 But he urged them strongly, so they turned his way and entered his house. He prepared a feast for them and baked unleavened bread, and they ate.

This is the first time the unleavened bread known as *matzah* is mentioned in the Torah. The term refers to bread that did not have sufficient time to rise. Just as the Jews ate matzah during the Passover exodus because they were in a rush to leave Egypt, Lot prepared matzah for his guests to be able to serve them quickly.

THERE WEREN'T EVEN TEN RIGHTEOUS PEOPLE IN SODOM

19.4 They had not yet lain down, when the townspeople, the men of Sodom, young and old—all the people to the last man—gathered about the house.

Sodom was so corrupt even the children and the elderly came—as we shall see in the next verse—to rape the visitors. An evil society breeds evil, including in its children. And although we think of elderly people as relatively harmless, that was not the case in Sodom. Moreover, from whom did the middle-aged and younger people of Sodom learn their behavior?

A modern-day analogy to the people of Sodom was provided by a Chinese author writing about China's Cultural Revolution (1966-1976), which led to three million deaths and a hundred million other victims: "The greatest horror of the Cultural Revolution...*was carried out by the population collectively. Almost everyone, including young children*, had participated in brutal denunciation meetings. Many had lent a hand in beating the victims" (italics added).[1]

19.5 And they shouted to Lot and said to him, "Where are the men who came to you tonight?

Sodom resembled twentieth-century totalitarian regimes, where state employees were stationed in apartment buildings to monitor everyone who entered the building, a level of oppression those fortunate to live in free societies have difficulty fathoming. I personally witnessed this during a trip to meet with dissidents in the Soviet Union in 1969—which is why I never met with a Soviet citizen in his or her apartment.

The sin that characterized Sodom's evil society was cruelty to strangers. In this instance, they intended to rape Lot's visitors. Conversely, in depicting Abraham's goodness, the Torah emphasizes Abraham's kindness to strangers—both to those who visited him and to the people of Sodom, on whose behalf he pleaded with God. The Torah contrasts Abraham with the people of Sodom, thereby teaching the supreme importance of kindness to strangers, a principle commanded more often than any other commandment in the Torah.

THE MEN OF SODOM SEEK TO RAPE THE STRANGERS

19.5 (cont.) Bring them out to us, that we may be intimate with them."

The word translated here as "be intimate with" is the Hebrew word *yada*, "to know." In biblical Hebrew, when the verb "to know" is used to describe a man "knowing" a woman or a woman "knowing" a man, it is always a euphemism for sexual intimacy.

Other examples from Genesis:

"And Adam *knew* his wife, and she conceived...." (Genesis 4:1).

"And Cain *knew* his wife; and she conceived...." (Genesis 4:17).

"And Adam *knew* his wife again; and she gave birth to a son... (Genesis 4:25).

"I have two daughters who have not *known* a man...." (Genesis 19:8).

Here the term "know" is used for male-male relations, and it means the same thing. There is no other way to understand the demand of the men of Sodom—they wanted to rape Lot's male guests. The men of Sodom were not interested in *getting to know* the guests—what foods they liked, their hobbies, or what brought them to Sodom. That is why Lot responded by suggesting the men do what they want with his daughters. He knew what the men wanted—that it wasn't to discuss the issues of the day. Indeed, from the casual way in which the men of Sodom made their demand and Lot's immediate understanding of what they wanted, it would appear homosexual rape was common there.

In demanding Lot "take them out," rather than demanding "let us in," the men of Sodom may have expected Lot to participate in their evil. In evil societies, it is difficult not to participate in evil. Human nature is to go along with the crowd. Hence, the importance of avoiding living among bad people, unless one is strong enough to work to make a bad society better.

WHAT WAS THE GREAT SIN OF SODOM AND GOMORRAH?

What was so evil about Sodom and Gomorrah that God destroyed the two cities?

The Bible supplies an answer through the Prophet Ezekiel: "Now this was the sin of your sister Sodom: She and her daughters were arrogant, overfed and unconcerned; they did not help the poor and needy. They were haughty and committed abomination before Me...." (Ezekiel 16:49-50).

The Hebrew word translated as "abomination" (*to'evah*) is the word the Torah uses to describe male homosexuality (Leviticus 18:22), among other sins. Because the one story told about Sodom and Gomorrah concerns homosexual rape, many Jews and Christians throughout history have identified the two cities' overriding sin with homosexuality. But while the one evil act described here in the Sodom story is attempted homosexual rape, it is clear from Ezekiel that the people of Sodom were guilty of evil in a variety of ways.

The Bible decided to depict homosexual rape of strangers as its one example of just how evil Sodom was. It is not a statement about homosexuality *per se*, as many traditionalists have regarded it. But it is also not a statement of poor treatment of strangers *per se*, as many in the contemporary period regard it.

19.6 So Lot went out to them to the entrance, shut the door behind him,

Lot's shutting the door served two purposes: to constitute a barrier between his guests and the mob and to prevent his guests and, more importantly, his daughters from hearing the suggestion he will offer the mob in his attempt to dissuade them from their plans for the visitors (see verse 8).

19.7 and said, "I beg you, my friends, do not commit such a wrong.

19.8 Look, I have two daughters who have not known a man. Let me bring them out to you, and you may do to them as you please; but do not do anything to these men, since they have come under the shelter of my roof."

Lot's offer strikes the reader as unbelievable in its depravity. Clearly, however, the men were not interested in women. Perhaps Lot knew this, and (viewing Lot's behavior in the most charitable light possible) knew the offer of his daughters would be rebuffed but hoped to use it to buy a little time.

As noted above, Lot's response of offering his virgin daughters is proof the men at the door wanted to be sexually intimate with the male visitors in Lot's house.

19.9 But they said, "Stand back! The fellow," they said, "came here as an alien, and already he acts the ruler! Now we will deal worse with you than with them."

"The fellow" is Lot. The men of Sodom consider Lot, a relatively new resident, an "alien." Like his guests, Lot is a stranger to whom the people of Sodom feel no moral obligation.

19.9 (cont.) And they pressed hard against the person of Lot, and moved forward to break the door.

19.10 But the men stretched out their hands and pulled Lot into the house with them, and shut the door.

19.11 And the people who were at the entrance of the house, young and old, they struck with blinding light, so that they were helpless to find the entrance.

The first "they" in this verse refers to the angels, who struck the people crowding the entrance to the house with blinding light.

19.12 Then the men said to Lot, "Whom else have you here?

The angels asked Lot who else was in his family so they could save everyone.

19.12 (cont.) Sons-in-law, your sons and daughters, or anyone else that you have in the city— bring them out of the place.

Since Lot had previously noted his daughters' virginity to the people of Sodom, as the next verses make clear, the two daughters Lot offered to the crowd were not Lot's only children. Apparently, Lot had four or more daughters, some of whom were married and two of whom were unmarried and living at home.

19.13 For we are about to destroy this place; because the outcry against them before the Lord has become so great that the Lord has sent us to destroy it."

19.14 So Lot went out and spoke to his sons-in-law, who had married his daughters, and said, "Up, get out of this place, for the Lord is about to destroy the city." But he seemed to his sons-in-law as one who jests.

It is quite understandable Lot's sons-in-law had trouble taking his warning seriously. Even if Lot were a particularly upstanding man—which he wasn't— it would be difficult to believe one's city was about to be destroyed. It may well be, as evidenced by Lot's own reluctance to leave (verse 16), that Lot himself was not completely convinced the messengers were speaking the word of God.

19.15 As dawn broke, the angels urged Lot on, saying, "Up, take your wife and your two remaining daughters,

The "remaining daughters" were the unmarried daughters whom Lot offered to the men of Sodom.

IT IS THE SIN THAT CAUSES THE SUFFERING—NOT THE PUNISHMENT

19.15 (cont.) lest you be swept away because of the iniquity of the city."

It is very important to note the Torah uses the word "sin" (here translated "iniquity") rather than "punishment," even though the destruction of Sodom was a punishment. The reason is when people do wrong and suffer as a result, *it is their sin, not their punishment, that brought on their suffering.*

This is true in both the personal and macro realms of life. Incarcerated violent criminals, for example, are notorious for blaming their situation on their punishment, not their sins. Cain, history's first killer, knew better: "My sin is too great to bear" (Genesis 4:13), he lamented. In many English translations, including this JPS translation, Cain's statement is rendered, "My *punishment* is too great to bear," but the Hebrew word literally means "sin," not "punishment." What Cain actually says is, "My *sin* is too great to bear."

> *When people do wrong and suffer as a result, it is their sin, not their punishment, that brought on their suffering.*

To provide a macro and contemporary example, many Japanese and others blame America for dropping the atom bomb on Hiroshima and Nagasaki, not Japan for its wars of aggression against America and many other countries, for its Nazi-like behavior against the people of China and Korea, and for its barbaric treatment of prisoners-of-war. But it was these sins of Japan that caused atomic weapons to fall on Japanese cities. Their sins caused their suffering, not the consequential punishment.

NO MATTER HOW BAD, MOST PEOPLE DON'T LEAVE THEIR HOMELANDS

19.16 Still he delayed.² So the men seized his hand, and the hands of his wife and his two daughters

Lot dawdled so long the angels had to grab him.

Ultimately, the angels had to coax him to leave six times:

1. They "urged" him.
2. They told him "[Get] up."
3. They told him to "take your wife."

4. They "seized his hand."
5. They "brought him out."
6. They "left" him outside the city.

One should not necessarily blame Lot. This is human nature. How many Jews stayed in post-1933 Germany as antisemitic law after antisemitic law was passed once Hitler and the Nazis came to power? It takes a lot—not just a Lot—to get people to leave their homes, their communities, everything they know, and flee to a foreign land.

WHY DID GOD SAVE LOT?

19.16 (cont.) —in the Lord's mercy on him—

Unlike Noah, who deserved to be saved, Lot was saved because God pitied him. Lot had the good fortune to be Abraham's nephew, which is what evoked God's pity to begin with—"God was mindful of Abraham, and removed Lot from the middle of the upheaval" (Genesis 19:29). Yale Bible scholar Professor Christine Hayes writes, "This is the first biblical instance of the doctrine of the merit of the righteous, the idea that an unrighteous person might be spared for the sake of, or on account of, the accrued merit of a righteous person....Lot is no prize himself, but he is saved from destruction on Abraham's account."[3]

In Hebrew, this term, what Hayes calls the "merit of a righteous person," is known as *zechut avot,* "merit of the patriarchs [or ancestors]." Moses invoked the patriarchs (Exodus 32:13) when he pleaded with God not to destroy the Israelites after the sin of the Golden Calf. To this day, Jews begin the thrice-daily *amidah* (central prayer recited while standing) with a reminder to God of the patriarchs. This is also true on the human level. Most of us treat people with extra consideration if we have a particular liking or respect for their parents or grandparents. The good we do and goodwill we engender can end up blessing the lives of our children and grandchildren.

19.16 (cont.) and brought him out and left him outside the city.

19.17 When they had brought them outside, one said, "Flee for your life! Do not look behind you, nor stop anywhere in the Plain; flee to the hills, lest you be swept away."

As we have seen, the angels had good reason to be concerned Lot wouldn't flee.

Lot may be regarded as an archetype of the person who has difficulty fleeing even as his life is at stake. This not only pertains to fleeing a terrible place; it also applies to leaving terrible situations—such as an abusive relationship or a city in the path of a hurricane. Refusing to leave a dangerous situation can kill a person, as will happen to Lot's wife.

19.18 But Lot said to them, "Oh no, my lord!

19.19 You have been so gracious to your servant, and have already shown me so much kindness in order to save my life; but I cannot flee to the hills, lest the disaster overtake me and I die.

Lot was still blasé about the angels' warnings despite their miraculous intervention (striking the men of Sodom with a blinding light) and their efforts to get him and his family out of the city. Lot seemed unmoved even by an obviously supernatural intervention. When comparing Lot to Abraham, it becomes evident that if we are disposed to seeing God in the world, we are more likely to see miracles when we encounter them; and if we are disposed not to see God in the world, we will not recognize miracles even when they occur before our eyes.

> *If we are disposed not to see God in the world, we will not recognize miracles even when they occur before our eyes.*

19.20 Look, that town there is near enough to flee to; it is such a little place! Let me flee there—it is such a little place—and let my life be saved."

19.21 He replied, "Very well, I will grant you this favor too, and I will not annihilate the town of

which you have spoken.

19.22 Hurry, flee there, for I cannot do anything until you arrive there." Hence the town came to be called Zoar.

> *Zoar* means "small place" [based on verse 20].

19.23 As the sun rose upon the earth and Lot went to Zoar,

What most matters is why, not how, the cities were destroyed. They were destroyed for the same reason God brought the Flood: God hates evil.

19.24 the Lord rained upon Sodom and Gomorrah sulfurous fire from the Lord out of heaven.

This verse mentions twice that God was the source of the fire that rained down, thereby emphasizing God, not nature, was responsible for the destruction of Sodom and Gomorrah.

Many scholars and lay people have sought to discover exactly how the cities were destroyed—was it an earthquake, fire, something else? I admit to not having much interest in this question. In my view, what most matters is why, not how, the cities were destroyed. They were destroyed for the same reason God brought the Flood: God hates evil.

19.25 He annihilated those cities and the entire Plain, and all the inhabitants of the cities and the vegetation of the ground.

> This description of the utter devastation—down to the very ground—explained to later readers the desolation of Sodom and Gomorrah and their environs.

WHY DID LOT'S WIFE STOP FLEEING?

19.26 Lot's wife looked back,

> This verse, translated literally, means "Lot's wife looked from behind him."
> The novelist and philosopher Rebecca Goldstein conjectures that "Lot's wife

had pity on her two older daughters who were left behind, and turned to see if they were following her. Maybe she is hoping against all hope that they didn't listen to their husbands who had mockingly dismissed Lot's plea that they leave."

Goldstein alternatively conjectures that Lot's wife may have deliberately provoked her fate in order to be with her daughters who had remained in Sodom. Such is the power of the maternal bond.

19.26 (cont.) and she thereupon turned into a pillar of salt.

Josephus, the first-century Jewish historian, claims to have actually seen the pillar of salt that was once Lot's wife. The imagery here is very powerful: Don't stay still, and don't look back. If you don't look forward and progress in life, you turn into a pillar. A friend who was teaching this Torah passage at a home for the aged recalled the observation of an eighty-five-year-old resident: "When you're always looking backwards, you become inorganic."

In life, one either progresses or regresses: that which doesn't grow contracts.

19.27 Next morning, Abraham hurried to the place where he had stood before the Lord,

19.28 And, looking down toward Sodom and Gomorrah and all the land of the Plain, he saw the smoke of the land rising like the smoke of a kiln.

What Does God "Remembered" Mean?

19.29 Thus it was that, when God destroyed the cities of the Plain and annihilated the cities where Lot dwelt, God was mindful of Abraham and removed Lot from the midst of the upheaval.

The Hebrew word translated here "was mindful of" is actually the Hebrew word "remembered." But God does not "remember" in the human sense because, unlike humans, God never forgets. The Torah uses this anthropomorphic term to mean God acknowledges something at a particular moment and then acts on it. When God "remembered Noah" (Genesis 8:1), He ended the flood. Similarly, Exodus

2:23-25 states God heard the groaning of the enslaved Israelites, and "remembered His covenant with Abraham and Isaac and Jacob." Obviously, God had not "forgotten" the covenant; God "remembered" means He was now going to take action.

In this instance, God "remembered" Abraham and took action on behalf of Abraham's nephew, Lot.

19.30 Lot went up from Zoar and settled in the hill country with his two daughters, for he was afraid to dwell in Zoar;

Lot may have feared settling in Zoar because he felt unwelcome there. Knowing he had fled the ashes of Sodom, the inhabitants of Zoar might have seen him as a bad omen, a harbinger of destruction wherever he went.

19.30 (cont.) he and his two daughters lived in a cave.

WHY DID LOT'S DAUGHTERS SLEEP WITH HIM?

19.31 And the older one said to the younger, "Our father is old, and there is not a man on earth to consort with us in the way of all the world.

Given that Lot's daughters were aware there were still other people living in the world—they had recently left Zoar, after all—they could not credibly believe all mankind except for them and their father had been wiped out. But this small remnant of Lot's family was, at this point, isolated from the few people living in nearby Zoar, clearly unwelcome in the little town. So, from their perspective, there really wasn't a man on earth for them to consort and make a family with.

ONCE AGAIN, THE PERILS OF ALCOHOL

19.32 Come, let us make our father drink wine, and let us lie with him,

All stories in the Torah, especially those that repeat a theme, are meant to teach some lesson.

One lesson, as in the case of Noah and his son (Genesis 9:20-25), is a warning against drunkenness. Neither the Torah nor later Judaism prohibited use of alcohol. In fact, wine consumption is mandated on the Sabbath and other holy days. The Torah distinguishes between responsible alcohol use and drunkenness.

The Jewish attitude toward wine can be summarized by a well-known Hebrew phrase: "respect it and suspect it" (*kab-dayhu ve'chash-dayhu*).

Given how often alcohol enables or even leads to child and spousal abuse and other violent crimes, including murder, it is understandable that some religions—most notably Islam and Mormonism—prohibit alcohol. The Jewish view is if alcohol, like most everything else in creation, is channeled to decent and holy ends, it need not be banned. This attitude has largely worked well for Jews, who historically have had low rates of alcoholism. But as Jews began drinking for pleasure rather than to celebrate holy days, their alcoholism rates increased. What is undeniable is the almost immeasurable amount of human suffering caused by alcohol. Ask anyone raised by an alcoholic parent, who has an alcoholic spouse or child, or anyone who has lost a loved one to a drunk driver.

A second lesson may be related to a recurring theme in the Book of Genesis "that which goes around, comes around." Lot offered his daughters to the men of Sodom for sexual use and now ends up himself being sexually used by them.

19.32 (cont.) that we may maintain life through our father."

19.33 That night they made their father drink wine, and the older one went in and lay with her father; he did not know when she lay down or when she rose.

> Lot must have been quite intoxicated since he had no recollection of what had happened. As in his forced flight from Sodom, things just seem to happen to the passive Lot.

19.34 The next day the older one said to the younger, "See, I lay with Father last night; let us make him drink wine tonight also, and you go and lie with him, that we may maintain life through our father."

19.35 That night also they made their father drink wine, and the younger one went and lay with him; he did not know when she lay down or when she rose.

19.36 Thus the two daughters of Lot came to be with child by their father.

19.37 The older one bore a son and named him Moab; he is the father of the Moabites of today.

The phrase "of today" signifies that Moab still existed at the time this verse was written—more evidence of the antiquity of the Torah text.

19.38 And the younger also bore a son, and she called him Ben-ammi; he is the father of the Ammonites of today.

The nations that descended from these incestuous encounters, Moab and Ammon, subsequently become great foes of Israel.

CHAPTER
20

20.1 Abraham journeyed from there to the region of the Negeb and settled between Kadesh and Shur. While he was sojourning in Gerar,

20.2 Abraham said of Sarah his wife, "She is my sister." So King Abimelech of Gerar had Sarah brought to him.

As in Egypt, Abraham was apparently afraid that if the reigning power in the region through which he was passing knew Sarah was his wife, he would be killed so that the ruler could take Sarah into his harem. To save his life, he again represented his wife as his sister.

20.3 But God came to Abimelech in a dream by night and said to him, "You are to die because of the woman that you have taken, for she is a married woman."

The Torah relates Abimelech saw God in a night-time dream perhaps to distinguish his encounter with God from that of Abraham, who saw God more directly in visions during waking hours. On the other hand, as Robert Alter writes, "This potentate [Abimelech] is immediately given a higher moral status than Pharaoh in chapter 12: to Pharaoh God speaks only through plagues, whereas Abimelech is vouchsafed direct address from God in a night-vision."

God's statement, which literally reads, "she is married to a man," implies Abimelech would have taken Sarah had God not intervened.

20.4 Now Abimelech had not approached her. He said, "O Lord, will You slay people even though innocent?

The Hebrew reads, "O, Lord, will you slay a *goy* even though righteous?"

The word *goy* means "nation," not "non-Jew," as it came to be used much later in Jewish life. Thus, in the Torah, *goy* refers to the Jewish nation as well as to non-Jewish nations. Exodus 19:6, for example, commands Israel to be "a holy *goy*."

Abimelech pleaded he was innocent—he would not have taken Sarah if he knew she was married. Just as Abraham in the case of Sodom (Genesis 18:25), Abimelech argued with God by appealing to God's universal moral standards.

20.5 He himself said to me, 'She is my sister!' And she also said, 'He is my brother.' When I did this, my heart was blameless and my hands were clean."

Abimelech responded to God accurately: Abraham and Sarah lied to him about their relationship.

He offered an honest plea to God and defended himself, though his words sound somewhat self-serving: If he was so innocent, why did he take Sarah without her consent? On the other hand, a king's taking women he wanted was so common in the ancient and medieval worlds, we should judge him according to the moral norms of his day (see the commentary concerning Noah being righteous "in his generations"—Genesis 6:9).

20.6 And God said to him in the dream, "I knew that you did this with a blameless heart, and so I kept you from sinning against Me. That was why I did not let you touch her.

God did not specify how He prevented Abimelech from being intimate with Sarah. It probably wasn't the dream that deterred Abimelech, since that would likely have taken place while asleep after having relations with her. We can therefore assume God did something physical to him to prevent Abimelech being physically intimate with her.

God's described adultery as a sin against "Me" (God), not against the woman's husband (Abraham). This is the first iteration of the Torah view that adultery is a sin against God, not only against one's spouse (see also Genesis 39:9 and the commentary on the Seventh Commandment in Exodus 20:13).

20.7 Therefore, restore the man's wife—since he is a prophet,

The Hebrew word translated as "prophet," *navi*, is more accurately translated "spokesperson." The biblical "prophet" was a spokesperson—a mouthpiece—for God. Biblical prophets only rarely prophesied in the sense of telling the future (see, for example, Jeremiah 30:1-3).

This is the first mention of this term in the Bible, and its only mention in Genesis.

20.7 (cont.) he will intercede for you—to save your life.

This prayer—asking a wronged party (Abraham) to pray that God forgive the person who wronged him (Abimelech)—is the first mention in the Bible of a prayer offered by one person on behalf of another. Abimelech will be forgiven if Abraham prays on his behalf.

20.7 (cont.) If you fail to restore her, know that you shall die, you and all that are yours."

20.8 Early next morning, Abimelech called his servants and told them all that had happened; and the men were greatly frightened.

"The men were greatly frightened"—of whom? Presumably God, not Abimelech. They recognized God as the source of the dream—a God with the power to impose grave consequences for sin and disobedience.

20.9 Then Abimelech summoned Abraham and said to him, "What have you done to us? What wrong have I done that you should bring so great a guilt upon me and my kingdom? You have done to me things that ought not to be done.

20.10 "What, then," Abimelech demanded of Abraham, "was your purpose in doing this thing?"

Abimelech faulted Abraham for causing him to sin. Abimelech had a point. He was annoyed that Abraham's (and Sarah's) lie misled him and put him in this dangerous position.

20.11 "I thought," said Abraham, "surely there is no fear of God in this place, and they will kill me because of my wife.

Not all Jewish religious commentators found Abraham's argument convincing. Nachmanides (Hebrew, Ramban), for example, questioned Abraham for immediately making this assumption. According to Nachmanides, Abraham should not have been suspicious of the king and people of Gerar in the same way he was previously suspicious of the Egyptian king and people because Gerar was not Egypt.

I find Abraham's argument persuasive. He knew how people acted in his time, especially in a place where there was no fear of God, especially toward strangers, and especially toward unmarried women.

GOD-FEARING IS A MORAL LABEL AND CAN APPLY TO PEOPLE OUTSIDE OF ONE'S OWN FAITH

By implication, Abraham acknowledged there can be good, God-fearing people outside of one's own religious group. This is an important lesson for people of all faiths: it is a life-changing moment in the life of a religious person when he meets members of other religions who are as religious and ethical as he thinks he is. When that happens we can begin to do as the Prophet Micah instructs, "Walk humbly with your God" (Micah 6:8).

This happened to me beginning in my thirties when, for ten years, I moderated a radio show every week featuring clergy and lay leaders of virtually every religion in the world. Meeting good and intelligent people of all these religions had a profound and permanent impact on me.

For much of Western history, decent men and women were often referred to as "God-fearing." It was a great compliment. But in our secular age, the term is almost never used. On the contrary, it is widely considered a foolish anachronism. Nevertheless, the concept is morally vital (see, for example, Exodus 1:15-17).

Even Voltaire (1694-1778), a passionate atheist and the godfather of the aggressively secular French Enlightenment, acknowledged: "I want my lawyer, my tailor, my servants, and even my wife to believe in God because it means that I shall be cheated, and robbed, and cuckolded less often. If God did not exist, it would be necessary to invent him."[1]

In the same vein, Rabbi J. David Bleich, a contemporary Orthodox Jewish writer, quoted a Jewish aphorism he heard as a child from his great-grandmother: "When you are riding in a horse and a wagon and pass the door of a church, if the driver does not cross himself, get off immediately."[2]

> *Voltaire (1694-1778), a passionate atheist and the godfather of the aggressively secular French Enlightenment, acknowledged: "I want my lawyer, my tailor, my servants, and even my wife to believe in God because it means that I shall be cheated, and robbed, less often."*

20.12 And besides, she is in truth my sister, my father's daughter though not my mother's; and she became my wife.

Abraham's argument here is pretty weak. Sarah was indeed his half-sister, but failing to acknowledge that she was also his wife made this a half-truth. They left out the more important half.

This is another example of the antiquity—and another argument for the veracity—of the Torah text. Given that later Torah law—Leviticus 18:9, 11; 20:17; Deuteronomy 27:22—prohibited marrying a half-sister, "it is inconceivable," Sarna rightly argues, "that a late author would invent a tale ascribing to the patriarch a practice abhorrent to the sexual morality of Israel as it found legal expression in the Torah codes."

20.13 So when God made me wander from my father's house,

> Abraham used the name for God, *Elohim*, followed by a plural verb, *hitu* ("made me wander") even though elsewhere it is always followed by a singular verb. Abraham did so not because he believed there is more than one God, but because in the world of polytheism he likely felt that Abimelech would be more apt to understand him if he spoke of God in the plural.

20.13 (cont.) I said to her, 'Let this be the kindness that you shall do me: wherever place we come to, say there of me: He is my brother.'"

20.14 Abimelech took sheep and oxen, and male and female slaves, and gave them to Abraham; and he restored his wife Sarah to him.

20.15 And Abimelech said, "Here, my land is before you; settle wherever you please."

20.16 And to Sarah he said, "I herewith give your brother a thousand pieces of silver;

> This is a rare instance of sarcasm in the Torah. Abimelech refers to Abraham as Sarah's brother, even though he now knows the true nature of their relationship. To best appreciate the sarcasm, read the verse aloud and emphasize the word "brother."

20.16 (cont.) this will serve you as vindication before all who are with you, and you are cleared before everyone."

20.17 Abraham then prayed to God, and God healed Abimelech and his wife and his slave girls, so that they bore children;

20.18 for the Lord had closed fast every womb of the household of Abimelech because of Sarah, the wife of Abraham.

21.1 The Lord took note of Sarah as He had promised, and the Lord did for Sarah as He had spoken.

It is noteworthy that the text does not read, "the Lord did for Abraham and Sarah as He had spoken," but only "did for Sarah." The promise of progeny, after all, was made to both. If the Torah were as sexist as some modern critics suggest, it likely would have mentioned only Abraham. But the Torah affirms the equal worth of the sexes—from the Creation story (where the woman is the final creation) to the demand that children honor both parents to the depiction of women as heroic—frequently more so than the men in their lives: Rebecca, Moses's mother Yocheved and sister Miriam, the daughter of Pharaoh, among others.

21.2 Sarah conceived and bore a son to Abraham in his old age, at the set time of which God had spoken.

21.3 Abraham gave his newborn son, whom Sarah had borne him, the name of Isaac.

Abraham named this son Isaac in accordance with God's prophecy in Gen. 17:19. The name means "laugh," and it reflects both Abraham's and Sarah's initial reactions to the news they would have a baby at their advanced ages. Although the name Isaac (Yitzchak in Hebrew) is common today, it would originally have been highly unusual to call a child "Laugh." Nonetheless, in modern Hebrew the word still means "he will laugh."

21.4 And when his son Isaac was eight days old, Abraham circumcised him, as God had commanded him.

21.5 Now Abraham was a hundred years old when his son Isaac was born to him.

21.6 Sarah said, "God has brought me laughter; everyone who hears will laugh with me."

First Sarah laughed when she heard she and Abraham would have a child (Genesis 18:9-12). Now she laughs at the fact that she really has given birth.

21.7 And she added, "Who would have said to Abraham that Sarah would suckle children! Yet I have borne a son in his old age."

Though it doesn't come across in translation, Sarah's statement in Hebrew reads like a little poem or ditty she has composed.

21.8 The child grew up and was weaned, and Abraham held a great feast on the day that Isaac was weaned.

Abraham was a wealthy man who could afford to throw a great party in honor of his son's weaning. Today, parties are often made on the eighth day, at the time of a child's circumcision. But in the ancient world, with its very high rate of infant mortality, it was only later—at the time of weaning, for example—that parents felt confident the child would survive and would throw a party in the child's honor.

21.9 Sarah saw the son whom Hagar, the Egyptian had borne to Abraham, playing.

The word "playing" (*mitzachek*) is another play on Isaac's name. Literally, it means "make to laugh." But it may also mean "mocking" or even have sexual connotations (as it does when used later to describe the Israelites' behavior around the Golden Calf—Exodus 32:6).

At this point, Ishmael was about sixteen years old and Isaac was about two. According to Genesis 16:16, Abraham was eighty-six years old when Ishmael was born, and according to Genesis 21:5, Abraham was one hundred when

Isaac was born. The brothers are thus fourteen years apart. Since a child is usually weaned at about two, this would make Ishmael about sixteen.

The older brother was probably just trying to amuse his little brother. But for whatever reason—and the following verse certainly offers one possible reason—this scene disturbed Sarah.

21.10 She said to Abraham, "Cast out that slave-woman and her son, for the son of that slave shall not share in the inheritance with my son Isaac."

There is no reason to believe Ishmael had done anything wrong. But now that Isaac has survived past the critical age of weaning, Sarah realized he will have competition for his inheritance, and she sought to eliminate it. She succeeded: Genesis 25:5 records at the end of Abraham's life that "he gave everything he had to Isaac."

21.11 The matter distressed Abraham greatly, for it concerned a son of his.

This translation downplays Abraham's internal reaction. The Hebrew does not say "distressed." It says, "the thing was very bad in his eyes."

Sarah's demand must have stunned Abraham. Ishmael was, after all, also his son—a son whom he loved and, furthermore, who was conceived at Sarah's behest. But she long since regretted her scheme (Genesis 16:4-6) and now wanted both Ishmael and his mother gone. That Sarah did not even deign to refer to Ishmael or his mother by their names must have further upset Abraham.

There are many things that can produce tension between a husband and wife. The raising of children is one of the biggest—particularly when one of them is a stepchild.

21.12 But God said to Abraham, "Do not be distressed over the boy or your slave; whatever Sarah tells you, do as she says, for it is through Isaac that offspring shall be continued through you.

God's instruction must have felt like another body-blow to Abraham, already reeling from the callousness of his wife's demand. According to Sarna, God told Abraham to listen to Sarah because she was right, even though her reasoning was ignoble. Though Sarah's intent was to banish Ishmael to safeguard her son's inheritance, God nevertheless supported her plan because it coincided with His ultimate purpose: that Isaac carries on Abraham's mission. It is possible that Sarah was also concerned with Isaac's divine destiny, since she heard the words of the three angels heralding his birth (Genesis 18:10). Still, it is disquieting that she demanded the expulsion of Ishmael and that she phrased her demand solely in terms of inheritance.

21.13 As for the son of the slave-woman, I will make a nation of him, too, for he is your seed."

Though God instructed Abraham to listen to Sarah, God reassured Abraham He would not neglect Ishmael. At the same time, God reinforced His support of Sarah by using precisely the same words Sarah had in referring to Ishmael and Hagar—"son of the slave-woman" (verse 10).

21.14 Early next morning Abraham took some bread and a skin of water,

A container made of animal skin.

21.14 (cont.) and gave them to Hagar. He placed them over her shoulder, together with the child,

Abraham placed the provisions over Hagar's, not Ishmael's, shoulder. Given that Ishmael was now sixteen years old, "together with the child" means that Abraham put the child in Hagar's care, not that Abraham put Ishmael on Hagar's shoulder.

21.14 (cont.) and sent her away. And she wandered about in the wilderness of Beer-sheba.

21.15 When the water was gone from the skin

How is Abraham's behavior to be explained? He gave Hagar meager supplies—some bread and water—and sent her and their son out into the desert. Shouldn't Abraham, this wealthy man, have sent Hagar and Ishmael away with far more provisions or at least accompanied by some of the large number of servants and retainers in his camp (see Genesis 14:14)? In retrospect, it would seem so. Perhaps he didn't think they needed more provisions or help because of God's reassurance that He would look after them. And perhaps, given his wife Sarah's resentment of Hagar and Ishmael, he did not want to seem overly protective of them. Wives have great influence over their husbands—even a husband who communicates directly with God.

21.15 (cont.) she left the child under one of the bushes,

21.16 and went and sat down at a distance, a bowshot away; for she thought, "Let me not look on as the child dies."

Hagar's behavior was even more confounding than Abraham's; one would expect a mother to remain with her child if she fears he is dying.

21.16 (cont.) And sitting thus afar, she burst into tears.

21.17 God heard the cry of the boy, and an angel of God called to Hagar from heaven and said to her, "What troubles you, Hagar? Fear not, for God has heeded the cry of the boy where he is.

Sarna notes that both of Abraham's sons were saved from death by an angel's voice from the heavens: Ishmael was saved when he was dying in the wilderness, and Isaac was saved in the next chapter as he lay on the altar (Genesis 22:12).

21.18 Come, lift up the boy and hold him by the hand, for I will make a great nation of him."

God promised Ishmael will be a great nation, but He does not promise him territory; Abraham's seed was promised both nationhood and territory. Ironically, Ishmael's descendants ended up with far more territory than Isaac's.

21.19 Then God opened her eyes and she saw a well of water. She went and filled the skin with water, and let the boy drink.

21.20 God was with the boy and he grew up; he dwelt in the wilderness and became a bowman.

21.21 He lived in the wilderness of Paran; and his mother got a wife for him from the land of Egypt.

Hagar was Egyptian, so it makes sense she arranged for her son to marry an Egyptian.

21.22 At that time Abimelech and Phicol, chief of his troops, said to Abraham, "God is with you in everything that you do.

21.23 Therefore swear to me here by God that you will not deal falsely with me or with my kith and kin, but will deal with me and with the land in which you have sojourned as loyally as I have dealt with you."

Having experienced both Abraham's dishonesty (about Sarah) and the patriarch's being under the protection of God, Abimelech was well aware Abraham had the upper hand. He therefore sought assurance Abraham would not again use deception or God's protection to take advantage of him.

WE CHOOSE WHEN TO FEEL HURT OR INSULTED

21.24 And Abraham said, "I swear it."

Abraham was in no way defensive. He well understood Abimelech's apprehensions. Many lesser people would be insulted if someone made them swear to be honest before engaging in a business dealing.

It is very important in life to know when to feel insulted or hurt and when not to. I have seen people feel insulted when store clerks checked their money to ensure it wasn't counterfeit. The best way to determine whether one was insulted is to react with one's mind, not one's feelings. If your money is examined, you are not being insulted because you were not unjustly targeted for special inspection. To put it another way, we *choose* whether to consider ourselves insulted. Abraham chose neither to be hurt or insulted. He knew he had earned Abimelech's mistrust.

21.25 Then Abraham reproached Abimelech for the well of water which the servants of Abimelech had seized.

For whatever reason, the Torah has said nothing about Abimelech's servants seizing of a well. We first learn about it in this verse.

21.26 But Abimelech said, "I do not know who did this; you did not tell me, nor have I heard of it until today."

21.27 Abraham took sheep and oxen and gave them to Abimelech, and the two of them made a pact.

THE NUMBER SEVEN

21.28 Abraham then set seven ewes of the flock by themselves,

The number seven figures prominently in this story, as it does throughout the Torah and in the Book of Genesis in particular.

The seven ewes are one example, as are Abimelech and Abraham's names, each of which is mentioned seven times. Another tie-in of the number seven is the men swearing an oath (verse 31), which in Hebrew is *shvua*, a word having the same root as the Hebrew word for "seven" (*sheva*). And although the name of the place where they make their oath, Beer-sheba, derives from the Hebrew word for oath, Beer-sheba also means "well number seven."

Seven often signifies completion or perfection. But, more than anything else, seven signifies either God's involvement or remembrance of the seven days of Creation.

21.29 and Abimelech said to Abraham, "What mean these seven ewes which you have set apart?"

21.30 He replied, "You are to accept these seven ewes from me as proof that I dug this well."

21.31 Hence that place was called Beer-sheba, for there the two of them swore an oath.

21.32 When they had concluded the pact at Beer-sheba, Abimelech and Phicol, chief of his troops, departed and returned to the land of the Philistines.

21.33 [Abraham] planted a tamarisk at Beer-sheba, and invoked there the name of the Lord, the Everlasting God.

21.34 And Abraham resided in the land of the Philistines a long time.

CHAPTER

22

THE ULTIMATE TEST OF ABRAHAM

22.1 Some time afterward, God put Abraham to the test.

(For one unconventional but provocative interpretation of this story—that this served as a lesson in empathy to Sarah for her treatment of Hagar and Ishmael—see the endnote.[1])

In this verse, God is rendered *Ha-Elohim*, "*the* God." In the great majority of cases, God is referred to as Elohim, but in more than a few instances, God is referred to as Ha-Elohim, "the" Elohim. I assume there is a reason but could not find one. However, I believe it is worth noting.

What is most important to note is the very first sentence of the Binding of Isaac story—"the God put Abraham to the test"—lets the reader know that God did not want Isaac sacrificed; He was only putting Abraham to a test. And, of course, this is shown at the end of the story when God stopped Abraham from going through with the sacrifice.

While this episode is known in Hebrew as *Akedat Yitzchak*, "the binding of Isaac," in Western literature it is usually referred to as "the sacrifice of Isaac," a misnomer that distorts the essence of the event, as God soon makes it clear that He never wants human beings to be sacrificed.

22.1 (cont.) He said to him, "Abraham," and he answered, "Here I am."

Abraham's response, the Hebrew word *Hineni* ("Here I am"), has become resonant among Jews as a statement of readiness to fulfill a calling, comparable to an enthusiastically offered "Yes, sir!"

GOD SAYS "PLEASE"

22.2 And He said, "Take your son, your favorite one, Isaac, whom you love,

Though the translation doesn't note it, there is a Hebrew word—*na*—in the text following the word "Take." Hamilton explains: "*Na*, which occurs more than sixty times in Genesis, is used only five times in the entire Old Testament when God speaks to a person. Each time God asks the individual to do something staggering, something that defies rational explanation or understanding. Here then is an inkling at least that God is fully aware of the magnitude of his test for Abraham."

WHY DIDN'T GOD JUST SAY, "TAKE ISAAC"?

Why does God use these descriptions—"your favorite (or 'only'), whom you love"—and not just say "Isaac"? Perhaps the purpose was to make the request/command all the more difficult for Abraham to obey.

22.2 (cont.) and go to the land of Moriah, and offer him there as a burnt offering on one of the heights that I will point out to you."

The Hebrew words used here for "go" (*lech-lecha*) were also the first words God said to Abraham when He told him to leave his father and go to another land (Genesis 12:1). Now God tells Abraham to take his son, leave his home, and go to another land with the same words. This presumably made God's order all the more compelling.

WHY DID ABRAHAM AWAKEN EARLY TO GO AND SACRIFICE HIS SON?

22.3 So early next morning,

Presumably, God appeared to Abraham at night, likely in a dream.

Why are we told Abraham awakened early? Some commentators cite this as the Torah's way of communicating Abraham was eager to perform God's commandments. Given that this command was to kill his beloved son, that is hard to imagine.

Perhaps Abraham could not sleep well that night.

Perhaps Abraham wished to get up before Sarah did.

And maybe there is a simpler reason: In the ancient world, one who sets out on a long journey leaves at the break of dawn. Leaving later than that is a waste of daylight.

WHY DIDN'T ABRAHAM ARGUE WITH GOD?

Abraham did not argue with God as he did in the case of Sodom. Why? Perhaps because Sodom seemed to be an affront to justice—God seemed ready to kill innocent people. But the command to sacrifice his son probably did not strike Abraham as unjust (even though Isaac was an innocent) because in the ancient world, child sacrifice was universally considered acceptable, even admirable (insofar as it showed devotion to one's god), and because children were regarded as possessions of parents. So, Abraham understandably may not have perceived the command to sacrifice Isaac as morally wrong but rather as a command from the God he believed in.

What might have most puzzled Abraham, therefore, was not his being told to sacrifice his child but being told to sacrifice the child whom God had promised would be the father of a nation. How could the commandment to sacrifice Isaac be reconciled with God's promise of a future nation emanating from Isaac? In not fully understanding God's ways, Abraham represented every believer who came after him.

In not fully understanding God's ways, Abraham represented every believer who came after him.

The ultimate reason Abraham did not argue with God is most likely this: His argument with God over destroying Sodom convinced him God is just and God knows what is best. Thus, after Sodom, Abraham never again argued with God.

WHY GOD TESTED ABRAHAM THIS WAY: THE UNIVERSALITY OF HUMAN SACRIFICE

Virtually every ancient society about which we have data had human sacrifice—the killing of human beings to propitiate their society's god(s).[2]

Why did only one book, one culture, one faith on earth abolish an evil practiced by every other society and faith in the world?

Only if one understands this can one understand why God would test Abraham in this way: "Are you, Abraham, willing to do for Me what all other human beings are prepared to do for their (false) gods?"

And only by understanding how universal human sacrifice was can one begin to appreciate how radically different the Torah was from every other society. And then, one must ask the most important question: Why did only one book, one culture, one faith on earth abolish an evil practiced by every other society and faith in the world?

Once again, one has two choices: this abolition came from uniquely moral—indeed superior—human beings, or it came from God. Given human behavior throughout history, I am much more inclined to believe the latter.

For a description of widespread human sacrifice that is far more recent (Central America, fourteenth to sixteenth centuries) than biblical times, see the endnote.[3]

The Torah repeatedly speaks of human, specifically child, sacrifice among the Canaanites. And archaeologists have "uncovered evidence of ritual human sacrifice in many ancient societies, including the ancient Greeks, the Vikings, the ancient Maya, and the Aztecs and the Incas, as well as in ancient China."[4]

The practice has not only been documented in ancient Africa but in contemporary Africa as well.[5]

GOOD PEOPLE MUST BE AS WILLING TO SACRIFICE AS BAD PEOPLE ARE

From God's perspective, the command to sacrifice Isaac was, as the Torah notes at the beginning of the chapter, a test. And what exactly was this test? As noted above, God was asking Abraham: "Will you, Abraham, be as obedient to me, the one God—the only God—of the world, as others are to their man-made local and multiple gods?"

That is a question innumerable people have had to answer throughout history: Will the good be as committed to what is good and true as the bad are to what is bad and false? History reveals the answer often in the negative. All too frequently, the decent have not fought the indecent until it was almost too late—and sometimes it was too late. Most good people are not fighters.

On the other hand, throughout history, innumerable people have indeed been prepared to make Abraham's sacrifice. Vast numbers of parents have willingly sent their children to fight and die for their beliefs. When the cause is moral, these people are doing God's will. The question, therefore, is not whether parents, even in our time, are prepared to sacrifice their children; it is whether they are doing so for a good and true cause or an evil and false one (as was the case with millions of German and Japanese parents during World War II, and the case with parents who celebrate their child's death when the child engaged in an Islamist suicide terror attack).

All the preceding notwithstanding, the ultimate message of this story is that human sacrifice is morally unacceptable to God. The good God introduced to the world by the Torah abhors child sacrifice.

22.3 (cont.) Abraham saddled his ass and took with him two of his servants and his son Isaac.

The Torah heightens the drama by continuing to emphasize the relationship between Abraham and Isaac ("his son") throughout this experience.

22.3 (cont.) He split the wood for the burnt offering, and he set out for the place of which God had told him.

22.4 On the third day Abraham looked up and saw the place from afar.

Abraham is not recorded as having said a word during this three-day journey. "He seems to move about his grim task with silent resignation, as if he were an automaton."[6]

Did they literally travel three days? Hamilton comments on the expression, "On the third day":

"'The third day' is often used in the Torah to refer to some ominous event, such as the execution of Hamor and the Shechemites (Genesis 34:25), the execution of Pharaoh's baker (Genesis 40:20), and Joseph testing his brothers (Genesis 42:18). It may be that one should take 'On the third day' in a similar way here. The expression is used not primarily for exact chronological purposes, but as an idiom to underscore the drama in the narrative."

Joseph Telushkin offers an alternative take on the length of the trip. "Why so long?" he asks, as God could have found a nearer place at which Abraham could have sacrificed Isaac. Most likely, God chose such a place to underscore the magnitude of the test. "In a moment of religious enthusiasm, Abraham might readily fulfill the divine command." People often say "yes" and, as time passes, regret having said so. But Abraham is forced to journey with Isaac a full seventy-two hours.

Further, as Abraham proceeds towards the mountain, he must be suffering additional trepidation, imagining what he will tell Sarah when he returns from the trip alone.

22.5 Then Abraham said to his servants, "You stay here with the ass. The boy and I will go up there; we will worship and we will return to you."

Abraham's use of the word "we" is puzzling: Didn't he assume that only he would return? Most likely, he wanted to spare Isaac the pain of knowing what was about to happen. It is also possible he was concerned Isaac might resist, or he suspected/hoped that it was all a test. Or all three possibilities might have been true.

22.6 And Abraham took the wood for the burnt offering and put it on his son Isaac. He himself took the firestone and the knife;

> Though we don't know Isaac's age at this point, this verse indicates he was old enough to carry the load of firewood up the mountain. The Torah here uses a very uncommon word for knife, *ma'achelet*, which literally means "feeder." It is a slaughtering knife—it "feeds" people—which underscores the reality of what is about to take place.

22.6 (cont.) and the two walked off together.

22.7 Then Isaac said to his father Abraham, "Father!"

> This dialogue is the only one between Abraham and Isaac recorded in the Torah. While the Torah does not explicitly state Isaac's age at the time of the *akedah*, this conversation, along with the previous verse, suggests he is a lad— perhaps approaching adolescence or early teens—rather than a young child, since he not only was able to carry the load of firewood but understood a sacrifice was about to be offered.

22.7 (cont.) And he answered, "Yes, my son."

> Abraham spoke gently and affectionately to Isaac, believing these were their final moments together. Abraham probably wanted to convey to Isaac how much he loved him, given what he (Abraham) was about to do.

22.7 (cont.) And he said, "Here are the firestone and the wood; but where is the sheep for the burnt offering?"

22.8 And Abraham said, "God will see to the sheep for His burnt offering, my son." And the two of them walked on together.

22.9 They arrived at the place of which God had told him. Abraham built an altar there; he laid out the wood; he bound his son Isaac; he laid him on the altar, on top of the wood.

This verse uses five verbs to describe the steps taken by Abraham (translating directly from the Hebrew): "came," "built," "spread," "bound," "put." One gets the sense that he methodically went through the necessary steps, in no rush, no doubt with a tremendous sense of dread. He must have been relieved that Isaac apparently, and remarkably, put up no resistance. With the brief exception of his questioning his father about the lack of a sacrificial animal, Isaac remained passive throughout this story, as he did at other times. (For an assessment of Isaac's life, see comment on Genesis 25:19.) On the other hand, if Abraham is to be honored for his obedience to God, Isaac must also be honored for his obedience to God—and to his father. After all, his father was an old man; if Isaac wished to resist him, it would have been easy to do so. Yet he didn't struggle, run away, or even verbally protest.

22.10 And Abraham picked up the knife to slay his son.

This verb, *shachat*, "to slaughter," is the same word that the Torah uses to refer to the slaughtering of animals for meat. The Torah does not use the euphemistic term "sacrifice" (*korban*) to describe what Abraham was prepared to do. The Torah's language is literal and explicit so as to impress upon the reader the terrible reality of what human sacrifice is really about: slaughter.

22.11 Then an angel of the Lord called to him from heaven: "Abraham! Abraham!" And he answered, "Here I am."

In the beginning of the story, it took the commanding authority of God Himself to get Abraham to go along with a plan to kill his son. But an angel—not God—is all that was needed to stop him from carrying out the plan. The angel called out to him twice because the matter was so very urgent: Abraham was about to plunge a knife into his son.

"This is nearly identical with the calling-out to Hagar in 21:17. In fact, a whole configuration of parallels between the two stories is invoked. Each of Abraham's sons is threatened with death in the wilderness, one in the presence of his mother, the other in the presence (and by the hand) of his father. In each case the angel intervenes at the critical moment, referring to the son fondly as *na'ar*, 'lad.' At the center of the story, Abraham's hand holds the knife; Hagar is enjoined to 'hold her hand' (the literal meaning of the Hebrew) on the lad. In the end, each of the sons is promised to become progenitor of a great people, the threat to Abraham's continuity having been averted" (Robert Alter).

22.12 And he said, "Do not raise your hand against the boy, or do anything to him.

Now we reach the ultimate message of this story: human sacrifice is morally unacceptable to God. The good God introduced to the world by the Torah abhors child sacrifice. This was another unique Torah contribution to human moral development. God had no interest in the sacrifice of Isaac—and has no interest in the sacrifice of any other human being. God had two interests here: to see if Abraham would pass the ultimate test of faith and to teach Abraham (and the rest of humanity) that the one true God prohibits human sacrifice. That is the essence of ethical monotheism: the one true God demands adherence to the one true morality.

This is the first (and most dramatic) example of this lesson, but not the only. The Torah repeatedly prohibits child sacrifice (another indication of how widespread human sacrifice was)—see Leviticus 18:21; 20:2-3; Deuteronomy 12:29-31; 18:9-10.

If God had required Abraham to go through with the sacrifice of Isaac, biblical religion/Judaism would have been just another pagan religion, differing from other religions only by having one god rather than many. But the difference between polytheism and the Torah's monotheism is not primarily the number of gods; it is in the moral nature of the Torah's God versus all other gods.

Prohibiting Abraham from sacrificing his son exemplified the triumph of ethical monotheism over paganism.

ESSAY: FAITH DEMANDS SACRIFICE

22.12 (cont.) For now I know that you fear God, since you have not withheld your son, your favorite one, from Me."

An obvious question is whether God meant this literally: Did the omniscient God not know whether Abraham would pass the test? In my view, a believer in the God of the Bible can hold either position—that God does not know what choices humans will make, since the human being, unlike everything else in the universe, has free will; or that God, existing outside of time, does know what humans will do before they do it.

If we take the latter view—that God knew what Abraham would do—the test was clearly not performed for God's benefit. Indeed, it may not have even been performed for Abraham's benefit. It does not seem to have benefitted him—and may well have cost him his marriage, as we shall see, and perhaps his son's trust.

Rather, the test was performed to teach the rest of us about the nature of faith—that it requires something of us; and to teach us that God does not want human sacrifice. But short of that, true religion does demand some sacrifice.

When any religious person says, "I am depriving myself of something because of a demand from God"—and that demand conforms with God's notions of the good and the just—that individual is demonstrating the nature of serious faith.

When Catholics deprive themselves of some joy during Lent; when Mormons abstain from coffee and alcohol and fast once a month; when Jews make a professional and monetary sacrifice in order to observe the Sabbath; when any religious person says, "I am depriving myself of something because of a demand from God"—and that demand conforms with God's notions of the good and the just—that individual is demonstrating the nature of serious faith.

In accordance with this requirement of true belief, millions of Jews throughout Jewish history have, in a sense, emulated Abraham. Given the repeated attempts throughout history to annihilate the Jewish people, every Jewish parent who chooses to remain a Jew knows that he or she might be subjecting his or her children or grandchildren to premature death simply by living as Jews.

Many years before writing this commentary, I was walking to my seat on an airplane in Phoenix, Arizona, when a woman in her mid-thirties stopped me. She told me she attended my previous night's lecture to the Jewish community of Phoenix. She explained she was a non-Jew married to a Jew, and though she attended my lecture, her husband refused to. He was the son of Holocaust survivors, and he was adamant about abandoning his Jewish identity and not raising their children as Jews. He had no desire to risk his children or future grandchildren being killed because they were Jews.

That man did not want to be an Abraham.

22.13 When Abraham looked up, his eye fell upon a ram, caught in the thicket by its horns. So Abraham went and took the ram and offered it up as a burnt offering in place of his son.

22.14 And Abraham named that site Adonai-yireh, hence the present saying, "On the mount of the Lord there is vision."

22.15 The angel of the Lord called to Abraham a second time from heaven,

22.16 and said, "By Myself I swear, the Lord declares: Because you have done this and have not withheld your son, your favored son,

As noted, every parent who has sent a child off to war was also "not withholding" their son (and now daughter). In effect, the child sacrifice test is one, unfortunately, that reoccurs in every age. The question, therefore, is not whether parents—and society as a whole—should ever be prepared to sacrifice a child; the question is whether the sacrifice is morally necessary. God's behavior at the story's end makes it clear that not all sacrifices are morally required or morally just.

"Sacrifice" is like "idealism." In and of itself, it is a morally neutral, not a morally positive, term. If somebody is an idealist for a good cause, that idealism will lead to good. But there is plenty of idealism for evil causes.

22.17 I will bestow my blessing upon you, and make your descendants as numerous as the stars of heaven and the sands on the seashore; and your descendants shall seize the gates of their foes.

Until now, Abraham was promised that his seed would be as numerous as the stars; now he is also told they will be as numerous as the sands on the seashore. Since people see far more grains of sand than stars in the sky, this verse greatly expands the magnitude of God's promise.

To ancients, this verse had to seem incredible—they could not believe the number of stars was comparable to the number of grains of sand. When they looked up, they saw far fewer stars in the sky than grains of sand on any seashore. But scientists now believe there are more stars in the universe than grains of sand on earth.

Nevertheless, while the equation of sand and stars is remarkable, both claims are meant to be dramatic, not mathematically precise. There are nowhere near as many descendants of Abraham as either stars in the sky or sands on the seashore. Indeed, there are not even that many human beings on earth.

22.18 All the nations of the earth shall bless themselves by your descendants, because you have obeyed My command."

Yet again, God emphasizes that Jewish chosenness is for the benefit of mankind (see, for example, Genesis 12:3). This is another reason the lessons of the Torah must be relevant to all people and should be taught to all people.

22.19 Abraham then returned to his servants, and they departed together for Beer-sheba; and Abraham stayed in Beer-sheba.

The word "stayed" in this context means "settled," which makes it clear that Abraham did not merely visit Beersheba; he made it his new home. This is highly significant in that it would mean that Abraham did not return to live with Sarah in Kiryat Arba (Hebron). In fact, the next time the Torah mentions Sarah (23:1), it is to chronicle her death in Kiryat Arba and to note that Abraham came from elsewhere (presumably Beersheba) to mourn her (Genesis 23:2). Rabbi Avraham Chen, an Israeli Orthodox scholar, raised the possibility that Abraham and Sarah lived apart in the aftermath of the *akedah,* perhaps because Sarah heard what had taken place and could not forgive her husband for what he had planned to do.

A mentor of mine, Rabbi Pinchas Peli, also believed the Torah makes clear Abraham and Sarah separated after the *akedah.* I can see no other explanation for the Torah not recording their ever speaking again, or their living in separate cities, many days' walking distance from one another.

Abraham, Isaac, and Sarah are one more of the many troubled families in Genesis. By describing every family in Genesis in such a way, the Torah does most of its readers a great service. It is calming to know even the matriarchs and patriarchs of the Bible had serious family problems. Those who have troubled families are therefore not alone; such families may well be the norm.

22.20 Some time later, Abraham was told, "Milcah too has borne children to your brother Nahor:

22.21 Uz the first-born, and Buz his brother, and Kemuel the father of Aram;

22.22 and Chesed, Hazo, Pildash, Jidlaph, and Bethuel"—

22.23 Bethuel being the father of Rebekah. These eight Milcah bore to Nahor, Abraham's brother.

Only one female name is listed here—Rebecca. Immediately after learning Isaac will not be sacrificed, we learn about the birth of his future wife, for it is through this couple that the line of God's people will continue.

22.24 And his concubine, whose name was Reumah, also bore children: Tebah, Gaham, Tahash, and Maacah.

Abraham's brother, Nahor, like Jacob later, had twelve sons.

CHAPTER
23

23.1 Sarah's lifetime—the span of Sarah's life—came to one hundred and twenty-seven years.

Regarding the number "127"—the number of years Sarah lived—whether or not one takes every lifespan in Genesis literally, the numbers are almost always significant in and of themselves (see the commentary on Genesis 47:28 concerning the lifespans of the three patriarchs). In this instance, the number "127" connotes 120 plus seven: 120 was the lifespan God ordained for human beings in Genesis 6:3 (Moses's age when he died); and seven is a sacred number that occurs repeatedly throughout the Torah: the days of creation, the weekly Sabbath, the Sabbatical year, etc.

If one holds the widely accepted view that the ages of people in Genesis usually convey meaning, Sarah's age at her death—120, the maximum lifespan (see commentary to Genesis 6:3 concerning exceptions to this rule) plus the sacred number seven—means she was a very important person. There is another indicator as well: Sarah, the Jewish people's founding matriarch, is the only woman in the Torah whose age at the time of her death is recorded.

23.2 Sarah died in Kiriath-arba—now Hebron—in the land of Canaan; and Abraham proceeded to mourn for Sarah, and to bewail her.

The word translated here as "proceeded" is the Hebrew word "came" or "went." This is important because it means Abraham travelled to where Sarah died in order to mourn her. That he had to travel from Beersheba, where he had settled after the *akedah* (see 22:19), to Kiryat Arba, where Sarah was living, clearly implies they were not living together at the time of her death. As noted in the previous chapter, it appears that Abraham and Sarah separated after Sarah learned of the near-sacrifice of Isaac (see commentary to Genesis 22:19): subsequent to that event, the Torah never mentions their being together.[1]

23.3 Then Abraham rose from beside his dead,

Abraham "rose" because he was sitting—"sitting *shiva*" ("sitting seven") days after the burial of an immediate relative.

23.3 (cont.) and spoke to the Hittites, saying,

The Hittites were the people living in this part of Canaan at the time.

23.4 "I am a resident alien among you; sell me a burial site among you, that I may remove my dead for burial."

Following Sarah's death, Abraham could have questioned God for promising him land in Canaan yet not giving him so much as a plot of land in which to bury his wife. Instead, he bought the land, thereby bringing about the fulfillment of God's promise through his own efforts.

Abraham's efforts to purchase the land that had already been promised to him by God provides a significant lesson: Even if God makes promises, humans may need to act to realize them, and to do so legally and morally—having God "on one's side" does not allow a person or a group either to do nothing or to act improperly. On the contrary, it is precisely those who claim God's providence who must act particularly decently. They have to earn the moral right to have God on their side by behaving as if they are on God's side. As Abraham Lincoln famously said, "My concern is not whether God is on our side; my greatest concern is to be on God's side, for God is always right."

As Abraham Lincoln famously said, "My concern is not whether God is on our side; my greatest concern is to be on God's side, for God is always right."

23.5 And the Hittites replied to Abraham, saying to him,

23.6 "Hear us, my lord: you are the elect of God among us.

Somehow the Hittites learned about God—presumably from Abraham, who earlier lived among them. We can assume Abraham spoke to them about God—precisely what Abraham's descendants should be doing today.

The Hittites treated Abraham with respect and graciousness. Once again, the greatest distinction in the Torah is between the moral and the immoral, not between Hebrew and non-Hebrew, the Jew and the non-Jew.

The greatest distinction in the Torah is between the moral and the immoral, not between Hebrew and non-Hebrew.

However, by the time of the Israelite conquest of Canaan, the moral life of the Hittites, as of the other Canaanite nations, had so deteriorated that they deserved to be vanquished.

23.6 (cont.) Bury your dead in the choicest of our burial places; none of us will withhold his burial place from you for burying your dead."

23.7 Thereupon Abraham bowed low to the people of the land, the Hittites,

Abraham demonstrated great respect and humility here and throughout this transaction.

23.8 and he said to them, "If it is your wish that I remove my dead for burial, you must agree to intercede for me with Ephron son of Zohar.

23.9 Let him sell me the cave of Machpelah that he owns,

This cave has enormous biblical and Jewish significance. The three patriarchs and three of the four matriarchs (all but Rachel) are buried in the cave. The final words spoken by Jacob before he died in Egypt were a request that his sons bury him in this cave. "After the Western Wall, it has remained throughout history the most sacred monument of the Jewish people" (Sarna).

23.9 (cont.) which is at the edge of his land. Let him sell it to me, at the full price, for a burial site in your midst."

23.10 Ephron was present among the Hittites; so Ephron the Hittite answered Abraham in the hearing of the Hittites, all who entered the gate of his town, saying,

23.11 "No, my lord, hear me: I give you the field and I give you the cave that is in it; I give it to you in the presence of my people. Bury your dead."

23.12 Then Abraham bowed low before the people of the land,

Abraham made sure the negotiation with Ephron took place publicly so that others would witness his legal acquisition of the land. The Torah repeats several times throughout this story that the transaction was performed in front of the Hittites to emphasize again and again that Abraham's right to the land was recognized by the local inhabitants. The fact this land was acquired in a legal sale is subsequently mentioned repeatedly in Genesis (Genesis 25:9-10; 49:30; 50:13).

23.13 and spoke to Ephron in the hearing of the people of the land, saying, "If only you would hear me out! Let me pay the price of the land;

Abraham refused Ephron's offer of the land as a free gift, insisting on paying the full price. He did not want anyone (such as a child or grandchild of Ephron) to later question or challenge his or his descendants' ownership.

29.13 (cont.) accept it from me, that I may bury my dead there."

23.14 And Ephron replied to Abraham, saying to him,

23.15 "My lord, do hear me! A piece of land worth four hundred shekels of silver—what is that between you and me?

Ephron made it sound as if four hundred shekels was a small sum—"What is that between you and me?"—but in actuality, it was a very large sum. Although it is very hard to draw monetary comparisons over millennia, it appears that a small plot of land, comparable in size to the Cave of Machpelah, was sold many centuries later for seventeen shekels (around 600 BCE, admittedly during an economic downturn—see Jeremiah 32:9).

23.15 (cont.) Go and bury your dead."

23.16 Abraham accepted Ephron's terms. Abraham paid out to Ephron the money that he had named in the hearing of the Hittites—four hundred shekels of silver at the going merchants' rate.

23.17 So Ephron's land in Machpelah, near Mamre—the field with its cave and all the trees anywhere within the confines of that field—passed

> The Torah explicitly states Abraham purchased not just the cave but also the area around it, so as to establish exactly which land belonged to him.

23.18 to Abraham as his possession, in the presence of the Hittites, of all who entered the gate of his town.

23.19 And then Abraham buried his wife Sarah in the cave of the field of Machpelah, facing Mamre—now Hebron—in the land of Canaan.

> This land was of great importance to Abraham because it was in Canaan: it represented a token title to the Promised Land and a symbol of possession.

23.20 Thus the field with its cave passed from the Hittites to Abraham, as a burial site.

> One more time, the Torah establishes Abraham's legitimate right to the land, which is the major purpose of this chapter. (Today, more than three thousand years later, the Jews' right to the patriarchs' and matriarchs' burial site is contested by many of the Jews' Arab neighbors).

CHAPTER 24

THE LONGEST CHAPTER IN GENESIS IS ABOUT... A MARRIAGE

Victor Hamilton makes an important point about this chapter: "It is interesting that the longest chapter in Genesis is given over to discussion of marriage and not, say, to the creation of the world or the covenant with Abraham."

There is a reason for this. As important as theology is, neither the Torah nor later Judaism is preoccupied with it. They are preoccupied with life.

The Torah's preoccupation is with living a morally good life and enjoying it. That is why, though the Torah alludes to the afterlife, it does not directly discuss it. So it makes sense the Torah would spend

> *From the Torah's perspective, it is better for a man to get married and know little about how the world was created than to never marry and know a great deal about how the world was created.*

more time on one man's marriage than on the creation of the world. From the Torah's perspective, it is better for a man to get married and know little about how the world was created than to never marry and know a great deal about how the world was created. (Ideally one does both.)

24.1 Abraham was now old, advanced in years,

Now that Abraham had acquired land in Israel, he sought to fulfill the second of God's promises to him: his descendants will have descendants. He therefore wanted to ensure his son Isaac, who seems to have possessed a passive disposition, gets married.

24.1 (cont.) and the Lord had blessed Abraham in all things.

24.2 And Abraham said to the senior servant of his household,

Jewish tradition holds that this is Eliezer, who was identified in Genesis 15:2 as Abraham's chief servant, but there is no textual evidence for this claim. Even though he remains anonymous, this servant deserves to be counted as one of the minor heroes of the Torah.

24.2 (cont.) who had charge of all that he owned,

The Hebrew word for "servant" (*eved*) is the same as "slave," denoting a broad category encompassing many levels of service. This verse is one of many examples in which "slave" does not do the word *eved* justice. This individual is called an *eved*, but he was obviously of very high status.

24.2 (cont.) "Put your hand under my thigh

In the ancient world, men made an oath with another man by holding that person's prized possession: his genitals. We get the English word "testify" from "testicle."[1] In our day, we consummate deals by signing contracts and shaking hands. While there was nothing sexual about the rite, this method might have been more effective. But I admit to a preference for handshakes and written contracts.

24.3 and I will make you swear by the Lord, the God of heaven and the God of the earth, that you will not take a wife for my son from the daughters of the Canaanites among whom I dwell,

Literally translated, the oath is taken in the name of "the Lord, the God of heaven and the God of the earth." While "God of heaven" is found in the Hebrew Bible almost two dozen times, this is the only time God is referred to as "the Lord, the God of heaven and the God of the earth." This singular usage serves to underscore how important it was to Abraham that his servant not take a Canaanite wife for Isaac.

Abraham was not trying to find his son a wife from within his clan; he insisted only that Isaac not marry a Canaanite. The Torah has contempt for the Canaanites, who were notorious for child sacrifice and other abominations. Later God specifically commanded the Jews not to act like Canaanites (see, for example, Leviticus 18:3).

The importance of shared values in a marriage is clear to any reader who is or has been married. But while shared values are necessary for a good marriage, they are not sufficient. Two people can share values but still not love one another.

24.4 but will go to the land of my birth and get a wife for my son Isaac."

Abraham did not tell his servant how to accomplish this task. As the servant entrusted with managing all of his possessions, Abraham had full confidence this man would devise an effective strategy to find an appropriate wife for Isaac, a woman who would serve as the vehicle for the succession of both Abraham's progeny and his religion.

The generally passive Isaac did not play a role in the choice of his wife, even though he was already forty (Genesis 25:20).

24.5 And the servant said to him, "What if the woman does not consent to follow me to this land, shall I then take your son back to the land from which you came?"

The servant didn't ask, "What if the woman does not consent to marry Isaac?" because before modern times (and in many countries even in modern times) few women had the right to choose their husbands. But in ancient societies, women could not always be forced to leave their people and country.

24.6 Abraham answered him, "On no account must you take my son back there!

Abraham's language is firm and direct. Canaan is the Promised Land and therefore Isaac, the conduit of God's promise, must remain there. (Abraham's wish was fulfilled; Isaac is the only one of the three patriarchs who never left the Promised Land.)

24.7 The Lord, the God of heaven, who took me from my father's house and from my native land, who promised me on oath, saying, 'I will assign this land to your offspring'—He will send His angel before you,

> Though Abraham informed his servant he could count on the help of an angel (a divinely appointed messenger), as we will see, no angel actually showed up. Perhaps Abraham had come to assume angels would appear at important moments. Or maybe this servant's competence carried the day and no angel was needed. Or perhaps a divine messenger did appear to the servant, and the servant did not recognize him as such. I do not believe this occurred, as the Torah would likely have made mention of it. I mention it only because I am certain this happens in all our lives—we miss a divinely ordained moment or messenger.

24.7 (cont.) and you will get a wife for my son from there.

24.8 And if the woman does not consent to follow you, you shall then be clear of this oath to me; but do not take my son back there."

24.9 So the servant put his hand under the thigh of his master Abraham and swore to him as bidden.

24.10 Then the servant took ten of his master's camels and set out, taking with him all the bounty of his master;

> "All the bounty of his master," gives the impression the servant took with him all of Abraham's wealth, an unlikely scenario. Richard Elliot Friedman, in his commentary on the Torah, renders the Hebrew more literally, and probably more accurately: "all of his lord's best things (*kol tuv*) were in his hand." What is clear is Abraham was very wealthy, and by sending a sample of his wealth, he hoped it would make a favorable impression on an intended wife's family.

24.10 (cont.) and he made his way to Aram-naharaim, to the city of Nahor.

24.11 He made the camels kneel down by the well outside the city,

at evening time, the time when women come out to draw water.

24.12 And he said, "O Lord, God of my master Abraham, grant me good fortune this day, and deal graciously with my master Abraham:

> The servant's request is the first individual petitionary prayer in the Torah.
>
> One lesson to be learned is anyone—not just an Abraham, but a servant—can talk to God and invite God into his or her life. Another lesson is the power of praying for the welfare of another—as the servant did here. Of course, one can pray to God on behalf of oneself, but there is something particularly noble about doing so on behalf of others.

24.13 Here I stand by the spring as the daughters of the townsmen come out to draw water;

> Presumably the servant reasoned the best place to find single women was by the well—the public square, so to speak—of the town.

24.14 let the maiden to whom I say, 'Please, lower your jar that I may drink,' and who replies, 'Drink, and I will also water your camels'—

> The servant brought ten camels with him (Genesis 24:10). If it took ten minutes for each camel to drink, a full watering would take at least an hour and forty minutes. This is a woman who would have to be quite generous with her time on behalf of a stranger, indicating a person of particular kindness.
>
> Here, as elsewhere in the Torah, decent treatment of the stranger is considered a paramount expression of goodness. When we do good for someone who knows us, there is always the possibility we can be repaid or at least acknowledged. But when we do good for a stranger, especially under circumstances where we will remain anonymous, the good we do cannot be repaid. This is true altruism.

ESSAY: GOODNESS IS MORE IMPORTANT THAN ANYTHING ELSE

The chief criterion here for choosing Isaac's spouse is goodness. This is the great lesson of this story. That should be the chief criterion for choosing a spouse, a friend, or a business partner. For most people, it is not. People place looks, personality, brains, wealth, or some other aspect of a person ahead of goodness—and often end up paying a terrible price for doing so. Goodness is not enough to ensure a happy marriage or friendship or partnership, but it is the single most important ingredient.

A rabbi I knew once told me he asked every couple who came to be married by him why they loved each other. One time, he told me, the woman said, "I love him because he's such a good dancer." He refused to conduct the wedding—he had little reason, he told me, to assume that marriage would last.

The odd thing about goodness is this: The thing almost everyone in the world most wants everyone else in the world to be is good. Yet, as a rule, what people most want for themselves is to be happy, smart, rich, famous, or powerful.

The Torah values goodness above all other human traits. In the Torah, God Himself identifies His essence as goodness (see Exodus 33:19 and the commentary there).

> *The thing almost everyone in the world most wants everyone else in the world to be is good. Yet, as a rule, what people most want for themselves is to be happy, smart, rich, famous, or powerful.*

That is the primary reason I not only revere the Torah but love it.

For decades, I have asked parents to ask their child, whether the child is fifteen or fifty years old: "What is it you think I—your mother (or father)—most want(ed) you to be: happy, smart, successful, or good?"

Innumerable parents have communicated to me their surprise when their child chose an answer other than "good." But it is not surprising. Few parents communicate to their child they care more about their child's goodness than about their grades or happiness or success. Frequently, when those children hear their parents bragging about them, it is usually about their intellectual, athletic, or artistic attainments, not their goodness. Far more parents have bragged to me about their child's attendance at a prestigious university than about their child's character. Why, then, would the children think their goodness is what matters most to their parents?

Another reason most people want to be something else more than they want to be good is they believe they are already good. Why aspire to become something you think you already are?

> *Why do most people think they are good? Because they assess their motives, not their behavior.*

Given how much meanness, dishonesty, and selfishness there is in the world, it is almost incredible how many people think they are good. And why do most people think they are good? Because they assess their motives, not their behavior or what results from it. And few people think they ever mean to do harm. Therefore, no matter how much bad people do, they continue to assess their motives—"I meant well"—rather than their actual behavior or the effects of their behavior. People assess *others* by their behavior or what that behavior produces; but they assess *themselves* by their motives.

How do you know if you are a good person?

One way is contained in a theory I developed regarding "life's three mirrors," the third of which reveals character.

LIFE'S THREE MIRRORS

If we want to see our face and body, we look into a mirror. That is the first mirror.

But what if we want to see our mind or our character? Are there mirrors for those?

It turns out there are.

The second mirror is the mirror of our mind. It is our writing. If you want to see your physical reflection, look at a mirror; if you want to see your mind, look at your writing. You will then be looking at a reflection of what is in your mind. And if your writing is not clear, it is most likely because your thinking is not clear.

I first came to realize this when I was in college and assigned to read essays and books whose writing was almost impossible to decipher. Like most students, I assumed the reason was my intellect was inferior to that of the writer—usually a professor. But I soon came to realize the problem wasn't mine; it was the writer's. The reason the writing was convoluted was the author's thinking was convoluted. This is disturbing to those who equate opacity with profundity.

Now, what if you want to see your character? What mirror is there for character?

The third mirror—the mirror of our character—is the people we attract into our lives. Good people attract good people; bad people do not. Of course, even good people will occasionally be fooled and bring bad people into their lives. But those who find they repeatedly attract people who cause them grief and who rarely attract quality people would do well to assess their character. If you assess your friends honestly and conclude they are good people, you are probably a good person. That's one of the main reasons they are in your life.

> *The mirror of our character is the people we attract into our lives. Good people attract good people; bad people do not.*

> *If you want to see your physical reflection, look at a mirror; if you want to see your mind, look at your writing.*

OBSERVE HOW A PERSON TREATS STRANGERS

24.14 (cont.) let her be the one whom You have decreed for Your servant Isaac. Thereby shall I know that You have dealt graciously with my master."

The servant devised a plan to test the character of a potential wife for Isaac—how does she treat strangers? This is a particularly good way to gauge the character of a potential spouse: observe how he or she treats strangers. It is often more instructive than observing how the person treats you. Someone you are dating will, of course, want to treat you well; this person wants something—love, sex, money, marriage—from you. It may therefore be more revealing of that individual's character to observe how he or she treats a stranger (a waiter, for example).

24.15 He had scarcely finished speaking, when Rebekah, who was born to Bethuel, the son of Milcah the wife of Abraham's brother Nahor,

> Rebecca was the daughter of Abraham's nephew. Abraham was, therefore, her great-uncle, which made Isaac her first cousin once removed. However, the servant did not yet know this.

24.15 (cont.) came out with her jar on her shoulder.

24.16 The maiden was very beautiful,

> Although the test itself was based on behavior, the servant decided to try it out on a beautiful woman first. The obvious reason is the powerful appeal of women's beauty. But there may be another reason: It is particularly impressive when a beautiful woman acts nobly, since she could easily rely on her beauty to impress people and get what she wants in life.

A particularly good way to gauge the character of a potential spouse: observe how he or she treats strangers (a waiter, for example).

24.16 (cont.) a virgin whom no man had known.

> The language of the Torah seems redundant. Isn't a virgin (*betulah*) by definition a woman "whom no man had known"? However, while *betulah* usually means "virgin," it does not always. In Joel 1:8, for example, we read, "Lament like a virgin girded with sackcloth for the husband of her youth."

It sometimes connotes a woman of marriageable age. To this day, a woman getting married for the first time is referred to in the Jewish marriage contract (*ketubah*) as a *betulah* (though no one today assumes all first-time brides are virgins). The Torah made Rebecca's status unambiguously clear by specifying that she was a *betulah* whom no man had known.

24.16 (cont.) She went down to the spring, filled her jar, and came up.

24.17 The servant ran toward her and said, "Please, let me sip a little water from your jar."

The servant asked for only a sip, purposely understating his request to see how the woman would react. Only a special person would respond by giving him his fill and offering water to his camels.

24.18 "Drink, my lord," she said, and she quickly lowered her jar upon her hand and let him drink.

This adverb, "quickly," appears again in verse 20; it reveals the kind of person Rebecca was. She didn't merely grant a stranger's request, she rushed to do so. In this regard, Rebecca was like her soon-to-be father-in-law, Abraham, who rushed to feed the strangers who passed near his tent (Genesis 18:6).

24.19 When she had let him drink his fill, she said, "I will also draw for your camels, until they finish drinking."

Rebecca didn't leave the servant there with the water and his camels; the Torah states three times between verses 19 and 22 she drew enough water for all the camels and waited for them to finish drinking.

Rebecca is "a continuous whirl of purposeful activity. In four short verses (Genesis 24:16, 18–20), she is the subject of eleven verbs of action and one of speech" (Alter).

24.20 Quickly emptying her jar into the trough, she ran back to the well to draw, and she drew for all his camels.

Rebecca's kindness to animals is another one of her virtues. Few Bible readers are aware there are more laws in the Torah legislating humane treatment of animals than there are, for example, about the Sabbath. To cite just two: It is forbidden to muzzle an ox while it is working in the field (Deuteronomy 25:4); the Torah regards muzzling an animal, thereby preventing it from eating any of the food it is threshing, as cruel. And the Ten Commandments ordains that one's animals rest on the Sabbath (Exodus 20:10).

> *Few Bible readers are aware there are more laws in the Torah legislating humane treatment of animals than there are, for example, about the Sabbath.*

In addition, refraining from cruelty to animals is one of the "Seven Noahide Laws," the laws the Jewish religion holds all mankind must observe; and it later became a significant factor in the laws of *kashrut*, which mandated slaughtering an animal in a manner that leads to its immediate demise to avoid undue suffering.

24.21 The man, meanwhile, stood gazing at her, silently wondering whether the Lord had made his errand successful or not.

The servant had yet to see whether the woman would actually wait for all his camels to drink as she had promised him.

24.22 When the camels had finished drinking, the man took a gold nose-ring weighing a half-shekel, and two gold bands for her arms, ten shekels in weight.

We have no reason to assume Rebecca regarded these gifts as anything related to a marriage proposal. But all that gold did make it clear the man behind these gifts was a man of great wealth.

24.23 "Pray tell me," he said, "whose daughter are you?

The servant still had no idea Rebecca was Abraham's relative. He gave her gifts not because of her family but because of her kindness.

24.23 (cont.) Is there room in your father's house for us to spend the night?"

24.24 She replied, "I am the daughter of Bethuel the son of Milcah, whom she bore to Nahor."

24.25 And she went on, "There is plenty of straw and feed at home, and also room to spend the night."

GRATITUDE: THE ROOT OF BOTH GOODNESS AND HAPPINESS

24.26 The man bowed low in homage to the Lord

The servant did not only make a request of God; he also offered a prayer of gratitude once his request had been granted. Prayers expressing gratitude are among the highest levels of prayer. Anyone can petition God (or people). The finest individuals are those who express gratitude after their request is fulfilled. It is almost impossible to overstate the power of gratitude. It is the root of both goodness and happiness. Ungrateful people cannot be either good or happy; indeed, such people are likely to be both bad and unhappy.

24.27 and said, "Blessed be the Lord, the God of my master Abraham, who has not withheld His steadfast faithfulness from my master. For I have been guided on my errand by the Lord, to the house of my master's kinsmen."

The servant didn't think he had stumbled across Rebecca's path by accident. He believed God had brought him to Rebecca, who was not just a fine young woman from the land of Abraham's birth but from his extended family as well.

24.28 The maiden ran and told all this to her mother's household.

24.29 Now Rebekah had a brother whose name was Laban. Laban ran out to the man at the spring—

Apparently, Rebecca's father didn't play much of a role in her household; her brother Laban was the source of authority.

24.30 when he saw the nose-ring and the bands on his sister's arms,

> The servant's wealth impressed Laban, who, we soon come to understand, greatly valued material possessions.

24.30 (cont.) and when he heard his sister Rebekah say, "Thus the man spoke to me." He went up to the man, who was still standing beside the camels at the spring.

24.31 "Come in, O blessed of the Lord," he said, "why do you remain outside, when I have made ready the house and a place for the camels?"

24.32 So the man entered the house, and the camels were unloaded. The camels were given straw and feed, and water was brought to bathe his feet and the feet of the men with him.

24.33 But when food was set before him, he said, "I will not eat until I have told my tale."

> Once again, the servant proved himself to be extraordinarily responsible and determined.

24.33 (cont.) He said, "Speak, then."

24.34 "I am Abraham's servant," he began.

24.35 "The Lord has greatly blessed my master, and he has become rich:

> The servant did not describe Abraham as God-fearing or as morally upright. He likely suspected Laban cared more about Abraham's wealth.

24.35 (cont.) He has given him sheep and cattle, silver and gold, male and female slaves, camels and asses.

24.36 And Sarah, my master's wife, bore my master a son in her old age, and he has assigned to him everything he owns.

24.37 Now my master made me swear, saying,

> When the servant recounted his master's instructions, he adjusted the details to suit his purpose. Abraham had his servant swear by "the Lord, the God of heaven and the God of the earth," but in relating the oath to Laban, the servant has thus far omitted all mention of God.

24.37 (cont.) 'You shall not get a wife for my son from the daughters of the Canaanites in whose land I dwell;

24.38 but you shall go to my father's house, to my kindred, and get a wife for my son.'

> The servant embellished the details of his instructions here. Abraham never told him Isaac was to marry a relative; he only said Isaac's wife should come from "the land of my birth." The servant's addition of this detail seems designed to make Laban think Rebecca—as a member of the extended family—is destined for his master's son.

24.39 And I said to my master, 'What if the woman does not follow me?'

24.40 He replied to me, 'The Lord, whose ways I have followed, will send His angel with you and make your errand successful; and you will get a wife for my son from my kindred, from my father's house.

> Once again, the servant relayed a detail Abraham did not include in his instructions. Nevertheless, this "detail" sticks in many readers' heads, who continue to think Abraham insisted his servant find a wife for Isaac from among his kinsmen.

24.41 Thus only shall you be freed from my adjuration: if, when you come to my kindred, they refuse you—only then shall you be freed from my adjuration.'

24.42 "I came today to the spring, and I said: O Lord, God of my master Abraham,

> Again, Abraham's oath had been in the name of "the Lord, the God of heaven and God of the earth." This time, the servant mentioned God, but minimally.

24.42 (cont.) if You would indeed grant success to the errand on which I am engaged!

24.43 As I stand by the spring of water, let the young woman who comes out to draw and to whom I say, 'Please, let me drink a little water from your jar,'

> Here, the servant faithfully related what happened; to impress Laban, this part of the story didn't need embellishing.

24.44 and who answers, 'You may drink, and I will also draw for your camels'—let her be the wife whom the Lord has decreed for my master's son.'

24.45 I had scarcely finished praying in my heart, when Rebekah came out with her jar on her shoulder, and went down to the spring and drew. And I said to her, 'Please give me a drink.'

24.46 She quickly lowered her jar and said, 'Drink, and I will also water your camels.' So I drank, and she also watered the camels.

24.47 I inquired of her, 'Whose daughter are you?' And she said, 'The daughter of Bethuel, son of Nahor, whom Milcah bore to him.' And I put the ring on her nose and the bands on her arms.

> The servant reversed the order of what actually happened. He said he first asked about Rebecca's family and then adorned her in jewelry, but in actuality, he adorned her before he knew she was a relative. The servant presumably wanted Laban to think Rebecca's family connection mattered greatly to him and to his master.

24.48 Then I bowed low in homage to the Lord and blessed the Lord, the God of my master Abraham, who led me on the right way to get the daughter of my master's brother for his son.

> For the third time, the servant claimed finding a relative was part of his original mission.

24.49 And now, if you mean to treat my master with true kindness, tell me; and if not, tell me also, that I may turn right or left."

The servant wasted no time in trying to get an answer from Laban. So anxious was he to accomplish his task, he wouldn't even eat until he was certain his mission has been completed successfully.

24.50 Then Laban and Bethuel answered,

At some point, Rebecca's father showed up to take part in the negotiation.

24.50 (cont.) "The matter was decreed by the Lord; we cannot speak to you bad or good.

The answer revealed the servant successfully convinced at least Laban that Rebecca was destined by God to marry his master's son.

24.51 Here is Rebekah before you; take her and go, and let her be a wife to your master's son, as the Lord has spoken."

24.52 When Abraham's servant heard their words, he bowed low to the ground before the Lord.

24.53 The servant brought out objects of silver and gold,

The servant knew that his work was not finished. After all, he didn't have to convince just Laban to consent to the marriage; he also had to convince Rebecca to agree to leave her family and people. In order to help accomplish this task, he now showered Rebecca with gifts of silver and gold, clearly communicating that she was being asked to join not only a wealthy and generous family, but one that also valued her kindness.

24.53 (cont.) and garments, and gave them to Rebekah; and he gave presents to her brother and her mother.

24.54 Then he and the men with him ate and drank, and they spent the night. When they arose next morning, he said, "Give me leave to go to my master."

24.55 But her brother and her mother said, "Let the maiden remain with us some ten days; then you may go."

Laban tried to delay Rebecca's departure, perhaps hoping to wrest more gifts from the servant. (Years later, he would successfully delay his nephew, Rebecca's son Jacob, by tricking him into working an extra seven years—Genesis 29:21-28). Rebecca's mother undoubtedly wanted to delay her daughter's departure simply out of maternal love. Twenty-four hours earlier, Rebecca was living at home with no thoughts of departure. Now a marriage proposal had been made, and Rebecca was being asked to leave immediately. For her mother, this was all happening too quickly.

24.56 He said to them, "Do not delay me, now that the Lord has made my errand successful.

The servant invoked God to intimidate Laban. Essentially, he was warning Laban, "If you start up with me, you're starting up with God."

24.56 (cont.) Give me leave that I may go to my master."

24.57 And they said, "Let us call the girl and ask for her reply."

Remarkably, given the time and place, Rebecca was asked to give her permission.

24.58 They called Rebekah and said to her, "Will you go with this man?" And she said, "I will."

Despite never having met her prospective husband, Rebecca assented to marry him. For whatever reasons, Rebecca was open to leaving her home and everything and everyone she had known. We cannot know for certain why she agreed to leave, but three possibilities suggest themselves. One, the servant did a remarkable job. Two, Rebecca was not unhappy to leave Laban and her parents. Three, between a future primarily consisting of watering camels and the wealth promised by this marriage proposal, the latter was far more appealing.

24.59 So they sent off their sister Rebekah and her nurse along with Abraham's servant and his men.

Given that we have no reason to think Rebecca is sickly, the nurse was likely her childhood nanny who had always remained close with her. Though unnamed here, we know this nurse's name was Deborah because her death is recorded in Genesis 35:8—a rare instance of the Torah recording the death of a non-famous person.

24.60 And they blessed Rebekah and said to her, "O sister! May you grow into thousands of myriads;

> To this day at Jewish weddings, these words of blessing are directed by the rabbi to a bride when she is veiled just prior to the wedding ceremony. (I suspect few Jews know this Jewish blessing was first offered by non-Jews.)

24.60 (cont.) May your offspring seize the gates of their foes."

24.61 Then Rebekah and her maids arose, mounted the camels, and followed the man. So the servant took Rebekah and went his way.

24.62 Isaac had just come back from the vicinity of Beer-lahai-roi, for he was settled in the region of the Negeb.

24.63 And Isaac went out walking in the field toward evening and, looking up, he saw camels approaching.

24.64 Raising her eyes, Rebekah saw Isaac. She alighted from the camel

24.65 and said to the servant, "Who is that man walking in the field toward us?" And the servant said, "That is my master." So she took her veil and covered herself.

> Rebecca's veiling of herself upon greeting her future husband is the origin of the custom of veiling the bride in the Jewish marriage ceremony.

24.66 The servant told Isaac all the things that he had done.

THE BIBLE'S FIRST REFERENCE TO LOVE

24.67 Isaac then brought her into the tent of his mother Sarah, and he took Rebekah as his wife. Isaac loved her,

The first reference to love in the Bible was Genesis 22:2, when God describes Abraham's love for his son Isaac. This is the second. The first described parent-child love; the second describes love for a spouse. These are the two greatest loves in life, and the Bible reflects the chronological order they follow.

According to this verse, Isaac first married Rebecca and then fell in love with her. In today's world, we think of love as a precondition for marriage, but in the ancient—and not-so-ancient—world, people married and then—hopefully—learned to love each other.

In a well-known scene from the musical *Fiddler on the Roof,* set in late nineteenth-century Russia, the dairyman, Tevye, struck by the romantic currents starting to affect his little village, turns to his wife and engages her in this dialogue:

> Tevye: Do you love me?
> Golde: I'm your wife!
> Tevye: I know. But do you love me?
> Golde: Do I love him? For twenty-five years I've
> lived with him, fought with him, starved with him.
> Twenty-five years my bed is his ...
> Tevye: Shh!
> Golde: If that's not love, what is?
> Tevye: Then, you love me!
> Golde: I suppose I do!
> Tevye: And I suppose I love you, too."

After a minute's reflection, Tevye continues: "It doesn't mean a thing, I know—but after twenty-five years, it's nice to know."

24.67 (cont.) and thus found comfort after his mother's death.

25.1 Abraham took another wife, whose name was Keturah.

25.2 She bore him Zimran, Jokshan, Medan, Midian, Ishbak, and Shuah.

Though this chapter follows the death of Sarah, it is unlikely it does so chronologically. As Sarna writes, "Over forty years earlier the patriarch [Abraham] had judged himself to be too old to sire children [Genesis 17:17]; it is hardly likely that he had six sons after the age of one hundred and forty. Hence, the present report does not relate to a time subsequent to Sarah's death and Isaac's marriage, but to many years before."

Richard Elliot Friedman refers to Keturah as "the most ignored significant person in the Torah." For one thing, as verse 2 records, one of the children she bore to Abraham was Midian, the ancestor of Jethro, Moses's greatest confidant and the father of Moses's wife, Tzipporah. In addition, Friedman notes, "The line of Levites who are descended from Moses [and Tzipporah]...derive from Abraham through both Sarah and Keturah."

25.3 Jokshan begot Sheba and Dedan. The descendants of Dedan were the Asshurim, the Letushim, and the Leummim.

25.4 The descendants of Midian were Ephah, Epher, Enoch, Abida, and Eldaah. All these were descendants of Keturah.

The purpose of these lists is to explain how these nations developed.

Given that Midian emerged as a bitter enemy of the Jews (see, for example, the Book of Numbers) this is another confirmation of the Torah's antiquity. A later Jewish author would not claim kinship between this hated nation and Abraham, the forefather of the Jewish people.

25.5 Abraham willed all that he owned to Isaac;

Abraham knew the heir of his tradition was to be his son Isaac.

25.6 but to Abraham's sons by concubines Abraham gave gifts while he was still living, and he sent them away from his son Isaac eastward, to the land of the East.

Although they would play no role in transmitting his heritage, Abraham treated the sons of his concubines generously. But he sent them away. He did not want them to influence Isaac, and he may have feared they would create trouble later, when, after Abraham's death, they realized they would not be co-heirs.

25.7 This was the total span of Abraham's life: one hundred and seventy-five years.

25.8 And Abraham breathed his last, dying at a good ripe age, old and contented;

This is a fulfillment of God's promise to Abraham that he will die in peace (Genesis 15:15). Abraham and Isaac are the only individuals in the Torah described as dying contented—unlike Moses, for example, who died deeply frustrated that he was unable to enter the Promised Land. In this sense, Abraham and Isaac are outliers—not only among personalities in the Torah, but among all humans. Most people die with at least some significant level of sadness—either because they die alone (or among strangers), too young, wracked with physical and/or emotional pain, fearing death, alienated from loved ones, or because their final years are unhappy ones. The list of reasons people die with sadness is a long one.

Given the rarity of happy endings to people's lives, it is vital we use happy memories to make our final days and years happier.

ESSAY: THE AFTERLIFE

25.8 (cont.) and he was gathered to his kin.

This idiomatic expression, "gathered to his kin," is also used to describe the deaths of Isaac, Ishmael, Jacob, Aaron, and Moses. The phrase strongly suggests the person has joined his/her kin in an afterlife. No other meaning of the phrase makes sense.

It cannot mean the dead person was buried with his kin—for two reasons. First, the expression "gathered to his kin" is used even when the person was not buried with his kin. In fact, the deaths of Abraham, Ishmael, Moses, and Aaron are each described as "gathered to his kin," yet none of them was buried in an ancestral grave. Second, the expression is used even before the person was buried. The individual is "gathered to his kin" upon dying, not upon being buried. Nor can the expression simply mean the person died because, as in this verse, the text has already stated the individual has died.

Abraham and Isaac are the only individuals in the Torah described as dying contented. In this sense, Abraham and Isaac are outliers—not only among personalities in the Torah, but among all humans.

Therefore, this expression must mean the person was united with his ancestors in the afterlife. Contrary to what many modern Jews believe, as the Encyclopedia Judaica, a major work of modern scholarship, states: "Judaism has always affirmed a belief in the afterlife." And, as we see here, this has likely been the case since the time of Abraham. Belief in the afterlife was not, as many scholars contend, a later adoption from Greek or Zoroastrian philosophy. Nahum Sarna, among others, refutes that contention:

"It would seem, therefore, that the existence of this idiom ["gathered to his kin"]…testifies to a belief that, despite his mortality and perishability, man possesses an immortal element that survives the loss of life. Death is looked upon as a transition to an afterlife where one is united with one's ancestors.

This interpretation contradicts the widespread, but apparently erroneous, view that such a notion is unknown in Israel until later times." (Italics added.)

Richard Elliott Friedman has offered another compelling argument for the Torah's affirmation of the afterlife. As many commentators have noted, the Torah is, among other things, a rejection of ancient Egypt and its values. Most prominent among Egypt's values was a preoccupation with the dead. Egypt's best-known symbols, the pyramids, were tombs; and Egypt's bible was *The Book of the Dead*. One would think, Friedman argues, that the Torah, in its desire to distinguish its values from those of Egypt, would have rejected the afterlife. But it never does.

Nevertheless, it also true that the Torah does not explicitly talk about the afterlife. The Torah wants human beings to focus on this life. Given how painful life has been for most people, it has always been tempting to ignore this world to the extent possible, and preoccupy oneself with the next.

Thus, in contradistinction to Egypt's holy work, *The Book of the Dead*, the Torah commands its followers to choose life: "I have set before you life and death, blessings and curses. Now *choose life*" (Deuteronomy 30:19, italics added). The Torah has been called throughout Jewish history a "Tree of Life" (*etz chayyim*). The Torah is so focused on this world, it forbids Jewish priests (*kohanim*) from having contact with dead bodies (Leviticus 21:1). I could find no other religion that forbade its priests from contact with the dead.

Since there is so much unjust suffering in this world, if God is just, there must be a place and time where ultimate justice prevails.

Beyond the Torah, there are another two compelling arguments for the existence of an afterlife:

First, unless the only reality is material, there is an immaterial reality. That immaterial reality is, first and foremost, God (other examples include the mind and information, which is conveyed through material—ink and paper, for example—but exists independently of it). And if there is an immaterial God, there is an immaterial reality—the human soul, for example.

Second, since there is so much unjust suffering in this world, if God is just, there must be a place and time where ultimate justice prevails—where the good are rewarded and the evil punished. That time and place can only be after this life. If people knew that if they acted badly in this world they would be immediately punished, there would no longer be free will (even career criminals don't commit crimes in the presence of police). So, then, *if God is just, it is axiomatic there is an afterlife.*

Jews who reject belief in the afterlife believe that Judaism has a different view of life and death. This was made clear to me at a funeral officiated by a Conservative rabbi. In his graveside remarks, he told the grieving family and friends of the deceased, "Judaism does not affirm a belief in an afterlife; rather, we live on through our good works and in the memories of loved ones."

The notion that human beings live on through their good works and the memories of loved ones—usually meaning a person's children and grandchildren—is largely meaningless, and often cruel.

That is what many, perhaps most, Jews believe today. But it is a mistake to equate what most Jews believe with what Judaism teaches. Most Jews do not observe the Sabbath, yet Judaism clearly teaches observance of the Sabbath, which is one of the Ten Commandments.

Meanwhile, the notion that human beings live on through their good works and the memories of loved ones—usually meaning a person's children and grandchildren—is largely meaningless, and often cruel. It is largely meaningless because, even if one has children and grandchildren, they, too, will die. And who really believes they will be remembered as more than a name, if that much, by their great-great-grandchildren? To take my own example, I know only the name—and little more—of one great-grandparent. Does that mean none of my other great-grandparents live on?

The notion we "live on" through the memories of loved ones means, at most, we live on for a hundred years. And then...what? If there is no afterlife, the answer is eternal oblivion.

The notion of living on through the memories of loved ones can also be cruel. What does one say to those who have no children? "Sorry, you don't live on"? Or "You'll live on as long as your friends are alive"?

This belief of living on through the memories of loved ones denies immortality to a large portion of the Jews murdered in the Holocaust—because for millions of them, all their loved ones, all those who had any memories of them, were also murdered.

Moreover, living on in anyone's memory—as beautiful and desirable as that is—is not the same as immortality. It is hardly a substitute for experiencing an afterlife. The American filmmaker Woody Allen put it best: "I don't want to achieve immortality through my work. I want to achieve it through not dying."

As regards living on through the good works one does, this, too, is rationally untenable. If one lives on through one's good works, clearly babies and most young children who die do not live on. Babies do not engage in good works. And the number of good works most children are capable of is minuscule.

As for the rest of us, the sad truth is bad works live on at least as long as, and often much longer than, good works. Indeed, if we live on through our work, Hitler, Stalin, and Mao, among others, will live on far longer than almost any good person who ever lived. Ask Holocaust survivors, their children, and their grandchildren how long Hitler's evil has lived on.

If we live on through our work, Hitler, Stalin, and Mao, among others, will live on far longer than almost any good person who ever lived.

If there is no afterlife, we don't live on. Period. Let's be honest enough to acknowledge this and not offer empty substitutes to make us feel better about dying. It is good to comfort people, but I am not alone in finding little comfort in the obviously meaningless or untrue.

Of course, none of this proves there is an afterlife. It means only that those who deny its existence should be courageous and honest enough not to offer palliatives in its place. If there is no afterlife, we return to dust and, with the exception of a few historical figures, are ultimately forgotten.

Those who doubt God's existence have every reason to doubt an afterlife. But for those who believe there is a just God, it is irrational to doubt an afterlife. And the God of the Torah is a just God. The first believer in this God, the first Jew, Abraham, established that (in his argument with God over Sodom).

What is the afterlife, and what happens there? There is no way for us mortals to know. All we can know is there is an afterlife.

I readily admit that my belief in a good God and an afterlife keep me sane. The thought that this life is all there is, that people are burned alive and that's their bad luck while their torturers get away with it and that's their good luck; that we form the most profound emotional bonds with family and friends yet will never be with them again after they or we die—such beliefs lie somewhere between depressing and maddening. It is difficult to understand how such beliefs do not drive people insane if they are sensitive to all the unjust suffering in the world.

The truth is it probably does drive many people a bit mad, which is why so many people, like the rabbi quoted at the beginning of this essay, concoct obviously untrue and sometimes unintentionally cruel substitutes such as living on through children's memories and through good works.

With the phrase, "gathered to his kin," the Torah offers us a hint—and substantial hope—there is something after this life. To its credit, the Torah spends no time on the subject. Think about the terrible effects resulting from preoccupation with the afterlife among those who believe slaughtering "infidels" ensures they will go straight to paradise. Preoccupation with the afterlife—including specific rewards, such as being greeted in heaven by seventy-two virgins—has been perhaps the single greatest driver of Islamist terror at the present time.

The Torah's view is we are supposed to be preoccupied with making *this* world as heavenly as possible. Those who live by its moral laws and values are best able to achieve that goal.

TO ISHMAEL'S CREDIT

25.9 His sons Isaac and Ishmael buried him in the cave of Machpelah, in the field of Ephron son of Zohar the Hittite, facing Mamre,

> Either Isaac and Ishmael got along with one another—the Torah never hints at a rift between them—or they reunited to bury their father. Either scenario is to the credit of Ishmael. He could easily have resented Isaac, whose birth set in motion events that culminated in his being forced to leave Abraham's house; and he could have easily resented his father Abraham, who sent him and his mother Hagar away for good. It is also possible, with the death of Sarah, who clearly bore great hostility to both Ishmael and his mother, Ishmael felt more comfortable reconnecting with Isaac.

25.10 the field that Abraham had bought from the Hittites; there Abraham was buried, and Sarah his wife.

> The Torah offers yet another reminder this cave was bought by Abraham and therefore was his rightful possession.

25.11 After the death of Abraham, God blessed his son Isaac. And Isaac settled near Beer-lahai-roi.

25.12 This is the line of Ishmael, Abraham's son, whom Hagar the Egyptian, Sarah's slave, bore to Abraham.

25.13 These are the names of the sons of Ishmael, by their names, in the order of their birth: Nebaioth, the first-born of Ishmael, Kedar, Adbeel, Mibsam,

25.14 Mishma, Dumah, Massa,

25.15 Hadad, Tema, Jetur, Naphish, and Kedmah.

25.16 These are the sons of Ishmael and these are their names by their villages and by their encampments: twelve chieftains of as many tribes.

Hamilton writes: "That Ishmael had so many children and that he enjoyed longevity are sure trademarks of the divine blessing."

He also notes the significance of twelve sons: Ishmael's twelve sons (see the prophecy of Genesis 17:20) parallel the twelve Aramean tribes (Genesis 22:20–24), the twelve Edomite tribes (Genesis 36:10–14), and the twelve tribes of Israel. "Perhaps the number twelve is dictated by the fact that each tribe was responsible to take a monthly turn in the maintenance of the central place of worship."

Once More, to Ishmael's Credit

25.17 These were the years of the life of Ishmael: one hundred and thirty-seven years; then he breathed his last and died, and was gathered to his kin.

This verse provides two more indications Ishmael must have been a good man. One is that despite his not being an Israelite, beginning with Abraham, the Hebrew Bible, which otherwise "only records the lifespans of the heroes of Israel" (Sarna), gives Ishmael's age at death. The second indication is the use of the phrase "gathered to his kin," which, aside from Ishmael, is used in the Torah to describe the deaths of only Abraham, Isaac, Jacob, Moses, and Aaron.

25.18 They dwelt from Havilah, by Shur, which is close to Egypt, all the way to Asshur; they camped alongside all their kinsmen.

Isaac, the Unknown Patriarch

25.19 This is the story of Isaac,

Isaac was overshadowed by his father Abraham and his son Jacob. However, references in the book of Amos to the "shrines of Isaac" and the "house of

Isaac" (see Amos 7:9, 16) suggest that a more extensive account of his life may have once existed.

One interesting difference is that, unlike both his father and son, whose names were changed—Abram to Abraham and Jacob to Israel—Isaac's name was never changed (perhaps because it was uniquely bestowed before his birth by God—Genesis 17:19).

Other differences:

Unlike other males of the period, Isaac remained monogamous throughout his life—and seems to have enjoyed a satisfying sensual life (see Genesis 26:8).

He was the only patriarch to engage in agriculture, a profession at which he was successful (Genesis 26:12).

He was the only patriarch never to set foot outside the Promised Land.

25.19 (cont.) son of Abraham. Abraham begot Isaac.

The Torah again states Abraham's paternity of Isaac. Some say the reason for this repetition is to reinforce the fact that Isaac was not the child of Abimelech and Sarah. But the Torah makes it clear Abimelech was not intimate with Sarah. Perhaps the repetition is there to make it crystal clear that the Abrahamic tradition runs through Isaac.

25.20 Isaac was forty years old when he took to wife Rebekah, daughter of Bethuel the Aramean of Paddan-aram, sister of Laban the Aramean.

25.21 Isaac pleaded with the Lord on behalf of his wife, because she was barren; and the Lord responded to his plea, and his wife Rebekah conceived.

The barrenness of Sarah and Rebecca is noted to reinforce the fact that their eventually conceiving children was an act of divine intervention.

25.22 But the children struggled in her womb, and she said, "If so, why do I exist?" She went to inquire of the Lord,

25.23 and the Lord answered her,

"Two nations are in your womb,

Two separate peoples shall issue from your body;

One people shall be mightier than the other,

God's words to Rebecca read in Hebrew like a poem.

Although God usually speaks to men in the Torah, here God speaks directly to a woman and transmits this important message about the destiny of Rebecca and Isaac's children to Rebecca alone. In fact, at this point, God has not yet spoken directly to Isaac.

ONCE AGAIN, THE YOUNGER OUTSHINES THE OLDER

25.23 (cont.) And the older shall serve the younger."

The final line of the prophecy makes clear Rebecca was privy to God's plan to make the younger twin the conduit of Abraham and Isaac's God-based monotheism. She will carry this knowledge with her when she later helps Jacob trick his father into bestowing on Jacob the "innermost blessing"—which Isaac intended to confer on his eldest son, Esau (chapter 27). This blessing from God to Rebecca makes clear that when Jacob maneuvered Esau into selling him his birthright, Jacob was putting God's plan into action.

In the Torah, the younger is repeatedly depicted as the more worthy and/or divinely chosen brother: Abel-Cain, Isaac-Ishmael, Joseph-his elder brothers, and Moses-Aaron, to cite the most obvious examples.

25.24 When her time to give birth was at hand, there were twins in her womb.

When God says something will happen, it happens.

25.25 The first one emerged red, like a hairy mantle all over; so they named him Esau.

25.26 Then his brother emerged, holding on to the heel of Esau; so they named him Jacob.

According to this verse, the name Jacob (*Yaakov*) comes from the Hebrew word *aykev*, which means "heel."

25.26 (cont.) Isaac was sixty years old when they were born.

As Isaac was forty when he married Rebecca (see verse 20), it was twenty years before the couple had children.

IS HUNTING A MORAL ISSUE?

25.27 When the boys grew up, Esau became a skillful hunter, a man of the outdoors; but Jacob was a mild man who stayed in camp.

Although they were twins, Jacob and Esau could not have been more different from one another. As every parent of more than one child knows, children are born with distinctive personalities.

The Torah implies a preference for Jacob's mild-mannered personality to Esau's roughness and fondness for hunting. As noted on a number of occasions, the Torah is greatly concerned with how human beings treat animals. As Sarna notes, hunting as a way of life was held in low esteem in Israel: "Near Eastern art often portrays kings and nobles in pursuit of game, but no Israelite or Judean king or hero is ever mentioned as engaging in this sport...."

Though I share the Torah's and later Judaism's view of hunting, I have known extremely fine individuals who hunt. These individuals enjoy the sport of hunting; they do not enjoy animal suffering. And nearly all of these people eat the animals they kill. I therefore do not equate all forms of hunting with low character. Moreover, given the low moral state of much animal slaughtering, those of us who do not hunt but eat animals are rarely in a position to condemn hunters. Having said this, I still could not bring myself to hunt.

25.28 Isaac favored Esau because he had a taste for game; but Rebekah favored Jacob.

In a world of food scarcity—which was most of the world through most of its history—families regarded whoever obtained food for the family as a hero. Isaac was no exception. But he favored Esau for more than obtaining food; Isaac "had a taste for game."

Whatever the reason, Isaac preferred the wrong son. It was his wife Rebecca who knew which son would carry on Abraham's and God's vision.

25.29 Once when Jacob was cooking a stew, Esau came in from the open wilderness, famished.

Jacob was a homebody who enjoyed domestic tasks such as cooking.

25.30 And Esau said to Jacob, "Give me some of that red stuff to gulp down, for I am famished"— which is why he was named Edom.

Esau actually said, "Give me some of the red red stuff." The Torah offers a play on words here: The Hebrew word for "red" (*adom*) sounds like *Edom*, which was the place where Esau's descendants would settle.

25.31 Jacob said, "First sell me your birthright."

25.32 And Esau said, "I am at the point of death, so of what use is my birthright to me?"

Esau actually said, "I'm going to die," just as a hungry teenager might say today, "I'm starving from hunger." But this was obviously an exaggeration; Esau was hardly on the brink of death. After a long day of hunting, Esau was, however, very hungry and tired.

Was Jacob Morally Wrong in Getting Esau to Sell the Birthright?

25.33 But Jacob said, "Swear to me first." So he swore to him, and sold his birthright to Jacob.

Jacob's behavior is often viewed as unscrupulous. But it is quite defensible. First of all, Jacob neither tricked nor threatened his brother; he simply saw an opening and tried to strike a deal, and Esau willingly complied. As the next verse importantly states, Esau could not have cared less about the birthright—"Esau had contempt for the birthright." And, of course, Esau had never earned the birthright—he just happened to leave their mother's womb a few minutes before Jacob did. It was pure chance that made Esau the firstborn, and therefore entitled to the best blessings his father had to bestow. Jacob was not bargaining to obtain some prized, let alone earned, possession of Esau.

To understand this defense of Jacob, let us imagine a man whose late father left him his personal collection of Shakespeare plays—not because the son had any reverence for Shakespeare, but because he was the firstborn. Now imagine the younger son did revere Shakespeare and offered his older brother a delicious meal for the Shakespeare collection at a moment of the older brother's weakness. Would that be wrong? And if so, why?

Jacob shared his father's values and valued the blessings that would come with the birthright. He asked for it in exchange for soup, and Esau readily agreed. And the Torah, in the very next verse, makes clear why he did.

25.34 Jacob then gave Esau bread and lentil stew; he ate and drank, and he rose and went away. Thus did Esau spurn the birthright.

Esau didn't have a second thought about selling the birthright to his brother. If he had cared at all or had any regret, he would have asked for it back once he regained his strength, arguing that it wasn't a fair trade; instead, he was content to leave with a full stomach. Lest there be any doubt in the reader's mind as to how little Esau valued the birthright, the concluding words of the chapter, rendered literally, read, "And Esau despised the birthright."

CHAPTER 26

26.1 There was a famine in the land—aside from the previous famine that had occurred in the days of Abraham—and Isaac went to Abimelech, king of the Philistines, in Gerar.

Isaac was on his way to Egypt in search of food in a time of famine, just as his father Abraham did. He stopped in Gerar on his way, believing he would be treated well there, since Abraham had entered into a contract of peace with the king of Gerar (Genesis 20:14-18).

WHAT DOES BELIEF IN GOD MEAN?

26.2 The Lord had appeared to him and said, "Do not go down to Egypt; stay in the land which I point out to you.

That is, in the Land of Israel.

God spoke very similar words to Abraham when He told him to go to the place that He would show him (Genesis 12:1). For both men, it was a test of faith. In Abraham's case, the test was to go to an unknown land. In Isaac's case, the test was whether he would trust God to provide food during a famine.

When we moderns speak of faith or belief in God, we are almost always referring to belief in God's existence. "Do you believe in God?" means "Do you believe God exists?" That is never a question in the Bible. Therefore, God was not testing Isaac (or Abraham before him) with regard to faith in His existence. That would have been absurd—who, after all, was speaking to them? The faith issue concerned God's promises, not His existence. Throughout the Bible, God's existence is a given. "Faith," therefore, always refers to acting upon a belief that God will do as He promises. The more precise English word would be "trust."

26.3 Reside in this land, and I will be with you and bless you; I will assign all these lands to you and to your heirs, fulfilling the oath that I swore to your father Abraham.

26.4 I will make your heirs as numerous as the stars of heaven, and assign to your heirs all these lands,

HUMANITY WILL BE BLESSED THROUGH THE JEWS

26.4 (cont.) so that all the nations of the earth shall bless themselves by your heirs—

The purpose of the Jewish people is to serve as a vehicle for God's blessing of the world, a theme that is stated five times in Genesis (12:3; 18:17-18; 22:16-18; 26:3-4; 28:10-14). That God wants a people to bless all mankind is another unprecedented idea in the Torah.

Many Jews, including those far removed from Jewish religious faith and practice, continue to believe in a universal mission for Jews. A good example was Walter Rathenau, the German foreign minister during the Weimar Republic (the German democracy that existed between the two World Wars):

"Do you know why we Jews were born into this world? In order to call every human being to Sinai. You don't want to go there? Well, if I don't call you, Marx will. If Marx doesn't, then Spinoza will. If not Spinoza, Christ will summon you."[1]

Rathenau's statement helps explain why Jews have disproportionately founded, led, or been involved in utopian causes such as Marxism and socialism. They have been influenced, often not consciously, by the Bible and Judaism's universal mission. However, nearly all of these Jews dropped commitment to God and Torah, and often wound up doing more harm than good for both humanity and the Jews. Jewish idealism without God, Torah and Israel (the three components of Judaism) has often been destructive, sometimes murderously so.

At the same time, Judaism without universal concerns has also not helped the world or fulfilled God's mission for the Jews. Jews need to take the Torah to the world and neither drop it nor hide it.

26.5 inasmuch as Abraham obeyed Me and he kept My charge: My commandments, My laws, and My teachings."

The prominent medieval commentator Nachmanides (Ramban) explained this verse in this way:

"'My charge' is faith in Divinity, that he believed in the unique God and that he kept this charge in his heart and he differed from the idolaters about it and called in the name of the Lord to bring back many to the service [of God].

"'My commandments' is like all that He had commanded him, in 'Go forth from your land,' and with the raising of his son [for a sacrifice] and the sending away of 'the maidservant and her son'.

"'My ordinances' is going in the ways of God, to be 'graceful and merciful' and 'to do righteousness and justice' and 'to command his children and his household' about [these things].

"'My laws' is circumcision on himself and on his children and servants, and all of the commandments of the Children of Noah, as they are the law to them."

26.6 So Isaac stayed in Gerar.

26.7 When the men of the place asked him about his wife, he said, "She is my sister," for he was afraid to say "my wife," thinking, "The men of the place might kill me on account of Rebekah, for she is beautiful."

This is the third time this situation arises in Genesis: first with Abraham in Egypt, then with Abraham in Gerar, and now with Isaac in Gerar. (As in the incident with Abraham, the king is named Abimelech; but given that many years have passed, this is likely a different King Abimelech—perhaps the son of the Abimelech whom Abraham had encountered).

26.8 When some time had passed, Abimelech king of the Philistines, looking out of the window, saw Isaac fondling his wife Rebekah.

> The word translated as "fondling" (*mitzachek*)—many translations say "caressing"—derives from the Hebrew word for laughter and depicts erotic activity. The Torah has a realistic attitude towards the erotic. It does not consider it dirty but rather as a part of life for enjoyment (in permitted ways, of course) and not only for procreation.
>
> Here we learn a little more about Isaac. Whatever passivity he may have exhibited elsewhere, Isaac seems to have been a passionate husband.

26.9 Abimelech sent for Isaac and said, "So she is your wife! Why then did you say: 'She is my sister?'" Isaac said to him, "Because I thought I might lose my life on account of her."

26.10 Abimelech said, "What have you done to us! One of the people might have lain with your wife, and you would have brought guilt upon us."

ON TRUSTING STRANGERS

26.11 Abimelech then charged all the people, saying, "Anyone who molests this man or his wife shall be put to death."

> This episode seems less dramatic than the previous two. There is no kidnapping of a wife, no gifts exchanged, no punishment is inflicted on the ruler, and there is no divine intervention. Perhaps this king, if he wasn't the same man with whom Abraham dealt, knew of or remembered what had happened with Abraham and Abraham's God and did not want to invite trouble on his kingdom.
>
> We assume Abimelech made this decree to protect Isaac and Rebecca because in Gerar, as in most places in the world, it was not uncommon to kill strangers and take their wives (which would mean Isaac's fear was legitimate). As we have seen throughout Genesis (e.g., chapter 19), the stranger was rarely treated decently in ancient Near Eastern societies—or, as far as we can ascertain, anywhere else

in the world—which makes the repeated Torah injunction to love and protect the stranger all the more remarkable.

One of life's puzzles is to know when one can trust a stranger. My own attitude has been to trust strangers in good societies unless they exhibit (through dress, speech, attitude, and, of course, behavior) reasons not to trust them. It is better to risk disappointment than never to trust. However, when visiting less decent societies, it may be wiser to be wary of strangers. One of the terrible evils of immoral governments and of crime-ridden societies is that they cause people to trust almost no one. In Communist East Germany, for example, it is estimated that up to two million people (out of a population of eleven million) were secret police (*Stasi*) or unofficial informers working for the regime.[2]

26.12 Isaac sowed in that land and reaped a hundredfold the same year.

Isaac was the only patriarch who engaged in agriculture. He was an unusually productive farmer and businessman (as related in the following verses).

26.12 (cont.) The Lord blessed him,

To Envy or to Emulate the Successful? That Is the Question.

26.13 and the man grew richer and richer until he was very wealthy:

26.14 he acquired flocks and herds, and a large household, so that the Philistines envied him.

26.15 And the Philistines stopped up all the wells which his father's servants had dug in the days of his father Abraham, filling them with earth.

As unlikely as it may seem, these three verses are among the most important in the Torah. They also demonstrate why the Torah is as relevant today as it was three thousand years ago—because it illuminates human nature, and human nature doesn't change.

These verses encapsulate Jewish and human history. Instead of emulating the successful, most people envy them, and then often wish to destroy their wealth—and sometimes even them.

The most notable exception to this unfortunate rule of human nature has been the American people. Until almost the present day, Americans tended to react to people who had attained material success not by resenting them but by wanting to know how they could emulate them. This seems to be changing as more Americans join others in resenting the economic success of other people. Like the Philistines here, most people would rather fill the wells of the world's Abrahams than learn how to dig wells with water.

> *The Torah is as relevant today as it was three thousand years ago—because it illuminates human nature, and human nature doesn't change.*

The envy of Abraham, Isaac, and their descendants is the theme of an important book by a major thinker, George Gilder. Titled *The Israel Test*, the book documents how envy of Israel's accomplishments has animated much of the hatred directed at the Jewish state. That envy has also been a significant factor in Jew-hatred for thousands of years.[3]

26.16 And Abimelech said to Isaac, "Go away from us, for you have become far too big for us."

This story is a paradigm of much of Jewish history. Jews arrive somewhere as strangers, become economically successful, and then are considered a threat to the original inhabitants, who then expel (and/or kill) the Jews.

26.17 So Isaac departed from there and encamped in the wadi of Gerar, where he settled.

26.18 Isaac dug anew the wells which had been dug in the days of his father Abraham and which the Philistines had stopped up after Abraham's death; and he gave them the same names that his father had given them.

Isaac used the same names to make clear that the wells belong to his family.

26.19 But when Isaac's servants, digging in the wadi, found there a well of spring water,

26.20 the herdsmen of Gerar quarreled with Isaac's herdsmen, saying, "The water is ours."

> The herdsman of Gerar could, of course, have tried to learn well-digging techniques from Isaac's herdsmen, but instead they became jealous and resentful.

26.20 (cont.) He named that well Esek, because they contended with him.

26.21 And when they dug another well, they disputed over that one also; so he named it Sitnah.

26.22 He moved from there and dug yet another well,

> Isaac was apparently a peace-loving man. Each time the herdsmen of Gerar disputed his claim after Isaac's men did the work, he moved away and dug another well. He was not a fighter like his father Abraham (see chapter 14) or his son Jacob.

26.22 (cont.) and they did not quarrel over it; so he called it Rehoboth, saying, "Now at last the Lord has granted us ample space to increase in the land."

26.23 From there he went up to Beer-sheba.

26.24 That night the Lord appeared to him and said, "I am the God of your father Abraham.

> God introduced Himself by referencing Isaac's father because the familial and tribal characteristics of religion were, at that point, meaningful to him. Before the Torah, no religion had posited a universal god.

> *Like the Philistines here, most people would rather fill the wells of the world's Abrahams than learn how to dig wells with water.*

26.24 (cont.) Fear not, for I am with you, and I will bless you and increase your offspring for the sake of My servant Abraham."

> Once again God says "Do not fear." As noted in the commentary to Genesis 15:1, this is the most frequent statement of God to man in the Hebrew Bible.

26.25 So he built an altar there and invoked the Lord by name. Isaac pitched his tent there and his servants started digging a well.

26.26 And Abimelech came to him from Gerar, with Ahuzzath his councilor and Phicol chief of his troops.

26.27 Isaac said to them, "Why have you come to me, seeing that you have been hostile to me and have driven me away from you?"

Peacemaker though he has been, Isaac finally had enough of the aggression and stood up for himself.

26.28 And they said, "We now see plainly that the Lord has been with you, and we thought: Let there be a sworn treaty between our two parties, between you and us. Let us make a pact with you

26.29 that you will not do us harm, just as we have not molested you but have always dealt kindly with you and sent you away in peace.

Given that Abimelech's herdsmen had dumped dirt into Isaac's wells, this was hardly a truthful statement. But it illustrates two common and unfortunate human traits:

One is to "rewrite history," to distort or even lie about the past in order to look good. The other is to assume that our motives are disinterested and pure when, in fact, they rarely are. Even when they are pure, it is actions—not motives—that matter most. And here, only once they realized God favored Isaac (verse 28) did their actions improve (if not their motives, which remained purely self-interested: they wanted to protect themselves against what they recognized as a superior force—the God of Isaac).

26.29 (cont.) From now on, be you blessed of the Lord!"

26.30 Then he made for them a feast, and they ate and drank.

26.31 Early in the morning, they exchanged oaths. Isaac then bade them farewell, and they departed from him in peace.

26.32 That same day Isaac's servants came and told him about the well they had dug, and said to him, "We have found water!"

26.33 He named it Shibah; therefore the name of the city is Beer-sheba to this day.

26.34 When Esau was forty years old, he took to wife Judith daughter of Beeri the Hittite, and Basemath daughter of Elon the Hittite;

26.35 and they were a source of bitterness to Isaac and Rebekah.

> By taking wives from among the pagan tribes, Esau confirmed he was unworthy of serving as the heir to the religious heritage of Abraham and Isaac.

CHAPTER
27

Chapter 27 describes the third conflict between the brothers Jacob and Esau. The first was in the womb and at birth (Genesis 25:21–28); the second was over the birthright (Genesis 25:29–34); and the third, in this chapter, is over the birthright blessing from their father Isaac. Every family in Genesis had profound conflicts. Families without conflict exist, but they are not the norm. One way to view the Torah and the rest of the Bible is as an instruction manual into how to elevate our lives despite our troubled origins.

27.1 When Isaac was old and his eyes were too dim to see, he called his older son Esau

That the Torah refers to Esau as Isaac's "older son" (*b'no ha-gadol*) rather than his "firstborn" (*b'choro*) strongly suggests the Torah views the sale of the birthright as valid. Esau will always be the chronologically older son (albeit by a matter of minutes), but the Torah no longer considers him to have the status of "firstborn."

27.1 (cont.) and said to him, "My son." He answered, "Here I am."

Esau answered with the Hebrew word *hineni*, which is the same response that Abraham gave to God (Genesis 22:1) and that Joseph will later give to Jacob (Genesis 37:13). This term, which is similar to "Yes, sir," shows Esau was a dutiful son. In fact, the Torah never depicts Esau as a bad person, only as unworthy of, and uninterested in, carrying on the Abrahamic monotheistic tradition.

27.2 And he said, "I am old now, and I do not know how soon I may die.

27.3 Take your gear, your quiver and bow, and go out into the open and hunt me some game.

This request provides another indication (as does Abraham's serving milk and meat to his guests—Genesis 18:8) the patriarchs were unfamiliar with many later Jewish laws. The laws of kosher slaughtering, which ordain that animals permitted for consumption be slaughtered with one smooth stroke that kills an animal almost instantly, would forbid shooting an animal intended for a meal with a bow and arrow since that could result in a prolonged death.

As noted, such records of pre-Jewish-law behaviors of the patriarchs should be welcomed by traditional believers. They are powerful evidence for the antiquity and therefore the authenticity of the Torah text. If the Torah had been written much later, it is highly unlikely that practices of the patriarchs that ran contrary to later Jewish ritual laws would have been included.

27.4 Then prepare a dish for me such as I like, and bring it to me to eat, so that I may give you my innermost blessing before I die."

We know Isaac favored Esau over Jacob because he liked the food Esau hunted and prepared for him (Genesis 25:28). One might have expected more substance from a biblical patriarch. This, then, is yet another example of the Torah putting truth above hagiography in its portrayal of biblical heroes.

It is clear from Rebecca's reaction (see the next three verses) this is no ordinary blessing but one of supreme importance. Both Jacob and Rebecca sensed Isaac's death was imminent.

The Hebrew rendered here as "so that I may give you my innermost blessing" literally means "so that my soul may bless you." The blessing came from the depths of Isaac's soul.

At this point, Esau could have confessed to his father he no longer possessed the birthright and may not have been deserving of this blessing. His failure to do so was also a form of deception, something rarely (if ever) mentioned in discussions of this episode.

27.5 Rebekah had been listening as Isaac spoke to his son Esau. When Esau had gone out into the open to hunt game to bring home,

27.6 Rebekah said to her son Jacob, "I overheard your father speaking to your brother Esau, saying,

27.7 'Bring me some game and prepare a dish for me to eat, that I may bless you, with the Lord's approval, before I die.'

In relating Isaac's instructions to Esau, Rebecca inserted the words "with the Lord's approval" to impress upon Jacob the blessing was part of a divine plan.

HUMAN INTERVENTION MAY BE WARRANTED TO BRING ABOUT GOD'S PLANS

27.8 Now, my son, listen carefully as I instruct you.

Rebecca was quite a woman. She was not only particularly kind (Genesis 24:15-25), she was particularly strong and decisive. The plan to ensure Jacob received the birthright blessing from Isaac was entirely her idea.

We have no reason to think she was a deceptive person. However, she had not forgotten God's statement to her that the older son would serve the younger. She realized if she did not intervene, Esau would receive the blessing God intended for Jacob (Genesis 25:23).

One might ask why God communicated only with Rebecca on the matter of the birthright. Perhaps it's because God is more likely to speak with those who are more likely to act on what God says.

Rebecca acted because human intervention is often warranted to bring about God's plans. That is likely why God told Rebecca what to expect for her sons. The idea that God alone will bring about all His aims is foreign to the Torah. On the contrary, humans are not allowed to do nothing and wait for God to act.

The idea that God alone will bring about all His aims is foreign to the Torah. On the contrary, humans are not allowed to do nothing and wait for God to act.

An example of religious people doing nothing while waiting for God to act involved Zionism, the late nineteenth and early twentieth century movement to re-establish the Jewish homeland in Israel. Many religious Jews did not originally join the Zionist movement, arguing that only God could re-establish the Jewish state. (By the time the modern state of Israel was declared in 1948, nearly all religious Jews acknowledged their error and came not only to support Israel but to become among its most fervent supporters.)

27.9 Go to the flock and fetch me two choice kids, and I will make of them a dish for your father, such as he likes.

27.10 Then take it to your father to eat, in order that he may bless you before he dies."

27.11 Jacob answered his mother Rebekah, "But my brother Esau is a hairy man and I am smooth-skinned.

27.12 If my father touches me, I shall appear to him as a trickster and bring upon myself a curse, not a blessing."

Jacob was more concerned with his father's reaction to detecting the deception than with the morality of deceiving him. A close reading of Jacob's words strongly implies he did not believe he was doing anything wrong. He did not say, "If my father touches me, he will realize that I am a trickster"; rather, he says, "I will *appear to him* as a trickster."

Jacob thought—not without merit—that his brother was the real trickster, since Esau was planning to claim the birthright blessing he had relinquished. Yet Jacob couldn't tell his father the truth because he knew his father favored Esau and would probably look askance at how Jacob had procured the birthright.

THE WOMAN IN THIS FAMILY IS THE STRONGEST PERSON IN IT

27.13 But his mother said to him, "Your curse, my son, be upon me! Just do as I say and go fetch them for me."

Rebecca was willing to take full moral responsibility for her plan—another example of her character and her strength. She was prepared to be judged by

God and to defend her actions before Him. Yet, though her plan was successful, in a certain sense, she was cursed by this event (though not necessarily by God—life has consequences for our behaviors independent of divine action). Subsequent to this episode, Jacob was forced to flee for his life, and though Rebecca believed he would be away for only a few days (see verse 44), he wound up being away for twenty years. The Torah does not record whether mother and son ever saw each other again.

27.14 He got them and brought them to his mother, and his mother prepared a dish such as his father liked.

27.15 Rebekah then took the best clothes of her older son Esau, which were there in the house, and had her younger son Jacob put them on;

27.16 and she covered his hands and the hairless part of his neck with the skins of the kids.

27.17 Then she put in the hands of her son Jacob the dish and the bread that she had prepared.

It is noteworthy that whenever this story is discussed, the culpability for the deception is placed on Jacob even though the plot was entirely conceived and orchestrated by his mother. Rebecca was clearly the active player. One example is described in this verse: She prepared the food and even placed it in her son's hands.

27.18 He went to his father and said, "Father."

Jacob probably wanted to speak as little as possible lest his father recognize his voice.

Or perhaps Jacob was nervously testing the waters. If Isaac recognized his voice and responded, "What is it you want, Jacob?" Jacob would likely have dropped the whole charade.

27.18 (cont.) And he said, "Yes, which of my sons are you?"

This was the first of four tests Isaac used to determine which son he was about to bless.

Isaac appears to have been suspicious from the very beginning. Many commentators, both modern and medieval, have suggested that throughout this episode, Isaac was subconsciously aware of Jacob's identity yet pretended to be deceived. In the view of these commentators, although Esau was his preferred son and the one he still regarded as the firstborn, Isaac nevertheless realized on some level that Esau was not the one to carry out God's promise to Abraham.

27.19 Jacob said to his father, "I am Esau, your first-born;

Having procured the birthright from Esau, claiming "first-born" status was not entirely a lie. But saying "I am Esau" was.

That being said, I do not believe Jacob found deceiving his father easy. He did what he did at the command of his mother, whose judgment he thoroughly trusted. He also probably assumed if his father understood the situation as Rebecca did, he would have come to a similar conclusion regarding the birthright.

27.19 (cont.) I have done as you told me. Pray sit up and eat of my game, that you may give me your innermost blessing."

In his imitation of Esau, Jacob spoke almost the exact words that Isaac had used and Esau would later use (see verse 31). The only significant difference between their statements is Jacob's use of the word *na* (translated here as "pray," and often translated as "please") in requesting his father sit up and eat. (See comments on the word *na* in Genesis 22:2.)

27.20 Isaac said to his son, "How did you succeed so quickly, my son?" And he said, "Because the Lord your God granted me good fortune."

Sarna criticizes Jacob for invoking God's name in an outright lie. In Jacob's defense, he undoubtedly believed—thanks to his mother—that God was behind the whole project. There is no reason to believe Jacob thought he was violating God's will in receiving Isaac's blessing.

27.21 Isaac said to Jacob, "Come closer that I may feel you, my son—whether you are really my son Esau or not."

> Still not convinced it is Esau before him, Isaac tried a second test, this time using his sense of touch to verify whom he is interacting with.

27.22 So Jacob drew close to his father Isaac, who felt him and wondered. "The voice is the voice of Jacob, yet the hands are the hands of Esau."

> This is one of the most famous lines in the Bible. Writers and speakers have used this phrase to describe confusion and/or deception for thousands of years. It beautifully describes what we call "mixed signals."

27.23 He did not recognize him, because his hands were hairy like those of his brother Esau; and so he blessed him.

A PLAUSIBLE DEFENSE OF JACOB'S DECEPTIVE BEHAVIOR

27.24 He asked, "Are you really my son Esau?" And when he said, "I am,"

> When a child reads this, the story can be—and ought to be—disturbing: How could Jacob so blatantly lie to his father? The Torah is written—as it must be—for both adults and children. Therefore, it is incumbent on adults to acknowledge its troubling aspects both for themselves and for their children. In this case, a parent can honestly say to a child it is almost always wrong to lie, and especially so to a parent. But Jacob can be defended for doing so here because he had legitimately obtained the birthright, and because the Torah makes clear its view that Esau spurned his birthright (Genesis 25:34). Had Esau been given the blessing, he would have obtained it through a lie (of omission, but a lie nevertheless). Moreover, the idea was hatched by Jacob's mother, Rebecca. Jacob was in a no-win situation: Whatever he did—whether he deceived his father or disobeyed his mother and allowed Esau to deceive Isaac—involved a moral and parental compromise.
>
> Finally, we have reason to believe that the end result was God's will. What was at stake here was nothing less than the survival of the nascent Abrahamic

monotheist ideal through the only one of the two sons of Isaac who cared about that ideal.

In order to do what is right, compromise is often—though certainly not always—necessary. Or to put it another way, those who wish to do good in this world cannot remain "pure." It is often necessary to get one's hands dirty. That is what Rebecca and Jacob did.

> *Those who wish to do good in this world cannot remain "pure." It is often necessary to get one's hands dirty. That is what Rebecca and Jacob did.*

27.25 he said, "Serve me and let me eat of my son's game
This is the third attempt by Isaac to ascertain which son is present, this time using his sense of taste.

27.25 (cont.) that I may give you my innermost blessing." So he served him and he ate, and he brought him wine and he drank.

27.26 Then his father Isaac said to him, "Come close and kiss me, my son";

27.27 and he went up and kissed him. And he smelled his clothes and he blessed him, saying, "Ah, the smell of my son is like the smell of the fields that the Lord has blessed.

The blind Isaac conducted his fourth test, using the last of his functioning senses—the sense of smell—to convince himself Esau was before him.

"The extent of Rebecca's cunning is thus fully revealed: one might have wondered why Jacob needed his brother's garments to appear before a father incapable of seeing them—now we realize she has anticipated the possibility that Isaac would try to smell Jacob: it is Esau's smell that he detects in Esau's clothing." (Alter)

27.28 May God give you
Of the dew of heaven and the fat of the earth,
Abundance of new grain and wine.

Isaac's blessing to Jacob was largely material, but Jacob's primary concern was to confer Abraham's spiritual legacy.

27.29 Let peoples serve you,
And nations bow to you;

YOUNGER BROTHERS IN THE TORAH

27.29 (cont.) Be master over your brothers,

> The Torah frequently undermines what were, at the time of its writing, universal beliefs and practices. In the ancient world, it was believed that great men were usually first-borns (to this day, kingship is bestowed on the first-born). With the preeminence of Jacob over Esau, the previous choice of Isaac over Ishmael, the subsequent preeminence of Joseph over his older brothers, and later of Moses over his older brother Aaron, the Torah asserts merit is more important than birth order. Indeed, to a statistically improbable extent, the great figures of the Bible are *not* first-born sons, culminating in the case of King David, Israel's most famous king, who was the youngest of eight sons.

27.29 (cont.) And let your mother's sons bow to you.

> "The plural ["mother's sons"], as in verse 37, simply emphasizes the comprehensive and absolute nature of Jacob's predominance." (Sarna)

27.29 (cont.) Cursed be they who curse you,

Blessed they who bless you."

> This is a restatement of what God had said to Abraham—"I will bless those who bless you, and curse him that curses you." This is in fact what has occurred for thousands of years: Those who have cursed the Jews have been cursed and those who have blessed the Jews have been blessed. (See the commentary to Genesis 12:3.)

27.30 No sooner had Jacob left the presence of his father Isaac—after Isaac had finished blessing Jacob—than his brother Esau came back from his hunt.

27.31 He too prepared a dish and brought it to his father. And he said to his father, "Let my father sit up and eat of his son's game, so that you may give me your innermost blessing."

27.32 His father Isaac said to him, "Who are you?" And he said, "I am your son, Esau, your first-born!"

Esau, too, is a deceiver. To his father's question, "Who are you?" Esau should simply have responded with his name. But by adding "your first-born," he laid claim to the blessing he wanted to receive.

Esau apparently either did not take seriously trading his birthright for a bowl of stew or he did not want to acknowledge there were consequences to the sale. Whichever the case, he omitted any mention of his changed status. Withholding that information was deceptive. And he knew it. Otherwise, he would have answered the question "Who are you?" by simply responding, "It's me—Esau."

27.33 Isaac was seized with very violent trembling.

Isaac was terrified by the prospect of being confronted by his son over so grievous a mistake.

27.33 (cont.) "Who was it then," he demanded, "that hunted game and brought it to me? Moreover, I ate of it before you came, and I blessed him; now he must remain blessed!"

In the ancient world, blessings were generally believed to be irrevocable. Isaac believed he could not fix the error by simply taking back his blessing to Jacob. On the other hand, it is plausible, though less likely, that Isaac was pretending the blessing could not be revoked. By way of illustration, let us Imagine some servant overheard Isaac promising to give Esau the blessing, and the servant then acted in the same deceptive manner as Jacob. Would Isaac say he couldn't withdraw the blessing from the servant? I do not know the answer, but I doubt such a blessing would be regarded as irrevocable.

27.34 When Esau heard his father's words, he burst into wild and bitter sobbing, and said to his father, "Bless me too, Father!"

The big, tough hunter was reduced to sounding like a child. It's hard not to feel sympathy for Esau.

27.35 But he answered, "Your brother came with guile and took away your blessing."

27.36 [Esau] said, "Was he, then, named Jacob that he might supplant me these two times? First he took away my birthright and now he has taken away my blessing!"

In his anguish, Esau acknowledged he no longer held the birthright—which undoubtedly came as news to his father.

Esau's criticism of Jacob here was not accurate, since the birthright and the blessing were not unrelated. Customarily, the son with the birthright receives the blessing, so Jacob has really supplanted Esau only once, not "two times."

27.36 (cont.) And he added, "Have you not reserved a blessing for me?"

Esau's only hope was to ask his father for an additional blessing.

27.37 Isaac answered, saying to Esau, "But I have made him master over you: I have given him all his brothers for servants, and sustained him with grain and wine. What, then, can I still do for you, my son?"

27.38 And Esau said to his father, "Have you but one blessing, Father? Bless me too, Father!" And Esau wept aloud.

Why was Esau so distraught? There is no definitive answer. He did, after all, "disdain the birthright" (Genesis 25:34). Was he simply agitated over not receiving the material blessings given to his brother Jacob? Or did he now care about all aspects of the birthright? Or is there another possibility? Perhaps he cared about it all along, but in a moment of hunger and weakness, he was flippant about it ("What good is a birthright if I'm dead of starvation?"). Maybe there's a lesson here about that: some things in life are so serious they should never be treated lightly—even in jest or when one is in a cross mood.

One thing is clear. On the previous occasion (the selling of the birthright in chapter 25), Esau exaggerated his hunger, demanded food like a barbarian, and showed no understanding of the birthright's significance. But now, on the day his father announced his intention to proffer the birthright blessing, Esau's behavior was appropriate. His father asked him to go hunting prior to receiving the blessing, and he willingly complied. He did not address his father in a boorish manner, for example, by asking for the blessing before going out to hunt the game. And even at this point, despite the pain he was feeling, he spoke respectfully to his father and made no angry accusations (*"What's the matter with you? How could you not tell me apart from Jacob?"*). All Esau could say was, "Bless me too, Father!" So, unlike the earlier circumstances in chapter 25, it is clear that, while the Torah favors Jacob, there is an undercurrent here of sympathy for Esau (Telushkin).

27.39 And his father Isaac answered, saying to him,

"See, your abode shall enjoy the fat of the earth
And the dew of heaven above.

If what Esau sought were the same material blessings his brother received, he did, in fact, receive them. There was obviously enough "fat of the earth" and "dew of heaven" for both brothers.

27.40 Yet by your sword you shall live,
And you shall serve your brother;

This had to be painful for Esau to take . . .

27.40 (cont.) But when you grow restive,
You shall break his yoke from your neck."

. . . but Isaac, in the end, offered him some consolation.

27.41 Now Esau harbored a grudge against Jacob because of the blessing which his father had given him,

Esau's anger would cause Jacob many problems throughout the rest of his life. Jacob long suffered the consequences of having persuaded Esau to relinquish the first-born blessing, but that does not necessarily mean he acted immorally. Nevertheless, here, as in so many other places, especially in the Book of Genesis, the Torah makes clear we must endure the consequences of our actions—good and bad alike. As the great Bible scholar Nehama Leibowitz puts it: "Sin and deceit, however justified, bring in their turn ultimate punishment." But this is sometimes true when we have not engaged in wrongdoing of any kind. It is in the nature of this world that sometimes when we do precisely the right or noble thing, we still suffer for it (hence the popular maxim, "No good deed goes unpunished").

27.41 (cont.) and Esau said to himself, "Let but the mourning period of my father come, and I will kill my brother Jacob."

Even at the moment of his greatest anger, Esau cared for his father. He would not kill his brother while Isaac was still alive, knowing the anguish that would cause his father.

The Torah does not present very positive models in Genesis of sibling relationships. The first two brothers in history were Cain and Abel, and Cain killed Abel. Generations later, while there was no fraternal hatred between Isaac and Ishmael, they were separated almost their entire lives. The schism between Jacob and Esau was followed by Jacob's sons, who were so alienated by their youngest brother, Joseph, they threw him into in a pit, plotted to have him sold off into slavery, and then covered it all up by deceiving their father into believing he had been killed by a wild animal. The Torah recognizes sibling relationships are frequently not loving ones.

27.42 When the words of her older son Esau were reported to Rebekah,

How did Rebecca find out what "Esau said to himself"? We are not told, but somehow (as mothers so often do) she knew. When someone is carrying around the depth of rage Esau felt toward Jacob, it's almost inevitable that he won't be able to conceal it or keep it entirely to himself—particularly someone like Esau who, with his unrestrained hunger and open weeping, is emotionally transparent.

27.42 (cont.) she sent for her younger son Jacob and said to him, "Your brother Esau is consoling himself by planning to kill you.

27.43 Now, my son, listen to me. Flee at once to Haran, to my brother Laban.

27.44 Stay with him a while, until your brother's fury subsides—

27.45 until your brother's anger against you subsides—

Rebecca thought Esau wouldn't remain angry at Jacob forever (the words translated as "stay with him a while," literally mean "a number of days"). With time, most people get over anger at a sibling. Or perhaps she was engaging in a mother's wishful thinking. Nothing means more to most parents than their children getting along with one another.

27.45 (cont.) and he forgets what you have done to him. Then I will fetch you from there. Let me not lose you both in one day!"

If Esau were to carry out his threat, not only would Jacob be dead, but Esau would then be condemned to death for murder. Even if that were not her concern, Rebecca may have well been referring to her emotional state if one son murdered the other. She could not have gone on loving the son who had murdered her other son (especially the one she favored). In this way, she would "lose both."

27.46 Rebekah said to Isaac, "I am disgusted with my life because of the Hittite women. If Jacob marries a Hittite woman like these, from among the native women, what good will life be to me?"

With this statement, reminiscent of Rebecca's hopelessness during the arduous pregnancy with her struggling twins—"If so, why do I exist?" (Genesis

25:22)—Rebecca prefaced her case to Isaac that Jacob should be sent away without mentioning the real reason: Esau was planning to kill him.

The end of this chapter hearkens back to the end of the previous chapter, which recounts that Esau took wives from among the Hittite women. Sarna believes her comment "is also calculated to allay any lingering uneasiness Isaac might be feeling about his unwitting blessing of Jacob." Esau's choice in wives was a sign he would not carry on the legacy of Abraham and Isaac. Jacob must be prevented from making the same mistake.

CHAPTER
28

28.1 So Isaac sent for Jacob and blessed him.

> This has to be one of the more remarkable, if not enigmatic, verses in the Torah. Just a few verses earlier, we were told Isaac trembled on learning he had been deceived into giving the blessing of the firstborn to Jacob—the wrong son. But now Isaac deliberately sought Jacob to again bless him.
>
> Has Isaac made peace—virtually overnight—with Jacob's deception and receiving of the birthright blessing meant for Esau? Did Rebecca, whom Isaac adored, convince him what transpired was a) her doing and b) God's will? We do not know.

28.1 (cont.) He instructed him, saying, "You shall not take a wife from among the Canaanite women.

> Rebecca's argument that Jacob must not follow in Esau's footsteps by marrying the local women (Genesis 26:34) was effective.

28.2 Up, go to Paddan-aram, to the house of Bethuel, your mother's father, and take a wife there from among the daughters of Laban, your mother's brother,

28.3 May El Shaddai bless you, make you fertile and numerous, so that you become an assembly of peoples.

28.4 May He grant the blessing of Abraham to you and your offspring, that you may possess the land where you are sojourning, which God assigned to Abraham."

28.5 Then Isaac sent Jacob off, and he went to Paddan-aram, to Laban the son of Bethuel the Aramean, the brother of Rebekah, mother of Jacob and Esau.

28.6 When Esau saw that Isaac had blessed Jacob and sent him off to Paddan-aram to take a wife from there, charging him, as he blessed him, "You shall not take a wife from among the Canaanite women,"

28.7 and that Jacob had obeyed his father and mother and gone to Paddan-aram,

28.8 Esau realized that the Canaanite women displeased his father Isaac.

Despite his heartbreak over losing the "innermost blessing," Esau continued to care about his father and his opinion of him; he wanted to be a dutiful son.

On Favoring One Child over Another

The Torah depicts no interaction between Rebecca and Esau. Given that children are very perceptive about their parents' feelings about them, Esau likely realized his mother's preference for Jacob from an early age and reacted by directing his attention and emotions toward his loving father. Rebecca was a kind human being, but being a kind person doesn't always translate into good parenting. The same goes for Isaac, whose preference for Esau was equally apparent (Genesis 25:28). Unfortunately, as is so often the case in parent-child relationships, Jacob wound up repeating the error of favoring one child over the others when he became a parent.

It is not easy to avoid repeating parental errors: our parents are generally the only parenting models we have. To paraphrase the British poet, Phillip Larkin: "They mess you up, your mom and dad; they may not mean to, but they do. They give you all the problems they had, and add a few—just for you." UCLA psychiatrist Dr. Stephen Marmer has said we would be good parents if we only repeated half our parents' mistakes.

28.9 So Esau went to Ishmael and took to wife, in addition to the wives he had, Mahalath the daughter of Ishmael son of Abraham, sister of Nebaioth.

Apparently seeking to please his father by balancing the mistake he made in marrying the Hittite women, Esau married a daughter of his uncle Ishmael (who had died—Genesis 25:17).

28.10 Jacob left Beer-sheba, and set out for Haran.

28.11 He came upon a certain place and stopped there for the night, for the sun had set. Taking one of the stones of that place, he put it under his head and lay down in that place.

One of the Hebrew terms for God is *ha-makom*, "The Place."

HUMAN-GOD CONTACT

28.12 He had a dream; a stairway was set on the ground and its top reached to the sky, and angels of God were going up and down on it.

The Hebrew word for "stairway" in this verse is used nowhere else in the Bible. But given a similar word in Akkadian, an ancient Semitic language, and in the context of the verse, it is assumed to be "stairway," though it is sometimes translated as "ladder."

We think of angels as residing in heaven and therefore descending to earth. Yet the Torah does not say that the angels were going "down and up," but "up and down." The reason may be found in the Hebrew word for angel, *malach*, which means "messenger." The angels of the Torah are divine messengers in human form, like the three men who appeared to Abraham in Genesis 18. Therefore, the angels are described here as going "up and down."

GOD IN OUR LIVES

28.13 And the Lord was standing at the top of it

An alternate translation is used by the JPS translation of 1917, the New English Bible, the New American Bible, and others: "And the Lord stood beside him"— that is, beside Jacob, not beside or on top of the stairway. I think this makes more sense. God was close to Jacob in the dream, not far off.

With regard to perceiving God in one's life, there are a number of possibilities:

1. God directly and unmistakably makes Himself known to an individual.
2. We call out to God and then clearly perceive His presence.
3. At some point, we decide to recognize God has acted in our life.
4. We believe—but are not certain—God has acted in our life.
5. God has acted in our life, but we are unaware of it.
6. We believe God acts in some people's—or even nations'—lives, but simply do not know if He has done so in our own.
7. We believe God knows us but does not necessarily intervene in our life.

In my view, all of these possibilities are theologically consistent with a Torah view of God. What would not be theologically acceptable is a God who does not know us. That would mean God does not care about us.

28.13 (cont.) and He said, "I am the Lord, the God of your father Abraham

God's reference to Abraham here is not as Jacob's literal father but as the founding father of Jacob's religion and people.

28.13 (cont.) and the God of Isaac: the ground on which you are lying, I will assign to you and to your offspring.

The Torah constantly repeats the centrality of the Land of Israel to the faith of Israel and the nation of Israel. God wants at least one place on earth to embody His holy and ethical will. That will become the task of His people, the people descended from Abraham, Isaac, and Jacob who came to be known as Jews. The Torah repeatedly warns that if God's people chosen for this task fail, they will be expelled from the land, just as the Canaanites were. It is to be the Holy Land.

28.14 Your descendants shall be as the dust of the earth; you shall spread out to the west and to the east, to the north and to the south. All the families of the earth shall bless themselves by you and your descendants.

Again, the Torah repeats the universal purpose of God's choosing Abraham and his descendants: to be a blessing to all the families of the earth.[1]

ESSAY: CAN WE EXPECT GOD TO PROTECT US?

28.15 Remember, I am with you: I will protect you wherever you go

God's promise to Jacob does not mean we can all expect God to protect us. It does not even mean God would protect Jacob from all pain and suffering; as we will see, Jacob suffered a great deal. What God was probably referring to was protecting Jacob from his greatest fears—being harmed by his brother Esau or harmed in a strange land.

God, as Maimonides argues, chooses certain people for specific divine roles and protects them until that role is carried out. Jacob was one such person.

Many people believe God will protect them from tragedy, and when it turns out they have not been protected, they lose not only trust in God but even belief in God's existence. That is one reason it is a bad idea to have such an image of God. Aside from being irrational, it too often leads to disillusionment and the consequent abandonment of faith and religiosity.

> *Many people believe God will protect them from tragedy, and when it turns out they have not been protected, they lose not only trust in God but even belief in God's existence. That is one reason it is a bad idea to have such an image of God.*

We cannot *expect* God to protect us, for two reasons:

First, that would mean God always intervenes in human affairs and in nature, thereby robbing human beings of freedom and depriving nature of the ability to function according to the laws of nature. In order for God to protect all of us from being hit by a drunk driver, He would have to rob all drivers of the ability to drive while intoxicated—or divert every wayward car from hitting us. In order to protect all of us from all illness, God would have to constantly intervene in nature. And what about protection from non-lethal mishaps? Does divine protection mean we could never fracture a leg? Have our feelings hurt? Where does one draw the line?

What, then, can we expect from God, if not to be protected? We can expect two things: God will honor His promises. And God will provide ultimate justice in an afterlife.

Second, with a few exceptions chosen by God, if God protects you or me, He will have to protect every decent person in the world. Otherwise, He would be an unfair and capricious God.

But, many people will respond, they are good people and deserve to be protected.

It is surely true that good people deserve to be protected. But if all good people were protected, we would be back to God depriving humans of free will, thereby rendering humans automatons and rendering life meaningless. Moreover, why would anyone expect to be protected given the enormous number of decent people who have not been protected?

The foregoing does not mean God never protects us or intervenes in any of our lives. I believe God intervenes in any number of people's lives. We simply cannot expect Him to.

What, then, can we expect from God, if not to be protected? I believe we can expect two things: God will honor His promises. And God will provide ultimate justice in an afterlife.

As an example of the former, many Jews and Christians see the return of the Jews to their homeland after almost two thousand years as a fulfillment of divine promises. And as regards the afterlife and its importance, see my essay at Genesis 25:8.

My relationship with God does not revolve around expectations of God (other than the two aforementioned exceptions). It revolves around trying to know and do what *God* expects of *me*.

28.15 (cont.) and will bring you back to this land. I will not leave you until I have done what I have promised you."

28.16 Jacob awoke from his sleep and said, "Surely the Lord is present in this place, and I did not know it!"

28.17 Shaken,

> Clearly, this encounter with God was an awe-inspiring experience.

28.17 (cont.) he said, "How awesome is this place! This is none other than the abode of God, and that is the gateway to heaven."

> Upon awakening from his dream, Jacob drew an understandable, but erroneous, conclusion: this particular place must be where God dwells on Earth.

28.18 Early in the morning, Jacob took the stone that he had put under his head and set it up as a pillar and poured oil on the top of it.

28.19 He named that site Bethel;

> Beth-El means "House of God."

28.19 (cont.) but previously the name of the city had been Luz.

ESSAY: ON MAKING DEALS WITH GOD

28.20 Jacob then made a vow, saying, "If God remains with me, if He protects me on this journey that I am making, and gives me bread to eat and clothing to wear,

28.21 and if I return safe to my father's house—the Lord shall be my God.

28.22 And this stone, which I have set up as a pillar, shall be God's abode; and of all that You give me, I will set aside a tithe for You."

To tithe is to give a tenth of one's produce or earnings to one's religion and/or to the needy.

Jacob's oath raises the issue of people making deals with God—something entirely understandable but theologically problematic.

There are two types of deals people make with God.

The first is: "God, if you do X for me, I will do Y for you (and/or for other people)." This type of deal is akin to paying a worker for services rendered: "If you fix my broken sink, I will pay you—and if you don't, I owe you nothing." In this case the "worker" is God, who is rendered essentially a celestial butler.

The second type of deal is the reverse: "If I do X, you will do Y." A common example would be: "God, if I keep your commandments—or, if I have the right faith—you will reward me."

The commandments example is common among Jews and the faith example among Christians.

With regard to the Jewish example, the commandments referred to are usually ritual commandments. Many believe they will (or should) be rewarded in this life—with good health, for example—for keeping the "commandments between man and God," i.e., ritual commandments such as keeping kosher or observing the Sabbath.

This type of deal with God is theologically unsound because the purpose of the laws "between man and God" is, or should be, encompassed within the practice of the commandment. In the words of the Talmud, "The reward for keeping a commandment is the keeping of the commandment."[2] The reward for keeping the Sabbath, for example, is having the Sabbath in one's life. Most people who observe the Sabbath would acknowledge the Sabbath greatly enriches their life.

Expecting to be rewarded with good health or long life because one keeps kosher or observes the Sabbath is not only theologically unsound, it reflects poorly on one's religiosity. It means that observing these laws does not give the individual a more rewarding, meaningful, or happier life.

One of the most telling things about a religion is whether its adherents are generally happy. If you meet religious people—of any religion—who radiate unhappiness, you can assume there is something wrong with either their religion or the way they live it. If their religion were all that good, they would surely radiate happiness, not misery. Conversely, when you meet happy religious people, you can assume their religion is impressive.

Few Christians believe right practice will bring them rewards in this world, but more than a few believe that with the right faith they will not contract serious illness or die prematurely. That is the Christian way of making deals with God.

Such deals can lead to another insidious consequence. Jews who believe proper practice of the commandments brings health and long life might well assume that a Jew who develops cancer or dies prematurely did not lead a proper religious life.

Similarly, Christians who believe proper faith brings health and long life might well assume that a Christian who receives a cancer diagnosis or dies prematurely did not have enough or proper Christian faith.

In both cases, this is terribly unfair—even cruel—to the religious person who is suffering from serious illness or prematurely dies.

"If I knew God, I'd be God," says a medieval Jewish proverb, and we therefore have no way of knowing why there are righteous people who suffer.

Finally, such thinking is profoundly irrational. It is difficult to imagine a religious Jew or faithful Christian who does not know of a religious Jew or faithful Christian who has suffered terribly and/or died prematurely.

> *If you meet religious people—of any religion—who radiate unhappiness, you can assume there is something wrong with either their religion or the way they live it.*

Likewise, all of us are aware of irreligious and even evil people who live a long and healthy life.[3]

The question remains: Did Jacob make such a deal with God? And if he did, was he wrong in doing so? The answer is, we cannot judge Jacob. He was taking his first steps toward an understanding of God (the very fact that he said, "God really is in this place, and I didn't know," demonstrates this). In this context, what he said was perfectly understandable.

CHAPTER

29

29.1 Jacob resumed his journey and came to the land of the Easterners.

29.2 There before his eyes was a well in the open.

> Wells were important meeting places in biblical times, often functioning as a sort of ancient dating site. Jacob's mother, Rebecca, was found at a well (Genesis 24:15-17), and Jacob first encountered the woman he married at a well. Generations later, Moses met his future wife at a well (Exodus 2:16-22).

29.2 (cont.) Three flocks of sheep were lying there beside it, for the flocks were watered from that well. The stone on the mouth of the well was large.

29.3 When all the flocks were gathered there, the stone would be rolled from the mouth of the well and the sheep watered; then the stone would be put back in its place on the mouth of the well.

29.4 Jacob said to them, "My friends, where are you from?" And they said, "We are from Haran."

> That was good news for Jacob. Haran, where his uncle's family lived, was his ultimate destination.

29.5 He said to them, "Do you know Laban the son of Nahor?" And they said, "Yes, we do."

29.6 He continued, "Is he well?" They answered, "Yes, he is; and there is his daughter Rachel, coming with the flock."

29.7 He said, "It is still broad daylight, too early to round up the animals; water the flock and take them to pasture."

29.8 But they said, "We cannot, until all the flocks are rounded up; then the stone is rolled off the mouth of the well and we water the sheep."

What was that all about? Jacob had just arrived, a newcomer, and here he is, instructing strangers on how to manage their flocks of sheep. It sounds like he was throwing out orders. What was happening? Jacob knew the main purpose of his sojourn (aside from avoiding Esau's seething rage and murderous plot) was to "take a wife from among the daughters of Laban" (Genesis 28.2), and he was just informed one of the daughters was approaching.

29.9 While he was still speaking with them, Rachel came with her father's flock; for she was a shepherdess.

29.10 And when Jacob saw Rachel, the daughter of his uncle Laban, and the flock of his uncle Laban, Jacob went up and rolled the stone off the mouth of the well, and watered the flock of his uncle Laban.

One way to anyone's heart—then and today—is through their animals. Then, it was cattle, sheep, or other livestock; today, it is pets.

A way for a man in particular to win a woman's heart is by acting manly. Until this point, we have not seen Jacob's physicality or masculinity; we only know him as "a mild man who stayed in camp" (Genesis 25:27). Now we see him demonstrate leadership and physical strength, which undoubtedly made an impression on Rachel.

This story presents Jacob as "the antithesis of his father [Isaac: instead of a surrogate [Abraham's servant], the bridegroom himself [Jacob] is present at the well, and it is he, not the maiden, who draws the water [in Isaac's story, Rebecca drew the water]" (Alter).

29.11 Then Jacob kissed Rachel,

Jacob fell in love with Rachel at first sight, and his kiss may or not have been the innocent kiss of a relative (they were cousins) given that this is the only instance in the Torah of a man kissing a woman who is neither his mother nor his wife.

29.11 (cont.) and broke into tears.

After a lengthy journey, fleeing his homeland for his life and trekking through what was undoubtedly, at times, treacherous territory, Jacob at last sensed he had reached safety and finally had the luxury of expressing pent-up emotions that had undoubtedly been building since he fled his parents' home. His tears of relief may have mingled with tears of joy at meeting this maiden who seemed to perfectly meet the requirements to become his wife.

29.12 Jacob told Rachel that he was her father's kinsman, that he was Rebekah's son; and she ran and told her father.

29.13 On hearing the news of his sister's son Jacob, Laban ran to greet him; he embraced him and kissed him,

This seems like a warm enough greeting, but Laban does not have a good reputation among Bible readers—for good reason, as will shortly be apparent. Due to this, the leading medieval Jewish commentator, Rashi, took a cynical view of Laban's behavior:

"'He ran to greet him'—thinking that Jacob was laden with money, for the servant of that household [Abraham's servant] had come there with ten camels fully laden [Genesis 24:10].

"'and embraced him'—when he saw that he had nothing with him, he thought, 'Perhaps he has brought gold coins and they are hidden away in his bosom!'"

29.13 (cont.) and took him into his house. He told Laban all that had happened,

29.14 and Laban said to him, "You are truly my bone and flesh." When he had stayed with him a month's time,

29.15 Laban said to Jacob, "Just because you are a kinsman, should you serve me for nothing? Tell me, what shall your wages be?"

Apparently, Jacob was put to work very shortly after he arrived at Laban's home.

29.16 Now Laban had two daughters; the name of the older one was Leah, and the name of the younger was Rachel.

29.17 Leah had weak eyes;

The meaning of this description is not fully clear. There are traditionally two ways of understanding this verse. The word translated here as "weak" really means "soft" more often than "weak," so very likely it means Leah had "soft" eyes, which would be a compliment. The other possibility—that Leah really did have "weak" eyes, meaning she had poor vision—implies she would constantly squint in order to see, a characteristic that would render her unattractive. The Torah here was doing one of two things: describing the positive attributes of both sisters, or contrasting their attractiveness.

THE UNFAIR (BUT UNDENIABLE) IMPORTANCE OF FEMALE BEAUTY

29.17 (cont.) Rachel was shapely and beautiful.

Whatever Leah's level of attractiveness, this seems to indicate that Rachel was the more beautiful of the two.

The Torah and the rest of the Hebrew Bible—the most dramatic example being the book "Song of Songs"—is not prudish. It treats sex as part of life and is therefore quite direct and honest on this matter. Thus, for example, it readily notes—as with Rachel here and Rebecca and Sarah before her—female beauty matters.

The extent to which female beauty matters is a painful and unfair fact of life. So much so, some people refuse to acknowledge it. They prefer to believe what really matters is "the inner beauty" of a woman. And, of course, that is what most matters in defining any human being—male or female. But we live in a physical world. And in this physical world, female physical beauty matters. Male looks also matter, but among humans (as opposed to, say, peacocks), it is the female that visually attracts the male, and it is obviously the first thing about a woman a man notices (for that matter, it is often the first thing about a woman that other women notice, too).

A man who loves a woman only for her beauty doesn't love *her*. Those relationships are doomed to end sooner or later—often sooner. But well-meaning parents and a well-meaning society do young women no favor by denying the importance of looks in attracting a man. And a woman does neither herself nor her marriage a favor if she denies the importance to her husband and therefore their marriage of her trying to remain physically attractive.

If I may offer a personal example, my late mother and father had a seventy-three-year love affair. One of many reasons was my mother aimed to look beautiful for my father every day of their married life. She took care of herself and put on makeup, styled her hair, and wore beautiful clothing every day. Due in no small part to her efforts, she retained her beauty until the day she died, at age eighty-nine.

It is often countered that men's looks are also important. But they are rarely as important as a man's personality, masculinity, brains, power, or wealth in attracting a woman. The power of the visual in men is simply far greater than the power of the visual in women. The fact that physical attractiveness is not distributed at all equally—as it wasn't between Rachel and Leah—is one of many built-in unfair features of life. Along with most women and many men, I wish it were otherwise. But the Torah never denies reality. It does, however, subtly evoke the reader's sympathy for the less attractive sister with its comment about her "soft" eyes and in its melancholy depiction of Jacob's greater love for Rachel.

29.18 Jacob loved Rachel; so he answered, "I will serve you seven years for your younger daughter Rachel."

29.19 Laban said, "Better that I give her to you than that I should give her to an outsider. Stay with me."

> Laban does not seem particularly enthusiastic about the match. His comment implies nothing positive about Jacob—he is simply a better choice than a non-family member as a future son-in-law.

29.20 So Jacob served seven years for Rachel and they seemed to him but a few days because of his love for her.

> If there is a more romantic sentence in world literature, I am unaware of it.
> (The Torah recognizes men can be just as romantic as women, and often more so.)

29.21 Then Jacob said to Laban, "Give me my wife, for my time is fulfilled, that I may cohabit with her."

> The Hebrew rendered here as "cohabit with her" is literally "come to her." The Torah could not be more explicit about his desire.

29.22 And Laban gathered all the people of the place and made a feast.

29.23 When evening came, he took his daughter Leah and brought her to him; and he cohabited with her.

29.24 Laban had given his maidservant Zilpah to his daughter Leah as her maid.

WORKING FOR—AND SLEEPING WITH—AN ILLUSION

29.25 When morning came, there was Leah!

> To the modern reader, it is difficult to understand how Jacob could have failed to realize he was sleeping with Leah rather than Rachel. But this was a primitive time and place: presumably the night was pitch dark, and the tent was in no way illuminated. Jacob may simply have had no way of seeing his wife's face.

Nevertheless, it is still hard to understand how Jacob could spend an intimate night with one of two sisters, and not know which one she was—if only by voice. One can imagine Leah minimized her speaking (just as Jacob minimized speaking when he deceived his father who, for a different reason, also could not see). When she did speak, Jacob might have said, paraphrasing his father Isaac, "the voice is the voice of Leah, but the body is the body of Rachel."

But there may be an additional explanation: Jacob was likely inebriated. There are two reasons to believe this. One is that the Hebrew word for "feast" (*mishteh*), alluded to in verse 22, comes from the Hebrew word "to drink" (*shata*). Undoubtedly, there was a good deal of drinking at Laban's feast. Two thousand years ago, the Roman Jewish historian Josephus wrote Jacob was "deluded by wine and the dark." A number of scholars point out the last time the Torah used the same words used here for "younger and older daughters," it did so to describe the daughters of Lot who had sexual relations with their inebriated father.[1]

This story has long captured people's imaginations and been applied to other areas of life. For example, the writer Arthur Koestler, a former Communist who eventually became an anti-communist, offered a powerful take on this text:

"I served the Communist Party for seven years—the same length of time as Jacob tended Laban's sheep to win Rachel his daughter. When the time was up, the bride was led into his dark tent; only the next morning did he discover that his ardors had been spent not on the lovely Rachel but on Leah. I wonder whether he ever recovered from the shock of having slept with an illusion."[2]

Koestler, like Jacob, had worked seven years for an illusion (Communism).

Jacob's being tricked by Laban in the darkness of night, and his consequent marriage to the sister he did not desire, is another of the many Genesis examples of "what goes around comes around." He was tricked because he could not see—just as he tricked his father, Isaac, who could not see.

Leah, too, undoubtedly harbored an illusion—that she could make Jacob love her during that night.

How many of us have not worked for a cause, a spouse, a friend, or a job that turned out to be an illusion? One has to assume this is common because there is a word for it: "disillusioned."

29.25 (cont.) So he said to Laban, "What is this you have done to me? I was in your service for Rachel! Why did you deceive me?"

Jacob appears to have confronted only Laban, not Leah, for the deception. And for good reason: it was Laban's scheme. He apparently knew his older daughter would be more difficult to marry off than his beautiful younger daughter. Leah likely found it difficult to disobey her father's wishes and, at least as important, undoubtedly had her own hopes and dreams of love.

29.26 Laban said, "It is not the practice in our place to marry off the younger before the older.

This can be viewed as another example of the Torah depicting a form of "what goes around, comes around" retribution. Jacob flouted the customary rules of older and younger siblings when he secured for himself Esau's birthright and blessing (and used deception to do so). Here he attempted something similar by seeking to wed a younger sister before the older sister had been married. Laban thwarted him (also by using deception) and deflected his complaint with a rebuke.

29.27 Wait until the bridal week of this one is over and we will give you that one too, provided you serve me another seven years."

Laban knew how to drive a hard bargain. What were Jacob's alternatives? He could refuse the deal, take the wife he now had but didn't want, and leave. Or he could agree and, though stuck with a wife he didn't love, would have the consolation of also having the wife he wanted and dearly loved. Of the two choices, the latter was clearly the better one.

29.28 Jacob did so; he waited out the bridal week of the one, and then he gave him his daughter Rachel as wife.

Many readers throughout the ages have mistakenly believed Jacob had to wait another seven years before marrying Rachel. Not so—the Torah clearly states

Jacob married Rachel only one week after marrying Leah. The seven additional years was the amount of time Jacob had to commit to work for Laban, not wait to marry Rachel.

That Jacob married sisters is one more argument for the antiquity of the Torah. Later Torah law expressly prohibited this practice (Leviticus 18:18).

29.29 Laban had given his maidservant Bilhah to his daughter Rachel as her maid.

29.30 And Jacob cohabited with Rachel also; indeed, he loved Rachel more than Leah. And he served him another seven years.

The Bible permits polygamy. But in almost every instance, it depicts a polygamous marriage as an unhappy marriage. The Bible assumes this is almost always the case. Deuteronomy 21:15 begins: "If a man has two wives, one loved and the other unloved [literally, "hated"]…" No husband in the Bible loves his two wives equally. (See I Samuel 1:4-6 for another example of an unhappy polygamous marriage.)

One learns moral ideals not only from the Torah's laws and principles, but at least as much from the Torah's and the Bible's later stories.

It is testimony to Jacob's good character that he fulfilled his seven-year obligation even though he was given Rachel as a wife after just one week.

> *One learns moral ideals not only from the Torah's laws and principles, but at least as much from the Torah's and the Bible's later stories.*

29.31 The Lord saw that Leah was unloved and he opened her womb; but Rachel was barren.

As He had with Hagar earlier, God took pity on Leah—the disadvantaged wife in a difficult situation—by providing her consolation.

29.32 Leah conceived and bore a son, and named him Reuben;

The name is from the Hebrew words, *"re'uh ben"*—"See, a son."

29.32 (cont.) for she declared, "It means: 'The Lord has seen my affliction'; it also means: 'Now my husband will love me.'"

29.33 She conceived again and bore a son, and declared, "This is because the Lord heard that I was unloved and has given me this one also"; so she named him Simeon.

> The name "Simeon" comes from the Hebrew word *shema*, which means "hear." His name, in effect, was "Heard"—as in, "God heard."

29.34 Again she conceived and bore a son and declared, "This time my husband will become attached to me, for I have borne him three sons." Therefore he was named Levi.

> The Hebrew word translated here as "attached" is *yi-laveh*, from which Leah derives the name Levi. She still yearns for Jacob's love.

29.35 She conceived again and bore a son, and declared, "This time I will praise the Lord." Therefore she named him Judah.

> At this point, Leah appears to have given up on Jacob's love; now she just praises God for giving her children (specifically sons). Her intent is to do what unhappy wives/mothers have done throughout history. She will concentrate her emotional life on her children.
>
> The ideal is for a mother and father to center their emotional lives on one another, not their children. That is best for them and for their children. But that doesn't always happen—either because the love between the parents is missing or because one of the parents (often the mother) is more interested in focusing energy and attention on the children than on the other spouse (who, being an adult, is erroneously thought to be less in need of attention).

29.35 (cont.) Then she stopped bearing.

> We don't know why, but perhaps Jacob, in an effort to appease the barren Rachel, ceased (for the time being) cohabiting with her. That may be why she

seems to have given up hope Jacob would ever love her. One could surely cry for Leah (even while acknowledging she participated in a nasty deception intended to steal the love of her sister's life).

CHAPTER

30

Essay: Is Life Meaningful without Children?

30.1 When Rachel saw that she had borne Jacob no children, she became envious of her sister; and Rachel said to Jacob, "Give me children, or I shall die."

Abraham expressed a similar sentiment to that of Rachel: "What can you give me," he asked God, "seeing that I die childless?" (Genesis 15:2).

Rachel believed that, without children, her life had no purpose and there was little point in going on. Rachel is hardly alone in this view. Her view has been that of most people—especially, but certainly not only, women—in just about every culture in history. Life without children has been deemed essentially worthless—even tantamount to death. As the Lion Handbook, a reference guide to the Bible, notes "Childlessness was always regarded as a calamity...."

For a typical view outside of the Western world, here is a Hindu echo of Rachel's perspective: "Orthodox Hindus do not approve of childlessness and consider it to be very inauspicious. Women without children have to face social discomfort and questioning looks from friends and relations. Newly married couples have to deal with peer pressure if they fail to produce children within a reasonable time after their marriage."[1]

Catholicism did honor one category of people who chose not to marry and thereby remain childless—priests, monks, and nuns. But outside these specific vows of celibacy, Christians were expected to marry (marriage is one of the seven sacraments of the Catholic Church) and to have children (traditional

Catholicism forbids Catholics from practicing birth control), and most Christians viewed not having children as much a tragedy as Jews and others have. (When one hears of a Christian family with four or more children, it is safe to assume they are religious.)

Within Jewish life, there has been both agreement and disagreement with Rachel's view.

On the one hand, the Talmud notes the commonly held view of childlessness as a form of death,[2] and as the classic 1902 Jewish Encyclopedia noted, "To be without children is regarded as the greatest curse"[3]

On the other hand, the Bible itself assures the childless that their lives are indeed precious and that God will profoundly compensate them: "For thus says the Lord, 'To the eunuchs who keep My Sabbaths, And choose what pleases Me, And hold fast My covenant, To them I will give in My house and within My walls a memorial, And a name better than that of sons and daughters; I will give them an everlasting name which will not be cut off'" (Isaiah 56:4-5).[4]

Rabbi Isaac Arama, a fifteenth-century Spanish rabbi known by the name of his Torah commentary, *Akedat Yitzchak*, taught there are two words in Hebrew for "woman," which denote two purposes: First, she is called *Isha* (woman), a being who was taken from man (see Genesis 2:23) and who, like man, can advance in intellectual and moral realms; and second, *Chava* (Eve, referring to the first woman, and hence "the mother of all the living"—Genesis 3:20), a being who, *unlike* man, is able to bear children. A barren woman is nonetheless capable of living as purposeful and fulfilling a life as a man, and therefore should not consider her life worthless if she cannot have children—her life is every bit as meaningful and worthwhile as that of a childless man. In other words, if a childless man can lead a meaningful life, so can a childless woman. Thus, the *Akedat Yitzchak* invokes the verses cited from Isaiah and then adds, "Rachel was no more dead because she was childless than Jacob would have been, if he were childless."

Of course, a woman who wishes to have children but cannot does not compare herself to childless men, but to women who have children. And that, to be sure, can be painful. It would be dishonest to deny that children can vastly enrich a person's life (it would also be dishonest to deny that children do not necessarily enrich a person's life—many children bring great pain to parents).

Nevertheless, the notion if a person does not have a child, he or she is essentially "dead" is intellectually, morally, and religiously absurd. It would mean that if we have no children, all the good we do is worthless, all the love we experience is pointless, that nothing short of a child—not even God, let alone a spouse, friends, work, religion, service to others, passions—makes life meaningful.

Nehama Leibowitz, one of the greatest Bible teachers of the twentieth century, had no children. It is therefore particularly interesting to read her take on Rachel's words, "Give me children, or I shall die." Leibowitz is not sympathetic: "This was a treasonable repudiation of her function, a flight from her destiny and purpose, shirking the duties imposed on her, not in virtue of her being a woman, but in virtue of her being a human being."[5]

All the preceding notwithstanding, having children (biologically or through adoption) should be a high priority in people's lives. The increasing trend in the Western world not to have children is a national death wish. So many men and women in the West (and other developed countries) are choosing not to have children that some nations' populations are in steep decline. Unless their birth rates are reversed, some nations will ultimately disappear (unless a vast number of people from other nations and cultures are brought in—in which case those nations will still disappear—they will be replaced by another nation). An undersupply of children also crushes nations' economies because there are too few young people to help support the older generation.

On the personal level, choosing not to have children is often a choice not to mature. Nothing matures people like marriage and raising children does.

Regarding Rachel's plea, "Give me children, or I shall die," Harold Kushner notes the tragic irony that it is while giving birth to her second son that Rachel dies (Genesis 35:16-20).

WHAT IS A MAN TO DO WHEN HIS WIFE LASHES OUT IN PAIN?

30.2 Jacob was incensed at Rachel,

Traditional Jewish commentators fault Jacob for failing to be more understanding of Rachel's anguish. However, there are at least two possibilities that would exonerate Jacob's anger. First, Rachel's demand implied that her husband was in some way withholding children from her. Second, by declaring that she would rather die than live without children, Rachel was essentially saying her life with her husband was worthless. Obviously, such a dispiriting comment would have deeply hurt Jacob, whose love for Rachel was so great he worked fourteen years in order to marry her.

An example of a different response comes from American history. The seventh president of the United States, Andrew Jackson, and his wife—coincidentally named Rachel—had no children. As reported in a biography of Jackson, "Rachel, according to a family story, cried: 'Oh, husband! How I wish I had a child!' With grace, Jackson said, 'Darling, God knows what to give, what to withhold: let's not murmur against Him.'"[6]

To be fair, the tone of Andrew Jackson's Rachel was more plaintive than accusatory. But the pained comment of Jacob's Rachel is also understandable: her husband already had children (through Leah).

It is probably fair to conclude that Rachel knew Jacob was no more at fault than she for her barrenness, and what she wanted from him was compassion. In general, men tend to be more oriented towards finding solutions (and Jacob was undoubtedly frustrated by his helplessness), whereas women want to know that their pain is heard.

30.2 (cont.) and said, "Can I take the place of God, who has denied you fruit of the womb?"

Jacob recognized everything is ultimately in God's hands. Unfortunately, he chose words that were virtually guaranteed to intensify Rachel's pain, implying that God Himself didn't want her to have children. I suspect even years later, after Rachel's premature death, Jacob regretted speaking to her so harshly. One of the cruelest things a believer can say to another believer is their suffering is their own fault and may even be God's will.

30.3 She said, "Here is my maid Bilhah.

Like Sarah, Rachel tried to solve her problem by offering a concubine to her husband.

30.3 (cont.) Consort with her, that she may bear on my knees and that through her I too may have children."

In the ancient world, "Placing the newborn on someone's knees was a gesture of adoption" (Alter).

30.4 So she gave him her maid Bilhah as concubine, and Jacob cohabited with her.

30.5 Bilhah conceived and bore Jacob a son.

Four of Jacob's twelve sons were born through concubines. These sons—Dan, Naftali, Gad, and Asher—were considered every bit as much tribes of Israel as the sons of Rachel and Leah. The fact that some were born to concubines rather than wives is irrelevant.

30.6 And Rachel said, "God has vindicated me; indeed, He has heeded my plea and given me a son." Therefore she named him Dan.

Though she was not the birth mother, Rachel was the one who reared Dan and the other sons born to Bilhah; therefore, like an adoptive mother today, she was considered their mother. "Dan" means "judged" or "vindicated."

30.7 Rachel's maid Bilhah conceived again and bore Jacob a second son.

"It seems that everybody except Rachel is able to conceive a child! To add to the hurt [and in a world that so favored sons], every other wife and concubine of Jacob is bearing him a son, not just a child" (Hamilton).

30.8 And Rachel said, "A fateful contest I waged with my sister; yes, and I have prevailed." So she named him Naphtali.

> This is one of the saddest lines in the Torah. It is actually pathetic—an indication of just how insecure Rachel was. She has already said she considered her life worthless without children; but now we see that having a child to nurture and love was not enough—she was in competition with her older sister. "Naphtali" comes from a Hebrew word meaning "to contest."

30.9 When Leah saw that she had stopped bearing, she took her maid Zilpah and gave her to Jacob as concubine.

30.10 And when Leah's maid Zilpah bore Jacob a son,

30.11 Leah said, "What luck!" So she named him Gad.

> "Gad appears as the name of the god of fortune and good luck. This pagan divinity is also mentioned in Isaiah 65:11" (Sarna).

30.12 When Leah's maid Zilpah bore Jacob a second son,

30.13 Leah declared, "What fortune!" meaning, "Women will deem me fortunate." So she named him Asher.

> To this day, in modern Hebrew the word *asher* means "fortunate" or "happy." A famous verse in Psalms 84:5 (84:4 in Christian texts) begins with this word: *ashrei yoshvei vey-te-cha*—"Happy are those who dwell in Your house."

30.14 Once, at the time of the wheat harvest, Reuben came upon some mandrakes in the field

> According to a common ancient superstition, the mandrake plant had the power to enhance sexual desire and induce pregnancy. Aphrodite, the Greek goddess of love, was known as "the lady of the mandrake." Mandrakes were customarily placed under the bridal bed in Germany. And in the *Song of Songs*, the maiden tells her lover she has stored up fragrant mandrakes for him (7:14).

Furthermore, *dodi*, the Hebrew word for "my beloved," is similar to *dudaim*, the Hebrew word for mandrake.

The Torah, however, ascribes no efficacy to these plants because it prohibits superstition. Superstition, at its essence, is a form of idol worship in that it implies something other than God—such as a black cat or a broken mirror—governs the world.

> *Superstition, at its essence, is a form of idol worship in that it implies something other than God—such as a black cat or a broken mirror—governs the world.*

30.14 (cont.) and brought them to his mother Leah.

Reuben probably felt bad for his mother because she was the less desired wife.

30.14 (cont.) Rachel said to Leah, "Please give me some of your son's mandrakes."

30.15 But she said to her, "Was it not enough for you to take away my husband,

It has been said that when it comes to self-justification, everyone is a genius. For Leah to accuse Rachel of taking Jacob from her when precisely the opposite was the case was an extraordinary act of self-justification.

It also manifests another common human trait: portraying oneself as the victim when one is, in fact, the victimizer.

30.15 (cont.) that you would also take my son's mandrakes?"

Clearly, it is not only brothers who do not get along in Genesis.

30.15 (cont.) Rachel replied, "I promise, he shall lie

As Nahum Sarna explains, the Hebrew word *shachav* (to "lie with" or to "lay"), when used in Genesis to refer to sexual relations, "never connotes a relationship of marital love but is invariably used in unsavory circumstances." Rachel offered Leah one night of sex with their mutual husband, not a night of lovemaking.[7]

30.15 (cont.) with you tonight, in return for your son's mandrakes."

Leah desired love above all else, but she clearly also desired more children; and despite her children through Bilhah, Rachel was still desperate to become pregnant. So the sisters struck this deal with one another.

30.16 When Jacob came home from the field in the evening, Leah went out to meet him and said, "You are to sleep with me, for I have hired you with my son's mandrakes."

The verb used here, *liskor,* means "to hire" in modern Hebrew as well. The term is used to refer to "renting" or "hiring"—a car, for instance, for a temporary period of time. Leah was so hungry for love she resorted to "hiring" her own husband for a night.

Despite Leah's role in deceiving Jacob into marrying her, it is difficult not to feel compassion for her lifelong pain at not being loved. She must have believed on some level sleeping with Jacob the first night would induce him to love her. But that proved to be a terrible mistake. We cannot manipulate people into loving us. Perhaps had she not tried to do so, she would have been able to marry a man who did love her—or at least wanted to make love to her.

30.16 (cont.) And he lay with her that night.

Jacob seems to have readily acquiesced to the women in his life: He did as his mother instructed in deceiving Isaac; he complied with Rachel when she told him to impregnate her maid servant; and he didn't argue when Leah announced she had "hired" him to sleep with her for the night.

30.17 God heeded Leah, and she conceived and bore him a fifth son.

Though Rachel was the one who ended up with the supposedly pregnancy-inducing mandrakes, she was not the next one to become pregnant. The Torah is making clear that magical formulas are powerless: the world is governed by God (see the language employed in verses 22-24).

30.18 And Leah said, "God has given me my reward for having given my maid to my husband." So she named him Issachar.

>Sachar in both biblical and modern Hebrew means "reward."

30.19 When Leah conceived again and bore Jacob a sixth son,

30.20 Leah said, "God has given me a choice gift; this time my husband will exalt me, for I have borne him six sons."

>One would think that by now Leah would have realized that no number of sons could induce her husband to fall in love with her. It is a fact of life that what evokes romantic love is somewhat mysterious; but whatever it is, it cannot be manipulated or controlled by human action. Sometimes love can be rekindled when it has faded over time and with life's vagaries, but for that to happen, it has to have been there in the first place. Throughout history, people have tried to make others love them, all to no avail. Such efforts guarantee only frustration and heartache and should be consciously avoided. One of the keys to happiness is to accept reality. In this regard, the beginning of the Serenity Prayer, authored by the American Christian theologian Reinhold Niebuhr (1892-1971) and used worldwide in Twelve-Step programs for addicts, is applicable to this (and so many other) aspects of life: "God, grant me the serenity to accept the things I cannot change."

30.20 (cont.) So she named him Zebulun.

30.21 Last, she bore him a daughter, and named her Dinah.

>After the birth of each of the sons, the Torah recounted the mother's explanation of her choice of name for that child. Only the daughter's name is not explained. This a good example of how one's attitude affects how one approaches Torah narrative: Does the lack of elaboration on Dinah's name reflect on the Torah as sexist? Or is the Torah simply describing the sexist reality that existed in the ancient world, where the birth of a daughter was deemed worthy of only a brief mention?

The strong and even heroic roles played by women in the Torah—from the matriarchs to the daughter of Pharaoh to the midwives who disobeyed Pharaoh—argue strongly for the latter explanation.

30.22 Now God remembered Rachel; God heeded her and opened her womb.

When the Torah describes God as "remembering," it does not mean God had previously forgotten. It means God has decided to act—often, from a human perspective, at long last.

The Torah explicitly states it was God who opened Rachel's womb lest there be any suspicion that the mandrakes were responsible.

30.23 She conceived and bore a son, and said, "God has taken away my disgrace."

30.24 So she named him Joseph, which is to say, "May the Lord add another son for me."

The Hebrew word for Joseph (*Yosef*) means "he will add," reflecting Rachel's desire for an additional son. She has just given birth to a son, and she names him "May the Lord add another son." Two reasons suggest themselves: She is in competition with her sister, and until the modern period, many children died at a very young age.

30.25 After Rachel had borne Joseph, Jacob said to Laban, "Give me leave to go back to my own homeland.

30.26 Give me my wives and my children, for whom I have served you, that I may go; for well you know what services I have rendered you."

In keeping with laws of the ancient world, Jacob spoke here as if he had the status of an indentured servant—almost a slave, in which case his wives and children would not automatically belong to him (see Exodus 21:2-4). But he was not a slave, nor was he an indentured servant. Why, then, did he seek permission to take them with him before leaving? Laban was his uncle, not his master; he had no claim of ownership on his wives or their children. The reason

Jacob had agreed to work fourteen years for his two wives was that he brought no money or property into the marriage. All that work for Laban was essentially a "bride-price," which he had long since paid. He had every right to leave with his family. But he apparently wanted to do so without burning bridges with his uncle and father-in-law; he wanted to go, and to take Laban's daughters and grandchildren with Laban's blessing.

30.27 But Laban said to him, "If you will indulge me, I have learned by divination that the Lord has blessed me on your account."

Laban acknowledged God was responsible for his having prospered—and the benefits he received were due entirely to Jacob's relationship with God.

30.28 And he continued, "Name the wages due from me, and I will pay you."

30.29 But he said, "You know well how I have served you and how your livestock has fared with me.

30.30 For the little you had before I came has grown to much, since the Lord has blessed you wherever I turned. And now, when shall I make provision for my own household?"

30.31 He said, "What shall I pay you?" And Jacob said, "Pay me nothing!

Jacob didn't want monetary wages. He wanted to be paid in the one commodity he knew how to manage and multiply.

30.31 (cont.) If you will do this thing for me, I will again pasture and keep your flocks:

30.32 let me pass through your whole flock today, removing from there every speckled and spotted animal—every dark-colored sheep and every spotted and speckled goat. Such shall be my wages.

These animals were rare, meaning Jacob was asking for only a handful of Laban's animals.

30.33 In the future when you go over my wages, let my honesty toward you testify for me: if there

are among my goats any that are not speckled or spotted or any sheep that are not dark-colored, they got there by theft."

30.34 And Laban said, "Very well, let it be as you say."

30.35 But that same day he removed the streaked and spotted he-goats and all the speckled and spotted she-goats—every one that had white on it—and all the dark-colored sheep, and left them in the charge of his sons.

30.36 And he put a distance of three days' journey between himself and Jacob, while Jacob was pasturing the rest of Laban's flock.

30.37 Jacob then got fresh shoots of poplar, and of almond and plane, and peeled white stripes in them, laying bare the white of the shoots.

30.38 The rods that he had peeled he set up in front of the goats in the troughs, the water receptacles, that the goats came to drink from. Their mating occurred when they came to drink,

30.39 and since the goats mated by the rods, the goats brought forth streaked, speckled, and spotted young.

> In the ancient world, it was believed the color of the rods by which farm animals mated would determine the color of their progeny. Although it is surprising to us today that the Torah devotes so many verses to flocks and rods, the extent of the detail is further evidence of the antiquity of the Torah. It was obviously written at a time when these beliefs governed animal husbandry practices.

30.40 But Jacob dealt separately with the sheep; he made these animals face the streaked or wholly dark-colored animals in Laban's flock. And so he produced special flocks for himself, which he did not put with Laban's flocks.

30.41 Moreover, when the sturdier animals were mating, Jacob would place the rods in the troughs, in full view of the animals, so that they mated by the rods;

30.42 but with the feebler animals he would not place them there. Thus the feeble ones went to Laban and the sturdy to Jacob.

30.43 So the man grew exceedingly prosperous, and came to own large flocks, maidservants and menservants, camels and asses.

CHAPTER
31

31.1 Now he heard the things that Laban's sons were saying: "Jacob has taken all that was our father's, and from that which was our father's he has built up all this wealth."

When they saw Jacob became rich, Laban's sons viewed Jacob's wealth as essentially stolen, despite the fact that a) Laban asked Jacob to name a price for his many years of service and b) that service resulted in great prosperity for Laban.

Laban had agreed to Jacob's request for the relatively rare speckled animals as payment. And even then Laban tried to limit Jacob's share by hiding the speckled (and spotted) animals—and entrusting them to his sons (Genesis 30:35-36) who presumably knew of their father's ploy to rob Jacob. Yet these sons were now accusing Jacob of cheating their father. Jacob's wealth, therefore, was entirely due to his own efforts and God's blessing.

Laban's sons were among the many throughout history who resent the success of others rather than seek to emulate it (recall the Philistines' reaction to Isaac's wealth in Genesis 26:15) and who believe people become rich only by taking wealth from others (see commentary to Genesis 26:13-15).

The subject of envy comes up often in Genesis because Genesis is about the human condition, and envy is all too human—as is exaggeration and arguing dishonestly: Laban's sons said, "Jacob has taken *all* that was our father's...." (emphasis added). When people do not have facts on their side, they often resort to inaccuracy and outright distortion. As a well-known lawyer's adage puts it: "If you have the law on your side, argue the law; if you have the facts, argue the facts; if you have neither, pound the table."

31.2 Jacob also saw that Laban's manner toward him was not as it had been in the past.

Laban's attitude toward Jacob had never been one of respect (see, for example, Genesis 29:19). That is why he was sure he could get away with tricking him regarding Leah and Rachel. However, Laban's attitude toward Jacob has now deteriorated. Perhaps it derived from Laban's subconscious guilt over taking advantage of Jacob; perhaps it came from the grumbling of his sons. Whatever the reason, relations were deteriorating between them, and Jacob needed to do something.

31.3 Then the Lord said to Jacob, "Return to the land of your fathers where you were born, and I will be with you."

Jacob already knew it was time to leave and had sought Laban's blessing (Genesis 30:26)—only to have Laban throw another delaying tactic in his path (Genesis 30:27-28). But now God Himself confirmed it was time for him to depart Laban's household and return to the Promised Land.

31.4 Jacob had Rachel and Leah called to the field, where his flock was,

It was time to make the case for leaving to his wives. Rachel, though younger and the second wife, is mentioned first because she was Jacob's beloved wife. To this day, more than three thousand years later, when Jews mention the names of the patriarchs and matriarchs, they are all mentioned in chronological order except for Rachel and Leah: "Abraham, Isaac, Jacob, Sarah, Rebecca, Rachel and Leah." Though this might seem unfair to Leah, it reflects subtle disapproval of Leah for having deceived Jacob into marrying her.

31.5 and said to them, "I see that your father's manner toward me is not as it has been in the past. But the God of my father has been with me.

Jacob spoke of God as a family or clan deity, terms he knew Rachel and Leah would readily understand. These women had grown up in a polytheistic world with a polytheistic father. Even after their many years with Jacob, it is unlikely they had become fully accustomed to the concept of a single and universal God.

Wide acceptance of monotheism even among the Hebrews/Israelites, let alone among non-Hebrews, was a very gradual process.

31.6 As you know, I have served your father with all my might;

31.7 but your father has cheated me, changing my wages time and again. God, however, would not let him do me harm.

Because He had a greater historical purpose for Jacob, God made an exception to the general rule of divine non-intervention in human affairs and saw to it that Jacob did not suffer the consequences of Laban's injustices.

31.8 If he said thus, 'The speckled shall be your wages,' then all the flocks would drop speckled young; and if he said thus, 'The streaked shall be your wages,' then all the flocks would drop streaked young.

31.9 God has taken away your father's livestock and given it to me.

By this, Jacob did not mean what Laban's sons meant when they grumbled about Jacob getting wealthy by "taking away" what had belonged to their father. Jacob began his own flock with only a very few animals—the spotted and speckled specimens that Laban hadn't been able to hide from him. But thereafter, far greater numbers of the flock than would ordinarily be expected to gave birth to speckled and spotted young, greatly increasing Jacob's livestock.

31.10 Once, at the mating time of the flocks, I had a dream in which I saw that the he-goats mating with the flock were streaked, speckled, and mottled.

31.11 And in the dream an angel of God said to me, 'Jacob!' 'Here,' I answered.

31.12 And he said, 'Note well that all the he-goats which are mating with the flock are streaked, speckled, and mottled; for I have noted all that Laban has been doing to you.

In the course of explaining to his wives that he had not cheated their father, Jacob attributed to God how greater-than-normal offspring were born to the flock (designated to him by his agreement with Laban)—not to the rods he used to manipulate the color of the flocks.

31.13 I am the God of Bethel, where you anointed a pillar and where you made a vow to Me.

Bethel was the name of the place where Jacob placed a rock under his head and dreamt of the stairway to heaven. The God of the whole world was not here identifying Himself as the God of Bethel and nowhere else; He was merely reminding Jacob of their encounter at Bethel many years before and of their mutual vows. God vowed to provide Jacob protection, and Jacob vowed that if God followed through on that promise and brought him safely back to the land of his birth, God would be his God, and he would tithe his wealth (Genesis 28:15-22).

31.13 (cont.) Now, arise and leave this land and return to your native land."'

31.14 Then Rachel and Leah answered him, saying, "Have we still a share in the inheritance of our father's house?

31.15 Surely, he regards us as outsiders, now that he has sold us and has used up our purchase price.

31.16 Truly, all the wealth that God has taken away from our father belongs to us and to our children. Now then, do just as God has told you."

Alter explains the daughters' lament: "Laban has evidently pocketed all of the fruits of Jacob's fourteen years of labor. His daughters thus see themselves reduced to chattel by their father, not married off but rather sold for profit, as though they were not his flesh and blood."

31.17 Thereupon Jacob put his children and wives on camels;

31.18 and he drove off all his livestock and all the wealth that he had amassed, the livestock in his possession that he had acquired in Paddan-aram, to go to his father Isaac in the land of Canaan.

BELIEF IN IDOLS AND BELIEF IN GOD

31.19 Meanwhile Laban had gone to shear his sheep, and Rachel stole her father's household idols.

Rashi theorized that Rachel stole the idols in an attempt to wean her father away from idol worship. But if she stole the idols to wean her father away from idol worship, Abraham ibn Ezra (a twelfth-century Spanish-Jewish biblical commentator) asks, why would she take them with her when she could have hidden them by, for example, burying them?

More likely, she stole them because she believed they would bring good fortune on the journey back to Jacob's homeland. Various modern commentators have offered another explanation: in keeping with ancient Near Eastern beliefs, Rachel sought thereby to declare Jacob, not Laban, head of their household.

These theories notwithstanding, there is a simpler explanation. Rachel surely believed in the God of Jacob, but she might well have still believed in the power of the idols with which she grew up. Throughout history, many people around the world combined traditional pagan beliefs with belief in the God of the Bible—a fusion of religious beliefs known as "syncretism." When people believe in many visible gods, it takes a very long time to get them to believe in one invisible God.

Rachel's behavior may have been similar to that of Niels Bohr, the Nobel-Prize winning physicist who was said to keep a rabbit's foot in his laboratory. When an astonished visitor asked, "But surely, professor, you don't believe in a rabbit's foot?" Bohr responded, "Of course not. But they say a rabbit's foot brings you luck whether you believe in it or not."

Rachel, who was desperately anxious to have a child (Genesis 30:1) and then desperately anxious to have a second child, might well have been open to utilizing all means toward procuring her goal, including mandrakes and, of course, Jacob's God, but perhaps also gods from her father's household. Whatever was in Rachel's mind, the Bible makes clear it was only when "God remembered Rachel" (Genesis 30:22) that she conceived.

31.20 Jacob kept Laban the Aramean in the dark, not telling him that he was fleeing,

31.21 and fled with all that he had. Soon he was across the Euphrates and heading toward the hill country of Gilead.

31.22 On the third day, Laban was told that Jacob had fled.

31.23 So he took his kinsmen with him and pursued him a distance of seven days, catching up with him in the hill country of Gilead.

31.24 But God appeared to Laban the Aramean in a dream by night and said to him, "Beware of attempting anything with Jacob, good or bad."

God told Laban to leave Jacob alone. A person as sly and selfish as Laban could not be trusted even when he believes his motives are good.

31.25 Laban overtook Jacob. Jacob had pitched his tent on the Height, and Laban with his kinsmen encamped in the hill country of Gilead.

31.26 And Laban said to Jacob, "What did you mean by keeping me in the dark and carrying off my daughters like captives of the sword?

Laban's accusation was disingenuous. As we know from verses 14-16, Rachel and Leah hardly regarded themselves as captives; they were fully supportive of Jacob's decision to leave. And as Jacob's wives, Jacob had every right to move away and take his family and belongings with him.

Alter notes the word Laban used, *nahag*, translated here and elsewhere as "carrying off," is usually reserved for animals, as in driving animals (see verse 18: "he drove (*nahag*) his livestock…"

ESSAY: ON LYING

31.27 Why did you flee in secrecy and mislead me and not tell me? I would have sent you off with festive music, with timbrel and lyre.

Laban lied claiming he would have given Jacob so gracious a sendoff. Jacob knew Laban was lying. But did Laban know?

Laban's statement to Jacob raises an intriguing question: Do liars believe their lies? Did Laban, when he made that claim, really believe he would have sent Jacob and his family off "with festive music"? The text does not answer this question, and readers are left to reach their own conclusion.

Analyzing lies and liars is not merely intriguing; it is morally significant.

Let us begin with people who do not know they are telling an untruth. The most obvious example—when a person says something that is mistaken—is not a lie; it is an error. For a false statement to be a lie, the person making the false statement must know it's false.

So, let us focus on the individual who is not simply making an occasional mistake but who habitually lies. For such people, lying can become so natural they believe it themselves; they have actually convinced themselves they are not lying. According to a study conducted by a professor of cognitive neuroscience at University College London: "People who tell small, self-serving lies are likely to progress to bigger falsehoods, and over time, the brain appears to adapt to the dishonesty."[1]

The brain adapting to dishonesty is another way of saying the individual no longer regards the lies he or she is telling as lies. It is therefore very difficult, if not impossible, for such people to change because, having done nothing wrong in their own mind, they recognize no reason to repent and therefore no reason to change.

In the present context, it is quite possible Laban believed himself when he said, "I would have sent you off with festive music, with timbrel and lyre."

Regarding such people, I will relate an anecdote. When I debated at the Oxford Union on the question of who posed the greater obstacle to peace, Israel or Hamas, one of my two opponents said, "Israel is doing to the Palestinians what the Nazis did to the Jews."

This was as blatant a lie as one could tell. Did she believe it?

The Nazis sought to murder every Jew in Europe, and they succeeded in murdering six million of them—two of every three Jews in Europe—within four years. These were not casualties of war; they were deliberate murders of non-combatants. The Nazi killing machine was organized and systematic. By contrast, including not only internal uprisings but all of Israel's wars with its Arab neighbors, the fifteen- to thirty thousand Palestinians killed since Israel's founding in 1948 were virtually all killed as a result of the numerous attempts, first by Arab armies and later by terrorist organizations like Hamas and Hezbollah, to kill as many Israelis as possible—and ultimately wipe Israel off the map. In the course of Israel's fraught relations with its Arab neighbors, there has been nothing remotely approximating the proportion, let alone the absolute number, of European Jews killed during World War II. And not only was there no Israeli policy of genocide, the opposite of genocide has taken place: During Israel's first seventy years, the population of Palestinians inside Israel *increased seven-fold.*

Did my opponent at Oxford, who holds a doctorate in Middle East history, not know all this? Did she really believe millions of Palestinian men, women, children, and babies have been rounded up and sent to death camps?

It is impossible to believe she did.

But those who hate Israel have become so used to repeating lies about Israel there was no voice in this woman—or in my other opponent, an anti-Israel Jewish professor—that asked, "Is this true?" (Alternatively, and this is probably the case, she regarded undermining and even destroying Israel as so worthwhile a goal it justified lying.)

So, then, do people who lie on behalf of their cause know they are being dishonest? Some do, and some do not. The test comes when they are shown their supporting data is not accurate—do they then stop making that argument? If they do, they are honest people who made an error; and errors are not lies. If they do not, they place ideology above truth. That, unfortunately, is not only common, it is probably the greatest source of mass evil in the world.

This needs to be emphasized: Big lies have been the greatest source of modern evil—the genocides and mass murders of the twentieth century. Vast numbers of Germans and other Europeans believed the lies told about Jews. Consequently, many Nazis believed that in murdering Jews—including babies and children—they were doing good. So, too, a vast number of people believed communist lies about "class enemies" and took part in the wholesale slaughter of men, women, and children in the Soviet Union, China, Cambodia, and elsewhere.

That is why—whether the lie is small or large, infrequent or frequent, told by an individual or told by masses of people—every person must ask himself whenever making any claim: Am I telling the truth? There is no more important question we can ask ourselves. Those who begin by justifying small lies—even just exaggerations—will, as the University College London study showed, end up telling bigger lies, and more and more often.

But what about lying on behalf of a *good* cause?

With few exceptions, that, too, leads to bad things.

The most obvious exception is lying to save an innocent life. A non-Jew who lied to Nazis as to the whereabouts of Jews the Nazis sought to murder was not only morally right in lying, but morally obligated to do so. It is a perverse moral standard that holds lying to a Nazi about where Jews are hiding is more immoral than telling the truth, thereby enabling a Nazi to murder Jews.

However, such circumstances are rare. One therefore has to be very careful about lying for a good cause. Rarely is so much at stake that lying becomes morally justifiable.

A particularly powerful example took place at the beginning of World War I when Allied propagandists made up stories of German atrocities to bolster the case for fighting Germany. It was right to fight the Germans, but most stories of German atrocities—German soldiers tossing infants in the air and impaling them on bayonets, cutting off children's hands, burning families alive, raping nuns—were lies; and when the war ended, that became known. As a result, during World War II, when *accurate* reports of German atrocities—against Jews and others—began to circulate, many in the West dismissed the reports, citing the false reports of World War I. Those who, with good motives, spread lies about German atrocities in World War I enabled many people two decades later to dismiss the true stories of German atrocities in World War II.

Given the overwhelming importance of truth, it is no wonder the Talmud states, "God's signature is truth."

31.28 You did not even let me kiss my sons and daughters good-by! It was a foolish thing for you to do.

Laban employed an age-old tactic: the best defense is a good offense.

31.29 I have it in my power to do you harm; but the God of your father said to me last night, 'Beware of attempting anything with Jacob, good or bad.'

Laban was clearly shaken by the appearance of Jacob's God in a vision the preceding night warning him against harming Jacob. Laban did not worship this God, but he saw that Jacob had faith in Him for good reason. He seemed to fear this God had the power to harm him.

In the ancient world, pagans were tolerant of everyone else's gods and even believed gods other than their own had powers. Only the Jews insisted there is only one God, and that He is the God of everyone.

31.30 Very well, you had to leave because you were longing for your father's house; but why did you steal my gods?"

31.31 Jacob answered Laban, saying, "I was afraid because I thought you would take your daughters from me by force.

> This was Jacob's answer to Laban's first question, "Why did you flee in secrecy and mislead me and not tell me?" (verse 27).

31.32 But anyone with whom you find your gods shall not remain alive! In the presence of our kinsmen, point out what I have of yours and take it." Jacob, of course, did not know that Rachel had stolen them.

> This is Jacob's answer to Laban's second question, "But why did you steal my gods?" (verse 30). Instead of simply assuring Laban that he did not take them, Jacob made an audacious pronouncement—one that must have terrified Rachel.
>
> We are all occasionally tempted to make these types of grandiose avowals, but they are risky and rarely necessary. Jacob's statement turned out to be highly risky—and unnecessary, as it did not deter Laban from searching Jacob's and all the other tents.

31.33 So Laban went into Jacob's tent and Leah's tent and the tents of the two maidservants; but he did not find them. Leaving Leah's tent, he entered Rachel's tent.

> Why didn't Laban believe Jacob's categorical denial that neither he nor anyone with him had stolen the idols?
>
> Because Laban regularly deceived people. People who lie assume everyone else does, too. People who cheat in business, for example, assume everyone else cheats; it's part of how they justify what they do: "If I don't, everyone else will take advantage of me." This is the built-in punishment of the dishonest: they go through life convinced they are constantly being deceived. Or, as George Bernard Shaw put it: "The liar's

"The liar's punishment is not in the least that he is not believed, but that he cannot believe anyone else."

punishment is not in the least that he is not believed, but that he cannot believe anyone else."

31.34 Rachel, meanwhile, had taken the idols and placed them in the camel cushion and sat on them; and Laban rummaged through the tent without finding them.

31.35 For she said to her father, "Let not my lord take it amiss that I cannot rise before you, for the period of women is upon me." Thus he searched, but could not find the household idols.

Laban did not try to look under the cushion because menstruation was considered such an impurity; he was reluctant even to touch it. Furthermore, it would have been inconceivable to him that Rachel would run the risk of menstruating while sitting on his gods.

31.36 Now Jacob became incensed

After twenty years of forbearance, Jacob finally lost his temper, and his pent-up grievances poured forth. Ironically, while Jacob's grievances against Laban were valid and Laban's were not, he exploded over the *one* complaint by Laban that had merit: someone from Jacob's camp *did* steal Laban's idols.

31.36 (cont.) and took up his grievance with Laban. Jacob spoke up and said to Laban, "What is my crime, what is my guilt that you should pursue me?

31.37 You rummaged through all my things; what have you found of all your household objects? Set it here, before my kinsmen and yours, and let them decide between us two.

Jacob was incensed at being unjustly accused of both theft and lying after all his years of faithful service despite Laban's mistreatment of him. Now the dam broke, and Jacob bared his soul.

31.38 These twenty years I have spent in your service, your ewes and she-goats never miscarried, nor did I feast on rams from your flock.

31.39 That which was torn by beasts I never brought to you; I myself made good the loss; you exacted it of me, whether snatched by day or snatched by night.

31.40 Often, scorching heat ravaged me by day and frost by night; and sleep fled from my eyes.

31.41 Of the twenty years that I spent in your household, I served you fourteen years for your two daughters,

> Only one of whom he wanted, Jacob could have added.

31.41 (cont.) and six years for your flocks; and you changed my wages time and again.

31.42 Had not the God of my father, the God of Abraham and the Fear of Isaac, been with me, you would have sent me away empty-handed. But God took notice of my plight and the toil of my hands, and He gave judgment last night."

> This is the real reason Jacob left without saying goodbye: he knew that Laban would have tried to prevent not only Jacob's family from leaving but his livestock as well.
>
> God's "judgment last night" refers to God's revelation to Laban to do Jacob no harm.

31.43 Then Laban spoke up and said to Jacob, "The daughters are my daughters, the children are my children, and the flocks are my flocks; all that you see is mine. Yet what can I do now about my daughters or the children they have borne?

> And here is the proof: Laban viewed his daughters and grandchildren as his rightful possessions. To him, Jacob was nothing more than an indentured servant, entitled to his own freedom after his years of service expired, but not to his wives, children, or flocks (see commentary on 30:26). But he also understood how limited were his options. His daughters had free will, and they preferred to go with their husband, and he was facing the will of Jacob's God, who wanted Jacob left unharmed to return with his family to the Promised Land.

31.44 Come, then, let us make a pact, you and I, that there may be a witness between you and me."

31.45 Thereupon Jacob took a stone and set it up as a pillar.

31.46 And Jacob said to his kinsmen, "Gather stones." So they took stones and made a mound; and they partook of a meal there by the mound.

31.47 Laban named it Yegar-sahadutha, but Jacob named it Gal-ed.

31.48 And Laban declared, "This mound is a witness between you and me this day." That is why it was named Gal-ed;

> *Gal* means "mound of rocks"; *ed* means "witness."

31.49 and [it was called] Mizpah, because he said, "May the Lord watch between you and me, when we are out of sight of each other.

31.50 If you ill-treat my daughters or take other wives besides my daughters—though no one else be about, remember, God Himself will be witness between you and me."

> Though his daughters didn't seem to think their father had much interest in them at this point ("Surely, he regards us as outsiders," verse 15), Laban revealed he was still a father who cared about his daughters. Few people, even among the indecent, do not have a special place in their heart for their children.

31.51 And Laban said to Jacob, "Here is this mound and here the pillar which I have set up between you and me:

31.52 this mound shall be witness and this pillar shall be witness that I am not to cross to you past this mound, and that you are not to cross to me past this mound and this pillar, with hostile intent.

31.53 May the God of Abraham and the god of Nahor"—their ancestral deities—"judge between us." And Jacob swore by the Fear of his father Isaac.

31.54 Jacob then offered up a sacrifice on the Height, and invited his kinsmen to partake of the meal. After the meal, they spent the night on the Height.

CHAPTER
32

Note to readers: In Christian Bibles, chapter 32 begins with verse 2 (and 32:1 is 31:55). Therefore, each verse in this chapter, following the Jewish enumeration of chapters, is one verse "ahead" of Christian Bibles. Thus, 32:2 here is 32:1 in Christian translations.

32.1 Early in the morning, Laban kissed his sons and daughters and bade them good-bye; then Laban left on his journey homeward.

> As Laban's adult sons (Genesis 31:1) are not going away with Jacob's family, "his sons" refers to his eleven grandsons. Laban kissed them and his daughters good-bye, but not Jacob, who is not even mentioned.

32.2 Jacob went on his way, and angels of God encountered him.

> The Hebrew word used for angels, *malachim*, is the same word used for "messengers" in verse 4. "Angels" are God's messengers.

32.3 When he saw them, Jacob said, "This is God's camp." So he named that place Mahanaim.

> Somehow Jacob understood these messengers were from God. Perhaps their presence was intended to mitigate—though it did not fully eliminate—Jacob's fear about his upcoming encounter with Esau.
>
> *Ma-ha-naim* is a variation on the Hebrew word for "camp," *ma-ha-neh*.

32.4 Jacob sent messengers ahead to his brother Esau in the land of Seir, the country of Edom,

> The word used for "messengers" (*malachim*) is the same word used in verse 2 and previously for angels sent by God to communicate with humans. This is the first

time in the Torah a human being is the one to send messengers (*malachim*). As a rule, when God send *malachim*, we call them "angels," and when human beings send them, we call them "messengers." In both cases, they appear as humans.

32.5 and instructed them as follows, "Thus shall you say, 'To my lord Esau,

Hoping to ingratiate himself with Esau, who, Jacob believed, had been angry with him for twenty years, Jacob instructed the messengers to use deferential, even obsequious, language. According to Nachmanides (Ramban), Jacob told his messengers to speak the way younger siblings spoke to older siblings in the ancient world. In that way, Jacob would publicly acknowledge Esau as his older brother. In the words of Nachmanides: "Now Jacob was showing Esau deference, as if that sale of the birthright meant nothing to him, and he was still acting toward Esau as the firstborn…to remove the hatred from Esau's heart."

32.5 (cont.) thus says your servant Jacob: I stayed with Laban and remained until now.

Jacob explained why he did not try to make peace with his brother sooner—he was detained in Laban's home for twenty years.

32.6 I have acquired cattle, asses, sheep, and male and female slaves; and I send this message to my lord in the hope of gaining your favor.'"

Jacob hoped to propitiate Esau by hinting that his possessions would be at Esau's disposal.

32.7 The messengers returned to Jacob, saying, "We came to your brother Esau; he himself is coming to meet you, and there are four hundred men with him."

This constituted a sizable regiment in the ancient world. In chapter 14, Abraham went into battle with 318 men against a group of kings who kidnapped his nephew Lot.

32.8 Jacob was greatly frightened; in his anxiety, he divided the people with him, and the flocks and herds and camels, into two camps,

32.9 thinking, "If Esau comes to the one camp and attacks it, the other camp may yet escape."

32.10 Then Jacob said, "O God of my father Abraham and God of my father Isaac, O Lord, who said to me, 'Return to your native land and I will deal bountifully with you'!

> Jacob reminded God that returning to his native land, where his allegedly angry brother resided, was God's idea.

32.11 I am unworthy of all the kindness that You have so steadfastly shown Your servant: with my staff alone I crossed this Jordan, and now I have become two camps.

EVERYONE HAS CRISES OF FAITH

32.12 Deliver me, I pray, from the hand of my brother, from the hand of Esau; else, I fear, he may come and strike me down, mothers and children alike.

32.13 Yet You have said, 'I will deal bountifully with you and make your offspring as the sands of the sea, which are too numerous to count.'"

> God had long ago promised Jacob He would "protect" him (Genesis 28:15) and, more recently, that he would "be with" him. Why, then, did Jacob feel the need to plea to God for protection from Esau and feel it necessary to remind God of His other promise—to give Jacob offspring "too numerous to count"?
>
> This is the Torah providing another example of the most devout individuals—*even those who had direct contact with God*—experiencing doubts. This is important for two reasons:
>
> First, it should comfort every one of us who ever has doubts. Given the nature of the world we inhabit—with its pain and suffering, the uncertainty engendered by an invisible God, and the knowledge of our mortality—doubts regarding God are entirely natural. Some people claim to never have doubts. I have to believe them, but I also have to believe they are rare.
>
> Second, it shows that even if God did appear to us, we would soon again have doubts. People imagine that God could make His existence so

clear, our faith would never again falter. As the case of Jacob makes clear, that is simply not so. In order for us to never doubt God—His existence, His goodness, or His trustworthiness—God would have to make His presence apparent at all times. But if God did that, the word "faith" would become meaningless; we would have virtually no free choice—who would disobey God in His presence?

32.14 After spending the night there, he selected from what was at hand these presents for his brother Esau:

Jacob was so affluent, he could gather together generous gifts from whatever happened to be most closely adjacent to him at the time.

32.15 200 she-goats and 20 he-goats; 200 ewes and 20 rams;

32.16 30 milch camels with their colts; 40 cows and 10 bulls; 20 she-asses and 10 he-asses.

32.17 These he put in the charge of his servants, drove by drove, and he told his servants, "Go on ahead, and keep a distance between droves."

32.18 He instructed the one in front as follows, "When my brother Esau meets you and asks you, 'Whose man are you? Where are you going? And whose [animals] are these ahead of you?'

32.19 you shall answer, 'Your servant Jacob's; they are a gift sent to my lord Esau; and [Jacob] himself is right behind us.'"

32.20 He gave similar instructions to the second one, and the third, and all the others who followed the droves, namely, "Thus and so shall you say to Esau when you reach him.

32.21 And you shall add, 'And your servant Jacob himself is right behind us.'" For he reasoned, "If I propitiate him with presents in advance, and then face him, perhaps he will show me favor."

A strategic thinker, Jacob wanted to present these gifts to Esau in the most dramatic way possible. Instead of giving his brother everything at once, he instructed his servants to present the livestock in "waves"—one drove at a time—to gradually overwhelm Esau with his largess and good will.

Jacob may have taken advantage of his brother two decades before in wresting the birthright from him, but now he is more than willing to generously share the abundance of the Lord's blessings with Esau.

32.22 And so the gift went on ahead, while he remained in camp that night.

32.23 That same night he arose, and taking his two wives, his two maidservants, and his eleven children, he crossed the ford of the Jabbok.

In the ancient world, crossing a river was a monumental task, considered to be laden with significance. The Jabbok (thought to be the modern-day Zarqa River in what is now Jordan) is particularly challenging because it has steep banks on both sides.

As regards the reference to Jacob's "eleven children," the Torah previously recorded that at this point, he had twelve—eleven sons and a daughter. In light of the importance attached to sons at the time, his daughter Dinah is not mentioned (his twelfth son, Benjamin, had not yet been born).

To the modern reader, this ignoring of the daughter in the family count is troubling. But while reflecting the reality of the era in which its stories take place, the Torah (and later books of the Bible) prominently features women as important, sometimes even dominant, figures.

In order for us to never doubt God, He would have to make His presence apparent at all times. But if God did that, the word "faith" would become meaningless.

32.24 After taking them across the stream, he sent across all his possessions.

32.25 Jacob was left alone.

> After getting his family to the other side, Jacob went back across the river to send everything else. That task completed, he remained alone, awaiting the encounter with his brother.

32.25 (cont.) And a man wrestled with him until the break of dawn.

> In addition to the struggle with Esau that Jacob believed was coming, he now found himself struggling with a mysterious being at this site.

32.26 When he saw that he had not prevailed against him,

he wrenched Jacob's hip at its socket, so that the socket of his hip was strained as he wrestled with him.

32.27 Then he said, "Let me go, for dawn is breaking." But he answered, "I will not let you go, unless you bless me."

> At some point, Jacob realized the being with whom he struggled was of divine origin and demanded from him a blessing.

32.28 Said the other, "What is your name?" He replied, "Jacob."

ESSAY: THE MEANING AND IMPORTANCE OF THE NAME "ISRAEL" ("STRUGGLE WITH GOD")

32.29 Said he, "Your name shall no longer be Jacob, but Israel, for you have striven with beings divine and human, and have prevailed."

> It is almost impossible to overstate the importance of the meaning of the name "Israel." It means "struggle (*yisra*) with God (*el*)." That God would bestow this name on His People could only mean God assumes—even expects—those who believe in Him to struggle with Him.

There are believers who think struggle with God—such as questioning, or even doubting, God—is impious. But God assures us it is not only not impious but expected, and it can be meritorious.

Abraham, the first believer in this universal God, the first Jew, engaged in a prolonged and strongly worded struggle with God (Genesis 18:23-32). And God in no way even hinted it was wrong of Abraham to do so. Why did God create humans with the capacity to think, reason, and challenge if He did not want or expect them to use those God-given abilities—in general and with regard to Him?

> *God may have had His own reasons for denying us certainty with regard to His existence and nature.*

How could a thinking and feeling human being never struggle with God? How can one personally experience unjust suffering—or observe the unjust suffering of others—and *not* struggle with God? Or get frustrated or angry with God? The Psalmist certainly does: "Why do You sleep, O Lord?...Why do You hide Your face, ignoring our affliction and distress?" (Psalms 44:24-25, Hebrew text; 23-24, Christian).

By giving His Chosen People the name "Struggle with God," (in Genesis 35:10, it is God Himself, not just the "divine being" of this chapter) God was not only giving people permission to struggle with Him; He was actually asking us to. Doing so makes our faith authentic. And it is that authenticity which keeps us from turning into religious automatons.

People who have no doubts about what they believe in—whether religious believers or believers in secular doctrines—easily become zealots who often do great harm.

In the words of the late Emanuel Rackman, a prominent modern Orthodox rabbi:

"Judaism encourages doubt even as it enjoins faith and commitment. A Jew dare not live with absolute certainty, because certainty is the hallmark of the fanatic and Judaism abhors fanaticism, and because doubt is good for the human soul, its humility.... God had His own reasons for denying us certainty with regard to His existence and nature. One apparent reason is that man's certainty with regard to anything is poison to his soul. Who knows this better than moderns who have had to cope with dogmatic Fascists, Communists, and even scientists?"[1]

We all at some time struggle with our earthly father and mother—why would we never struggle with our Heavenly Father?

Struggle means our relationship with God is real: Is there any person we love with whom we have never struggled? Why would it be different with God? Likewise, we all at some time struggle with our earthly father and mother—why would we never struggle with our Heavenly Father?

(Many modern readers object to gender-based language in referring to God—such as "Heavenly Father" and "He." See the essay "Why God Is Depicted in Male Terms," in Genesis 1:1.)

I will never forget paying a *shiva* call—visiting a Jew during the seven-day mourning period (*shiva* means "seven") following the death of an immediate relative—to a young Chabad rabbi (who would be considered an "ultra-Orthodox" Jew). He had suddenly lost his wife and he, along with their seven young children, was emotionally devastated. When I walked into his home, he looked at me, sighed, and cited a famous Yiddish lament, "Mahn tracht und Gott lacht"—"Man plans and God laughs."

This is an example of a pious person being real. The lament is a dark sentiment regarding God. But it in no way signified a diminution in the rabbi's faith in God. He was simply acknowledging the reality of "struggle with God." He had God's permission, even invitation, to do so.

At the same time, "struggle with God" also demands that non-believers struggle with their non-belief. The Torah is, in essence, telling any secular Jew who wishes to take being a Jew seriously that he, too, must struggle with God; he must struggle with his atheism or agnosticism and struggle to believe. To paraphrase Elie Wiesel, "A Jew can love God or fight with God, but he cannot ignore God."

The term "secular Jew" may need explanation. Many non-Jews find the term "secular Jew," or "Jewish atheist," difficult to comprehend: there is, for example, no such thing as a "Christian atheist." That is because Christianity is a religion, not a people. A Christian, by definition, is a person who holds Christian beliefs, but a Jew is a Jew even if he is an atheist because Jews are both a people and a religion.

I suspect many more Jewish and Christian believers wrestle with faith than atheists wrestle with atheism. (See the essay "Is it OK for believers to have doubts?" at Genesis 12:12.)

That "Israel" means "struggle with God" is a distinguishing feature of Judaism and the Torah. This was illustrated in my early days of broadcasting when a Muslim woman called my radio show.

She said: "You say we can ask you anything. Is that correct?"

"Yes," I responded.

"So, I would like to know: Why aren't you a Muslim?"

I told her I was honored by her call—by her belief that I had enough knowledge about Islam to give a thoughtful answer (she was aware I had studied Islam and Arabic).

I responded, "My answer lies in the words for each religion—'Islam' and 'Israel.' 'Islam' means 'submit to God' and 'Israel' means 'struggle with God.' I would rather struggle with God than submit to God."

The woman contemplated that for a moment, then simply responded: "Thank you."

I was touched by that woman—that, as a believing Muslim, she found the answer completely valid. Muslims are not taught to struggle with God. Nor, in my experience, are many Christians, even though Genesis is as much a part of the Christian Bible as it is the Hebrew Bible.

> *The Torah is, in essence, telling any secular Jew who wishes to take being a Jew seriously that he, too, must struggle with God; he must struggle with his atheism or agnosticism.*

I am often surprised by how many Christians—many of whom know the Old Testament better than many religious Jews—do not know that "Israel" means "struggle with God."

To anyone seeking religious guidance, I believe just knowing the meaning of the word "Israel" should elicit intellectual respect for the Torah. No other religious book or secular doctrine demands its adherents struggle with it.

32.30 Jacob asked, "Pray tell me your name." But he said, "You must not ask my name!" And he took leave of him there.

The first thing humans want to know about strangers is who they are. Moses later asked God the same question at the burning bush. God offered only a terse and cryptic response: "I am what I am" (Exodus 3:13-14). Man cannot know God's name because divinity is unknowable. As an anonymous medieval Hebrew philosopher put it, *lu yadativ, hayitiv,* "If I knew God, I'd be God."

32.31 So Jacob named the place Peniel, meaning, "I have seen a divine being face to face,

Peniel literally means "the face of God."

The Hebrew here says "God" (Elohim) not "divine being," as translated. Yet, in the last chapter of the Torah (Deuteronomy 34:10), the Torah writes, "Never again did there arise in Israel a prophet like Moses—whom the Lord singled out, face to face." How then did Jacob see God "face to face"? For one thing, Jacob did not see God face to face; Jacob saw a divine being (hence the present translation, "divine being"). Second, it is Jacob who says he saw God face to face, not the Torah. From Jacob's perspective, the divine being was essentially "God."

32.31 (cont.) yet my life has been preserved."

It is an innovation of the Torah that a person cannot see God and live (Exodus 33:20).

32.32 The sun rose upon him as he passed Penuel,

The Hebrew is Penuel, and is the same place as Peniel.

32.32 (cont.) limping on his hip.

HOW TO PRESERVE NATIONAL MEMORY

32.33 That is why the children of Israel to this day do not eat the thigh muscle that is on the socket of the hip, since Jacob's hip socket was wrenched at the thigh muscle.

> To this day, kosher butchers remove the sciatic nerve from meat. This practice is an example of the centrality of physical signs and rituals in the Torah and in Jewish tradition. As I understand it, the Torah's laws—ritual and moral—have three primary purposes (some of the laws fit into all three categories, but each fits into at least one):
>
> 1. To produce a moral individual.
> 2. To bring holiness into one's life.
> 3. To preserve Jewish national memory.

The removal of the sciatic nerve falls into the third category. These laws of national memory are a major reason Jews, unlike other nations and religions from the ancient world, have survived for more than three thousand years. A nation without a memory will cease to exist.

As a general rule, the Torah believes people can best internalize a value (or memory) through physical representation. For instance, instead of just being told to remember they were slaves in Egypt, Jews are instructed to eat bread that has not risen (matzah)—as the Israelites did when they fled Egypt—for seven days each year (Passover) and to observe a Passover Seder, where they are to eat bitter herbs so as to "remember" the bitterness of slavery.

The Torah and Judaism are behaviorist in their approach to life. How we behave is ultimately more important than how we think or feel. This is one of the greatest differences between the Torah and the contemporary mind, which attaches far more importance to how people feel. That the behavioral approach is superior should be obvious upon a moment's reflection. Do we care more about how people feel about us or how they treat us? Are the poor helped more by compassionate words or by compassionate deeds?

33.1 Looking up, Jacob saw Esau coming, accompanied by four hundred men. He divided the children among Leah, Rachel, and the two maids,

> Jacob was fearful because he had reason to assume Esau was still angry with him—and Esau's four hundred men only exacerbated his fear.

33.2 putting the maids and their children first, Leah and her children next, and Rachel and Joseph last.

> In a rather unsubtle demonstration of his favoritism, Jacob divided his camp in the order of his love for them, placing his treasured wife Rachel and her son Joseph in the back so that they would be the last to be harmed should enemy forces attack.

33.3 He himself went on ahead

> Despite his fear, Jacob showed courage by confronting Esau head-on.

33.3 (cont.) and bowed low to the ground seven times until he was near his brother.

> Jacob's gesture may have been a demonstration of respect for his older brother, but it was also clearly an act of self-humiliation. The Hebrew phrase "bowed low to the ground" (vayishtachu artza) denotes a full-length proneness of the body in submission to a superior authority (Sarna).
>
> Jon Levenson, a professor of Bible at Harvard University, notes the irony in this situation: "The scene reverses the dominance of Jacob over Esau prophesied in Genesis 25:23 and 27:29, 37 [which predicted Esau will bow to Jacob]."[1]

33.4 Esau ran to greet him. He embraced him and, falling on his neck, he kissed him; and they wept.

The age-old maxim "time heals all wounds" seems to have been in operation here. Both Esau and Jacob were overcome with sincere affection and emotional catharsis. Esau was not a bad man, and the Torah never portrays him as such. It is true Esau did not care about spiritual matters, and he was a gruff man of the earth; but the Torah never depicts him as mean-spirited. Moreover, he was a devoted son—which in my book and, more importantly, this Book—counts for a lot: honoring one's parents is one of the Ten Commandments.

In addition to reacting to this emotional moment—reuniting with his only sibling after twenty years—Jacob's tears must have been at least partially out of profound relief that his brother's greeting was one of familial love, not hostility or, worse, violence.

33.5 Looking about, he saw the women and the children. "Who," he asked, "are these with you?" He answered, "The children with whom God has favored your servant."

Jacob, not wanting to take any chances, continued to speak to his brother in submissive terms.

I have long wondered how Esau reacted to Jacob addressing him as "my lord" and to Jacob referring to himself as "your servant." While younger brothers were expected to show deference to their older sibling(s), Jacob's language went well beyond the expected standard. Bowing low to the ground seven times and speaking of himself in so servile a manner are not the normal manners or language a younger brother would use upon meeting an older brother, even after a long separation. Did Esau not wonder, "What is all this servile language and behavior about?" And if he did, why didn't he suggest Jacob speak normally to him?

I can offer two possible explanations. One is that Esau was not a particularly introspective man who would have thought deeply about this. The other is that he may have liked it.

33.6 Then the maids, with their children, came forward and bowed low;

33.7 next Leah, with her children, came forward and bowed low; and last, Joseph and Rachel came forward and bowed low.

When Jacob's servants and family members saw the extent to which Jacob honored his older brother, they took their cues from him and paid similar respect. These bows would have demonstrated to Esau that Jacob had effectively conveyed to his family how much he respected his brother.

Alternatively, and perhaps more likely, they all shared Jacob's apprehension of Esau, and therefore sought to honor him as much as possible. They undoubtedly understood the reason Jacob had divided them up into separate camps prior to the meeting.

33.8 And he asked, "What do you mean by all this company which I have met?"

Esau wanted to know why Jacob had sent ahead such an extraordinary array of gifts.

33.8 (cont.) He answered, "To gain my lord's favor."

This was quite an honest answer on Jacob's part.

33.9 Esau said, "I have enough, my brother; let what you have remain yours."

And this was quite an honorable answer on Esau's part.

33.10 But Jacob said, "No, I pray you; if you would do me this favor, accept from me this gift; for to see your face is like seeing the face of God, and you have received me favorably.

Some readers might regard Jacob's comment that seeing Esau's face was like seeing God's face as Jacob being willing to say anything to gain Esau's favor. But it may have been authentic. Jacob had asked God for a warm and friendly welcome, and in Jacob's view, his prayer was directly answered. It may well have seemed to Jacob as if God were greeting him.

JACOB OWES ESAU AMENDS

33.11 Please accept my present which has been brought to you, for God has favored me and I have plenty." And when he urged him, he accepted.

The Hebrew word translated here as "my present" is actually the Hebrew word "my blessing." Thus, Hebrew readers would not have missed the power of what Jacob was, in effect, saying: "While I once took your blessing, I now give back to you a blessing."

But the word was likely also a reminder of the history between the brothers. Esau accepted Jacob's gifts but did not offer any gifts of his own in return. Perhaps Esau, who saw himself as having been cheated out of his blessing, did not feel he owed Jacob anything.

Richard Elliott Friedman writes: "Unlike biblical interpreters who try to defend Jacob's earlier actions, Jacob himself is pictured as (1) not trying to make any excuses, and (2) trying to make amends." As one of those who does offer a defense of Jacob's earlier actions, I nevertheless acknowledge that Jacob needed to make amends.

33.12 And [Esau] said, "Let us start on our journey, and I will proceed at your pace."

33.13 But he said to him, "My lord knows that the children are frail and that the flocks and herds, which are nursing, are a care to me; if they are driven hard a single day, all the flocks will die.

33.14 Let my lord go on ahead of his servant, while I travel slowly, at the pace of the cattle before me and at the pace of the children, until I come to my lord in Seir."

Though they had just concluded a warm reunion, Jacob had little interest in traveling with his brother (or, as will become clear, in meeting up with him in Esau's land, Seir). While Jacob seemed truly happy to have reconciled with Esau, he deemed it best if they each went their separate ways. Jacob probably believed, in the words of an old expression, "they buried the hatchet, but each one remembers where the hatchet was buried." Too much exposure to each other might fray their fragile truce.

33.15 Then Esau said, "Let me assign to you some of the men who are with me." But he said, "Oh no, my lord is too kind to me!"

> Esau offered some of his men to protect Jacob who, traveling with women, young children, and large flocks, was vulnerable to bandits. Though he made it this far without encountering trouble, perhaps Esau knew something about the nature of some of the people in the region. There was probably a reason he had an army of four hundred men.

33.16 So Esau started back that day on his way to Seir.

33.17 But Jacob journeyed on to Succoth, and built a house for himself and made stalls for his cattle; that is why the place was called Succoth.

> This appears to confirm that despite what he'd said in verse 14, Jacob had no intention of meeting up with Esau in Seir.
>
> Succoth is a Hebrew word which means "booths" or "little houses."

33.18 Jacob arrived safe in the city of Shechem which is in the land of Canaan—having come thus from Paddan-aram—and he encamped before the city.

33.19 The parcel of land where he pitched his tent he purchased from the children of Hamor, Shechem's father, for a hundred kesitahs.

33.20 He set up an altar there, and called it El-elohei-yisrael.

> This Hebrew phrase means "El, God of Israel."

CHAPTER
34

34.1 Now Dinah, the daughter whom Leah had borne to Jacob, went out to visit the daughters of the land.

> The Torah explains why Dinah was out on her own: she was not looking for men or for trouble (which for young women is often the same thing). As the sole daughter with eleven brothers, she understandably wanted to meet and befriend other women. Nevertheless, in many traditional cultures, it was (and is to this day) risky for an unmarried young woman to venture out on her own.

34.2 Shechem son of Hamor the Hivite, chief of the country, saw her, and took her and lay with her by force.

> These three verbs describe the three stages of a rape: a man sees a woman, takes her sexually by force, and causes her to suffer. The Hebrew word translated here as "by force" (*vayina-e-hah*) literally means "he made her suffer." The use of this word makes it clear Dinah in no way wanted what happened to her, and it was therefore rape.[1]

RAPE FOLLOWED BY LOVING WORDS

34.3 Being strongly drawn to Dinah daughter of Jacob, and in love with the maiden, he spoke to the maiden tenderly.

> After raping Dinah, Shechem fell in love with her. This juxtaposition of violence and love is, unfortunately, a realistic portrayal of more than a few men's behavior.

Shechem "spoke to the maiden tenderly" in order to convince her to marry him—either because he really did think he loved her or because he hoped her agreement to marry him would render him acceptable to her family, who would then not seek to exact revenge for the rape. In any case, he clearly was not confident that his feelings were reciprocated by Dinah, for he kept her under a kind of house arrest (Telushkin; see verse 26).

Although most ancient societies had laws against raping women of their own tribe or clan, there was rarely, if ever, an explicit prohibition against raping women of other clans. Thus, Shechem would not necessarily think that he had done anything morally wrong in violating a foreign woman, but he would surely recognize that Dinah's clan would view his behavior as inexcusable.

The idea people owe decent behavior to members of other groups was one of the Torah's radical moral innovations. Indeed, the commandment to love the stranger is the most frequently repeated commandment in the Torah.

34.4 So Shechem said to his father Hamor,

Hamor is the Hebrew word for "donkey." Shechem was therefore the "son of a donkey," something that would have greatly amused the ancient Israelites who recounted this story.

34.4 (cont.) "Get me this girl as a wife."

Shechem's blunt language reflected Shechem's—and his world's—view of women: they were property to be acquired.

34.5 Jacob heard that he had defiled his daughter Dinah; but since his sons were in the field with his cattle, Jacob kept silent until they came home.

34.6 Then Shechem's father Hamor came out to Jacob to speak to him.

34.7 Meanwhile Jacob's sons, having heard the news, came in from the field. The men were distressed

and very angry, because he had committed an outrage in Israel by lying with Jacob's daughter—a thing not to be done.

34.8 And Hamor spoke with them, saying, "My son Shechem longs for your daughter. Please give her to him in marriage.

> Hamor's manner of speaking skirted the fact that his son had already done much more than simply "long for" Dinah. He made it seem as if nothing untoward had taken place. This is a common defensive human trait: minimizing our misbehavior or that of a relative (especially a child).

34.9 Intermarry with us: give your daughters to us, and take our daughters for yourselves:

> Hamor proposed an exchange of daughters who would presumably have no say in the matter. However, even in such ancient cultures, women's wishes were not always disregarded. Laban and Bethuel, Rebecca's father and brother, had initially negotiated Rebecca's marriage to Isaac without any input from her (Genesis 24:50-51); but then, before the deal was finalized, they said, "Let us call the young woman and ask for her reply." Only after Rebecca was asked, "Will you go with this man [Abraham's emissary and negotiator]?" and she answered, "I will" did she set out on the journey to meet and marry Isaac (Genesis 24:57-61). The Talmud subsequently ruled, "A father is forbidden to marry off his daughter while she is a minor. He must wait until she is grown up and says, "I want so-and-so."[2]

34.10 You will dwell among us, and the land will be open before you; settle, move about, and acquire holdings in it."

> Hamor sweetened the proposal, hoping that even if Jacob and his sons know what was done to Dinah, their desire for peace, land, and wealth would enable them to overlook it.

34.11 Then Shechem said to her father and brothers, "Do me this favor, and I will pay whatever you tell me.

Determined to do whatever it takes to win the woman he desires, Shechem further sweetened his father's proposal. Underlying his offer was the assumption that Jacob and his sons could be bought.

34.12 Ask of me a bride-price ever so high, as well as gifts, and I will pay what you tell me; only give me the maiden for a wife."

There are two possibilities for Shechem's offer of a "blank check": either he really was in love with Dinah or he was afraid of Jacob's clan and would do whatever it took to assuage their anger.

34.13 Jacob's sons answered Shechem and his father Hamor—speaking with guile because he had defiled their sister Dinah—

Dinah was being held in the town of Shechem, so her family would say whatever they deemed necessary, and negotiate any agreement, to get her back. The Torah tells us Jacob's sons answered "with guile" because they had a plan that hinged on pretending they didn't know their sister had been defiled by Shechem.

34.14 and said to them, "We cannot do this thing, to give our sister to a man who is uncircumcised, for that is a disgrace among us.

Every nation has a derogatory way of referring to other nations, and the ancient Israelites were no exception: To them, the term "uncircumcised" signified a man who was on a lower level—certainly not an appropriate match for one of their daughters.

34.15 Only on this condition will we agree with you; that you will become like us in that every male among you is circumcised.

34.16 Then we will give our daughters to you and take your daughters to ourselves; and we will dwell among you and become as one kindred.

34.17 But if you will not listen to us and become circumcised, we will take our daughter and go."

34.18 Their words pleased Hamor and Hamor's son Shechem.

34.19 And the youth lost no time in doing the thing, for he wanted Jacob's daughter. Now he was the most respected in his father's house.

> The Hebrew term used here to describe Shechem, "youth," is *na'ar*, the male equivalent of *na'arah*, the word used to describe Dinah (verse 3, translated here as "maiden"). He was, therefore, about as young as she. Avraham Even-Shoshan, author of what is generally regarded as the most authoritative Hebrew dictionary, defines *na'ar* as a term that generally refers to a young person between ages twelve and fifteen (though that may not necessarily accurately define the term as the Torah always uses it).[3] In other words, this was probably not a fully grown adult man who took Dinah.

> Shechem was his father's favorite son, which explains Hamor's willingness to go to great lengths to get him the woman he now claimed to love.

34.20 So Hamor and his son Shechem went to the public place of their town and spoke to their fellow townsmen, saying,

> Having struck a deal with Jacob's sons, Hamor was now in a difficult position with respect to his fellow townsmen. Though he was chief of Shechem (verse 2), that did not give him the authority to command the townsmen to circumcise themselves. He could only try to persuade them it was in their best interest to do so.

34.21 "These people are our friends; let them settle in the land and move about in it, for the land is large enough for them; we will take their daughters to ourselves as wives and give our daughters to them.

> Hamor and Shechem conveniently neglected to mention they had also promised Jacob's sons full property rights and as much money as they wanted—money Hamor would likely acquire from taxing the townspeople. They also neglected to mention the reason they made this deal, as the townsmen would never agree to circumcise themselves for the sake of one young man's love interest—or

worse, to help extricate him from the consequences of his wrongdoing against a foreign woman and her clan.

34.22 But only on this condition will the men agree with us to dwell among us and be as one kindred: that all our males become circumcised as they are circumcised.

34.23 Their cattle and substance and all their beasts will be ours, if we only agree to their terms, so that they will settle among us."

This promise was completely fabricated; Jacob's sons never agreed to give up their possessions and livestock. Apparently, the Hivites (understandably) did not respond favorably when Hamor and Shechem told them they should agree to circumcise themselves, so father and son came up with this additional incentive.

Only by acknowledging how bad the human condition is does one appreciate how necessary the rest of the Torah is.

Jacob's sons were deceiving Hamor and Shechem, and Hamor and Shechem in turn were deceiving their clan. Genesis is filled with people deceiving other people—because Genesis describes the human condition. Only by acknowledging how bad the human condition is does one appreciate how necessary the rest of the Torah is. It provides the moral guidelines to solve the problems of the human condition.

34.24 All who went out of the gate of his town heeded Hamor and his son Shechem, and all males, all those who went out of the gate of his town, were circumcised.

Once they thought the payoff would be riches, the townsmen were willing to circumcise themselves. People will endure a great deal of pain for a great deal of money.

34.25 On the third day, when they were in pain, Simeon and Levi, two of Jacob's sons, brothers of Dinah, took each his sword, came upon the city unmolested, and slew all the males.

This was a clear instance of clan violence. The brothers exacted massive revenge against an entire town of innocent people (there is nothing in the text that implicates the townspeople in Shechem's crime).

Simeon and Levi were Dinah's full brothers (all three were children of Leah). Though the text doesn't say so, given the amount of violence they inflicted, it is reasonable to assume they were not alone.

Even though Simeon and Levi were foreigners bearing swords, the inhabitants of Shechem allowed them to enter "unmolested" because of the deal they had made—a betrayal of trust that makes the brothers' behavior all the more reprehensible.

34.26 They put Hamor and his son Shechem to the sword, took Dinah out of Shechem's house, and went away.

There is a plausible defense of Simeon and Levi: they did not believe Shechem would release their sister without a wedding. Therefore, they had to rescue her, and could do so only while the citizenry was disabled. Furthermore, following the mores of the time and place, these brothers knew they could not kill only Shechem and his father, the clan's chief; leaving any of the male Shechemites alive would have led to a counterattack.

The problem with this defense is the brothers didn't make it! In verse 31, they stated their only reason was Dinah's and their family's honor. We, today, would argue the family's honor was defiled by their mass killing, not by the rape of Dinah. But they didn't live today; they lived three thousand years ago.

This culture of "honor," of "saving face" through revenge killing, still operates in much of the region to the present day. The Torah sought to replace it with God's values—including trial by courts of law before meting out penalties; punishment of only the wrongdoer, not his entire clan; and punishment proportional to the crime.

34.27 The other sons of Jacob came upon the slain and plundered the town, because their sister had been defiled.

34.28 They seized their flocks and herds and asses, all that was inside the town and outside;

34.29 all their wealth, all their children, and their wives, all that was in the houses, they took as captives and booty.

Whatever justification there could conceivably have been for the killings, there was no conceivable justification for the kidnapping and the looting.

34.30 Jacob said to Simeon and Levi, "You have brought trouble on me, making me odious among the inhabitants of the land, the Canaanites and the Perizzites; my men are few in number, so that if they unite against me and attack me, I and my house will be destroyed."

For reasons that are not clear, Jacob's criticism was directed at Simeon and Levi alone, even though the behavior of his other sons was also abhorrent. But Simeon and Levi started the whole terrible process. Whatever the reason, this was a failure on Jacob's part: Instead of censuring his sons for committing evil, Jacob complained they had endangered his household. In short, Jacob responded not with moral outrage, but with pragmatic rebuke. To be fair, however, Jacob did morally rebuke these two sons on his deathbed.

The heartlessness displayed toward the town of Shechem by Jacob's sons, and their disregard for its impact on their father, foreshadowed the heartlessness they later displayed in the treatment of their younger brother, Joseph, and the effect it had on their father (Genesis 37:18-27). Cruelty leads to more cruelty.

This story makes the Israelites appear odious. Nevertheless the Torah includes it. The Torah is an honest and balanced portrayal of the Israelites and of the full range of human behavior (which the Torah seeks to influence). Its honesty about the Jews and about humanity is a major reason I believe the Torah is true.

34.31 But they answered, "Should our sister be treated like a whore?"

Like their grandfather, Laban, the brothers employed the principle that the best defense is a good offense. They essentially said to their father, "Should we allow our sister—your daughter—to be violated by a stranger and married off to her rapist just so that our household can be safe and secure?"

Presented this way, the brothers undermined Jacob's pragmatic rebuke. Though their defense did not justify killing innocent people or plundering the town and its remaining inhabitants—innocent women and children—Jacob could think of nothing to say in response. Not until many years later, on his deathbed, did Jacob strongly condemn these two sons on moral grounds: "Their weapons are tools of violence. Let not my person be included in their council... For when angry they slay men... Cursed be their anger so fierce, and their wrath so relentless"—Genesis 49:5-7).

PHYSICAL REMINDERS TO BE GRATEFUL

35.1 God said to Jacob, "Arise, go up to Bethel and remain there; and build an altar there to the God who appeared to you when you were fleeing from your brother Esau."

This is the only time God told a patriarch to build an altar. All other times, the patriarchs spontaneously built one.

Perhaps God wanted Jacob to have a physical reminder of His intervention on Jacob's behalf "when you were fleeing from your brother Esau." Gratitude must be constantly fed (unlike resentment, which lives on naturally), and physical reminders are essential.

The Torah is filled with commandments consisting of physical reminders—e.g., eating unleavened bread (matzah) for the seven days of Passover each year (which symbolizes, among other things, it is better to live in freedom and eat poor food than to remain in slavery even if one eats well) and building booths on the Festival of Booths (Succot/Tabernacles) to remind the Israelites forever of the booths in which they dwelled in the wilderness after God took them out of slavery in Egypt.

> *Gratitude must be constantly fed (unlike resentment, which lives on naturally).*

Every good trait must be taught, and no trait is more essential to goodness than gratitude. That's why good parents repeatedly remind their children over and over to say, "Thank you" when something is done on their behalf.

MONOTHEISM WAS NOT ADOPTED OVERNIGHT

35.2 So Jacob said to his household and to all who were with him, "Rid yourselves of the alien gods in your midst, purify yourselves, and change your clothes.

Perhaps Jacob was referring to the idols Rachel had stolen from her father's house (Genesis 31:19), or perhaps these were gods his clan had picked up from the polytheistic inhabitants of Shechem (or both).

It undoubtedly comes as a surprise to some readers that members of Jacob's household kept idols for such a long time. But the Torah does not leave out embarrassing details about its heroes, and it makes the point that establishing ethical monotheism among the Israelites was neither fast nor easy.

HOW TORAH MONOTHEISM CHANGED THE WORLD

This is the first time that the Torah draws a contrast between the God of Israel and other gods. Biblical monotheism and the Torah's denial of all other gods served as the single most important moral and intellectual advance in history. See the commentary on Exodus 8:6, in which I offer fifteen world-transforming consequences of biblical monotheism. For the reader's convenience, I will briefly list them here.

The God introduced by the Torah:

1. Is the first god in history to have been entirely above and beyond nature.
2. Brought universal morality into the world.
3. Means "good" and "evil" are not individual or societal opinions but objectively real.

4. Morally judges every human being.

5. Gives humanity hope.

6. Introduced holiness—the elevation of humans from animal-like to beings created in God's image.

7. Gives every individual unprecedented self-worth.

8. Is necessary for human brotherhood.

9. Began the long journey to belief in human equality.

10. Is incorporeal (no body; not physical).

11. Teaches us the physical realm is not the only reality.

12. Means there is ultimate meaning to existence and to each of our lives.

13. Gives human beings free will.

14. Teaches might is not right.

15. Made human moral progress possible.

ON REGARDING GOD AS PROVIDER

35.3 Come, let us go up to Bethel, and I will build an altar there to the God who answered me when I was in distress and who has been with me wherever I have gone."

Jacob spoke of God in personal terms, focusing on what God had done for him. Gratitude is powerful, as it is the mother of both goodness and happiness. Neither is possible without gratitude. (This is an instance of a virtue that is rewarded in this world since gratitude is a prerequisite for happiness.)

But a word of caution is appropriate here. The view of God as provider can lead to problems—to regarding God as a sort of "celestial butler," a heavenly being whose purpose is to provide for us whenever we need something. This is not only unsophisticated; it can be dangerous to one's faith. If God's primary role is to do things for us, what happens when He doesn't? People may stop believing in Him. If the Provider stops providing, maybe there is no Provider.

> *If God's primary role is to do things for us, what happens when He doesn't?*

God failing to "deliver" as expected is one of the most common reasons people stop believing in God.

This is not Jacob's sole understanding of God, but if one has only the view of God expressed by Jacob here, one is inviting potentially major theological difficulties.

35.4 They gave to Jacob all the alien gods that they had, and the rings that were in their ears, and Jacob buried them under the terebinth that was near Shechem.

The modern Etz Chayyim Torah commentary explains these were no ordinary pieces of jewelry, but apparently talismans adorned with pagan symbols.

"Jacob intuitively senses that the continued presence of these gods is irreconcilable with the new life he has found in Yahweh. The whole incident must be read as an illustration of Jacob's religious maturation" (Hamilton).

35.5 As they set out, a terror from God fell on the cities round about, so that they did not pursue the sons of Jacob.

35.6 Thus Jacob came to Luz—that is, Bethel—in the land of Canaan, he and all the people who were with him.

35.7 There he built an altar and named the site El-bethel, for it was there that God had revealed Himself to him when he was fleeing from his brother.

35.8 Deborah, Rebekah's nurse, died, and was buried under the oak below Bethel; so it was named Allon-bacuth.

Given that we know nothing about Deborah, this detail seems hardly worthy of mention. She had appeared in the biblical narrative once before: she was the unnamed nurse—presumably a childhood nanny who worked and cared for Rebecca throughout her life—whom Rebecca took with her when she accompanied Abraham's servant back to Canaan to marry Isaac (Genesis 24:59). As a last tie to Rebecca's childhood, this death must have mattered to her.

Sarna contends more details were known about Deborah at some earlier point in Jewish history, so her death would have interested early readers.

It is, to say the least, interesting that Deborah's death is mentioned but Rebecca's is not. Rebecca and Leah are the only two of the matriarchs and patriarchs whose deaths are not recorded. The Torah notes only that Rebecca and Leah were buried in the Cave of Machpelah along with the patriarchs and Sarah (Genesis 49:31).

35.9 God appeared again to Jacob on his arrival from Paddan-aram, and He blessed him.

GOD DIRECTLY AFFIRMS JACOB'S NAME-CHANGE TO ISRAEL

35.10 God said to him,
"you whose name is Jacob,
You shall be called Jacob no more,
But Israel shall be your name."
Thus He named him Israel.

Jacob's name-change was already decreed in Genesis 32:29. But it was a messenger of God, not God Himself, who made the announcement.

35.11 And God said to him,
"I am El Shaddai.
Be fertile and increase;
A nation, yea an assembly of nations,
Shall descend from you.

"Assembly of nations" most likely refers to all nations that eventually affirm God, not biological descendants (see "from your loins" below). A similar promise was expressed in God's blessing to Abraham: "All the families of the earth shall bless themselves by you" (Genesis 12:3).

35.11 (cont.) Kings shall issue from your loins.

These kings which "issue from your loins" does refer to biological descendants.

35.12 The land that I assigned to Abraham and Isaac

I assign to you;

And to your offspring to come

Will I assign the land."

Although God is universal, the Land of Israel is designated for the Israelite/Jewish people.

35.13 God parted from him at the spot where He had spoken to him;

35.14 and Jacob set up a pillar at the site where He had spoken to him, a pillar of stone, and he offered a libation on it and poured oil upon it.

35.15 Jacob gave the site, where God had spoken to him, the name of Bethel.

35.16 They set out from Bethel; but when they were still some distance short of Ephrath, Rachel was in childbirth, and she had hard labor.

35.17 When her labor was at its hardest, the midwife said to her, "Have no fear, for it is another boy for you."

35.18 But as she breathed her last—for she was dying—she named him Ben-oni; but his father called him Benjamin.

Ben-oni is generally understood to mean "Son of Mourning."

Jacob's name for his new son, Benjamin (Binyamin) has at least three possible interpretations:

1. Yamin is the Hebrew word for "right," so Binyamin could mean "Son of My Right Hand," a symbol of dexterity, power, and protection.

2. Rashi notes that the word yamina referred to the South in ancient languages, so Binyamin could mean "Son of the South," where this boy was born. He alone of Jacob's sons is born in Canaan.

3. Rashbam notes that the Hebrew word yamin may be understood as yamim (see Daniel 12:13), which is Hebrew for "days"; thus Jacob, who is now an old man, could be naming Benjamin "Son of my Days."

Whatever interpretation one accepts, if *oni* means "mourning" (or "my sorrow"), it is easy to understand why Jacob would not be pleased with that name. Among other reasons, he would not want his son saddled with a name that would forever remind him and those who knew him that his birth caused, or at least accompanied, his mother's death.

35:19 Thus Rachel died. She was buried on the road to Ephrath—now Bethlehem.

35.20 Over her grave Jacob set up a pillar; it is the pillar at Rachel's grave to this day.

35.21 Israel journeyed on, and pitched his tent beyond Migdal-eder.

WHY DOES REUBEN SLEEP WITH HIS FATHER'S CONCUBINE?

35.22 While Israel stayed in that land, Reuben went and lay with Bilhah, his father's concubine;

Reuben slept with Bilhah, who had been Rachel's servant, in an effort to ensure she would not supplant Leah as the new chief wife now that Rachel has died. "The Talmud saw in the story an intention on the part of Reuben to defile the slavegirl of his mother's dead rival, Rachel, and so to make her sexually taboo to Jacob" (Alter).

Reuben was very dedicated to his mother Leah, as the earlier incident with the mandrakes showed (Genesis 30:14).

35.22 (cont.) and Israel found out.

Though Jacob later criticized and punished Reuben for his behavior, he apparently said nothing at the time of this incident.

However, at the end of Jacob's life, his awareness of his son's behavior was reflected in the blessings he gave his sons: He rebuked Reuben, his firstborn, and denied him his birthright hegemony over the other sons/tribes—"for you ascended your father's bed" (Gen 49:3–4).

35.22 (cont.) Now the sons of Jacob were twelve in number.

35.23 The sons of Leah: Reuben—Jacob's first-born—Simeon, Levi, Judah, Issachar, and Zebulun.

35.24 The sons of Rachel: Joseph and Benjamin.

35.25 The sons of Bilhah, Rachel's maid: Dan and Naphtali.

35.26 And the sons of Zilpah, Leah's maid: Gad and Asher. These are the sons of Jacob who were born to him in Paddan-aram.

35.27 And Jacob came to his father Isaac at Mamre, at Kiriath-arba—now Hebron—where Abraham and Isaac had sojourned.

35.28 Isaac was a hundred and eighty years old

35.29 when he breathed his last and died. He was gathered to his kin in ripe old age;

> The phrase "gathered to his kin" was previously used in recounting Abraham's death (see 25:8). Now Isaac joined his deceased relatives in the afterlife. (To understand why "gathered to his kin" implies the afterlife, see the essay in Genesis 25:8.)

ESAU WAS NOT A BAD MAN

35.29 (cont.) and he was buried by his sons Esau and Jacob.

> Once again, Esau proved himself to be a respectful and dutiful son. Though he was not the right person to carry on the monotheist tradition, he was a decent human being. I believe he is unfairly maligned by some later commentaries on the Bible. The Torah may well share this opinion because it lists Esau first here: "This seems rather to be a sign of recognition, compassion, and compensation to Esau for his displacement by Jacob" (Friedman).

CHAPTER
36

GOD AND THE TORAH CARE ABOUT ALL NATIONS (AND INDIVIDUALS)

36.1 This is the line of Esau—that is, Edom.

Though Esau's line is not a part of the covenantal community, the Torah devotes an entire chapter to the genealogy of his descendants—because he, too, was the recipient of divine promises. As is made clear repeatedly in the Torah, God cares not only about the Jewish people but about all people, including the descendants of Esau, some of whom became Israel's archrivals. As Victor Hamilton writes, Chapter 36 "is given over exclusively to genealogy—Esau's family and lists of Edomite leaders. Illustrative of the Bible's interest in the development and history of other nations is the inclusion of forty-three verses that trace meticulously the proliferation and history of the Edomites."

Jon Levenson makes an additional telling point about the extensive genealogy here: "The attention given to Esau's family suggests considerable fraternal feeling for him." The Torah even commands the Israelites not to hate Edomites (the descendants of Esau) "for he is your kinsman" (Deuteronomy 23:8, 23:7 in Christian texts).

36.2 Esau took his wives from among the Canaanite women—Adah daughter of Elon the Hittite, and Oholibamah daughter of Anah daughter of Zibeon the Hivite—

Isaac, unhappy with Esau's choice of Canaanites wives (Genesis 26:34-35), instructed his other son, Jacob, not to marry a Canaanite (Genesis 28:1). In the aftermath of this appeal to Jacob, Esau, in deference to his father, married a cousin, Mahalath, the daughter of Ishmael (Genesis 28:9), and therefore Abraham's granddaughter. The wives mentioned here, though, are Canaanites, and Esau's children (except for Reuel—verse 4) appear to have descended from his Canaanites wives.

36.3 and also Basemath daughter of Ishmael and sister of Nebaioth.

36.4 Adah bore to Esau Eliphaz; Basemath bore Reuel;

36.5 and Oholibamah bore Jeush, Jalam, and Korah. Those were the sons of Esau, who were born to him in the land of Canaan.

36.6 Esau took his wives, his sons and daughters, and all the members of his household, his cattle and all his livestock, and all the property that he had acquired in the land of Canaan, and went to another land because of his brother Jacob.

Esau at this point had such a congenial attitude toward his brother he was willing to inconvenience himself and move away for Jacob's sake. He could just as easily have said, "Look—there isn't enough room here for both of us, this is my lifelong home; *you* go over to the next land and settle there with your flocks."

36.7 For their possessions were too many for them to dwell together, and the land where they sojourned could not support them because of their livestock.

36.8 So Esau settled in the hill country of Seir—Esau being Edom.

36.9 This, then, is the line of Esau, the ancestor of the Edomites, in the hill country of Seir.

36.10 These are the names of Esau's sons: Eliphaz, the son of Esau's wife Adah; Reuel, the son of Esau's wife Basemath.

36.11 The sons of Eliphaz were Teman, Omar, Zepho, Gatam, and Kenaz.

THE TORAH AND LATER JUDAISM'S ATTITUDES
TOWARD CONVERSION

36.12 Timna was a concubine of Esau's son Eliphaz; she bore Amalek to Eliphaz. Those were the descendants of Esau's wife Adah.

Though the following commentary is not based on anything actually written in the Torah, I am including it to elucidate an important aspect of later Jewish history. Many non-Jews have regarded the Jews as a closed community—meaning one that does not welcome, let alone seek, converts. Many Jews have held a similar view, and as time went on, Jews made conversion to Judaism as difficult as possible. This, to be fair, was in large measure due to the widespread antisemitism in the Christian and Muslim worlds. Understandably, but unfortunately, this led to increasing insularity within Jewish life. And this in turn led to greater and greater discouragement of conversion to Judaism.

In light of this, I note an important observation from the Talmud and later rabbinic sources:

The words "Timna was a concubine" appear to hold little, if any, significance. But a long-standing rabbinic tradition used those words to make a point whose lesson remains as significant today as when it was first made.

According to this ancient Jewish tradition, Timna had been attracted to the beliefs of the patriarchs, but all three—Abraham, Isaac, and Jacob—discouraged her from converting. At that point, she became a concubine to Eliphaz, Esau's son, and gave birth to Amalek (this verse, Genesis 36:12), the father of the nation of Amalek, which became ancient Israel's greatest enemy (Exodus 17:8-16; Deuteronomy 25:17-19).

The preeminent Jewish commentator Rashi concluded the patriarchs badly erred in distancing Timna; they should have encouraged her conversion.[1]

In other words, Jewish tradition took three seemingly insignificant words and transformed them into an epic lesson: Jews should not discourage anyone sincerely interested in becoming a Jew from doing so. This is particularly remarkable in light of later Jewish tradition which actively discouraged would-be converts to Judaism.

At the same time, it is also worth repeating that neither the Torah nor later Judaism ever taught that everyone needs to become a Jew. The Jewish desire is that all people come to believe in the God of the Torah and His moral rules (e.g., the Ten Commandments and the Seven Laws of Noah). Nevertheless, as the Talmudic passage cited here (and by Rashi in the eleventh century) makes clear, Jews should have been, and should be today, more receptive to making converts.

36.13 And these were the sons of Reuel: Nahath, Zerah, Shammah, and Mizzah. Those were the descendants of Esau's wife Basemath.

36.14 And these were the sons of Esau's wife Oholibamah, daughter of Anah daughter of Zibeon: she bore to Esau Jeush, Jalam, and Korah.

36.15 These are the clans of the children of Esau. The descendants of Esau's first-born Eliphaz: the clans Teman, Omar, Zepho, Kenaz,

36.16 Korah, Gatam, and Amalek; these are the clans of Eliphaz in the land of Edom. Those are the descendants of Adah.

36.17 And these are the descendants of Esau's son Reuel: the clans Nahath, Zerah, Shammah, and Mizzah; these are the clans of Reuel in the land of Edom. Those are the descendants of Esau's wife Basemath.

36.18 And these are the descendants of Esau's wife Oholibamah: the clans Jeush, Jalam, and Korah; these are the clans of Esau's wife Oholibamah, the daughter of Anah.

36.19 Those were the sons of Esau—that is, Edom—and those are their clans.

36.20 These were the sons of Seir the Horite, who were settled in the land: Lotan, Shobal, Zibeon, Anah,

36.21 Dishon, Ezer, and Dishan. Those are the clans of the Horites, the descendants of Seir, in the land of Edom.

36.22 The sons of Lotan were Hori and Hemam; and Lotan's sister was Timna.

36.23 The sons of Shobal were these: Alvan, Manahath, Ebal, Shepho, and Onam.

36.24 The sons of Zibeon were these: Aiah and Anah—that was the Anah who discovered the hot springs in the wilderness while pasturing the asses of his father Zibeon.

36.25 The children of Anah were these: Dishon and Anah's daughter Oholibamah.

36.26 The sons of Dishon were these: Hemdan, Eshban, Ithran, and Cheran.

36.27 The sons of Ezer were these: Bilhan, Zaavan, and Akan.

36.28 And the sons of Dishan were these: Uz and Aran.

36.29 These are the clans of the Horites: the clans Lotan, Shobal, Zibeon, Anah,

36.30 Dishon, Ezer, and Dishan. Those are the clans of the Horites, clan by clan, in the land of Seir.

36.31 These are the kings who reigned in the land of Edom before any king reigned over the Israelites.

36.32 Bela son of Beor reigned in Edom, and the name of his city was Dinhabah.

36.33 When Bela died, Jobab son of Zerah, from Bozrah, succeeded him as king.

36.34 When Jobab died, Husham of the land of the Temanites succeeded him as king.

36.35 When Husham died, Hadad son of Bedad, who defeated the Midianites in the country of Moab, succeeded him as king; the name of his city was Avith.

36.36 When Hadad died, Samlah of Masrekah succeeded him as king.

36.37 When Samlah died, Saul of Rehoboth-on-the-river succeeded him as king.

36.38 When Saul died, Baal-hanan son of Achbor succeeded him as king.

36.39 And when Baal-hanan son of Achbor died, Hadar succeeded him as king; the name of his city was Pau, and his wife's name was Mehetabel daughter of Matred daughter of Me-zahab.

36.40 These are the names of the clans of Esau, each with its families and locality, name by name: the clans Timna, Alvah, Jetheth,

36.41 Oholibamah, Elah, Pinon,

36.42 Kenaz, Teman, Mibzar,

36.43 Magdiel, and Iram. Those are the clans of Edom—that is, of Esau, father of the Edomites— by their settlements in the land which they hold.

CHAPTER

37

37.1 Now Jacob was settled in the land where his father had sojourned, the land of Canaan.

37.2 This, then, is the line of Jacob:

> The Torah announces "the line of Jacob" and then immediately proceeds to the story of Joseph, moving Jacob off center-stage. The remainder of the book of Genesis constitutes the longest single story about an individual (other than Moses, of course) in the Torah. It is widely considered by secular scholars of literature one of the most compelling and profound human stories ever written.

37.2 (cont.) At seventeen years of age, Joseph tended the flocks with his brothers,

> Rachel had died, and the motherless Joseph was placed in the care of his older brothers, who were expected to look after him.

37.2 (cont.) as a helper to the sons of his father's wives Bilhah and Zilpah.

> Until now, Bilhah and Zilpah have been referred to as "maidservants" (see, for example, Genesis 33:2) and "concubines" (Genesis 35:22). Now that Rachel has died, and perhaps Leah as well (her death is not recorded, though Jacob alluded to it on his deathbed—Genesis 49:31), Bilhah and Zilpah have risen in status and are described as "wives."

37.2 (cont.) And Joseph brought bad reports of them to their father.

This is the first of several reasons that Joseph's brothers hated him: He was a snitch. We do not know what he reported to their father, but his reporting antagonized them.

If People Learned from Others' Mistakes... the World Would Be a Beautiful Place

37.3 Now Israel loved Joseph best of all his sons,

This is a second reason Joseph's brothers hated him: He was the clear favorite son of their father. As will soon become apparent, Jacob made no effort to disguise his favoritism. Given the family chaos he had experienced as a result of his own father favoring his older brother Esau (and his mother favoring him), one would think Jacob would have learned not to (at least openly) favor one of his sons. But if human beings all learned from others' mistakes, the world would be a beautiful place. One way to describe the human condition is this: people rarely learn from others' lives. We seem to be programmed to learn only from our own mistakes (and even that is hardly guaranteed). Learning from others' mistakes is a good definition of wisdom.

If human beings all learned from others' mistakes, the world would be a beautiful place. We seem to be programmed to learn only from our own mistakes.

37.3 (cont.) for he was the child of his old age;

Benjamin was the child of Jacob's old age, not Joseph. But Benjamin was still a young child and had probably not yet developed much of a personality. More significantly, Jacob's beloved wife, Rachel, died while giving birth to Benjamin, so (irrational as it would have been) Jacob may have felt some ambivalence toward him. Whatever the reason, Joseph was Jacob's favorite.

37.3 (cont.) and he had made him an ornamented tunic.

This is a third reason Joseph's brothers hated him: He received a special garment as a sign of their father's love for him. The Talmud is not generally critical of the patriarchs' behavior, but it views this gift with great disapproval:

"A man should never single out one of his children for favored treatment, for because of two extra coins' worth of fine silk, which Jacob gave to Joseph and not to his other sons, Joseph's brothers became jealous of him, and one thing led to another until our ancestors became slaves in Egypt."[1]

WHEN FAMILY COMMUNICATIONS BREAK DOWN

37.4 And when his brothers saw that their father loved him more than any of his brothers, they hated him so that they could not speak a friendly word to him.

The Hebrew word translated here as "friendly" (*l'shalom*) could be literally translated as "of peace." What happened to Jacob's family is one of the most destructive things that can happen to a family—family members either not speaking civilly to one another or not speaking to each other at all. This breakdown in communication enables family members to demonize one another (or is the end result of demonization—as in the many cases of one parent alienating a child from the other parent after divorce). That is what enabled Joseph's brothers to contemplate murdering him or selling him into slavery without speaking a single word to him (Genesis 37:18-27).

37.5 Once Joseph had a dream which he told to his brothers;

Joseph's dreams came from God, but his youthful arrogance and lack of judgment led him to brag about the dreams to his brothers.

37.5 (cont.) and they hated him even more.

37.6 He said to them, "Hear this dream which I have dreamed:

37.7 There we were binding sheaves in the field, when suddenly my sheaf stood up and remained upright; then your sheaves gathered around and bowed low to my sheaf."

THE BROTHERS' RESENTMENT OF JOSEPH

37.8 His brothers answered, "Do you mean to reign over us? Do you mean to rule over us?"

Though Joseph is primarily known for being an interpreter of dreams—Pharaoh's dreams being the most famous (Genesis 41)—these first two dreams were so transparent they required no explanation. The brothers immediately understood them, and they ignited their fury.

Note that the brothers did not dismiss Joseph or his dreams; they took them seriously and hated Joseph both for having them and for boasting about them. Though Jews have never boasted about their belief they are God's Chosen People (there is nothing to boast about—it is not a claim of superiority, and it has led to unspeakable suffering), the brothers' reactions to Joseph foreshadowed much of the world's reactions to the Jews' belief in being the Chosen People. The world did not dismiss the belief with ridicule. On the contrary, they took the claim seriously and hated the Jews for it—so much so that many non-Jews have sought to destroy the Jews, just as Joseph's brothers sought to destroy Joseph, either by killing him or selling him into slavery.

37.8 (cont.) And they hated him even more for his talk about his dreams.

This is the third time in five verses the Torah mentions the brothers' hatred of Joseph.

37.9 He dreamed another dream

The dreams associated with Joseph—both the two recorded here and the four dreams he later interpreted—came in pairs, the second reinforcing the first to demonstrate their seriousness. In the ancient world, not every dream was taken as a divine message. But if a dream recurred (usually in more than one form), it was presumed to be an omen. The Talmud commented that "a dream not interpreted is like a letter not read."[2]

37.9 (cont.) and told it to his brothers, saying, "Look, I have had another dream: And this time, the sun, the moon, and eleven stars were bowing down to me."

> Like the first dream, the meaning of this one was immediately apparent: The sun and the moon referred to Joseph's father and mother, and the eleven stars to his brothers.

37.10 And when he told it to his father and brothers,

> Unlike his first dream, which he related only to his brothers, Joseph shared this second dream with his father as well.

37.10 (cont.) his father berated him.

> Finally, even Jacob became angry with his favorite son. Perhaps he realized that his favoritism had gotten out of control—that he'd created a bit of a monster and wanted his other children to see that he, too, could get angry with Joseph. Or perhaps he was outraged by Joseph's suggestion that he—the father—would bow down to his son (see next verse).

IS JACOB'S APPARENT REFERENCE TO JOSEPH'S DEAD MOTHER A TORAH INCONSISTENCY?

37.10 (cont.) "What," he said to him, "is this dream you have dreamed? Are we to come, I and your mother and your brothers, and bow low to you to the ground?"

> Jacob tried to dismiss the legitimacy of Joseph's dream as absurd. One detail might seem puzzling: Given that Joseph's mother was, at this point, no longer living, how could she bow down to him? One answer is that dreams—even God-sent dreams—rarely correspond precisely to reality. Or, perhaps it did make sense in that the dream was meant to show that the entire family—including even their late mother—revolved around Joseph.
>
> However, many scholars, including Robert Alter, believe Jacob's reaction does constitute a Torah inconsistency: How could Jacob refer to "your mother" bowing down if she was in fact dead? In Robert Alter's words: "This particular

episode seems to assume, in flat contradiction of the preceding narrative, that Rachel is still alive.... Attempts to rescue consistency on the ground that dreams may contain incoherent elements are unconvincing, because it is a perfectly lucid Jacob who assumes here that Rachel is still alive."

Alter may be right about there being a contradiction here. But I don't think so. Alter, a fine scholar with great admiration for the Torah, like most modern secular scholars, believes the Torah is composed of documents edited much later by a Redactor (editor). While it would be foolish to assume that a later Redactor would catch and remove every possible inconsistency in the Torah, this alleged inconsistency is so glaring—a man presumably referring to his dead wife as still alive—one simply has to wonder how an editor would let it pass.

And even if one assumes a later Redactor edited various documents, Jacob's statement does not necessarily constitute an inconsistency. There is another explanation that makes perfect sense: Jacob may be referring to Bilhah, who had raised Joseph as a mother. This possibility was long ago suggested by Rashi and Ibn Ezra and repeated in our time by Sarna.

But assuming the reference is, in fact, to Rachel, Rashi makes another argument that I find convincing: Precisely by including the reference to his mother, who of course could not "come...and bow low to you," Jacob was making clear just how absurd Joseph's dream was in the hope that his brothers would simply dismiss it rather than envy and further hate him for it.

ENVY AND FESTERING ANGER LEAD TO BAD OUTCOMES

37.11 So his brothers were wrought up at him,

The Hebrew actually says his brothers "were envious of him." Envy is poisonous. It almost always leads to bad behavior.

So does anger that is allowed to fester. Despite their increasing hatred, the Torah does not record the brothers expressing this hatred to Joseph. And this unexpressed anger ultimately proved more destructive than angry speech: when finally expressed, it was expressed in deeds, not in words.

The danger of unexpressed anger is reflected in the later biblical story of Absalom, King David's son, who was enraged—with cause—at his older brother, Amnon. For two years, "Absalom didn't utter a word to Amnon, good or bad," and then, when Amnon's guard was down, Absalom arranged to have him assassinated (II Samuel 13:22-29).

The Torah law, "You shall not hate your brother in your heart" (Leviticus 19:17) addresses this issue. When anger is kept in our heart, it festers—and can become toxic.

This does not mean we should blow up at every person with whom we are angry. People who do so will end up with no friends and no love. We need to know when to express anger, toward whom to express it, and how.

But anger should not be allowed to fester. We should either let it go or properly express it.

37.11 (cont.) and his father kept the matter in mind.

Jacob took both Joseph's dreams and his brothers' reactions to them seriously.

37.12 One time, when his brothers had gone to pasture their father's flock at Shechem,

Jacob Tries to Have His Sons Get Along

37.13 Israel said to Joseph, "Your brothers are pasturing at Shechem. Come, I will send you to them." He answered, "I am ready."

37.14 And he said to him, "Go and see how your brothers are and how the flocks are faring, and bring me back word."

The Hebrew once again uses the word "peace" (*shalom*). Jacob sent Joseph to find out about the peace of his brothers. Since we already know the brothers could not interact with Joseph peacefully, his mission was doomed.

It is unlikely Jacob was oblivious to the tension between the brothers and Joseph, though we can surmise he was unaware of just how deep their hostility was. This is probably why he sent Joseph to check on "the peace of your brothers." This is an example of something parents frequently do—try to engineer their children's lives, especially to have them get along. But parental engineering almost never works, and as happens here, it all too easily leads to the very opposite result: greater alienation.

37.14 (cont.) So he sent him from the valley of Hebron. When he reached Shechem,

37.15 a man came upon him wandering in the fields. The man asked him, "What are you looking for?"

37.16 He answered, "I am looking for my brothers. Could you tell me where they are pasturing?"

To his credit, Joseph, a devoted son, did not give up when he had difficulty finding his brothers. Knowing his brothers intensely disliked him, he could have easily chosen to return home and told his father he couldn't find them.

GOD OR COINCIDENCE: FAITH IS A CHOICE

37.17 The man said, "They have gone from here, for I heard them say: Let us go to Dothan." So Joseph followed his brothers and found them at Dothan.

Joseph did not have to describe his brothers to the man; as soon as Joseph explained he was looking for his brothers, the man immediately knew both who and where they were. Although Joseph, unlike Abraham, Isaac, and Jacob, would never be directly addressed by God and, also unlike the patriarchs, will make no sacrifices to God, God's hand was clearly involved throughout Joseph's life. And as his life progressed, Joseph would see this hand of God operating (see comment on Genesis 39:8) if for no other reason than there were simply too many "coincidences" in his life.

We, too, have the choice of attributing fortuitous events in our lives—like Joseph's meeting this stranger—to either random coincidence or to God. Whose life has not been deeply influenced by seemingly serendipitous events? Were they entirely random? Like faith itself, seeing or not seeing God is a choice.

Much of life is shaped by choices we make. We do not choose what happens to us; we choose how to react to what happens to us.

Since we can neither prove nor dis-prove God's presence in our lives, whether or not we see God's hand is a decision. The same holds true regarding whether to live a religious or secular life. And, for the most part, we even choose whether or not to be happy. As Abraham Lincoln, who led a life filled with tragedy, famously said, "We are as happy as we make up our mind to be."

> *We do not choose what happens to us; we choose how to react to what happens to us.*

Finally, this is especially true with regard to faith. Whether to believe is largely a choice. If we wait until someone or something convinces us there is a God, we will probably wait forever. Choose to act happy, and you will likely be happy (or at least happier). Choose to live a God-centered life, and you will ultimately have faith (or at least be less skeptical). As Menachem Mendel Schneerson, the Lubavitcher Rebbe, would say, "Faith is like the body; it has to be fed."

37.18 They saw him from afar, and before he came close to them they conspired to kill him.

The brothers began conspiring to kill Joseph while he was still far off in the distance. It is easier to loathe people and plot against them when we are not actually confronted with them. When we interact with them, they often become sympathetic human beings. The surest way to preserve hatred—and negative stereotypes—is to avoid dealing face-to-face with those we hate.

But the principle operates in the opposite direction and must also be guarded against: when interacting with truly bad people, they can also become sympathetic figures, and we can easily be fooled into thinking they are good people.

37.19 They said to one another, "Here comes that dreamer!

37.20 Come now, let us kill him and throw him into one of the pits; and we can say, 'A savage beast devoured him.' We shall see what comes of his dreams!"

> Joseph's brothers had plenty of reason for ill will toward him: their father's obvious favoritism of him, his "snitching" on them to Jacob, the special gift of a tunic only to Joseph. But Joseph's dreams of superiority over his entire family, and the confident and arrogant way he related them, had become the overriding focus of the brothers' resentment. They could not stop Jacob from loving Joseph more than the rest of them, but they could ensure Joseph's dreams never came true.

37.21 But when Reuben heard it, he tried to save him from them. He said, "Let us not take his life."

37.22 And Reuben went on, "Shed no blood! Cast him into that pit out in the wilderness, but do not touch him yourselves"—intending to save him from them and restore him to his father.

> Reuben tried to thwart the plot. Whether this was because, as the oldest brother, he was the one whom Jacob would hold most responsible for Joseph's fate or simply because he had a conscience we cannot know. But the Torah makes clear that Reuben's intention was to return to the pit, rescue Joseph, and send him home (see verse 29).

37.23 When Joseph came up to his brothers, they stripped Joseph of his tunic, the ornamented tunic that he was wearing,

> Like the dreams, the tunic made the brothers furious. "Only now do we learn that Joseph has the bad judgment to wear on his errand the garment that was the extravagant token of his father's favoritism. Thus he provokes the brothers' anger, and they strip him—not part of their original plan...." (Alter)
>
> If they couldn't kill the dreamer, they could at least get rid of this prominent and hated symbol of their father's favoritism. The cruelty is also increased— Joseph is thrown nearly naked into the pit.

37.24 and took him and cast him into the pit. The pit was empty; there was no water in it.

37.25 Then they sat down to a meal.

> In Telushkin's view, "there are few more damning lines in the Bible. These men have just thrown their brother into a pit, where they intend to leave him until he died of hunger or thirst (the Bible emphasizes that the pit had no water). And then they sat down and enjoyed a meal."

37.25 (cont.) Looking up, they saw a caravan of Ishmaelites coming from Gilead, their camels bearing gum, balm, and ladanum to be taken to Egypt.

37.26 Then Judah said to his brothers, "What do we gain by killing our brother and covering up his blood? After all, he is our brother, our own flesh." His brothers agreed.

37.27 Come, let us sell him to the Ishmaelites, but let us not do away with him ourselves.

> Now it was Judah arguing on behalf of saving Joseph's life, though his suggestion to sell Joseph into slavery hardly casts him in a favorable light. Indeed, later Torah law regards selling a person into slavery as a capital crime (Exodus 21:16). If Joseph was aware that it was Judah who suggested selling him into slavery, it would make sense that decades later he could fully forgive Judah only when Judah offered to become a slave to spare Benjamin that fate (Genesis 44:33-45:5).
>
> Earlier, Reuben argued on behalf of sparing Joseph (verse 21-22). Some Bible scholars see a Torah contradiction here: first, Reuben tries to save Joseph, and then Judah is described as trying to save Joseph's life. But why assume a contradiction (or two different stories)? Isn't it possible that Judah and Reuben, both of whom may have had a conscience—at least with regard to the ultimate sin of murdering their brother—independently devised ways to save Joseph?

37.28 When Midianite traders passed by, they pulled Joseph up out of the pit. They sold Joseph for twenty pieces of silver to the Ishmaelites, who brought Joseph to Egypt.

Most people, having just read Judah's suggestion to sell Joseph to the Ishmael-ites, believe that's what happened—that Joseph was sold into slavery by his brothers. But that is not what the Hebrew text says. In the Hebrew, "they pulled Joseph up out of the pit" refers to the Midianite traders, not to Joseph's broth-ers. Some translations have contributed to this misperception by placing the brothers in the verse. For example, the New International Version (NIV) reads: "So when the Midianite merchants came by, his brothers pulled Joseph up out of the cistern and sold him for twenty shekels of silver to the Ishmaelites, who took him to Egypt." But the Hebrew text makes no mention of Joseph's broth-ers in this verse.

It was the Midianites and then the Ishmaelites who sold Joseph into slavery, not the brothers. The brothers simply left him in the pit (see comment on the next verse). Joseph, however, apparently believed his brothers had sold him into slavery (Genesis 45:4).

These Midianite traders may be viewed as Joseph's good luck or as mes-sengers sent by God to save Joseph from dying in the pit. The Torah narrative clearly sees the hand of God.

37.29 When Reuben returned to the pit and saw that Joseph was not in the pit, he rent his clothes.

Reuben's return to the pit to rescue Joseph would seem to confirm the brothers were not the ones who sold Joseph into slavery. If they had, why would Reuben have returned to the pit? He would have known he wasn't there, and he also would have known that Joseph wasn't dead.

Reuben saw the empty pit and concluded that some ill fate had befallen Joseph. Perhaps he assumed Joseph was dead, even though there was no body in the pit or anywhere else. Perhaps he simply did not know what to think. Whether in frustration and fear (over how his father would react to his favorite son missing) or in mourning over his brother's presumed death, Reuben ripped his clothes.

37.30 Returning to his brothers, he said, "The boy is gone! Now, what am I to do?"

37.31 Then they took Joseph's tunic, slaughtered a kid, and dipped the tunic in the blood.

Sarna points out the irony in the brothers' use of a kid's blood to deceive their father: It was a kid that Rebecca asked Jacob to bring her so that she could prepare Isaac's favorite dish, and it was a kid's skin she covered Jacob's arms with to deceive Isaac (see Genesis 27:9, 16). As Jacob deceived his father with a kid, he will now be deceived by his sons using a kid—yet another of the myriad instances of payback in the book of Genesis.

37.32 They had the ornamented tunic taken to their father, and they said, "We found this. Please examine it; is it your son's tunic or not?"

Referring to him as "your son" rather than "our brother," Jacob's sons did not hide their contempt for Joseph or their anger toward their father over his favoritism.

37.33 He recognized it, and said, "My son's tunic! A savage beast devoured him! Joseph was torn by a beast!"

Jacob quickly moved through three stages of escalating horror: First, he realized he was looking at the tunic that belonged to Joseph, covered in blood; from that, he concluded Joseph had been killed; and finally, he inferred Joseph's death was terror-filled and torturous.

The brothers did not actually tell their father that Joseph had been devoured by a wild beast. Instead, they presented him with their manufactured "evidence" and let Jacob come to this logical, but incorrect, conclusion on his own. They probably prided themselves on having technically not lied to their father. (Along similar lines, they did not actually sell their brother into slavery; they simply left him in a pit to be picked up by slave traders.)

Their ruse worked: Never in his life did Jacob hold his other sons responsible for Joseph's "death."

37.34 Jacob rent his clothes, put sackcloth on his loins, and observed mourning for his son many days.

The millennia-old Jewish practice of tearing a garment when mourning a close relative who has died (*kriah*) is practiced to this day.

37.35 All his sons and daughters

Thus far, the Torah has mentioned Jacob having one daughter. The verse probably refers to Jacob's daughters-in-law. The Torah has mentioned one of Jacob's daughters by name—Dinah. But, as Genesis 46:7 notes, Jacob had other daughters.

37.35 (cont.) sought to comfort him;

One has to wonder whether, seeing their father's unspeakable grief, the brothers felt remorse for what they had done. There is, of course, no way to know. But they will—eventually.

37.35 (cont.) but he refused to be comforted, saying, "No, I will go down mourning to my son in Sheol."

In biblical times, Sheol was the name of the place to which it was believed people went after death. It is obviously some aspect of an afterlife, but we do not know exactly what the name signified.

37.35 (cont.) Thus his father bewailed him.

37.36 The Midianites, meanwhile, sold him in Egypt

This verse seems to contradict verse 28, which states that the Midianites sold Joseph to the Ishmaelites who were the ones who took him to Egypt, but the contradiction is due to the translation. What the Hebrew more accurately says here is, "The Midianites sold him *toward* Egypt." In other words, the Midianites were as responsible for Joseph's sale to Egypt as were the Ishmaelites.

37.36 (cont.) to Potiphar, a courtier of Pharaoh and his chief steward.

Joseph was ultimately sold to the highest official in the court of the Egyptian king—another instance where one can either see great luck or the hand of God.

38.1 About that time Judah left his brothers and camped near a certain Adullamite whose name was Hirah.

> Judah, who came up with the idea to sell Joseph into slavery, may have considered himself particularly responsible for Joseph's disappearance and the subsequent unending grief of his father. The other brothers possibly even came to blame him for suggesting that they sell Joseph into slavery (37:27). This could explain his decision to distance himself from his brothers.

38.2 There Judah saw the daughter of a certain Canaanite whose name was Shua, and he married her and cohabited with her.

> Judah married a Canaanite woman, which was prohibited by Abraham (Genesis 24:3) and by later Torah law (Deuteronomy 7:3).[1] This is yet another argument for the antiquity of the Torah: as Sarna notes, "later tradition would hardly have invented the uncomfortable account about his [Judah's] marriage to one [a Canaanite]."

38.3 She conceived and bore a son, and he named him Er.

38.4 She conceived again and bore a son, and named him Onan.

38.5 Once again she bore a son, and named him Shelah; he was at Chezib when she bore him.

38.6 Judah got a wife for Er his first-born; her name was Tamar.

38.7 But Er, Judah's first-born, was displeasing to the Lord, and the Lord took his life.

The Torah does not specify Er's offense. It says, "evil in the Lord's eyes," translated here as "displeasing to the Lord." This is not common in the Torah: when God takes a person's life, the reason is almost always given. But it must have been a grave offense—Er is the first named individual in the Bible whose life God takes as punishment.

It should be noted the two letters of his name spelled backwards spell out the word *ra* ("evil"). This may be coincidence, but I doubt it. Noah's two-consonant name backwards spells *chen*, "favor," as in, "he found favor in God's eyes." And here Er was "evil in God's eyes."

"BROTHER-IN-LAW" (LEVIRATE) MARRIAGE

38.8 Then Judah said to Onan, "Join with your brother's wife and do your duty by her as a brother-in-law, and provide offspring for your brother."

The duty Judah invoked refers to an ancient law known as "levirate marriage," known in Hebrew as *yibbum*. *Levir* is the Latin word for "brother-in-law." This law obligated a man whose brother had died childless to marry and impregnate his brother's widow. The resulting child was customarily given the dead brother's name and was considered to be a successor to the dead brother's line. At that time, the surviving brother had no choice in the matter, nor was the widow free to decline marriage to her dead husband's brother.

The Torah later modified this tradition by allowing a brother to refuse to marry his brother's widow (though he would then have to partake in a public ceremony, *halitzah*, in which the late brother's widow removed the man's sandal and spat at him because he refused to "preserve his brother's name in Israel"—see Deuteronomy 25:5-10). As this incident with Tamar predates the Torah, *halitzah* may not have been an option, leaving a brother with no choice but to marry his late brother's widow.

As primitive as it might sound to us today, levirate marriage was a way to help a widow have both children and economic security.

38.9 But Onan, knowing that the seed would not count as his,

> The child would be legally viewed as that of his late brother, Er.
>
> Genesis contains story after story of brothers who mistreat brothers—in this case, even a dead brother. Whatever the reason—a birthright blessing, envy, parental favoritism, and now money—brothers seem to be in constant conflict.

WHAT WAS ONAN'S SIN?

38.9 (cont.) let it go to waste whenever he joined with his brother's wife, so as not to provide offspring for his brother.

> Onan's sin was making sure not to impregnate Tamar when he slept with her. In so doing, he cheated Tamar, cheated his father and father-in-law, and cheated his late brother. He cheated Tamar by preventing her from having children; his father and father-in-law by pretending to fulfill the obligation of levirate marriage; and his late brother by denying him an heir and the "preservation of his name in Israel."
>
> We do not know Onan's motivation. The most probable explanation is he did not want to produce a child who would eventually inherit his late brother's estate. As the Jewish Encyclopedia (1906) explained, "If the levirate union resulted in male issue, the child would succeed to the estates of the deceased brother." Therefore, a son attributable to Er meant there would be a third heir upon the death of Judah. At that point, Judah had two heirs—Onan and Shelah. But if Er had an heir, that child would share in the inheritance of Judah's estate.
>
> Some traditional Jewish and Christian teachings interpreted Onan's sin as masturbation, which is the origin of the term "onanism." However, the Torah clearly states Onan's sin was his refusal to complete sexual relations with Tamar, thereby depriving her of any offspring, refusing to perpetuate his dead brother's name, and by implication, using Tamar solely for his sexual gratification.

Therefore, Onan's sin was not masturbation. However, though the Torah does not mention masturbation, later Jewish religious law's opposition to masturbation was based on this story. Later Christian opposition was and is largely based on the New Testament's prohibition against lusting after a woman one is not married to (Matthew 5:28) and Christianity's permitting of sexual activity solely between a husband and wife.[2]

38.10 What he did was displeasing to the Lord, and He took his life also.

DECEPTIONS IN GENESIS

Genesis contains story after story depicting deception. Er's deception of Tamar and Judah is only the most immediate example. If this book of the Bible were not named Genesis, it might well be named "Deceptions."

Abraham deceived Pharaoh.

Abraham deceived Abimelech.

Jacob and Rebecca deceived Isaac.

Laban and Leah deceived Jacob.

Rachel deceived Laban.

Simeon and Levi deceived the Shechemites.

Joseph's brothers deceived Jacob.

Onan deceived Tamar and Judah.

Judah deceived Tamar.

Tamar deceived Judah.

Potiphar's wife deceived Potiphar.

Joseph deceived his brothers.

38.11 Then Judah said to his daughter-in-law Tamar, "Stay as a widow in your father's house until my son Shelah grows up"—for he thought, "He too might die like his brothers." So Tamar went to live in her father's house.

This is a rare instance of the Torah telling us what someone is thinking. Under the levirate marriage law there was apparently no mechanism for releasing a widow to marry outside her husband's family (specifically, her brother-in-law) if her deceased husband had a living brother. Shelah, who at this point was still a minor, was next in line to provide his dead brother's widow with a child once he was old enough to marry. But given what had already happened to his two sons who had married her, Judah felt she brought bad luck. So, he sent her home to her father.

38.12 A long time afterward, Shua's daughter, the wife of Judah, died.

The Torah mentions the death of Judah's wife to let the reader know Judah's subsequent behavior takes place only once he is again an unmarried man. This verse also notes that this was "a long time afterward"—long enough for Shelah to have reached a marriageable age.

38.12 (cont.) When his period of mourning was over, Judah went up to Timnah to his sheepshearers, together with his friend Hirah the Adullamite.

38.13 And Tamar was told, "Your father-in-law is coming up to Timnah for the sheep shearing."

TAMAR'S ACTING LIKE A PROSTITUTE

38.14 So she took off her widow's garb, covered her face with a veil, and, wrapping herself up, sat down at the entrance to Enaim, which is on the road to Timnah; for she saw that Shelah was grown up, yet she had not been given to him as wife.

Tamar realized her father-in-law was not going to permit his last remaining son to marry her. Consequently, she would not only be cheated out of having children but also out of the economic security of marriage. So, having waited years to marry Shelah and aching for a child, she decided to take matters into her own hands.

Once again, we find a woman in the Bible taking the initiative in a patriarchal world. Examples include Rebecca's behavior in Genesis 27, when she sees her husband is about to make a major blunder; and Naomi's and Ruth's behavior in the Book of Ruth, Chapter 3.

While the Torah condemns prostitution (see Leviticus 19:29), it does not condemn Tamar for acting like a prostitute, seducing her father-in-law, and sleeping with him. Rather Tamar is portrayed as a victim—of deceit, having been deprived of the possibility of having a child; and as acting on behalf of a just cause—desiring a child to which she, a twice-married woman, had twice been deprived. Indeed, the Bible later describes the birth of Perez, the son born to Tamar and Judah, as a blessing (Ruth 4:12): "Through the offspring the Lord gives you by this young woman, may your family be like that of Perez, whom Tamar bore to Judah."

38.15 When Judah saw her, he took her for a harlot; for she had covered her face.

Prostitutes apparently covered their face at that time and in that place—or Judah would have recognized her.

38.16 So he turned aside to her by the road and said, "Here, let me sleep with you"—for he did not know that she was his daughter-in-law. "What," she asked, "will you pay for sleeping with me?"

38.17 He replied, "I will send a kid from my flock." But she said, "You must leave a pledge until you have sent it."

38.18 And he said, "What pledge shall I give you?" She replied, "Your seal and cord, and the staff which you carry."

Tamar was very clever in making this request. It ultimately saved her life.

The seal was a small stone with writing cut into it that could make an impression in a wax or tallow seal on a document and serve as a form of identification; the cord was a custom-made article of clothing; and the staff was carved, therefore probably a unique item. Alter notes the contemporary equivalent would be asking for "a person's driver's license and credit cards."

38.18 (cont.) So he gave them to her and slept with her, and she conceived by him.

38.19 Then she went on her way. She took off her veil and again put on her widow's garb.

38.20 Judah sent the kid by his friend the Adullamite, to redeem the pledge from the woman; but he could not find her.

> Hirah the Adullamite was the very definition of a good friend—a person to whom you can tell anything, even something humiliating, and who will stay loyal to you.

38.21 He inquired of the people of that town, "Where is the cult prostitute, the one at Enaim, by the road?" But they said, "There has been no prostitute here."

> In this verse, Judah's friend referred to Tamar as a *kedesha*, but in verse 15, she was described as a *zonah*. Both words mean "prostitute." The former is widely perceived as referring to cult prostitution and *zonah* as referring to regular prostitution. But some major biblical scholars, including Professor Leeor Gottlieb of Bar-Ilan University and Edward Lipinski, professor of ancient Near East culture and religion at the Katholieke Universiteit Leuven in Belgium, claim there is no proof of cult prostitution in ancient Canaan.[3]

38.22 So he returned to Judah and said, "I could not find her; moreover, the townspeople said: There has been no prostitute here."

38.23 Judah said, "Let her keep them, lest we become a laughingstock.

> Judah spoke in the plural, as if what he did reflected on his friend Hirah as well as on himself.

38.23 (cont.) I did send her this kid, but you did not find her."

> Judah made an honorable attempt to find Tamar. (He also had an interest in having his belongings returned to him.)

38.24 About three months later, Judah was told, "Your daughter-in-law Tamar has played the harlot;

in fact, she is with child by harlotry." "Bring her out," said Judah, "and let her be burned."

Judah had apparently forgotten about his visit with the harlot in the same region Tamar had gone to live in her father's house. This news rang no alarm bell in his mind.

While Tamar was designated to be married to Judah's third son Shelah, Judah's rush to judgment and demand for a particularly cruel punishment reflected poorly on his character—particularly since it was he who withheld from her the one man to whom she was permitted. His calling for Tamar's execution probably reflected more on his perception of Tamar having dishonored his family's name (by sleeping with a man outside his family) than on law.

38.25 As she was being brought out, she sent this message to her father-in-law, "I am with child by the man to whom these belong." And she added, "Examine these: whose seal and cord and staff are these?"

To her great credit, Tamar did not publicly accuse Judah.

38.26 Judah recognized them, and said, "She is more in the right than I, inasmuch as I did not give her to my son Shelah."

Judah immediately realized what had happened and immediately admitted he was at fault—for preventing Shelah from marrying Tamar.

As time goes on Judah appears to become an honorable man:

Earlier, Judah had attempted to save Joseph's life (Genesis 37:26-27).

In this verse he immediately described Tamar as "more in the right" than he was. He could have continued to demand her execution (after all, he now possessed the incriminating evidence).

And later, in dealing with Joseph as governor of Egypt, Judah volunteered to become a lifelong slave for the sake of his brother Benjamin and his father Jacob.

Throughout history, there have been otherwise honorable men who have sinned in the sexual arena (and, remember, Judah was unmarried, he did not know the identity of the woman who posed as a prostitute, and he would have no reason to assume this "prostitute" was either betrothed or married).

The Torah may be telling us not to be too quick to judge in this regard or, at the very least, not to assess a person's honor on the basis of sexual sin alone. To cite one other biblical example, of all the inhabitants of Canaan, it was a prostitute, Rahab, who hid the Israelite spies and thereby enabled the Israelites to enter the Promised Land.

Among those who regard Tamar's behavior in a negative light, there is another lesson in these examples: God uses flawed individuals to show His redemptive powers or, as Christians often put it, God's grace.

38.26 (cont.) And he was not intimate with her again.

38.27 When the time came for her to give birth, there were twins in her womb!

38.28 While she was in labor, one of them put out his hand, and the midwife tied a crimson thread on that hand, to signify: This one came out first.

This story is an obvious echo of the birth of Esau and Jacob. Also, by having twins, both Er and Onan now had sons to replace them, which was the purpose of *yibbum*.

38.29 But just then he drew back his hand, and out came his brother; and she said, "What a breach you have made for yourself!" So he was named Perez.

Perez (*Peretz*) is Hebrew for "breach."

According to the genealogy recorded in the fourth chapter of the Book of Ruth, Perez later became the ancestor of David (Ruth 4:17) and, therefore, the ancestor of the Messiah. The Messiah thus stems from a strange and non-indigenous line: He will be the descendant of both a Canaanite woman (Tamar) and a Moabite woman (Ruth), two nations that were historic enemies of Israel. This is one of the moral lessons of the Torah: moral values matter more than national identity.

38.30 Afterward his brother came out, on whose hand was the crimson thread; he was named Zerah.

39.1 When Joseph was taken down to Egypt, a certain Egyptian, Potiphar, a courtier of Pharaoh and his chief steward, bought him from the Ishmaelites who had brought him there.

39.2 The Lord was with Joseph,

> Of the two primary names for God in the Torah—"the Lord" (YHVH, *Adonai*) and "God" (*Elohim*)—"the Lord" connotes the more personal aspect of God while *Elohim* connotes the universal God, the Creator. "The Lord" is used here and throughout most of this chapter because God is involved in the personal— looking after Joseph.

Joseph as a Paradigm of the Jewish People

39.2 (cont.) and he was a successful man;

> The story of Joseph is a paradigm of the Jewish experience. From being thrown into a pit and then being sold by traders into slavery in a foreign land, he met with considerable success before being wrongfully imprisoned, then released, and once again rose to success, this time on a grand scale. Jewish history follows the same pattern: Jews are persecuted; the moment they are emancipated, they achieve social and professional success; then they are subjugated again; and when given another chance, they rise again.
>
> Like Joseph, the Jewish people have been remarkably successful in foreign societies. The primary reason has been the Jews' values: strong and stable family life (nearly universal marriage and children); near-universal literacy, even

among women; emphasis on the life of the mind; delayed gratification (for example, keeping one's children in school as long as possible rather than sending them out to work); and an aversion to violence. These values ultimately derive from the Torah and later Judaism. There is no other way to explain the success and, more importantly, the influence of the Jews, one of the world's smallest peoples.

Regarding the Jews' influence, Winston Churchill wrote this in 1920:

"We owe to the Jews a system of ethics which, even if it were entirely separated from the supernatural, would be incomparably the most precious possession of mankind, worth in fact the fruits of all wisdom and learning put together. On that system and by that faith there has been built out of the wreck of the Roman Empire the whole of our existing civilization."[1]

39.3 And when his master saw that the Lord was with him and that the Lord lent success to everything he undertook,

39.4 he took a liking to Joseph. He made him his personal attendant and put him in charge of his household, placing in his hands all that he owned.

Potiphar comes across as an entirely decent man. Despite the terrible suffering inflicted by Egyptians on the Israelites, the Torah repeatedly depicts individual Egyptians sympathetically or even heroically (the daughter of Pharaoh and the Egyptian midwives in Exodus).

39.5 And from the time that the Egyptian put him in charge of his household and of all that he owned, the Lord blessed his house for Joseph's sake, so that the blessing of the Lord was upon everything that he owned, in the house and outside.

This is reminiscent of the success God bestowed on Laban's house because of Jacob's presence (see Genesis 30:27).

39.6 He left all that he had in Joseph's hands and, with him there, he paid attention to nothing save the food that he ate.

The ancient Egyptians had particular dietary practices (see Genesis 43:32), for which reason Potiphar would not have wanted Joseph in charge of his food, but he entrusted Joseph with every other aspect of his household management. The verse can also be interpreted as meaning Joseph took care of every aspect of Potiphar's life; all that Potiphar had to concern himself with was what he ate.

39.6 (cont.) Now Joseph was well built and handsome.

Literally translated, this verse states Joseph was "well-built and good to look at." Both Sarah and Rachel were described this way, but this is the only time the Torah used these words to describe a man—probably because Joseph is the only male in the Bible whose looks played a significant role in the fate that befell him.

39.7 After a time, his master's wife cast her eyes upon Joseph and said, "Lie with me."

Potiphar's wife is surprisingly direct. Typical gender roles were reversed in this encounter: The woman was the person in the position of power and the one who sought inappropriate sexual relations while the man was particularly good-looking, in the vulnerable position, and the one who said no.

39.8 But he refused.

Every word or group of words in the Torah has a corresponding musical notation—known as *trope*—which indicates how that word should be chanted. The Hebrew word for "refused," *va'yi'ma'en*, is marked by the longest musical note in the trope (*shalshelet*). When chanted, a part of the word is chanted over and over as if it read, "and he refu—u—u—u—sed." The most plausible explanation is Joseph rebuffed Mrs. Potiphar's advances over and over (see verse 10).

ESSAY: WHY WAS JOSEPH CONSIDERED PARTICULARLY RIGHTEOUS?

It is primarily because of his rejection of Mrs. Potiphar's attempt to seduce him that Jewish tradition appended the title of "righteous" to Joseph's name (*Yosef ha-Tzaddik*). The rabbis, being male, understood how difficult it is for a man to resist a woman's invitation to be with her.

A second reason Joseph was given the greatest title Judaism can bestow was his having saved Egypt from a calamitous and deadly famine.

A third reason, offered in a modern commentary by Rabbi Shmuel Goldin, is that all three patriarchs (Abraham, Isaac, and Jacob) and two of the four matriarchs (Sarah and Rebecca) received direct messages from God. By the time of Joseph, however, this was no longer the case: None of Jacob's twelve sons experienced a direct revelation from God. Yet Joseph again and again made reference to God and honored God before others:

- When Mrs. Potiphar tried to seduce him, he said to her (in the next verse), "How then could I do this most wicked thing, and sin before God?"

- When his two fellow prisoners complained there was no one to interpret their dreams, Joseph responded: "Surely God can interpret! Tell me your dreams" (Genesis 40:8).

- When Pharaoh said to Joseph, "I have heard it said of you that for you to hear a dream is to tell its meaning," Joseph replied: "Not I! God will see to Pharaoh's welfare." And Pharaoh was convinced: after hearing Joseph's interpretations and advice, Pharaoh said to his courtiers, "Could we find another like him, a man in whom is the spirit of God?" (Genesis 41:38).

- When Joseph revealed himself to his brothers, who had so grievously sinned against him, he assured them that they had nothing to fear from him: "Do not be distressed or reproach yourselves because you sold me hither; it was to save life that God sent me ahead of you" (Genesis 45:5).

Goldin concludes: "Joseph is a *tzaddik* because he is the first of our ancestors to maintain his faith while living in a non-prophetic era—an era when God is silent. Joseph emerges as the paradigm for our lives.... Our challenge, like his, is to see God's hidden hand in the world around us and to determine our role in the unfolding divine plan."

> *"This is what makes Joseph a tzaddik. In a world in which God is silent, in a world in which God appears absent, Joseph sees God everywhere."*

And, as Rabbi Ian Pear appends, "This is what makes Joseph a *tzaddik* [particularly righteous]. In a world in which God is silent, in a world in which God appears absent, Joseph sees God everywhere."

WHY JOSEPH REFUSED MRS. POTIPHAR

39.8 (cont.) He said to his master's wife, "Look, with me here, my master gives no thought to anything in this house, and all that he owns he has placed in my hands.

39.9 He wields no more authority in this house than I, and he has withheld nothing from me except yourself, since you are his wife. How then could I do this most wicked thing, and sin before God?"

Joseph gave Mrs. Potiphar three reasons he would not sleep with her: It would be ungrateful of him to betray his master, who had treated him so generously; she was the wife of another man; adultery is a sin against God.

The last reason is of particular interest, in that Joseph lived centuries before the Ten Commandments were given. How did he know adultery was a "sin before God"? One possible answer may lie in Joseph's use of "Elohim"—the universal name of God—when he told Mrs. Potiphar adultery is "a sin before God." As this is the only time in the narrative *Elohim* is used, it had to have been deliberate. Sleeping with a married woman was regarded as wrong in Egyptian culture, and Joseph was thereby telling Mrs. Potiphar that adultery was a sin against the God of everyone—Hebrews and Egyptians alike.

All three reasons Joseph gave for refusing Mrs. Potiphar involved her being a married woman. That raises an interesting question: Would Joseph have said no to a single woman?

39.10 And much as she coaxed Joseph day after day, he did not yield to her request to lie beside her, to be with her.

39.11 One such day, he came into the house to do his work. None of the household being there inside,

39.12 she caught hold of him by his garment and said, "Lie with me!" But he left his garment in her hand and got away and fled outside.

39.13 When she saw that he had left it in her hand and had fled outside,

39.14 she called out to her servants and said to them, "Look, he had to bring us a Hebrew

Realizing her own vulnerability, the conniving Mrs. Potiphar shifts blame onto her husband—"*he* had to bring us a Hebrew." And by referring to Joseph as "a Hebrew," she emphasized Joseph's alien status, hoping prejudice against foreigners would help turn the servants against him.

39.14 (cont.) to dally with us!

The Hebrew word used here for "dally" (*litzachek*) literally means "to play," but it also connotes laughter, sometimes mockery, and often sexual innuendo, as in the story of Isaac and Rebecca (Genesis 26:8).

39.14 (cont.) This one came to lie with me;

When talking to the servants, Potiphar's wife accused Joseph of coming to "lie" with her. She later used a different verb when she recounted the incident to her husband. Investigators often ask victims and witnesses to retell their story several times, paying careful attention to such inconsistencies. They are often the hallmark of a made-up story.

39.14 (cont.) but I screamed loud.

> Perhaps Egyptian law was similar to that of Deuteronomy 22:23-27, which stipulates that a woman who cried out could claim to have been taken against her will.

39.15 And when he heard me screaming at the top of my voice, he left his garment with me and got away and fled outside."

39.16 She kept his garment beside her, until his master came home.

> Potiphar is referred to not as her husband but as Joseph's master in order to emphasize Potiphar had complete power over Joseph.

39.17 Then she told him the same story, saying, "The Hebrew slave whom you brought into our house came to me to dally with me;

39.18 but when I screamed at the top of my voice, he left his garment with me and fled outside."

39.19 When his master heard the story that his wife told him, namely, "Thus and so your slave did to me," he was furious.

> "Furious" toward whom? Joseph or his wife? (See below.)

DID POTIPHAR BELIEVE HIS WIFE?

39.20 So Joseph's master had him put in prison, where the king's prisoners were confined.

> Joseph's punishment was relatively mild. One would think that a slave accused of the attempted rape of, or even of just carrying on an affair with, the mistress of the house would be executed if not tortured and then executed. Perhaps the fact that Potiphar let him off relatively easily implies that he did not fully believe his wife. The Torah does not record any dialogue between Potiphar and Joseph—perhaps because Potiphar was afraid to hear the other side of the story lest he find it convincing. If this presumption is accurate, the previous verse, noting that Potiphar was "furious," suggests the possibility it was his wife

toward whom he was furious—for initiating the whole thing and for costing him the best servant and manager of household affairs he ever had.

39.20 (cont.) But even while he was there in prison,

39.21 the Lord was with Joseph: He extended kindness to him and disposed the chief jailer favorably toward him.

39.22 The chief jailer put in Joseph's charge all the prisoners who were in that prison, and he was the one to carry out everything that was done there.

39.23 The chief jailer did not supervise anything that was in Joseph's charge, because the Lord was with him, and whatever he did the Lord made successful.

No matter what his situation, Joseph found a way to prosper. He was gifted with a talent for organizing and management, and God saw to it that these skills were recognized and rewarded. In prison, as in Potiphar's house, he was quickly placed in charge and granted executive authority.

CHAPTER

40

40.1 Some time later, the cupbearer and the baker of the king of Egypt gave offense to their lord the king of Egypt.

40.2 Pharaoh was angry with his two courtiers, the chief cupbearer and the chief baker,

> These were important roles in ancient Egypt. The literal translation of "cup-bearer" is "officer in charge of drinks." Ancient Egyptian documents testify to how important that person was in Pharaonic Egypt. The king's baker was also very important. Bread was not only an Egyptian staple; Egypt is widely regarded as the birthplace of leavened bread.[1]

40.3 and put them in custody, in the house of the chief steward, in the same prison house where Joseph was confined.

40.4 The chief steward assigned Joseph to them, and he attended them. When they had been in custody for some time,

40.5 both of them—the cupbearer and the baker of the king of Egypt, who were confined in the prison—dreamed in the same night, each his own dream and each dream with its own meaning.

> For the same reason Jacob took note of Joseph's dreams once he had a pair of them (Genesis 37:5-11), the cupbearer and baker became particularly interested in their dreams once they realized the two dreams had taken place on the same night. Two dreams with similarities occurring in the same night was considered doubly significant.

40.6 When Joseph came to them in the morning, he saw that they were distraught.

40.7 He asked Pharaoh's courtiers, who were with him in custody in his master's house, saying, "Why do you appear downcast today?"

40.8 And they said to him, "We had dreams, and there is no one to interpret them."

In times past, and particularly in the ancient world, people attached much greater significance to dreams than we do today. Therefore, having "no one to interpret them" caused Joseph's prison mates to be distraught. "A dream without an accompanying interpretation is like a diagnosis without a prognosis" (Hamilton).

Of course, those with a Freudian outlook still attach significance to dreams—but as explanations of our past or present, not as predictors of our future.

SEEING ONE'S TALENTS AS GIFTS FROM GOD

40.8 (cont.) So Joseph said to them, "Surely God can interpret! Tell me [your dreams]."

Joseph made clear to the king's courtiers that it is only God who can interpret dreams. He did not claim any powers of soothsaying or divination. Life humbles most people, and it is becoming increasingly apparent the formerly arrogant young Joseph is becoming a changed person.

That Joseph attributed his ability to interpret dreams to God is another reason he is regarded as a particularly righteous human being. How people who have special talents view their talents defines their character and often their life. Unfortunately, most gifted individuals do not regard their special abilities as gifts from God (or even as a gift from nature, for that matter). They simply bask in the glory their gift brings them as if *they* are the source, not the recipients, of their talents.

Regarding one's special talents as gifts from God has two important moral benefits. The first is humility. Seeing one's talents as gifts from God is the antidote to arrogance. If you believe God gave you the talent to become a great singer, a brilliant scientist, a gifted athlete, etc., you regard yourself as very lucky because you realize that other people might work as hard as you and not achieve anywhere near your level of success. That is humility. Arrogant people are insufferable, and as a result have no real friends. The very gifted who are arrogant have many sycophants, but no true friends.

> *Seeing one's talents as gifts from God is the antidote to arrogance.*

The second moral benefit of regarding one's special talent a gift from God is that one will use it in the service of God, not just in the service of self. One area in which this makes all the difference in the world is the arts. The greatest composer, Johann Sebastian Bach, wrote all his music "for the greater glory of God." And it shows. In modern times, which have become largely godless, composers have written music to glorify their own name, not God's. And it also shows.

40.9 Then the chief cupbearer told his dream to Joseph. He said to him, "In my dream, there was a vine in front of me.

40.10 On the vine were three branches. It had barely budded, when out came its blossoms and its clusters ripened into grapes.

40.11 Pharaoh's cup was in my hand, and I took the grapes, pressed them into Pharaoh's cup, and placed the cup in Pharaoh's hand."

Scholars have noted this dream involves units of three. The vine has three branches. Three verbs are used to describe the growth of the vine and the branches: "budded," "out came," and "ripened." Three times in verse 11 the cupbearer mentions Pharaoh and three times the cup. And in verse 11, the cupbearer cites himself three times: "I took," "I pressed," "I placed."

40.12 Joseph said to him, "This is its interpretation:

Richard Elliot Friedman comments: "The significance of dreams in human experience—and the significance of dream interpretation especially—is reflected by this fact: the first divine power possessed by a human in the Tanakh (Hebrew Bible, or Old Testament) is the interpretation of dreams."

40.12 (cont.) The three branches are three days.

40.13 In three days Pharaoh will pardon you and restore you to your post; you will place Pharaoh's cup in his hand, as was your custom formerly when you were his cupbearer.

The Hebrew actually says, "In three days Pharaoh will lift your head..." Virtually all translations except this one includes these words.

WE CANNOT RELY ON MIRACLES

40.14 But think of me when all is well with you again, and do me the kindness of mentioning me to Pharaoh, so as to free me from this place.

Joseph did not rely solely on God; and he was theologically right to do so. People should not expect miracles from heaven; they should do everything in their power to improve their situation. As a well-known religious aphorism commonly (but uncertainly) attributed to the great Catholic theologian Augustine teaches: "Pray as if everything depends on God; work as if everything depends on you."

There's a waggish tale that well illustrates this point.

A very religious man was once caught in rising floodwaters. He climbed onto the roof of his house and trusted God to rescue him. A neighbor rowed by in a canoe and said, "The waters will soon be above your house. Hop in, and we'll paddle to safety."

"Thank you," replied the religious man. "But I've prayed, and I have faith that God will save me." Shaking his head, the neighbor rowed away.

A short time later, the police came by in a powerboat. "The waters will soon be above your house. Hop in, and we'll take you to safety."

"No, thanks," replied the religious man. "God will save me." The police went on to look for others who wanted saving.

The floodwaters continued to rise, threatening to submerge the house. A rescue helicopter spotted the man sitting on the peak of his rooftop with the water closing in. Hovering overhead, the pilot let down a rope ladder and called out through a bullhorn, "The waters will soon be above your house! Climb the ladder, and we'll fly you to safety."

"No, thanks," shouted the religious man. "I've prayed to God and I'm sure he will save me!" The pilot reluctantly flew away.

Finally, the floodwaters swept over the rooftop, carrying the man into the floodwaters where he drowned. When he arrived in heaven, he demanded an audience with God. Ushered before God's throne, he said, "Lord, what happened? I prayed for you to save me, I trusted you to save me, and you let me drown!"

The Lord replied, "First, I sent you a canoe. Next, I sent you a powerboat. And then, I sent you a helicopter! What more did you expect?"

There are at least two reasons we cannot rely on miraculous intervention.

First, if we could rely on miracles, we would sit back and wait for God to do whatever we needed. Second, if we rely on miracles, we are bound to be disappointed—in God. And that will often lead to abandonment of faith in God.

40.15 For in truth, I was kidnapped from the land of the Hebrews; nor have I done anything here that they should have put me in the dungeon."

The Hebrew word translated here as "dungeon" (*bor*) is the same word used to describe the hole in the ground into which Joseph's brothers threw him and is usually translated as "pit." Joseph's word choice thus highlights the commonality between those two experiences.

40.16 When the chief baker saw how favorably he had interpreted, he said to Joseph, "In my dream, similarly, there were three openwork baskets on my head.

The poor chief baker. After hearing Joseph's optimistic interpretation of the cupbearer's dream, he was anxious to get Joseph's take on his dream, which "similarly" had the element of three. Unfortunately for him, the similarities ended there.

40.17 In the uppermost basket were all kinds of food for Pharaoh that a baker prepares; and the birds were eating it out of the basket above my head."

In their respective dreams, the cupbearer served Pharaoh while the baker served the birds—a distinction calling for markedly different interpretations.

40.18 Joseph answered, "This is its interpretation:

Joseph interpreted the baker's dream without any attempt to break the news gently. Instead, his words came across as if he were in a trance, which was appropriate given that he considered himself merely a conduit for God's message. As his total lack of affect suggested, he was not the one in control of what he was saying. Nevertheless, given that he was predicting a man's impending execution, Joseph comes across as somewhat cold-blooded.

40.18 (cont.) The three baskets are three days.

40.19 In three days Pharaoh will lift off your head and impale you upon a pole;

Joseph's ominous interpretation of the baker's dream began with the same words as did his favorable interpretation of the cupbearer's dream (verse 13). He told both men Pharaoh "will lift your head." The poor baker undoubtedly got excited. However, whereas Joseph told the cupbearer Pharaoh will lift his head and "restore you to your post," Joseph told the baker Pharaoh will lift his head and "impale it on a pole" (the Hebrew actually reads, "will hang you on a tree").

40.19 (cont.) and the birds will pick off your flesh."

One can only imagine the shock this news must have caused, and the depth of the baker's dejection. He must have felt deep regret at having confided his dream to Joseph. (Not doing so would not have changed anything for him, but now he had to live the next three days in dread of his impending doom.) The baker's fate must have seemed doubly horrific in a society that revered the dead body: In addition to being hanged, his body would be mutilated.

40.20 On the third day—his birthday—Pharaoh made a banquet for all his officials, and he singled out his chief cupbearer and his chief baker from among his officials.

This is the only birthday mentioned in the Hebrew Bible.

40.21 He restored the chief cupbearer to his cup bearing, and he placed the cup in Pharaoh's hand;

40.22 but the chief baker he impaled—just as Joseph had interpreted to them.

MEMORY MUST BE DELIBERATELY KEPT ALIVE

40.23 Yet the chief cupbearer did not think of Joseph; he forgot him.

The Hebrew reads "did not remember," rather than "did not think of." Therefore, the verse sounds redundant—"the cupbearer did not remember Joseph; he forgot him." The Torah is deliberately redundant, perhaps to emphasize the egregiousness of the cupbearer's ingratitude. In the ancient world, someone who correctly and positively interpreted a dream was believed to have helped make the positive dream come true.[2] Therefore the cupbearer had even more reason to be grateful to Joseph.

The cupbearer's behavior reflected people's tendency to make generous promises to those who help them when they are in distress but then quickly forget them when their situation improves. That people have short memories is a cliché for good reason. American humorist and social commentator Will Rogers once quipped, "The short memories of the American voters is what keeps our politicians in office."

People need to keep memory alive by deliberately thinking about people or events—or they will forget everything and anything—good, bad, even evil.

That is why holidays commemorating great people and great events are so important. And that is why teaching history is so important. At this time in America, few young people know about the founding of their country, and therefore have little appreciation of how special it is. As a consequence, they have little gratitude for their immense good fortune to live in America. And few young people almost anywhere in the world know anything about the greatest evils of the twentieth century, Nazism and Communism. The Torah repeatedly commands "remember" (*zachor*)—both the good (the Exodus) and the evil ("what Amalek did to you").

Without remembering good, the most important moral trait—gratitude—cannot be sustained. And without remembering evil, people are likely—and, in many cases, destined—to repeat it.

CHAPTER
41

41.1 After two years' time, Pharaoh dreamed that he was standing by the Nile,

> The cupbearer forgot Joseph, who languished in prison another two years.

41.2 when out of the Nile there came up seven cows, handsome and sturdy, and they grazed in the reed grass.

41.3 But presently, seven other cows came up from the Nile close behind them, ugly and gaunt, and stood beside the cows on the bank of the Nile;

41.4 and the ugly gaunt cows ate up the seven handsome sturdy cows. And Pharaoh awoke.

41.5 He fell asleep and dreamed a second time:

> As noted, dreams were considered to have great significance when occurring in pairs.

41.5 (cont.) Seven ears of grain, solid and healthy, grew on a single stalk.

41.6 But close behind them sprouted seven ears, thin and scorched by the east wind.

41.7 And the thin ears swallowed up the seven solid and full ears. Then Pharaoh awoke: it was a dream!

41.8 Next morning, his spirit was agitated, and he sent for all the magicians of Egypt, and all its

wise men; and Pharaoh told them his dreams, but none could interpret them for Pharaoh.

These dreams were so rich in detail and in clear, if undefined, symbolism it is hard to imagine none of Pharaoh's "wise men" and "magicians" were able to offer some interpretation. It is likely they tried. The problem was none were able to interpret the dreams to Pharaoh's satisfaction.

41.9 The chief cupbearer then spoke up and said to Pharaoh, "I must make mention today of my offenses.

Finally, the cupbearer remembered Joseph!

41.10 Once Pharaoh was angry with his servants, and placed me in custody in the house of the chief steward, together with the chief baker.

41.11 We had dreams the same night, he and I, each of us a dream with a meaning of its own.

41.12 A Hebrew youth was there with us, a servant of the chief steward; and when we told him our dreams, he interpreted them for us, telling each of the meaning of his dream.

41.13 And as he interpreted for us, so it came to pass: I was restored to my post, and the other was impaled."

41.14 Thereupon Pharaoh sent for Joseph, and he was rushed from the dungeon.

Pharaoh was immediately amenable to the cupbearer's suggestion that he call upon Joseph because of his trust in the cupbearer and because none of his wise men could interpret the dreams. Pharaoh was clearly desperate.

41.14 (cont.) He had his hair cut and changed his clothes, and he appeared before Pharaoh.

This was done in order to make Joseph look as presentable possible—and perhaps to make him look as Egyptian as possible: "In the ancient Near East, only the Egyptians were clean-shaven, and the verb used here can equally refer to shaving the head, or close-cropping it, another distinctive Egyptian practice" (Alter).

41.15 And Pharaoh said to Joseph, "I have had a dream, but no one can interpret it. Now I have heard it said of you that for you to hear a dream is to tell its meaning."

41.16 Joseph answered Pharaoh, saying, "Not I! God will see to Pharaoh's welfare."

As he had with the cupbearer and the baker, Joseph immediately emphasized he was merely a mouthpiece for God. And, as always when talking to non-Hebrews, Joseph used the universal name for God, Elohim.

41.17 Then Pharaoh said to Joseph, "In my dream, I was standing on the bank of the Nile,

41.18 when out of the Nile came up seven sturdy and well-formed cows and grazed in the reed grass.

41.19 Presently there followed them seven other cows, scrawny, ill-formed, and emaciated—never had I seen their likes for ugliness in all the land of Egypt!

Pharaoh, emotionally agitated, added his strong personal reaction in recounting his dream. He may also have added these words in an attempt to help Joseph interpret it.

41.20 And the seven lean and ugly cows ate up the first seven cows, the sturdy ones;

41.21 but when they had consumed them, one could not tell that they had consumed them, for they looked just as bad as before.

This detail was also not mentioned in the original description of the first dream. Here again, Pharaoh inserted his own impressions.

41.21 (cont.) And I awoke.

41.22 In my other dream, I saw seven ears of grain, full and healthy, growing on a single stalk;

41.23 but right behind them sprouted seven ears, shriveled, thin, and scorched by the east wind.

41.24 And the thin ears swallowed the seven healthy ears. I have told my magicians, but none has an explanation for me."

> As in verse 8, Pharaoh was likely saying no one offered an explanation that satisfied him. That is the reason for the words "for me."

41.25 And Joseph said to Pharaoh, "Pharaoh's dreams are one and the same: God has told Pharaoh what He is about to do.

41.26 The seven healthy cows are seven years, and the seven healthy ears are seven years; it is the same dream.

41.27 The seven lean and ugly cows that followed are seven years, as are also the seven empty ears scorched by the east wind; they are seven years of famine.

41.28 It is just as I have told Pharaoh: God has revealed to Pharaoh what He is about to do.

41.29 Immediately ahead are seven years of great abundance in all the land of Egypt.

41.30 After them will come seven years of famine, and all the abundance in the land of Egypt will be forgotten. As the land is ravaged by famine,

41.31 no trace of the abundance will be left in the land because of the famine thereafter, for it will be very severe.

41.32 As for Pharaoh having had the same dream twice, it means that the matter has been determined by God, and that God will soon carry it out.

41.33 Accordingly, let Pharaoh find a man of discernment and wisdom, and set him over the land of Egypt.

Here, Joseph shifted from interpreting the dreams to offering advice. Clearly, Joseph was now a man of great confidence. He was just released from prison and was already comfortable advising the god-king of Egypt. His confidence, in turn, was a testament to his certainty that his interpretations and advice came from God.

Was Joseph so confident as to be shrewdly recommending himself as the "man of discernment and wisdom" to be "set over the land of Egypt"? It would seem so.

41.34 And let Pharaoh take steps to appoint overseers over the land, and organize the land of Egypt in the seven years of plenty.

41.35 Let all the food of these good years that are coming to be gathered, and let the grain be collected under Pharaoh's authority as food to be stored in the cities.

41.36 Let that food be a reserve for the land for the seven years of famine which will come upon the land of Egypt, so that the land may not perish in the famine."

41.37 The plan pleased Pharaoh and all his courtiers.

Pharaoh was pleased that Joseph did not just interpret his dreams but also offered a solution to the looming crisis they foretold. Pharaoh was likely also impressed by Joseph's self-confidence and charisma (qualities that apparently had their effect on Potiphar's wife).

That Pharaoh immediately believed his dreams were about Egypt, not about himself, marks him as a great leader. Great leaders—and Pharaoh's behavior throughout this episode shows him in a very positive light—put their people's concerns above their own. It is one reason great leaders are rare.

41.38 And Pharaoh said to his courtiers, "Could we find another like him, a man in whom is the spirit of God?"

41.39 So Pharaoh said to Joseph, "Since God has made all this known to you, there is none so discerning and wise as you.

41.40 You shall be in charge of my court, and by your command shall all my people be directed; only with respect to the throne shall I be superior to you."

This is reminiscent, on a much grander scale, of Joseph's master, Potiphar, placing Joseph in charge of his estate (Genesis 39:6).

41.41 Pharaoh further said to Joseph, "See, I put you in charge of all the land of Egypt."

41.42 And removing his signet ring from his hand, Pharaoh put it on Joseph's hand; and he had him dressed in robes of fine linen, and put a gold chain about his neck.

41.43 He had him ride in the chariot of his second-in-command, and they cried before him, "Abrek!" Thus he placed him over all the land of Egypt.

41.44 Pharaoh said to Joseph, "I am Pharaoh; yet without you, no one shall lift up hand or foot in all the land of Egypt."

While Pharaoh showered Joseph with praise and prizes, Joseph, who was so talkative and confident when explaining Pharaoh's dreams, said nothing. The likely reason is whereas earlier he had been speaking words God put in his mouth, now that he was no longer speaking God's words, his meteoric rise from a prison cell to second-most-powerful man in Egypt left him dumbstruck.

41.45 Pharaoh then gave Joseph the name Zaphenath-paneah;

The exact meaning of this ancient Egyptian name is unknown, though it undoubtedly signified something grandiose. In the Targum, one of the oldest translations of the Torah, it is interpreted as "the man to whom mysteries are revealed," while the historian Josephus translated it, somewhat similarly, as "the revealer of secrets."[1] Whatever the name means, it testifies to the Torah's antiquity.

41.45 (cont.) and he gave him for a wife Asenath daughter of Poti-phera, priest of On. Thus Joseph emerged in charge of the land of Egypt.

41.46 Joseph was thirty years old when he entered the service of Pharaoh king of Egypt. Leaving Pharaoh's presence, Joseph traveled through all the land of Egypt.

41.47 During the seven years of plenty, the land produced in abundance.

41.48 And he gathered all the grain of the seven years that the land of Egypt was enjoying, and stored the grain in the cities; he put in each city the grain of the fields around it.

41.49 So Joseph collected produce in very large quantity, like the sands of the sea, until he ceased to measure it, for it could not be measured.

41.50 Before the years of famine came, Joseph became the father of two sons, whom Asenath daughter of Poti-phera, priest of On, bore to him.

ESSAY: IN OUR PERSONAL LIFE IT IS GOOD TO FORGET

41.51 Joseph named the first-born Manasseh, meaning, "God has made me forget completely my hardship and my parental home."

This is one of the most important verses in the Torah. Take it seriously, and it will change your life. There are three elements to it:

1. Joseph willfully forgot his childhood pain.

Joseph wanted to forget the pain of his family experience. This is evidence of Joseph's burgeoning psychological health and maturity. Most of us would do well to do the same with regard to our childhood pain. Few people grow up without family pain; and few people do well remembering that pain. One of the healthiest people I know is an adult woman who was molested by her father. If anyone has the right to remember their childhood pain and to resent their parent(s), she (and so many other molested women and men) does. Yet she chose to move on in life. She even forgave her father even though he never apologized.

Joseph wanted to forget the pain of his family experience. Most of us would do well to do the same with regard to our childhood pain.

In America in the 1990s, there was a popular psychotherapeutic movement known as "Recovered Memory." In therapy or under hypnosis, suppressed memories of childhood trauma would allegedly be recovered. While some recovered memories were accurate, some memories were not, and some were exaggerated. Whatever the case, the impact was almost always negative because the recovered memories almost inevitably alienated people from their parents and tore families apart.[2]

That movement was in many ways the opposite of Joseph's approach to childhood/family pain—try to forget (meaning, do not dwell on it) and try to move on.

In the previous chapter, I wrote how important memory is—so as to remain grateful for the good done to us or others and to learn from the evil done to us or others. But in our personal lives, it is often best to remember only the good and to forget the painful.

2. The role of having a child in that process.

It may be that the birth of his first child was what most enabled Joseph to forget the pain of his own childhood.[3] When family relations during one's childhood are emotionally troubled, they can leave an emotional hole—a hole that can later be somewhat or even entirely filled by having a child of one's own. For example, a man whose relationship with his father left an emotional hole might be able to fill that hole through a relationship with his own son. In this way, he still will have had a loving father-son relationship—but with him as father rather than son.

3. The role of God in this process.

Joseph notes it was God who enabled him to forget those family hardships. That, too, is critically important. Every addict who has become sober through a twelve-step program attributes his or her recovery to God (or at least to a "Higher Power"). The magnitude of the mistake the modern world has made in thinking we (individually and especially as a society) can thrive—morally or psychologically—without God is difficult to overstate. Demonstrating that fact is a primary reason for this commentary.

> *The magnitude of the mistake the modern world has made in thinking we (individually and especially as a society) can thrive without God is difficult to overstate.*

41.52 And the second he named Ephraim, meaning, "God has made me fertile in the land of my affliction."

41.53 The seven years of abundance that the land of Egypt enjoyed came to an end,

41.54 and the seven years of famine set in, just as Joseph had foretold. There was famine in all lands, but throughout the land of Egypt there was bread.

41.55 And when all the land of Egypt felt the hunger, the people cried out to Pharaoh for bread; and Pharaoh said to all the Egyptians, "Go to Joseph; whatever he tells you, you shall do."

Note that Pharaoh did not tell the Egyptian people, "Go to Zaphenath-paneah," the name Pharaoh had given to Joseph. He told the Egyptian people to "Go to Joseph." Indeed, the Egyptian name is never used again. Why Pharaoh would refer to Joseph by his Hebrew name when speaking about him to the Egyptian people is, of course, not knowable. But there are at least three possibilities:

1. Pharaoh did so out of respect to Joseph.
2. In case Joseph's policies were unpopular, the Egyptian people would then blame a Hebrew, not Pharaoh.
3. Pharaoh had gained respect for the God of Joseph— see, for example, verse 39.

41.56 Accordingly, when the famine became severe in the land of Egypt, Joseph laid open all that was within, and rationed out grain to the Egyptians. The famine, however, spread over the whole world.

"The whole world" meant the Near East, the world which the Torah is describing. The phrase is not necessarily literally true, any more than "as everyone knows," means all the billions of people on earth know.

41.57 So all the world came to Joseph in Egypt to procure rations, for the famine had become severe throughout the world.

CHAPTER
42

42.1 When Jacob saw that there were food rations to be had in Egypt, he said to his sons, "Why do you keep looking at one another?

> After years of grieving for Joseph, Jacob has gathered his strength and once again spoke as the patriarch of the family. He asked the question we should all ask when there is an ongoing and unaddressed problem: "Why am I—why are we—not doing something to solve it?" Too often, we just "keep looking at one another" waiting (hoping) for something to change.

42.2 Now I hear," he went on, "that there are rations to be had in Egypt. Go down and procure rations for us there, that we may live and not die."

42.3 So ten of Joseph's brothers went down to get grain rations in Egypt;

42.4 for Jacob did not send Joseph's brother Benjamin with his brothers, since he feared that he might meet with disaster.

> Jacob has apparently shifted his favoritism from the lost Joseph to Benjamin, his youngest. He would not part from him: to lose his only other child from his beloved Rachel would be too much to bear. The death of Rachel during childbirth and presumed death of Joseph may have left Jacob fearing this branch of the family was cursed or, at the very least, prone to tragedy.

42.5 Thus the sons of Israel were among those who came to procure rations, for the famine extended to the land of Canaan.

42.6 Now Joseph was the vizier of the land; it was he who dispensed rations to all the people of the land. And Joseph's brothers came and bowed low to him, with their faces to the ground.

The Hebrew words repeat those of Joseph's childhood dreams, in which his brothers' sheaves in the field gathered around and bowed down to his sheaf, and the sun, moon, and stars in the sky bowed low to him (Genesis 37:5-11).

42.7 When Joseph saw his brothers, he recognized them; but he acted like a stranger toward them,

Joseph knew that as soon as his brothers realized that the brother they betrayed was in control of the food supply, they would beg forgiveness. But that would tell him nothing about their character, and it is their character Joseph wanted to test: specifically, were they repentant for the evil they committed against him? To determine this, he needed to keep his identity hidden for as long as possible.

42.7 (cont.) and spoke harshly to them.

Why did Joseph speak harshly to his brothers? The obvious reason is what they had done to him. It is also possible he noticed Benjamin was missing and wondered if they done something to that brother, the other son of Rachel, as they had to him?

42.7 (cont.) He asked them, "Where do you come from?" And they said, "From the land of Canaan, to procure food."

42.8 For though Joseph recognized his brothers, they did not recognize him.

Joseph was unrecognizable to his brothers for many reasons. He was seventeen years old when his brothers last saw him; he was now thirty-nine (he was thirty when appointed vizier of Egypt, and an additional nine years passed since then—the seven years of plenty and two years of famine). In addition, he was Egypt's highest official, he was dressed in Egyptian garb, and he was speaking to them in Egyptian. And, of course, they were sure he was long dead.

42.9 Recalling the dreams that he had dreamed about them, Joseph said to them, "You are spies, you have come to see the land in its nakedness."

42.10 But they said to him, "No, my lord! Truly, your servants have come to procure food.

42.11 We are all of us sons of the same man; we are honest men; your servants have never been spies!"

42.12 And he said to them, "No, you have come to see the land in its nakedness!"

42.13 And they replied, "We your servants were twelve brothers, sons of a certain man in the land of Canaan; the youngest, however, is now with our father, and one is no more."

> They did not lie to Joseph by telling him the story they allowed their father to believe—that a wild animal had devoured their brother; they told him as much as they knew. Nor did they say "this brother was dead" because, in truth, they did not know what had happened to Joseph. All they said was—literally translated—"he isn't" (*einenu*). But, of course, they didn't tell the whole story: "We got rid of him."

42.14 But Joseph said to them, "It is just as I have told you: You are spies!

42.15 By this you shall be put to the test: unless your youngest brother comes here, by Pharaoh, you shall not depart from this place!

> Joseph was preparing to test his brothers to see if they had remorse for what they had done to him. What sort of test would demonstrate whether the brothers were repentant? A good answer is provided in the definition of repentance later written by Maimonides in his Code of Jewish Law:
>
> "What constitutes complete repentance? He who is confronted by the identical situation in which he transgressed and it lies within his power to commit the transgression again but he nevertheless abstains...out of repentance and not out of fear [of being caught]....[For example,] if he had relations with

a woman forbidden to him and he is subsequently alone with her, still in the full throes of his passion for her and his virility unabated…If he abstains and does not sin, this is a true penitent."[1]

Joseph's plan was to engineer a test placing his brothers in a situation similar to the one in which they betrayed him, a situation in which they could save themselves by abandoning their youngest brother, Benjamin to a life of slavery (see Genesis 44:10, 33). Would they protect Benjamin or themselves?

42.16 Let one of you go and bring your brother, while the rest of you remain confined, that your words may be put to the test whether there is truth in you. Else, by Pharaoh, you are nothing but spies!"

As in the previous verse, Joseph spoke like a true Egyptian, swearing not in the name of God but in the name of Pharaoh.

Though Joseph accused the brothers of being spies, his "test" had nothing to do with their being spies. It was about the missing brother Benjamin. First, he invented a ruse to force them to bring Benjamin to Egypt. Then he could proceed with his test.

42.17 And he confined them in the guardhouse for three days.

42.18 On the third day Joseph said to them, "Do this and you shall live, for I am a God-fearing man.

This last statement, "I am a God-fearing man," is the Bible's quintessential characteristic of a decent person, of someone who can be trusted (see, for example, Genesis 20:11 and Exodus 1:17). For an explanation as to why "God-fearing" is vital to a moral life, see the essay, "The Moral Significance of Fearing God" in Exodus 1:17.

The use of this Israelite phrase by Joseph likely both startled and puzzled them.

42.19 If you are honest men, let one of you brothers be held in your place of detention, while the rest of you go and take home rations for your starving households;

Joseph gave the appearance he was softening. He had previously told his brothers one of them could go home while the rest remained confined (see verse 16); now he required that only one remain and the rest could go. Perhaps he thought following through with his original plan—imprisoning nine brothers and allowing only one to return home—would be emotionally devastating to his father, so much so that he might die of a broken heart.

42.20 but you must bring me your youngest brother, that your words may be verified and that you may not die." And they did accordingly.

42.21 They said to one another, "Alas, we are being punished on account of our brother,

> This was the first indication the brothers truly felt guilty for what they had done to Joseph. Evidently, they were guilt-ridden enough to associate their present predicament with the crime they committed twenty-two years earlier.

42.21 (cont.) because we looked on at his anguish, yet paid no heed as he pleaded with us. That is why this distress has come upon us."

> The brothers' words revealed Joseph had begged them not to throw him into the pit, or to release him once they had done so. Probably both. This detail, which was not related in the Torah's original account of the incident (chapter 37), reveals the callousness of the brothers' treatment of Joseph. Not only did they leave him to die, they sat down to eat while their brother cried out to them (Genesis 37:23-25).

42.22 Then Reuben spoke up and said to them, "Did I not tell you, 'Do no wrong to the boy'? But you paid no heed. Now comes the reckoning for his blood."

42.23 They did not know that Joseph understood, for there was an interpreter between him and them.

> Listening to his brothers' conversation—which his brothers thought he couldn't understand, Joseph learned his eldest brother tried to save his life. One can only

imagine what Joseph felt and the difficulty he experienced trying to keep it inside. The emotion and drama are reasons the story of Joseph and his brothers is considered one of the greatest stories in all literature.

The emotion and drama are reasons the story of Joseph and his brothers is considered one of the greatest stories in all literature.

42.24 He turned away from them and wept.
Through all his tribulations, the Torah never reports Joseph breaking down and crying—not when his brothers threw him into the pit, not when he was sold into slavery, not when Potiphar sent him to prison—until now.

And why wouldn't he be moved? He heard their expressions of guilt and remorse, he learned Reuben tried to intervene, he was beginning to believe his brothers weren't bad people after all, and he imagined for the first time that his family had returned to him. Family reconciliations generate some of the most powerful emotions humans experience. Even if great love never returns, reconnecting in any fashion is immeasurably superior to permanent alienation.

42.24 (cont.) But he came back to them and spoke to them; and he took Simeon from among them and had him bound before their eyes.
Why Simeon? Under normal circumstances, Joseph would have kept the first born in Egypt. But Joseph now knew the first born—Reuben—had tried to save him. So, Joseph chose the second-born son, Simeon, to remain behind in Egypt while his brothers returned home.

42.25 Then Joseph gave orders to fill their bags with grain, return each one's money to his sack, and give them provisions for the journey; and this was done for them.

42.26 So they loaded their asses with the rations and departed from there.

42.27 As one of them was opening his sack to give feed to his ass at the night encampment, he saw his money right there at the mouth of his bag.

42.28 And he said to his brothers, "My money has been returned! It is here in my bag!" Their hearts sank; and, trembling, they turned to one another, saying, "What is this that God has done to us?"

The brothers were distressed because money they had brought to pay for the rations was now back in one of their bags along with the grain and provisions for the journey home. What were they to think? Were they being framed so that they would appear to be criminals? Or was something else going on, involving them in a larger-than-life drama being orchestrated by a higher power? Whatever the case, they were experiencing circumstances beyond their control.

42.29 When they came to their father Jacob in the land of Canaan, they told him all that had befallen them, saying,

The brothers told their father what had taken place but left out a few important details. They did not tell him about being imprisoned for three days, that Simeon was being held hostage, or about the money that was returned to them. And they certainly didn't mention their discussion of their culpability for what they did to Joseph.

42.30 "The man who is lord of the land spoke harshly to us and accused us of spying on the land.

42.31 We said to him, 'We are honest men; We have never been spies!

42.32 There were twelve of us brothers, sons by the same father; but one is no more, and the youngest is now with our father in the land of Canaan.'

Family reconciliations generate some of the most powerful emotions humans experience. Even if great love never returns, reconnecting in any fashion is immeasurably superior to permanent alienation.

42.33 But the man who is lord of the land said to us, 'By this I shall know that you are honest men: leave one of your brothers with me, and take something for your starving households and be off.

42.34 And bring your youngest brother to me, that I may know that you are not spies but honest men. I will then restore your brother to you, and you shall be free to move about in the land.'"

> The brothers further softened their account, telling their father the vizier wanted them to return with Benjamin to confirm they were "honest men." But that is not all that Joseph said to them. He told them they needed to return with Benjamin so that they "shall live" (verse 18) and "not die" (verse 20).

42.35 As they were emptying their sacks, there, in each one's sack, was his money-bag! When they and their father saw their money-bags, they were dismayed.

> Now they learned the money had not been returned to only one of them but to all of them. The Hebrew word translated here as "they were dismayed" (*vayiroo*) literally means "they were afraid." The brothers were afraid of the consequences of leaving Egypt with provisions for which—they now discovered—they had not paid. And they were afraid because some very strange things were happening to them.

42.36 Their father Jacob said to them, "It is always me that you bereave: Joseph is no more and Simeon is no more, and now you would take away Benjamin. These things always happen to me!"

> "Always" is a bit exaggerated. But one can well understand Jacob's anguish and fear. As Hamilton writes, "Each time (chapters 37 and 42) Jacob's sons have left home, they have returned to their father minus a brother (Joseph, Simeon) . . . ."

42.37 Then Reuben said to his father, "You may kill my two sons if I do not bring him back to you.

> Taken literally, this is surely one of the strangest statements in the Bible. It is hard to imagine Reuben is really offering Jacob permission to kill his sons, who are also Jacob's grandsons—and harder to imagine that Jacob would want to take advantage of the offer. Reuben simply felt compelled to reassure his father in the strongest way possible that Benjamin would return.
>
> Alter writes: "This is not the only moment in the story when we sense that Reuben's claim to preeminence among the brothers as firstborn is dubious, and

he will be displaced by Judah, the fourth-born." And Sarna notes: "Reuben assumes leadership for the last time."

42.37 (cont.) Put him in my care, and I will return him to you."

42.38 But he said, "My son must not go down with you, for his brother is dead and he alone is left.
It sounds as if Jacob said Benjamin was his only remaining son. One hopes he meant Benjamin was the only one left of Rachel's two sons. But it was nevertheless a hurtful thing to say to his other sons.

42.38 (cont.) If he meets with disaster on the journey you are taking, you will send my white head down to Sheol in grief."
Sheol is generally understood to be the place where the dead reside (see also Genesis 37:35). Jacob did not believe he would be able to go on living should anything happen to Benjamin on the proposed journey back to Egypt.

CHAPTER
~9 43 C~

43.1 But the famine in the land was severe.

43.2 And when they had eaten up the rations which they had brought from Egypt, their father said to them, "Go again and procure some food for us."

43.3 But Judah said to him,

> Judah was apparently now the brothers' spokesman. Reuben, the oldest, chose to remain silent. He might have lost credibility with his over-the-top offer of his sons' lives as a guarantee he would bring Benjamin back safely (Genesis 42:37). In addition, Reuben had long before angered his father by sleeping with Bilhah, Jacob's concubine (Genesis 35:22).
>
> As regards brothers two and three, Simeon and Levi, Simeon was being held hostage in Egypt, and both had likely been discredited after they slaughtered the male inhabitants of Shechem—actions which infuriated Jacob (see Genesis 34:30 and Genesis 49:5-7).
>
> Judah, brother number four, stepped forward and assumed leadership.

43.3 (cont.) "The man warned us, 'Do not let me see your faces unless your brother is with you.'

43.4 If you will let our brother go with us, we will go down and procure food for you;

43.5 but if you will not let him go, we will not go down, for the man said to us, 'Do not let me see your faces unless your brother is with you.' "

43.6 And Israel said, "Why did you serve me so ill as to tell the man that you had another brother?"

43.7 They replied, "But the man kept asking about us and our family, saying, 'Is your father still living? Have you another brother?'

In truth, Joseph never asked this; the brothers volunteered the information about their younger brother (Genesis 42:13). But now, in self-defense against their father's accusation, the brothers made up this detail.

43.7 (cont.) And we answered him accordingly. How were we to know that he would say, 'Bring your brother here'?"

This is a legitimate argument. Why would it have occurred to the brothers that if they told the Egyptian vizier they had another brother, he would insist they bring him to Egypt?

43.8 Then Judah said to his father Israel, "Send the boy in my care, and let us be on our way, that we may live and not die—

Judah echoed Jacob's words when he initially sent the brothers to Egypt to procure rations, "that we may live and not die" (Genesis 42:2). Using someone's own words against them in an argument is very effective.

43.8 (cont.) you and we and our children.

43.9 I myself will be surety for him;

Judah used legal terminology, guaranteeing his father that he would bear full responsibility for Benjamin.

43.9 (cont.) you may hold me responsible: if I do not bring him back to you and set him before you, I shall stand guilty before you forever.

Judah's presentation was rather more sober and realistic than Reuben's wild offer of his two sons' lives. It is often tempting to speak as Reuben did—to use drama or exaggeration to make a point. It may work the first time and even on subsequent occasions. But once a person acquires a reputation for exaggeration or melodrama, his credibility is lost.

43.10 For we could have been there and back twice if we had not dawdled."

Judah again echoed Jacob's words when Jacob rebuked the sons for dawdling instead of leaving immediately to procure provisions (Genesis 42:1), thereby offering a subtle rebuke of Jacob, who was now causing them to dawdle by withholding Benjamin.

43.11 Then their father Israel said to them, "If it must be so, do this: take some of the choice products of the land in your baggage, and carry them down as a gift for the man—some balm and some honey, gum, ladanum, pistachio nuts, and almonds.

43.12 And take with you double the money, carrying back with you the money that was replaced in the mouths of your bags; perhaps it was a mistake.

43.13 Take your brother too;

Jacob may simply have been too pained by the separation from Benjamin to mention him by name. Calling him "your brother" created for Jacob some psychological distance. Or he may have wanted to emphasize to his sons that Benjamin is their brother so that they remember their responsibility for him.

43.13 (cont.) and go back at once to the man.

43.14 And may El Shaddai dispose the man to mercy toward you, that he may release to you your other brother,

Jacob's reference to Simeon simply as "your other brother" demands explanation. According to Nachmanides, Jacob avoided any mention of Simeon by name because he was still angry at Simeon and Levi for their murderous violence in Shechem following the rape of their sister Dinah (chapter 34). Whether or not Nachmanides' theory is correct, the Torah does not record Jacob mentioning

Simeon by name during the entire time his son was captive in Egypt. It is even possible that, had it not been for his family's dire need for food, Jacob would have allowed Simeon to languish in captivity. Jacob only asked his sons to return to Egypt when food ran out. In effect, Jacob said, "While you're out picking up food, pick up your brother, too."

And we know that, at the end of his life, Jacob had only harsh words for Simeon (and Levi—Genesis 49:5-7).

43.14 (cont.) as well as Benjamin. As for me, if I am to be bereaved, I shall be bereaved."

Jacob's remark expressed total resignation. He was preparing himself for the worst, which may well be the best emotional strategy at such a difficult juncture.

43.15 So the men took that gift, and they took with them double the money as well as Benjamin. They made their way down to Egypt, where they presented themselves to Joseph.

The brothers appear to have been granted immediate access to the most important man in Egypt aside from Pharaoh. Joseph must have issued instructions that he be informed if this group from Canaan returned.

43.16 When Joseph saw Benjamin with them, he said to his house steward, "Take the men into the house; slaughter and prepare an animal, for the men will dine with me at noon."

Joseph instructed his Egyptian steward to prepare food for his Israelite brothers. Since an Egyptian would not have been capable of slaughtering meat in a kosher manner, this verse has troubled those traditional Jewish commentators who believe the Israelites—or, at least, their leaders—kept the laws of Kashrut even before those laws were written. There is no reason to believe such laws were observed centuries before they were given. If anything, inclusion of such details should be welcomed as testimony to the Torah's historical authenticity—since, as I note on a number of occasions, if the Torah had been written much later, it is unlikely stories of the founding Jews failing to observe Jewish ritual laws would have been included.

43.17 The man did as Joseph said, and he brought the men into Joseph's house.

43.18 But the men were frightened at being brought into Joseph's house. "It must be," they thought, "because of the money replaced in our bags the first time that we have been brought inside, as a pretext to attack us and seize us as slaves, with our pack animals."

> This is another rare instance of the Torah relating what someone is thinking. What they thought at first blush makes sense: Why would the most powerful man in Egypt invite them—lowly foreigners in need—into his house? Was it a trap? But Hamilton makes an excellent argument that their fear was unfounded: "It never dawns on the brothers that Joseph has enough authority to have them arrested on the spot without having to resort to a dinner invitation."

43.19 So they went up to Joseph's house steward and spoke to him at the entrance of the house.

43.20 "If you please, my lord," they said, "we came down once before to procure food.

43.21 But when we arrived at the night encampment and opened our bags, there was each one's money in the mouth of his bag, our money in full. So we have brought it back with us.

43.22 And we have brought down with us other money to procure food. We do not know who put the money in our bags."

43.23 He replied, "All is well with you; do not be afraid. Your God, the God of your father, must have put treasure in your bags for you.

> Since an Egyptian would not have said such a thing, let alone invoked the name of God on his own, Joseph undoubtedly told the steward what to say. And what he said must have further added to the brothers' belief that strange things (perhaps divinely ordained?) were happening to them.

43.23 (cont.) I got your payment." And he brought out Simeon to them.

One would think the brothers would have been elated to see their brother healthy and safe, but no reaction by them is recorded. (And given that Simeon was undoubtedly treated well, and well fed, while in Egypt, he may not have been all that elated to see his brothers.)

43.24 Then the man brought the men into Joseph's house; he gave them water to bathe their feet, and he provided feed for their asses.

43.25 They laid out their gifts to await Joseph's arrival at noon, for they had heard that they were to dine there.

43.26 When Joseph came home, they presented to him the gifts that they had brought with them into the house, bowing low before him to the ground.

On this visit, all eleven brothers bowed down to Joseph, just as predicted in the second of his youthful dreams (Genesis 37:9), another—perhaps the most explicit—indicator of the divine element in the Joseph story.

43.27 He greeted them, and he said, "How is your aged father of whom you spoke? Is he still in good health?"

43.28 They replied, "It is well with your servant our father; he is still in good health." And they bowed and made obeisance.

Though the translation does not note this, the word *shalom* ("peace") appears three times in these two verses. Whereas once the brothers could not speak a word of *shalom* to Joseph (Genesis 37:4), now, as one commentator put it, there is "a veritable burst of shaloms."[1]

43.29 Looking about, he saw his brother Benjamin, his mother's son, and asked, "Is this your youngest brother of whom you spoke to me?" And he went on, "May God be gracious to you, my boy."

The Hebrew words are "my son," not "my boy." Why would Joseph refer to Benjamin, who, after all, is not all that much younger than he, as "my son"? It was probably to keep up the act of the Egyptian superior who had no idea who these Hebrews were.

43.30 With that, Joseph hurried out, for he was overcome with feeling toward his brother and was on the verge of tears; he went into a room and wept there.

43.31 Then he washed his face, reappeared, and—now in control of himself—gave the order, "Serve the meal."

ESSAY: DOES "CHOSEN" MEAN SUPERIOR?

43.32 They served him by himself, and them by themselves, and the Egyptians who ate with him by themselves; for the Egyptians could not dine with the Hebrews, since that would be abhorrent to the Egyptians.

The Egyptians regarded themselves as a superior race. Foreigners were viewed as unclean, and therefore Egyptians ate only with fellow Egyptians. This Egyptian particularism probably asserted itself even more strongly in this situation because the Hebrews were shepherds, an occupation viewed by the Egyptians as abhorrent (Genesis 46:34).

Had the Egyptians lived and dined alongside the Hebrews, they might have seen these foreigners as equal human beings and might not have later enslaved them. Arguably, the most unique commandment in the Torah is to love the stranger (for example, Leviticus 19:34), which involves learning to see ourselves in people who are different. Perceiving others as real people—as "real" as we are—makes it very difficult to mistreat them.

The Egyptians' belief in their racial and religious superiority was not unique. Almost every people in history, including the Jews, has considered itself in some way exalted. However, there are at least four significant differences between the Jews' belief in their chosenness and other nations' beliefs in their superiority.

First, the Jewish notion of chosenness never meant Jews were inherently superior to any other people. The Hebrew Bible goes out of its way to make that clear. As the Prophet Amos said, "For Me, O Israelites, you are just like the Ethiopians, declares the Lord" (Amos 9:7).

Second, no central text of any group, or bible of any religion, depicts its own group as negatively as the Jewish Bible often depicts Jews. The Torah, to cite but one of many examples, repeatedly depicts the newly freed Israelite slaves as ingrates and malcontents (Exodus 16:2-3, Numbers 11:4-6, among other places). In addition, aside from the right to the Holy Land (which itself was permitted only once the Canaanites had sunk to a particularly low moral and ethical level), the Bible makes clear that chosenness confers no special rights, only increased obligations, on Jews: "You alone have I singled out of all the families of the earth; that is why I will call you to account for all your iniquities" (Amos 3:2).

Third, one could not convert to a group that was race- or ethnicity-based. A non-Egyptian could not "convert" to becoming an Egyptian. There was a racial element to the Egyptians'—and all other groups'—exalted status. In contrast, Jews have always accepted members of other nations and races. Therefore, Jewish chosenness could not possibly have a racial element. Anyone who joins the Jewish people becomes Chosen.

Fourth, whereas the claimed superiority of any ethnic or national group was never believed by any other ethnic or national group, vast numbers of non-Jews have believed, or at the very least suspected, Jewish chosenness may well be true.

43.33 As they were seated by his direction, from the oldest in the order of his seniority to the youngest in the order of his youth, the men looked at one another in astonishment.

Things kept getting stranger.

First, their money mysteriously reappeared in their bags. Then the vizier's steward told them their God must have put it there. Then they were invited to a meal in the home of Egypt's most powerful official—why would he take any interest in them? Now, the vizier seated them according to their birth order. That could not have been an accident. How could he have known? They had to have begun to suspect the steward was right—God was playing a role in their lives.

43.34 Portions were served them from his table; but Benjamin's portion was several times that of anyone else.

It seems Joseph was continuing the unfortunate family tradition of displaying favoritism—here fed by the fact that Benjamin was his only full (as opposed to half-) brother and was also the only brother not present while the terrible crime was committed against him.

The Hebrew word translated here as "several" is actually the Hebrew word "five."

43.34 (cont.) And they drank their fill with him.

The Hebrew states that "they drank and became drunk with him."

Another riddle for the brothers: Why would the second-most powerful man in the most powerful country in the world as they knew it have a private meal, and even get drunk, with them?

CHAPTER
44

44.1 Then he instructed his house steward as follows, "Fill the men's bags with food, as much as they can carry, and put each one's money in the mouth of his bag.

Although this translation uses "money" rather than silver, a number of commentators have pointed out the word "silver" is mentioned twenty times between chapters 42 and 45. These twenty mentions reflect the repeated notion in Genesis that what goes around comes around: Joseph was sold for twenty pieces of silver (Genesis 37:28), and he now used silver—mentioned twenty times—to force his brothers to confront what they had done to him. It is one of the many unlikely numerical coincidences in the Torah that seem to embed a "code" of single authorship.

44.2 Put my silver goblet in the mouth of the bag of the youngest one, together with his money for the rations." And he did as Joseph told him.

44.3 With the first light of morning, the men were sent off with their pack animals.

44.4 They had just left the city and had not gone far, when Joseph said to his steward, "Up, go after the men! And when you overtake them, say to them, 'Why did you repay good with evil?

ANOTHER PRE-TORAH PRACTICE

44.5 It is the very one from which my master drinks and which he uses for divination.

Divination (contacting the "divine" to foretell the future and to learn answers to otherwise unanswerable questions) was a widespread pagan practice the Torah later condemned and outlawed (Leviticus 19:26 and Deuteronomy 18:9-10). "So important was divination in Mesopotamia that divinatory texts developed into the largest single category of Akkadian literature in terms of sheer number of texts."[1]

The Torah's inclusion of this detail is yet another example of one of the Hebrews in Genesis not observing later Jewish Law—a compelling argument for the authenticity of the text. If the Torah had been written much later, as I frequently note, there would have been no mention of a great figure such as Joseph—virtually a patriarchal figure—acknowledging he engaged in divination (in verse 15).

44.5 (cont.) It was a wicked thing for you to do!'"

44.6 He overtook them and spoke those words to them,

Joseph will continue testing his brothers—have they really changed?

44.7 And they said to him, "Why does my lord say such things? Far be it from your servants to do anything of the kind!

44.8 Here we brought back to you from the land of Canaan the money that we found in the mouths of our bags. How then could we have stolen any silver or gold from your master's house!

The brothers offered Joseph's steward a compelling defense: If they were truly thieves, why would they have returned the money they found in their bags after their last visit to Egypt?

44.9 Whichever of your servants it is found with shall die; the rest of us, moreover, shall become slaves to my lord."

Earlier, Reuben offered to have Jacob kill his sons if he did not bring Benjamin back (see 42.37). Before that, Jacob made a similarly rash declaration when Laban accused him of stealing his household idols: "But anyone with whom you find your gods shall not remain alive" (Genesis 31:19, 32), unaware that it was his wife Rachel who took the idols. And now we have another instance of playing with fate by making an over-the-top promise.

44.10 He replied, "Although what you are proposing is right, only the one with whom it is found shall be my slave; but the rest of you shall go free."

> The steward, knowing this was a ruse, ignored the offer to put to death the brother found with the goblet.

44.11 So each one hastened to lower his bag to the ground, and each one opened his bag.

44.12 He searched, beginning with the oldest and ending with the youngest; and the goblet turned up in Benjamin's bag.

44.13 At this they rent their clothes.

> When the brothers realized they would have to return home without Benjamin, they responded as Reuben had when he discovered Joseph missing from the pit (Genesis 37:29) and as Jacob had when he beheld Joseph's blood-soaked tunic (Genesis 37:34).

44.13 (cont.) Each reloaded his pack animal, and they returned to the city.

44.14 When Judah and his brothers reentered the house of Joseph, who was still there, they threw themselves on the ground before him.

44.15 Joseph said to them, "What is this deed that you have done? Do you not know that a man like me practices divination?"

> Aside from restating that Joseph claimed to practice divination, the purpose of Joseph saying this was to further intimidate the brothers with regard to his (Joseph's) divine powers—"You can't fool me," he was telling his brothers. Of course, the truth was Joseph did have Divine power on his side.

44.16 Judah replied, "What can we say to my lord? How can we plead, how can we prove our innocence? God has uncovered the crime of your servants. Here we are, then, slaves of my lord, the rest of us as much as he in whose possession the goblet was found."

> Judah wisely omitted the brothers' earlier promise to have whichever one of them was found with the goblet put to death.

44.17 But he replied, "Far be it from me to act thus! Only he in whose possession the goblet was found shall be my slave; the rest of you go back in peace to your father."

> Joseph was testing his brothers: Would they abandon the favored youngest brother (again)?

44.18 Then Judah went up to him and said, "Please, my lord, let your servant appeal to my lord, and do not be impatient with your servant, You who are the equal of Pharaoh.

44.19 My lord asked his servants, 'Have you a father or another brother?'

44.20 We told my lord, 'We have an old father, and there is a child of his old age, the youngest; his brother is dead,

> Of course, Judah was referring to Joseph, whom the brothers assumed to be dead.

44.20 (cont.) so that he alone is left of his mother, and his father dotes on him.'

> Judah and his brothers were well aware of Jacob's preference for Benjamin. However much this irritated them, Judah used it in hope of eliciting Joseph's sympathy for their father and allowing Benjamin to return.

44.21 Then you said to your servants, 'Bring him down to me, that I may set eyes on him.'

44.22 We said to my lord, 'The boy cannot leave his father; if he were to leave him, his father would die.'

44.23 But you said to your servants, 'Unless your youngest brother comes down with you, do not let me see your faces.'

44.24 When we came back to your servant my father, we reported my lord's words to him.

44.25 "Later our father said, 'Go back and procure some food for us.'

44.26 We answered, 'We cannot go down; only if our youngest brother is with us can we go down, for we may not show our faces to the man unless our youngest brother is with us.'

44.27 Your servant my father said to us, 'As you know, my wife bore me two sons.

44.28 But one is gone from me, and I said: Alas, he was torn by a beast! And I have not seen him since.

> Hertz points out this was the first time Joseph learned what the brothers reported had happened to him. But the last words attributed to Jacob by Judah, "and I have not seen him since," strongly suggest that, on some level, Jacob was not sure Joseph had died. When a child's death is assumed but not proven, most parents will cling to hope—however remote—that their child is still alive.

44.29 If you take this one from me, too, and he meets with disaster, you will send my white head down to Sheol in sorrow.'

44.30 "Now, if I come to your servant my father and the boy is not with us—since his own life is so bound up with his—

44.31 when he sees that the boy is not with us, he will die, and your servants will send the white head of your servant our father down to Sheol in grief.

44.32 Now your servant has pledged himself for the boy to my father, saying, 'If I do not bring him back to you, I shall stand guilty before my father forever.'

"LOVE THE STRANGER" AND "LOVE YOUR NEIGHBOR"—BOTH BEGIN WITH FAMILY

44.33 Therefore, please let your servant remain as a slave to my lord instead of the boy,

Judah offered himself in place of Benjamin. As demonstrated earlier by his immediate admission that he had wronged Tamar, Judah turned out to be impressive. He offered himself as a lifelong slave in place of Benjamin to keep his word to Jacob that Benjamin would return to him.

Judah has learned the meaning of family responsibility. Two great lessons of family life are teaching people how to care for others and how to live with people who may be completely unlike them. It is often much easier to treat friends well than family well. We choose our friends, not our family. For many—perhaps most—people, "Love the stranger" starts at home.

Perhaps most striking in this passage is that Judah, the brother who years earlier advocated selling Joseph as a slave (Genesis 37:26-27), was now prepared to become a slave in order to spare another brother the same fate. His noble offer convinced Joseph the test had gone far enough. Having seen solid evidence his brothers had truly changed, he could now reconcile with them.

Judah is the archetype of the true penitent—the person who confronts the same situation in which he had previously acted wrongly and now acts decently (see comment to Genesis 42:15). In the words of a famous Talmudic teaching: "In the place where penitents stand, even the most righteous do not stand."[2] In other words, an even higher level of righteousness is ascribed to the one who has sinned and repented than to the one who has always been righteous. An old Jewish teaching suggests that it was because of Judah's willingness to risk his own freedom to spare Benjamin a life of slavery the Jewish people was named for him (Judah's Hebrew name is *Yehuda*; the Hebrew word for "Jew" is *Yehudi*).

> *For many—perhaps most—people, "Love the stranger" starts at home.*

44.33 (cont.) and let the boy go back with his brothers.

44.34 For how can I go back to my father unless the boy is with me? Let me not be witness to the woe that would overtake my father!"

CHAPTER

45

45.1 Joseph could no longer control himself

Now that they had passed his tests, Joseph was emotionally overcome—by his brothers' presence, their suffering, their pain (and his), and their moral growth. They were not the same people who had thrown him into a pit and then sat down to a meal while he cried out for help.

45.1 (cont.) before all his attendants, and he cried out, "Have everyone withdraw from me!" So there was no one else about when Joseph made himself known to his brothers.

45.2 His sobs were so loud that the Egyptians could hear, and so the news reached Pharaoh's palace.

45.3 Joseph said to his brothers, "I am Joseph. Is my father still well?"

Joseph spoke now without an interpreter, communicating directly with his brothers in their language. That, along with his knowledge that they were responsible for their lost brother's disappearance (next verse), made it impossible not to believe what would otherwise have been incredible: this Egyptian ruler was their brother.

45.3 (cont.) But his brothers could not answer him, so dumbfounded were they on account of him.

"Dumbfounded" is surely an understatement. The brothers were undoubtedly in a state of shock. They had assumed Joseph was either long dead (life expectancy for slaves in ancient societies was short) or had irretrievably disappeared. How could a seventeen-year-old boy who was presumably sold into slavery become, aside from Pharaoh, the most powerful person in Egypt? It made no sense. Yet, here he was, undeniably the man he claimed to be. As the American writer Mark Twain once remarked: "Truth is stranger than fiction because fiction has to make sense."[1]

45.4 Then Joseph said to his brothers, "Come forward to me." And when they came forward, he said, "I am your brother Joseph,

These words, "I am Joseph your brother," were echoed by Pope John XXIII, whose given name was Joseph Roncalli, when he greeted Jewish leaders at the Vatican in 1960.

These words, "I am Joseph your brother," were echoed by Pope John XXIII, whose given name was Joseph Roncalli, when he greeted Jewish leaders at the Vatican in 1960. The Pope used this great biblical story of reconciliation in an attempt to reconcile the Roman Catholic Church with the Jewish people, whom it had often persecuted. These words, which so deeply surprised and moved Joseph's brothers, greatly surprised and moved the twentieth-century descendants of Joseph and his brothers.

45.4 (cont.) he whom you sold into Egypt.

ESSAY: GOD AND FREE WILL

45.5 Now do not be distressed or reproach yourselves because you sold me hither; it was to save life that God sent me ahead of you.

Now that Joseph believed his brothers truly regretted what they had done to him, he told them they were not ultimately responsible for what they did—they were actors in the divine drama that led to his prominence in Egypt.

This raises one of life's most important questions: How much free will do we have?

Religious people who believe in divine intervention—such as Joseph describes here—need to address this question.

Atheists have an answer: human beings do not have free will. If, as atheists contend, we are only material beings, like the stellar dust of which we are composed, we cannot have free will. As matter doesn't make choices, neither do we. Everything we do is determined by our genes and by neurons firing according to scientific principles. For the atheist, the assertion that human beings have free will is wishful thinking and self-delusion. Human beings are essentially rocks with self-consciousness and therefore have no more free will than rocks.

Here is the atheist position on free will as described in The Humanist by a prominent contemporary atheist thinker:

"There's a desperate charm to that idea [free will] but we're quite beyond it now. The mechanisms of decision making, the chemistry of empathy, the physics of neural plasticity, each gnaws away every day at the few remaining supports of a free will model of individuality. We are forced to either redefine free will to something existent but meaningless, or chuck the idea altogether and make peace with finding the subtle joys of our exquisite programmability."[2]

But this position makes sense only in the abstract. When any of us—atheists, believers, agnostics—think about it, the idea we have no more free will than a rock strikes us as absurd. If you decide to forego dessert to keep your weight down, is that decision entirely programmed? Do students who cheat on tests have no choice but to do so? Are we to believe that no one who does good and no one who does evil is in any way responsible for what they do?

If we do believe these things, all discussion of good and evil is meaningless—calling a person or an act evil is no more meaningful than calling the earth evil after an earthquake. And moral instruction is pointless—we'll respond to such instruction as we are programmed to—so why teach good and evil? (And if teaching about good and evil does influence people, it means we do have free

If there is no free will, life is pointless; we are all here acting out a preprogrammed script we had no hand in writing.

will.) Finally, if there is no free will, life is pointless; we are all acting out a pre-programmed script we had no hand in writing.

Only if we have non-material consciousness (and/or a soul) can we make decisions that are not entirely determined by genes and environment. Therefore, as ironic as it may sound to a secular person, only a God-based understanding of human life allows for free will.

Only a God-based understanding of human life allows for free will.

The problem for believers is how to believe in both divine intervention and free will. If Joseph was right about God leading the brothers to abandon him to his fate in a pit, where was the brothers' free will?

There is no perfect answer because believers are not prepared to abandon either belief in divine intervention or free will. But there are imperfect answers. One is that moral free will and divine providence co-exist, but only God knows precisely how they mesh. Another is most believers recognize God does not always intervene but does so at times of His choosing for His purposes. I find both responses rationally acceptable.

In any event, Joseph was magnanimous in telling his brothers not to reproach themselves for what they did to him. But it is quite a bit easier, we must admit, to forgive—and to see God's hand—when things turn out as well as they did for Joseph.

45.6 It is now two years that there has been famine in the land, and there are still five years to come in which there shall be no yield from tilling.

45.7 God has sent me ahead of you to ensure your survival on earth, and to save your lives in an extraordinary deliverance.

Joseph's statement reflects Maimonides' view (a view shared by many, if not most, believers) that on occasion God intervenes in human affairs and uses human beings as vehicles to carry out His plans.

45.8 So, it was not you who sent me here, but God; and He has made me a father to Pharaoh, lord of all his household, and ruler over the whole land of Egypt.

45.9 "Now, hurry back to my father and say to him: Thus says your son Joseph, 'God has made me lord of all Egypt; come down to me without delay.

45.10 You will dwell in the region of Goshen, where you will be near me—you and your children and your grandchildren, your flocks and herds, and all that is yours.

45.11 There I will provide for you—for there are yet five years of famine to come—that you and your household and all that is yours may not suffer want.'

45.12 You can see for yourselves, and my brother Benjamin for himself, that it is indeed I who am speaking to you.

45.13 And you must tell my father everything about my high station in Egypt and all that you have seen; and bring my father here with all speed."

45.14 With that he embraced his brother Benjamin around the neck and wept, and Benjamin wept on his neck.

> Joseph had special affection for Benjamin because, in addition to being his beloved mother's only other child, he was the only brother not involved in the original attack on him.

45.15 He kissed all his brothers and wept upon them; only then were his brothers able to talk to him.

> To Joseph's credit, he did not only embrace Benjamin but embraced and wept upon all his brothers. One would wish that all who read this would find it possible to reconcile with family members from whom they are estranged and whose wrongs are likely far less evil than those committed by Joseph's brothers.

45.16 The news reached Pharaoh's palace: "Joseph's brothers have come." Pharaoh and his courtiers were pleased.

45.17 And Pharaoh said to Joseph, "Say to your brothers, 'Do as follows: load up your beasts and go at once to the land of Canaan.

45.18 Take your father and your households and come to me; I will give you the best of the land of Egypt and you shall live off the fat of the land.'

Pharaoh, indebted to Joseph for saving his kingdom from starvation, welcomed Joseph's family to Egypt to avoid starvation and live well. In other words, he wanted to do for Joseph's family what Joseph had done for Egypt.[3]

45.19 And you are bidden [to add], 'Do as follows: take from the land of Egypt wagons for your children and your wives, and bring your father here.

45.20 And never mind your belongings, for the best of all the land of Egypt shall be yours.'"

45.21 The sons of Israel did so; Joseph gave them wagons as Pharaoh had commanded, and he supplied them with provisions for the journey.

45.22 To each of them, moreover, he gave a change of clothing; but to Benjamin he gave three hundred pieces of silver and several changes of clothing.

Again Joseph gave Benjamin special treatment. While Joseph's preference for Benjamin is understandable (see commentary on verse 14), Joseph apparently learned little from his own experience how destructive such favoritism can be.

45.23 And to his father he sent the following: ten he-asses laden with the best things of Egypt, and ten she-asses laden with grain, bread, and provisions for his father on the journey.

45.24 As he sent his brothers off on their way, he told them, "Do not be quarrelsome on the way."

The Hebrew word translated here as "quarrelsome" (tirgizu) means "get angry" in modern Hebrew. The literal meaning is "to shake." In biblical Hebrew, it is used to mean "to fear" (see Exodus 15:14, Deuteronomy 2:25, 1 Samuel 14:15). "Joseph's remark would mean, "Don't fear on the way." It is an expression of the newly repaired familial relations" (Gottlieb).

45.25 They went up from Egypt and came to their father Jacob in the land of Canaan.

45.26 And they told him, "Joseph is still alive; yes, he is ruler over the whole land of Egypt." His heart went numb, for he did not believe them.

Jacob's reaction to his sons' news was shock and disbelief because the news that Joseph was not only alive and well but also the ruler of Egypt was literally unbelievable. Moreover, these same sons had brought him the blood-soaked tunic twenty years before, leading Jacob to conclude Joseph was dead. Though he never confronted them about it, he had to have wondered what had really happened to his beloved son and what his other sons knew about it.

The brothers have reaped the inevitable consequence of lying—being doubted when telling the truth. Many adolescents and teens lie to their parents, and when their parents respond even to the truth with skepticism, they angrily protest, "You don't trust me!" To which the appropriate response is, "Why should I?"

45.27 But when they recounted all that Joseph had said to them, and when he saw the wagons that Joseph had sent to transport him, the spirit of their father Jacob revived.

45.28 "Enough!" said Israel. "My son Joseph is still alive! I must go and see him before I die."

CHAPTER
46

46.1 So Israel set out with all that was his, and he came to Beer-sheba, where he offered sacrifices to the God of his father Isaac.

46.2 God called to Israel in a vision by night: "Jacob! Jacob!" He answered, "Here."

46.3 And He said, "I am God, the God of your father.

> Isaac was specifically mentioned probably because this was the place he had built an altar (Genesis 26:24-25). That God identified Himself as "the God of your father" may imply Jacob still had a relatively provincial understanding of God—as simply the God of his father. God speaks to people in terms they can understand. Though aware intellectually that God is universal—the Creator of heaven and earth—Jacob nevertheless understood God in the way most natural to him: primarily as the God of his father. Later, when Moses asked God for His name at the burning bush, God provided a much more sophisticated self-description (see Exodus 3:14).

ESSAY: HOW NOT TO BE AFRAID

46.3 (cont.) Fear not to go down to Egypt,

> In addition to having a natural fear of the unknown, Jacob may have been afraid of dying on alien soil and/or of leaving the Promised Land, especially since God had forbidden his father Isaac from doing so (Genesis 26:1-3).

God told Abraham, Isaac, and (later) Moses to "fear not"—though the Torah never states they were afraid. But God knows what we think and feel. God knows us better than we know ourselves. For the decent, that should be reassuring; for the indecent, it ought to be disquieting. But it often doesn't work that way because decent people often think they are worse than they are, and indecent people almost always think they are better than they are. For example, few groups have as high a self-esteem as do violent criminals. Three American professors of psychology reported:

> *Decent people often think they are worse than they are, and indecent people almost always think they are better than they are.*

"Violent men seem to have a strong sense of personal superiority.... Favorable self-regard is linked to violence in one sphere after another. Murderers, rapists, wife beaters, violent youth gangs, aggressive nations, and other categories of violent people are all marked by strongly held views of their own superiority.... When large groups of people differ in self-esteem, the group with the higher self-esteem is generally the more violent one."[1]

The influence of fear on the human psyche and on human behavior is too often overlooked. Harold Kushner (author of *When Bad Things Happen to Good People*) was approached after a speech one night by a man who asked him what sentence God repeats more than any other in the Bible. Kushner guessed it was the verse about being kind to the widow, stranger and orphan. The man shook his head. "Not even close," he said. "The sentence God repeats more than any other is: 'Fear not.'"

Kushner went home, looked up the phrase, and discovered the man was right.

Of course, the same Torah and Bible do tell us to fear *God*—because when people fear a good, moral, judging God, they are more likely to behave properly. This is borne out first and foremost by common sense: fear of punishment is the primary deterrent to crime. A society that meted out no punishments for crime would be overrun by crime. And common sense is confirmed by academic research. As reported in a major academic study, societies in which people believe in hell have fewer crimes:

"In a large analysis of 26 years of data consisting of 143,197 people in 67 countries, psychologists found significantly lower crime rates in societies where many people believe in hell compared to those where more people believed in heaven.

"'The key finding is that, controlling for each other, a nation's rate of belief in hell predicts lower crime rates, but the nation's rate of belief in heaven predicts higher crime rates, and these are strong effects,' lead author Azim Shariff, professor of psychology and director of the Culture and Morality Lab at the University of Oregon said in a university news release."[2]

Another study by Shariff found that "students were more likely to cheat when they believed in a forgiving God than a punishing God."[3]

Shariff concludes, "It's possible that people who don't believe in the possibility of punishment in the afterlife feel like they can get away with unethical behavior. There is less of a divine deterrent." Though one would think that people who believe in heaven also believe in hell, it turns out that many people are certain that they are destined for heaven and have no fear whatsoever they will go to hell; therefore, the threat of hell as a punishment for evil behavior has no deterrent effect on their behavior.

There is another benefit that accrues from fear of God: When we fear God, we are less likely to fear people. That not only provides the benefit of living a less fearful life, it also helps to supply people with the moral courage to do what is right at personal risk (see the essay, "The Moral Significance of Fearing God," in the commentary to Exodus 1:17).

Students were more likely to cheat when they believed in a forgiving God than a punishing God.

When we believe in and fear God (and in an afterlife), we are not only less likely to fear people, we are also less likely to fear anything—even death, the most universal fear.

In sum, it is highly significant God says "Fear not" far more often than anything else He says in the Bible. Too many people's behaviors and states of emotional well-being are affected by inappropriate fear.

46.3 (cont.) for I will make you there into a great nation.

46.4 I Myself will go down with you to Egypt, and I Myself will also bring you back; and Joseph's hand shall close your eyes."

God promised Jacob that Joseph would be at his deathbed. For most people, dying alone is one of life's greatest fears. What, then, could be more reassuring to Jacob than to know his beloved son Joseph would be at his side when he dies?

Every human being dies. What distinguishes one person's death from another's is how they die.

God's emphatic promise—made twice in this one verse—that He would accompany Jacob on his journey ("I Myself") is a direct result of the Torah's utterly new idea that God is not located in one place. This is one of the many characteristics of the God introduced by the Torah that had no parallel in human history. (Fifteen unique characteristics are listed in the essay, "The God of the Torah: The Most Important Idea in World History," in the commentary to Exodus 8:6.)

As Alter notes, in the polytheistic view, the gods' activities "were imagined to be limited to the territorial borders of the deity's worshippers. By contrast, this God solemnly promises to go down with His people to Egypt and to bring them back up."

46.5 So Jacob set out from Beer-sheba. The sons of Israel put their father Jacob and their children and their wives in the wagons that Pharaoh had sent to transport him;

46.6 and they took along their livestock and the wealth that they had amassed in the land of Canaan. Thus Jacob and all his offspring with him came to Egypt:

46.7 he brought with him to Egypt his sons and grandsons, his daughters and granddaughters—all his offspring.

46.8 These are the names of the Israelites, Jacob and his descendants, who came to Egypt.

The Torah lists the names of Jacob's descendants to make clear the national significance of their migration. This is how the Israelites all ended up in Egypt, where they would be enslaved for hundreds of years. The Torah lists many names of the non-famous, as it does elsewhere, because the less well-known are also significant and worthy of memorializing. Unlike many people, the Torah does not equate fame with significance. "The majority of these grandsons are but names, included in genealogies but absent from narratives. Nevertheless, God has a role for each—for the famous and for the otherwise unknown" (Hamilton).

WHY FEW WOMEN ARE LISTED

Some contemporary readers will be offended by the omission from this list of women's names (with the exceptions of Dinah [verse 15] and, for reasons unknown, Serah [verse 17]). But given how often the Torah portrays women as primary actors and how insistent it is on the equal worth of men and women, the omission has nothing to do with devaluation of females. It is simply listing men as representing households, as was customary throughout the world until very recently. When I was a child, I recall asking my parents—in the United States of America, where women had more equality and status than almost anywhere else in the world— why letters to my mother were addressed to

> *The Torah lists many names of the non-famous because unlike many people, the Torah does not equate fame with significance.*

"Mrs. Max Prager" rather than to "Mrs. Hilda Prager." They explained this was simply how married women were usually addressed, and my mother, a very strong and independent woman who ran a four-hundred bed nursing home, couldn't have cared less (though, for the record, it did bother me). Given the ever-changing social mores of society, it would have been impossible for the Torah—or for any text written today—to meet the social standards of every future society. What is eternal about the Torah are its values and wisdom, not its genealogical lists.

46.8 (cont.) Jacob's first-born Reuben;

46.9 Reuben's sons: Enoch, Pallu, Hezron, and Carmi.

46.10 Simeon's sons: Jemuel, Jamin, Ohad, Jachin, Zohar, and Saul the son of a Canaanite woman.

46.11 Levi's sons: Gershon, Kohath, and Merari.

46.12 Judah's sons: Er, Onan, Shelah, Perez, and Zerah—but Er and Onan had died in the land of Canaan; and Perez's sons were Hezron and Hamul.

46.13 Issachar's sons: Tola, Puvah, Iob, and Shimron.

46.14 Zebulon's sons: Sered, Elon, and Jahleel.

46.15 Those were the sons whom Leah bore to Jacob in Paddan-aram, in addition to his daughter Dinah. Persons in all, male and female: 33.

46.16 Gad's sons: Ziphion, Haggi, Shuni, Ezbon, Eri, Arodi, and Areli.

46.17 Asher's sons: Imnah, Ishvah, Ishvi, and Beriah, and their sister Serah. Beriah's sons: Heber and Malchiel.

46.18 These were the descendants of Zilpah, whom Laban had given to his daughter Leah. These she bore to Jacob—16 persons.

46.19 The sons of Jacob's wife Rachel were Joseph and Benjamin.

46.20 To Joseph were born in the land of Egypt Manasseh and Ephraim, whom Asenath daughter of Poti-phera priest of On bore to him.

46.21 Benjamin's sons: Bela, Becher, Ashbel, Gera, Naaman, Ehi, Rosh, Muppim, Huppim, and Ard.

46.22 These were the descendants of Rachel who were born to Jacob—14 persons in all.

46.23 Dan's son: Hushim.

46.24 Naphtali's sons: Jahzeel, Guni, Jezer, and Shillem.

46.25 These were the descendants of Bilhah, whom Laban had given to his daughter Rachel. These she bore to Jacob—7 persons in all.

46.26 All the persons belonging to Jacob who came to Egypt—his own issue, aside from the wives of Jacob's sons—all these persons numbered 66.

46.27 And Joseph's sons who were born to him in Egypt were two in number. Thus the total of Jacob's household who came to Egypt was seventy persons.

"Seventy" may be a precise number; but it may also signify completeness. It is ten times seven, the Torah number that represents completion, divinity, and Creation. Here it represents the complete people of Israel going to Egypt, where their fate will be lived out as foretold by God to Abraham in Genesis 15:13. There are ten other times the Hebrew Bible describes groups as numbering "seventy."[4]

To offer a (light-hearted) glimpse into Torah numerology about "seven," Hamilton points out the seventh son of Jacob listed here is Gad, and the sum of the numerical values assigned to the two Hebrew letters of Gad (*gimmel* and *daled*) equals seven.

46.28 He had sent Judah ahead of him to Joseph, to point the way before him to Goshen. So when they came to the region of Goshen,

> Goshen is a region of Egypt located on the eastern delta of the Nile River, where the Israelites ended up living for hundreds of years.

46.29 Joseph ordered his chariot and went to Goshen to meet his father Israel; he presented himself to him and, embracing him around the neck, he wept on his neck a good while.

> The Hebrew literally states that Joseph "wept on his neck *more*," a powerful descriptive phrase that does not appear anywhere else in the Torah. Joseph was indescribably overcome with emotion at being reunited with his father.

46.30 Then Israel said to Joseph, "Now I can die, having seen for myself that you are still alive."

> Jacob would live yet another seventeen years with Joseph, bookending the seventeen years he had with Joseph before he vanished from Jacob's life.

46.31 Then Joseph said to his brothers and to his father's household, "I will go up and tell the news to Pharaoh, and say to him, 'My brothers and my father's household, who were in the land of Canaan, have come to me.

46.32 The men are shepherds; they have always been breeders of livestock, and they have brought with them their flocks and herds and all that is theirs.'

46.33 So when Pharaoh summons you and asks, 'What is your occupation?'

46.34 you shall answer, 'Your servants have been breeders of livestock from the start until now, both we and our fathers'—so that you may stay in the region of Goshen. For all shepherds are abhorrent to Egyptians."

> Numerous scholars note there is no extra-biblical evidence suggesting Egyptians abhorred shepherds. But Rashi points out that sheep were Egyptian deities, and the twelfth-century commentator Ibn Ezra offers the explanation that ancient Egyptians, "like modern Hindus," did not eat meat.

Yet another Jewish commentary, *Daat Zekenim*, a compendium of commentaries published in 1783 in Italy, states: "The Egyptians hated sheep meat, i.e. mutton, just as they hated goats' meat. This was something not unique to the Egyptians. This is also why they could not sit at the same table as the Hebrews when the latter were being served lamb.... The Hebrews claimed that they would insult the Egyptians if they slaughtered their animals as service to their God inside the boundaries of the land of Egypt."

Whatever the explanation, ancient Egyptian xenophobia is well documented, and at the very least, Joseph was referring to that.

CHAPTER

47

47.1 Then Joseph came and reported to Pharaoh, saying, "My father and my brothers, with their flocks and herds and all that is theirs, have come from the land of Canaan and are now in the region of Goshen."

47.2 And selecting a few of his brothers, he presented them to Pharaoh.

47.3 Pharaoh said to his brothers, "What is your occupation?" They answered Pharaoh, "We your servants are shepherds, as were also our fathers.

> As Joseph had instructed them, the brothers told Pharaoh the truth about their occupation, despite potential Egyptian hostility.

47.4 We have come," they told Pharaoh, "to sojourn

> In using the Hebrew word *lagur*, translated here as "to sojourn" but literally meaning "to reside," Joseph's brothers identified themselves as resident strangers ("resident aliens" in modern parlance)—residents, but not citizens, of the country. This is in accord with God's prophecy to Abraham: "Know that your offspring will be resident strangers (*gerim*) in a land that is not theirs" (Genesis 15.13).

THE MORAL POWER OF EMPATHY

Awareness of their ancestors' status in Egypt—first as strangers, then as slaves—left a deep imprint on the Jewish consciousness. Thus, the repeated Torah injunction to "love the stranger because you were strangers in the land of Egypt" (see, for example, Exodus 22:20 (22:21 in the Christian Bible), Exodus 23:9, Leviticus 19:34, and Deuteronomy 10:19.)

This Torah law is predicated on the principle that empathy is a prerequisite for living morally. It is probably fair to say that universal empathy would end evil. Yet many people lack empathy, and why they do is one of the riddles of life. How can a person see another person suffer, let alone deliberately inflict suffering, and not feel empathy?

> *It is probably fair to say that universal empathy would end evil. Yet many people lack empathy, and why they do is one of the riddles of life.*

Since it is impossible for people with empathy to understand people who lack empathy, one can draw only one of two conclusions. Either some people are born without the ability to empathize, or they are people who can empathize—but only with those who are like them.

I think many—but not all—people in the first group can be taught some degree of empathy. As for the second group, they need to be taught that people unlike them are just as human as they are and suffer just as they do. When people regard those unlike them as less than fully human—as Jews are viewed by antisemites, blacks by racists, or land owners and the "bourgeoisie" by Communists—empathy cannot exist.

47.4 (cont.) in this land, for there is no pasture for your servants' flocks, the famine being severe in the land of Canaan. Pray, then, let your servants stay in the region of Goshen."

47.5 Then Pharaoh said to Joseph, "As regards your father and your brothers who have come to you,

47.6 the land of Egypt is open before you: settle your father and your brothers in the best part of the land; let them stay in the region of Goshen. And if you know any capable men among them, put them in charge of my livestock."

Pharaoh kept his promise to Joseph (Genesis 45:17-18), allowing his father and brothers to live in the best part of the land—and even asked that some of them be put in charge of the royal livestock.

47.7 Joseph then brought his father Jacob and presented him to Pharaoh; and Jacob greeted Pharaoh.

47.8 Pharaoh asked Jacob, "How many are the years of your life?"

47.9 And Jacob answered Pharaoh, "The years of my sojourn [on earth] are one hundred and thirty.

LIFE IS A JOURNEY—TO WHERE?

When Pharaoh asked Jacob about the years of his life, Jacob responded with the years of his "sojourn," speaking of life as a journey.

Alter observes that is indeed one of the two meanings of this response: "Jacob's life has been a series of wanderings or 'sojournings,' not a sedentary existence in one place." The other meaning, Alter writes, is "human existence is by nature a sojourning, a temporary dwelling between non-being and extinction."

Alter's use of the term "extinction" rather than "death" is instructive. As a secular man, Alter assumes extinction upon death is our fate. This in no way reflects on his commentary, which is both scholarly and illuminating. Moreover, it is to his credit that he wrote "extinction." Many people who believe there is no afterlife do not honestly confront the consequence of that belief: oblivion awaits us after death.

Many people who believe there is no afterlife do not honestly confront the consequence of that belief: oblivion awaits us after death.

JACOB DESCRIBES HIS LIFE AS BRIEF AND HARD. HE SPEAKS FOR MOST OF US.

47.9 (cont.) Few and hard have been the years of my life, nor do they come up to the life spans of my fathers during their sojourns."

Jacob briefly described his life as if he were talking to a long-lost friend, not the king of Egypt. He regarded his years as having been few and difficult. The difficult part is easy to understand. From his youth, since his schism with his twin brother Esau, struggle and pain had been hallmarks of his life. And he regarded his years as "few" because he assumed he would soon die and compared his 130 years to his father's 180 and his grandfather's 175. His assumption, however, was wrong; he lived to 147.

Jacob was no stoic. He tended to regard himself as a victim and let others—even Pharaoh—know it. Here is Alter's view of Jacob's summation of his life:

"[Jacob] achieved everything he aspired to achieve: the birthright, the blessing, marriage with his beloved Rachel, progeny, and wealth. But one measure of the profound moral realism of the story is that although he gets everything he wanted, it is not in the way he would have wanted, and the consequence is far more pain than contentment. From his 'clashing' (Genesis 25:22) with his twin in the womb, everything has been a struggle. He displaces Esau, but only at the price of fear and lingering guilt and long exile. He gets Rachel, but only by having Leah imposed on him, with all the domestic strife that entails, and he loses Rachel early in childbirth. He is given a new name by his divine adversary, but comes away with a permanent wound. He gets the full solar-year number of twelve sons, but there is enmity among them (for which he bears some responsibility), and he spends twenty-two years continually grieving over his favorite son, who he believes is dead. This is, in sum, a story with a happy ending that withholds any simple feeling of happiness at the end."

In other words, given Jacob's response to Pharaoh, it would appear he did not subscribe to the well-known saying, "All's well that ends well."

The truth is much of humanity could sum up their lives the way Jacob did—too few years, and hard. Such is life. Jacob was real. The Torah is real.

47.10 Then Jacob bade Pharaoh farewell, and left Pharaoh's presence.

47.11 So Joseph settled his father and his brothers, giving them holdings in the choicest part of the land of Egypt, in the region of Rameses, as Pharaoh had commanded.

47.12 Joseph sustained his father, and his brothers, and all his father's household with bread, down to the little ones.

47.13 Now there was no bread in all the world, for the famine was very severe; both the land of Egypt and the land of Canaan languished because of the famine.

47.14 Joseph gathered in all the money that was to be found in the land of Egypt and in the land of Canaan, as payment for the rations that were being procured, and Joseph brought the money into Pharaoh's palace.

47.15 And when the money gave out in the land of Egypt and in the land of Canaan, all the Egyptians came to Joseph and said, "Give us bread, lest we die before your very eyes; for the money is gone!"

47.16 And Joseph said, "Bring your livestock, and I will sell to you against your livestock, if the money is gone."

47.17 So they brought their livestock to Joseph, and Joseph gave them bread in exchange for the horses, for the stocks of sheep and cattle, and the asses; thus he provided them with bread that year in exchange for all their livestock.

47.18 And when that year was ended, they came to him the next year and said to him, "We cannot hide from my lord that, with all the money and animal stocks consigned to my lord, nothing is left at my lord's disposal save our persons and our farmland.

47.19 Let us not perish before your eyes, both we and our land. Take us and our land in exchange for bread, and we with our land will be serfs to Pharaoh; provide the seed, that we may live and not die, and that the land may not become a waste."

47.20 So Joseph gained possession of all the farm land of Egypt for Pharaoh, every Egyptian having sold his field because the famine was too much for them; thus the land passed over to Pharaoh.

47.21 And he removed the population town by town, from one end of Egypt's border to the other.

This verse is not easy to understand. The Hebrew may mean "town by town" (or "city by city") as translated here; it actually states the population was moved "*to* towns [or "cities"]. But the Hebrew is not the problem: Joseph's policy may be. Why did he move whole populations? Perhaps it was to more effectively distribute seed; alternately (and more darkly), it could have been done to ensure they understood the land no longer belonged to them. But, despite Joseph's intent to feed the Egyptian people during a prolonged famine, his economic policies (described here and in the remainder of the chapter) transformed Egypt into a feudal state. The Egyptian people gave up their freedom and became serfs of the state.

Whether or not Egypt became a totalitarian state, what is known for certain is that all modern totalitarian states have been created with the promise that the people would be better fed (and better clothed, and better educated, and given better medical care). But it doesn't work. People who forfeit liberty for food end up both unfree and poorly fed.

47.22 Only the land of the priests he did not take over, for the priests had an allotment from Pharaoh, and they lived off the allotment which Pharaoh had made to them; therefore they did not sell their land.

47.23 Then Joseph said to the people, "Whereas I have this day acquired you and your land for Pharaoh, here is seed for you to sow the land.

47.24 And when harvest comes, you shall give one-fifth to Pharaoh, and four-fifths shall be yours as seed for the fields and as food for you and those in your households, and as nourishment for your children."

> Leeor Gottlieb has a positive take on Joseph's plan: "Joseph ingeniously 'negotiates' a deal in which the people are led to feel that Pharaoh is entitled to everything, but in his compassion is going to take 'only' twenty percent and they will remain with eighty percent as a form of salary for their work on what is now Pharaoh's land."

47.25 And they said, "You have saved our lives! We are grateful to my lord, and we shall be serfs to Pharaoh."

47.26 And Joseph made it into a land law in Egypt, which is still valid, that the fifth should be Pharaoh's; only the land of the priests did not become Pharaoh's.

47.27 Thus Israel settled in the country of Egypt, in the region of Goshen; they acquired holdings in it, and were fertile and increased greatly.

LIFESPANS IN GENESIS MEAN MUCH MORE THAN THE NUMBER OF YEARS LIVED

47.28 Jacob lived seventeen years in the land of Egypt, so that the span of Jacob's life came to one hundred and forty-seven years.

> As explained in this commentary on a number of occasions, though not readily discernible to readers, lifespans in Genesis often have a significance beyond their literal number. The lifespans of the three patriarchs provide another such example:
> Abraham lived to 175, which is 5^2 x 7.
> Isaac lived to 180, which is 6^2 x 5.
> Jacob lived to 147, which is 7^2 x 3.

In this series, the squared number (5, then 6, then 7) increases by one in each case, while the coefficient (7, then 5, then 3) decreases by two in each case. And the sum of the factors is the same in each case: seventeen (5+5+7, 6+6+5, 7+7+3).

These patterned lifespans exist to suggest a divine element to the lifespans of the patriarchs.

47.29 And when the time approached for Israel to die, he summoned his son Joseph and said to him, "Do me this favor, place your hand under my thigh

The placing of one's hand under the thigh of another when making a contract is explained in Genesis 24:2.

47.29 (cont.) as a pledge of your steadfast loyalty: please do not bury me in Egypt.

47.30 When I lie down with my fathers, take me up from Egypt and bury me in their burial-place." He replied, "I will do as you have spoken."

47.31 And he said, "Swear to me." And he swore to him. Then Israel bowed at the head of the bed.

48

48.1 Some time afterward, Joseph was told, "Your father is ill." So he took with him his two sons, Manasseh and Ephraim.

48.2 When Jacob was told, "Your son Joseph has come to see you," Israel summoned his strength and sat up in bed.

48.3 And Jacob said to Joseph, "El Shaddai

> As explained in the commentary to Genesis 17:1, "In the modern period, it is sometimes noted this name for God—Shaddai—appears to be related to the Hebrew word *shaddayim* (breasts), and may refer to a feminine aspect of God." However, the notion that Shaddai comes from *shaddayim* is not borne out in the scholarly literature.
>
> Regarding God's "gender," the God of the Torah and the other books of the Bible is incorporeal and is therefore neither male nor female. From Genesis 1:1 on, God is both desexualized and de-gendered—another radical departure from all other Near Eastern religions and the other religions of the world, which depicted gods as either super-men or, in the case of goddesses, super-women. Nonetheless, the Torah and later Judaism portray God in masculine terms. For an explanation, see the essay, "Why God is Depicted as Male" (Genesis 1).

48.3 (cont.) appeared to me at Luz in the land of Canaan, and He blessed me,

48.4 and said to me, 'I will make you fertile and numerous, making of you a community of peoples; and I will assign this land to your offspring to come for an everlasting possession.'

God is the center of Jacob's message to Joseph. Whatever Jacob's weaknesses, he accomplished at least two great things: he kept the Israelite clan together and kept the concept of an invisible and just God alive.

And we are reminded yet again that the land of Canaan is for Jacob's descendants. There is to be one place on earth where God's presence is particularly felt. That's why the term "Holy Land" is used to describe the Land of Israel by Jews and Christians to this day.

48.5 Now, your two sons, who were born to you in the land of Egypt before I came to you in Egypt, shall be mine; Ephraim and Manasseh shall be mine no less than Reuben and Simeon.

Jacob adopted Joseph's sons into the clan of Israel as if they were his own sons and not his grandsons, thereby giving Joseph (through these two sons) a double portion in the inheritance.

Jacob had twelve sons—who became the twelve tribes of Israel. However, neither Joseph nor Levi were given their own lands. Joseph's two sons, Ephraim and Manasseh—as a result of their adoption by Jacob in this verse—had their own lands; and Levi, being the tribe of the priests, had no land.

48.6 But progeny born to you after them shall be yours;

If Joseph has any more children, they will be Joseph's children, they will not be considered Jacob's—only Ephraim and Manasseh are to be so considered.

48.6 (cont.) they shall be recorded instead of their brothers in their inheritance.

48.7 I [do this because], when I was returning from Paddan, Rachel died, to my sorrow, while I was journeying in the land of Canaan, when still some distance short of Ephrath; and I buried her there on the road to Ephrath"—now Bethlehem.

According to Nachmanides, because Jacob planned to ask Joseph (and his other children) to bury him in the Cave of Machpelah (Genesis 49:29-30;

50:5), he felt he needed to justify why he did not bury Rachel in the cave. He explained he was travelling when Rachel suddenly died (while giving birth to Benjamin—Genesis 35:16-21); therefore, he was unable to take her body to the family tomb.

48.8 Noticing Joseph's sons, Israel asked, "Who are these?"

The reason for this question, as verse 10 explains, is that Jacob was by now almost blind.

48.9 And Joseph said to his father, "They are my sons, whom God has given me here."

"Here" refers to Egypt.

He did not say, "Asenath [his wife] has given me." Once again, Joseph ascribed his blessings to God.

48.9 (cont.) "Bring them up to me," he said, "that I may bless them."

48.10 Now Israel's eyes were dim with age; he could not see. So [Joseph] brought them close to him, and he kissed them and embraced them.

48.11 And Israel said to Joseph, "I never expected to see you again, and here God has let me see your children as well."

A relatively rare, and therefore all the more moving, statement of gratitude by Jacob.

48.12 Joseph then removed them from his knees,

Apparently Ephraim and Manasseh are still young children.

48.12 (cont.) and bowed low with his face to the ground.

As Hamilton writes, "Joseph may be the second most powerful man in Egypt, but he never loses his respect for his father." This is another reason to regard Joseph as a particularly impressive individual.

48.13 Joseph took the two of them, Ephraim with his right hand–to Israel's left–and Manasseh with his left hand–to Israel's right–and brought them close to him.

48.14 But Israel stretched out his right hand and laid it on Ephraim's head, though he was the younger, and his left hand on Manasseh's head–thus crossing his hands–although Manasseh was the first-born.

As was the case in just about every society, the right hand was considered more important than the left. For a biblical example, see Exodus 15:6 ("Your right hand, O Lord, glorious in power"). In English, the word "left" derives from the Anglo-Saxon *lyft*, which means "weak" or "useless."

Therefore, when offering a blessing, a father would place his right hand on the older child and his left on the younger. But Jacob placed his right hand on Ephraim, treating the younger son as if he were the firstborn.

We do not know why Jacob did this, favoring the younger over the older, but it is certainly in keeping with the Torah's (God's?) attempt to undo all traditional societies' preference for the firstborn. This "reversed" blessing may, therefore, have been God's will—how else explain Jacob's prophecy (verse 19) regarding Ephraim surpassing Manasseh, who thus joins Cain, Ishmael, Esau, Reuben, and Zerah in having their firstborn status undermined.

48.15 And he blessed Joseph,

Jacob is, of course, blessing Manasseh and Ephraim, not Joseph. According to a traditional explanation of this verse, the Torah states Joseph is being blessed because the ultimate blessing for parents is to know their children are blessed. I might add that nothing so moves parents as when they see their own parent's love for their children.

48.15 (cont.) saying,
"The God in whose ways my fathers Abraham and Isaac walked,
The God who has been my shepherd from my birth to this day–

48.16 The Angel who has redeemed me from all harm–

> "The Angel" may be another reference to God or to God's messenger(s) who have helped guide Jacob's life.

48.16 (cont.) Bless the lads.
In them may my name be recalled,
And the names of my fathers Abraham and Isaac,
And may they be teeming multitudes upon the earth."

48.17 When Joseph saw that his father was placing his right hand on Ephraim's head, he thought it wrong;

> Seeing his younger son being favored by his father, Joseph may have feared Jacob was making the same mistake with Ephraim and Manasseh, Jacob made with him (Joseph).

48.17 (cont.) so he took hold of his father's hand to move it from Ephraim's head to Manasseh's.

48.18 "Not so, Father," Joseph said to his father, "for the other is the first-born; place your right hand on his head."

48.19 But his father objected, saying, "I know, my son, I know. He too shall become a people, and he too shall be great. Yet his younger brother shall be greater than he, and his offspring shall be plentiful enough for nations."

48.20 So he blessed them that day, saying, "By you shall Israel invoke blessings, saying: God make you like Ephraim and Manasseh." Thus he put Ephraim before Manasseh.

> To this day, Jewish fathers bless a son on Shabbat eve by placing their hands over their son's head and reciting this prayer. The Shabbat eve blessing for daughters is linked to the matriarchs: "May God make you like Sarah, Rebecca, Rachel, and Leah."

48.21 Then Israel said to Joseph, "I am about to die; but God will be with you and bring you back to the land of your fathers.

48.22 And now, I assign to you one portion more than to your brothers, which I wrested from the Amorites with my sword and bow."

According to Sarna, "Amorites" is a generic term for pre-Israelite peoples of Canaan. Jacob wanted Joseph to know he fought for the territory he is now giving him (though the Torah never mentions this battle).

CHAPTER

❧ 49 ❧

49.1 And Jacob called his sons and said, "Come together that I may tell you what is to befall you in days to come.

> This chapter is popularly thought of as Jacob blessing his sons. But his words are more prophecy and moral criticism than blessing.
>
> Though many of Jacob's predictions may not have significance to us today, they would have meant a great deal to the ancient Israelites who still retained tribal identities.

49.2 Assemble and hearken, O sons of Jacob;
Hearken to Israel your father:

49.3 Reuben you are my first-born,
My might and first fruit of my vigor,
Exceeding in rank
And exceeding in honor.

49.4 Unstable as water, you shall excel no longer;
For when you mounted your father's bed,
You brought disgrace—my couch he mounted!

> Jacob cursed Reuben—"you shall excel no longer"—for sleeping with his (Jacob's) concubine Bilhah following the death of Rachel (Genesis 35:22). Here, as in several other of his "blessings" (particularly to his three oldest sons), Jacob rebuked his sons for vile behavior.

49.5 Simeon and Levi are a pair;

> The Hebrew actually states Simeon and Levi "are brothers." All of Jacob's sons
> are brothers, but these two were linked as partners in crime.

THE IMPORTANCE OF JACOB'S CONDEMNATION OF SIMEON AND LEVI

49.5 (cont.) Their weapons are tools of lawlessness.

49.6 Let not my person be included in their council,

Let not my being be counted in their assembly.

For when angry they slay men,

And when pleased they maim oxen.

> As Genesis 34 relates, Simeon and Levi avenged the rape of their sister Dinah
> by killing not only Dinah's rapist but all the male inhabitants of Shechem as
> well. Although Jacob did not condemn them on moral grounds at the time
> (Genesis 34:30), he did so now. This condemnation is important and impressive.
> It is another example of the Torah's preoccupation with good and evil—not Jew
> and non-Jew, believer and non-believer, rich and poor, family and non-family,
> or any other non-morality-based division of humanity.
>
> Jacob's harsh censure of Levi in particular provides another example of the
> historicity of the Torah. The Levites became the most elite tribe in Israel, among
> whom were the priests (*kohanim*), God's elect who enjoyed a privileged status
> because of their role in the Temple service. Given this exalted status, had the
> Torah been written in a later period, it is unlikely to have depicted Levi in such
> a negative light.

ON CONTROLLING ANGER

49.7 Cursed be their anger so fierce,

And their wrath so relentless.

Anger is directly related to both good and evil. The difference is the answer to five questions:

What am I angry about?

Is the anger justified?

Is the anger proportionate to the offense?

What behavior will my anger lead me to do?

Do I control my anger, or does my anger control me?

Jacob condemned Simeon and Levi because they allowed justified anger to lead them to unjustifiable behavior—mass killing.

Whether people get angry is not what reveals their character; it is what they get angry about and how they express it.

A Talmudic saying states we can judge a person by how he acts with regard to "his pocket; his anger; and his cup."[1]

"Pocket" refers to monetary matters, and "cup" refers to alcohol. The Hebrew is a play on these three words which sound almost identical—"*kiso*" (his pocket"), *ka'aso* ("his anger"), and *koso* ("his cup").

Telushkin makes a compelling argument that people with bad tempers who tell themselves they cannot control their anger are usually deceiving themselves: Mugging victims, for example, feel intense anger at their mugger, but virtually all of them—even those with bad tempers—politely hand over their money rather than curse or fight the attacker. They control their behavior, proving they *can* do so—when they want to.

Telushkin offers a second example: If people with anger issues were offered a million dollars to significantly reduce the number of times they expressed excessive anger over a six-month period, most would become adept at controlling their temper. But in the absence of million-dollar incentives, people destroy marriages, family relationships, and friendships—things worth far more than a million dollars.

> *Whether people get angry isn't what reveals their character; it is what they get angry about and how they express it.*

This was Jacob's message to Simeon and Levi: They *chose* not to control their rage. Therefore, "Cursed be their anger so fierce."

49.7 (cont.) I will divide them in Jacob,
Scatter them in Israel.

49.8 You, O Judah, your brothers shall praise;
Your hand shall be on the nape of your foes;
Your father's sons shall bow low to you.

Judah received a particularly favorable blessing, second only to that of Joseph. Judah's character was demonstrated by his acknowledgment he was guilty in the incident with his daughter-in-law Tamar (Genesis 38:26) and in becoming the brothers' spokesman when Jacob feared parting with Benjamin (Genesis 43:2-5). In addition, it was Judah who convinced Jacob if the family did not go to Egypt, it would perish; and it was Judah who pledged to safeguard Jacob's youngest son, Benjamin. Finally, in Egypt, it was Judah's speech, the longest in Genesis, that moved Joseph to forgive his brothers (44:18-34).

Beginning with King David, all legitimate rulers of Israel, up to and including the Messiah, were and will be from the tribe of Judah.

49.9 Judah is a lion's whelp;
On prey, my son, have you grown.
He crouches, lies down like a lion,

The phrase "Lion of Judah" comes from this blessing. The lion became the symbol of the tribe of Judah.

49.9 (cont.) Like the king of beasts—who dare rouse him?

49.10 The scepter shall not depart from Judah,

Gunther Plaut notes that Jacob's blessing of Judah focused on the future because God's designs for the Jewish people would be carried out through him. The tribe of Judah survived the Babylonian destruction and deportation of the Israelites in 586 BCE. It made the survival of the Jews possible. It is from Judah that the Jews get their name.

49.10 (cont.) Nor the ruler's staff from between his feet;
So that tribute shall come to him
And the homage of peoples be his.

49.11 He tethers his ass to a vine,
His ass's foal to a choice vine;
He washes his garment in wine,
His robe in blood of grapes.

49.12 His eyes are darker than wine;
His teeth are whiter than milk.

49.13 Zebulun shall dwell by the seashore;
He shall be a haven for ships,
And his flank shall rest on Sidon.

49.14 Issachar is a strong-boned ass,
Crouching among the sheepfolds.

49.15 When he saw how good was security,

And how pleasant was the country,
He bent his shoulder to the burden,
And became a toiling serf.

49.16 Dan shall govern his people,
As one of the tribes of Israel.

540 THE RATIONAL BIBLE: GENESIS

49.17 Dan shall be a serpent by the road,
A viper by the path,
That bites the horse's heels
So that his rider is thrown backward.

49.18 I wait for Your deliverance, O Lord!

49.19 Gad shall be raided by raiders,
But he shall raid at their heels.

49.20 Asher's bread shall be rich,
And he shall yield royal dainties.

49.21 Naphtali is a hind let loose,
Which yields lovely fawns.

49.22 Joseph is a wild ass,
A wild ass by a spring
—Wild colts on a hillside.

49.23 Archers bitterly assailed him;
They shot at him and harried him.

49.24 Yet his bow staved taut,
And his arms were made firm
By the hands of the Mighty One of Jacob—
There, the Shepherd, the Rock of Israel—

> Though "The Rock of Israel" is a well-known description of God (it even appears in Israel's Declaration of Independence), the expression does not derive from this verse, in which the word is "stone" (*even*); it comes instead from in 2 Samuel 23:3, where the word is "rock" (*tzur*).

49.25 The God of your father who helps you,
And Shaddai who blesses you
With blessings of heaven above,
Blessings of the deep that couches below,
Blessings of the breast and womb.

49.26 The blessings of your father
Surpass the blessings of my ancestors,
To the utmost bounds of the eternal hills.
May they rest on the head of Joseph,
On the brow of the elect of his brothers.

49.27 Benjamin is a ravenous wolf;
In the morning he consumes the foe,
And in the evening he divides the spoil."

49.28 All these were the tribes of Israel, twelve in number, and this is what their father said to them as he bade them farewell, addressing to each a parting word appropriate to him.

49.29 Then he instructed them, saying to them, "I am about to be gathered to my kin. Bury me with my fathers in the cave which is in the field of Ephron the Hittite,

> The Torah frequently uses this expression, "gathered to one's kin," to refer to death. It almost definitely alludes to the existence of an afterlife. (The commentary about this phrase and the afterlife is at Genesis 25:8.)

49.30 the cave which is in the field of Machpelah, facing Mamre, in the land of Canaan, the field that Abraham bought from Ephron the Hittite for a burial site—

> Chapter 23 first described Abraham's negotiations with Ephron the Hittite for the Cave of Machpelah. The Torah states again and again this land, the first formal acquisition of land by Jews in Israel, was purchased legally and it therefore belongs to the Jewish people. (It is referred to yet again in the next chapter—Genesis 50:13.)

49.31 There Abraham and his wife Sarah were buried; there Isaac and his wife Rebekah were buried; and there I buried Leah—

49.32 the field and the cave in it, bought from the Hittites."

49.33 When Jacob finished his instructions to his sons, he drew his feet into the bed and, breathing his last, he was gathered to his people.

The Torah is, among other things, the story of the Jewish people, not of any one individual. It is therefore appropriate Jacob dies not at the very end of Genesis but in the penultimate chapter. The last chapter will continue the story of the Israelites. The one exception, fittingly, is Moses, whose death is recorded at the end of the final chapter of Deuteronomy, the last book of the Torah.

Death is described here as "gathered to his people." Once again, it cannot mean being buried near one's people. None of Jacob's people were buried in Egypt; and, as being "gathered to his people" takes place immediately upon "breathing his last," it clearly preceded burial.

CHAPTER

50

50.1 Joseph flung himself upon his father's face and wept over him and kissed him.

> Only Joseph's reaction to Jacob's death is reported. Did Joseph mourn Jacob's death more than all his brothers? Hamilton offers this thought: "That Joseph alone flung himself on his father's face may be intended as a fulfillment of an earlier word to Jacob by God that it would be Joseph who would close the eyes of his father (Genesis 46:4). It would appear that 'such honor is reserved beforehand to the survivor acknowledged to have been closest to the departed.'"[1]

50.2 Then Joseph ordered the physicians in his service to embalm his father, and the physicians embalmed Israel.

> In Nahum Sarna's view, the Torah specifically mentions the role of the physicians in Jacob's embalming to disassociate it from Egyptian religion. Egyptians were embalmed by priests in a religious ritual, but Jacob was embalmed by physicians. It was, so to speak, a secular embalming.

50.3 It required forty days, for such is the full period of embalming. The Egyptians bewailed him seventy days;

50.4 and when the wailing period was over, Joseph spoke to Pharaoh's court, saying, "Do me this favor, and lay this appeal before Pharaoh:

50.5 'My father made me swear, saying, "I am about to die. Be sure to bury me in the grave which I made ready for myself in the land of Canaan." Now, therefore, let me go up and bury my father; then I shall return.'"

Given that we have every reason to assume Joseph had always maintained a particularly close relationship with Pharaoh (see, for example, Genesis 45:16-20), it may be worth noting he did not go to Pharaoh directly but made his request through a member of Pharaoh's court. Perhaps Joseph feared Pharaoh would be offended by Joseph not burying his father in Egypt (Joseph emphasized this was his father's request).

To provide a modern example, it was reported that France's President Charles De Gaulle was upset when a prominent member of the French branch of the Rothschild family chose to be buried in Israel (a tradition among some Jews) rather than in France.

50.6 And Pharaoh said, "Go up and bury your father, as he made you promise on oath."

Though Joseph did not make his request directly to Pharaoh, Pharaoh responded directly to Joseph.

50.7 So Joseph went up to bury his father; and with him went up all the officials of Pharaoh, the senior members of his court, and all of Egypt's dignitaries,

50.8 together with all of Joseph's household, his brothers, and his father's household; only their children, their flocks, and their herds were left in the region of Goshen.

50.9 Chariots, too, and horsemen went up with him; it was a very large troop.

50.10 When they came to Goren ha-Atad, which is beyond the Jordan, they held there a very great and solemn lamentation; and he observed a mourning period of seven days for his father.

The Hebrew word for seven is *shiva*, the term that is used to describe the seven-day Jewish ritual of mourning for the dead. Jewish law obligates Jews to mourn for seven days following the death of an immediate relative (mother, father, son, daughter, brother sister, spouse). This verse suggests the *shiva* mourning ritual predates the Torah.

50.11 And when the Canaanite inhabitants of the land saw the mourning at Goren ha-Atad, they said, "This is a solemn mourning on the part of the Egyptians." That is why it was named Abel-mizraim, which is beyond the Jordan.

> *Abel* means "mourning." *Mizraim* means "Egypt."

50.12 Thus his sons did for him as he had instructed them.

50.13 His sons carried him to the land of Canaan, and buried him in the cave of the field of Machpelah, the field near Mamre, which Abraham had bought for a burial site from Ephron the Hittite.

> Every time the Torah mentions the Cave of Machpelah, it reiterates it was purchased legally by Abraham from the Hittites (see Genesis 23). It is as if the Torah foresaw the Jews' right to this land would be continually contested.

50.14 After burying his father, Joseph returned to Egypt, he and his brothers and all who had gone up with him to bury his father.

50.15 When Joseph's brothers saw that their father was dead, they said, "What if Joseph still bears a grudge against us and pays us back for all the wrong that we did him!"

> Even though Joseph's brothers had lived on good terms with him in Egypt for the past seventeen years, they were still worried that Joseph had not fully forgiven them for their betrayal of him—and that now, with their father dead, Joseph would feel free to express his anger.

50.16 So they sent this message to Joseph,
"Before his death your father left this instruction:

50.17 So shall you say to Joseph, 'Forgive, I urge you, the offense and guilt of your brothers who treated you so harshly.' Therefore, please forgive the offense of the servants of the God of your father."

Jacob never left any such instruction. Nor is there any reason to believe Jacob ever knew what his sons did to Joseph. Like many parents, Jacob was likely better off not knowing all the details of his children's lives. (But, then, what did Joseph tell his father happened to him all those years away? We will never know.)

Like many parents, Jacob was likely better off not knowing all the details of his children's lives.

We can assume the brothers fabricated this "instruction" from Jacob to stop Joseph from unleashing anger he kept in check while Jacob was alive.[2]

What makes the lie transparent is it makes no sense. If Jacob had been concerned that Joseph might seek revenge against his brothers, he, not the brothers, would have been the one to make this appeal to Joseph. But the brothers, still ridden with guilt, were thrown into panic by Jacob's death.

Note that in their fabricated "message," the brothers referred to Jacob as "your" father, not "our" father to reinforce the gravity of the message.

By invoking the God of Joseph's father, the brothers added a religious obligation to their message: "You, Joseph, owe good treatment of us not only for the sake of your father but of the God of your father."

50.17 (cont.) And Joseph was in tears as they spoke to him.

Telushkin suggests he cried because he realized that even seventeen years after their reconciliation and all the good will he had shown them, his brothers still feared him.

50.18 His brothers went to him themselves, flung themselves before him,

Just as predicted in Joseph's childhood dreams, the brothers once again prostrated themselves before him.

50.18 (cont.) and said, "We are prepared to be your slaves."

The brothers repeated the offer Judah made to Joseph almost two decades earlier—to be his slaves (Genesis 44:33). Once again in Genesis, what goes around comes around. The brothers who plotted to sell Joseph into slavery now offered themselves as Joseph's slaves.

50.19 But Joseph said to them, "Have no fear! Am I a substitute for God?

50.20 Besides, although you intended me harm, God intended it for good, so as to bring about the present result—the survival of many people.

50.21 And so, fear not. I will sustain you and your children."

Thus he reassured them, speaking kindly to them.

> This reassurance of, and kindness to, his brothers is further evidence Joseph had turned out to be a truly good man. Of the many good traits among human beings—kindness, integrity, courage, loyalty—forgiveness is one of the most beautiful. That is why we have the saying, "To err is human, to forgive is divine."

50.22 So Joseph and his father's household remained in Egypt. Joseph lived one hundred and ten years.

> In the Jewish tradition, the ideal lifespan is 120 years (Moses's lifespan, as recorded in Deuteronomy 34:7). In the Egyptian tradition it was 110 years. Egyptologists have identified twenty-seven places in ancient Egyptian documents where this figure of 110 is mentioned—an example of the veracity and antiquity of the Torah.

50.23 Joseph lived to see children of the third generation of Ephraim; the children of Machir son of Manasseh were likewise born upon Joseph's knees.

50.24 At length, Joseph said to his brothers, "I am about to die.

> Logically, Joseph could not have been speaking to his brothers since they, or at least most of them, would have died by this time. He was, after all, the second youngest brother of the twelve, and he was already 110 years old. The Torah is likely referring to the tribes descended from his brothers. For a study of the number "110" and its relationship to the years lived by Joseph's father (Jacob), grandfather (Isaac), and great-grandfather (Abraham), see the endnote.[3]

50.24 (cont.) God will surely take notice of you and bring you up from this land to the land that He promised on oath to Abraham, to Isaac, and to Jacob."

50.25 So Joseph made the sons of Israel swear, saying, "When God has taken notice of you, you shall carry up my bones from here."

Joseph's words allude to the time when God will decide to deliver the Israelite slaves from Egypt. The book of Genesis thereby ends by setting the stage for the slavery and the Exodus, the primary stories of the next book of the Torah. Thus, at the very moment the Torah is preparing to introduce us to a terrible period in Jewish history, it is also assuring us that period will end.

Unlike his father Jacob's burial in Canaan, Joseph recognized it was imperative he be buried in Egypt. His burial in Canaan would have called into question his loyalty to Egypt and might thereby imperil his family's security, whose only claim to Egyptian hospitality was their kinship with Joseph. It is also likely Joseph, who owed so much to this decent Pharaoh, did not want to insult him.

For here, unlike the Pharaoh in the next book of the Bible, was a good Pharaoh. And the very fact that the Torah could portray a good Pharaoh—given the suffering inflicted on the Israelites by a future Pharaoh—demonstrates one of the great and original teachings of the Torah: the only division among human beings that matters is moral, not ethnic, national, or economic. Or, as Viktor Frankl put it in his classic work *Man's Search for Meaning*, "there are two races of men in this world, but only these two—the 'race' of the decent man and the 'race' of the indecent man."

50.26 Joseph died at the age of one hundred and ten years; and he was embalmed and placed in a coffin in Egypt.

NOTES

1. "In the beginning God created the heavens and the Earth" is how almost all translations translate this verse. Because I concur with this rendering—and because it is probably the most famous verse in the Bible—I use it here. It is the one time in *The Rational Bible* I change the English translation used in this commentary (published in 1962 by the Jewish Publication Society). That translation renders Genesis 1:1 "When God began to create," a translation favored by many modern scholars. The endnote explains why I prefer the traditional translation.

2. Francis S. Collins, Ph.D. in physical chemistry, Yale University, director of the National Human Genome Research Institute, director of the National Institutes of Health, member National Academy of Sciences. Author of *Belief: Readings on the Reason for Faith*, HarperOne, 2010; *The Language of God: A Scientist Presents Evidence for Belief*, Free Press, 2006; Jennifer Wiseman, Ph.D. in astronomy, Harvard University, Senior Project Scientist for the Hubble Space Telescope, NASA Goddard Space Flight Center. See *Gutsy Girls: Strong Christian Women Who Impacted the World: Jennifer Wiseman*, 2017; Hugh Ross, Ph.D. in astrophysics, University of Toronto. Author of *Improbable Planet: How Earth Became Humanity's Home*, Baker Books 2016; *Navigating Genesis: A Scientist's Journey through Genesis 1-11*, RTB Press, 2014; Stephen C. Meyer, Ph.D. in history and philosophy of science, Cambridge University. Author of *Signature in the Cell: DNA and the Evidence for Intelligent Design*, HarperOne, 2009; Douglas Axe, Ph.D. in chemical engineering, California Institute of Technology, postdoctoral and research scientist positions at the University of Cambridge, the Cambridge Medical Research Council Centre, and the Babraham Institute in Cambridge. Author of *Undeniable: How Biology Confirms Our Intuition That Life Is Designed*, 2018.

3. Stephanie Garry, "Statistics don't lie in this case," *Politifact*, June 23, 2008.

4. See, for example, Sarah Hall, "Crime linked to absent fathers," *The Guardian*, April 5, 2001.

5. http://www.mnpsych.org/index.php?option=com_dailyplanetblog&view=entry&category=industry%20news&id=54:father-absent-homes-implications-for-criminal-justice-and-mental-health-professionals.

6. Coley, R. L. Medeiros, B. L., "Reciprocal longitudinal relations between nonresident father involvement and adolescent delinquency," *Child Development* 78, 132-147, 2007.

7. T. L. Snell and D. C. Morton, "Women in prison: Survey of prison inmates," 1994. U.S. Department of Justice, 1991.

8. M.A. Hill and J. O'Neill, "Underclass behaviors in the United States: Measurement and analysis of determinants." City University of New York, 1993.

9. C. Harper and S. McLanahan, "Father absence and youth incarceration," *Journal of Research on Adolescence* 14, 369-397, 2004.

10. Jesse Emspak, "Early Earth's Atmosphere Was Surprisingly Thin," *Scientific American*, May 14, 2016.

11. Quoted in Space.com, November 8, 2013.

12. *New Scientist*, May 8, 2017.

13. Physicist Gerald Schroeder's words to me. This is also the view of another religious (Christian) scientist and Bible scholar, the astrophysicist Hugh Ross.

14. With regard to people who denigrate their accomplishments, the twentieth-century rabbi Chazon Ish—a man renowned for his scholarship and moral character—said: "People are mistaken in thinking that humility means to think of yourself as an ignorant boor even when such is surely not the case. *Humility means that a person realizes his true worth.*"

15. Among Schroeder's books are *Genesis and the Big Bang*, Bantam Doubleday, 1990; *The Science of God*, Free Press 1997 (Amazon's bestselling book in physics/cosmology in 1998).

16. The Orthodox Jewish scientist Schroeder has a novel take: "Actually the Hebrew is 'great reptiles,' not 'sea monsters' and the irony of this is the first Torah translation, the Septuagint, 2200 years ago, was into Greek. Had the Greek been faithful to the Hebrew, 'great reptiles' would translate into the Greek as *dino* ['big' or 'terrible'] *saurus* ['reptiles']—'dinosaurus.'"

17. Scott A. Shay, *In Good Faith: Questioning Religion and Atheism*, Post Hill Press, 2018.

18. The Talmud states that every person should walk around saying, "For my sake the world was created" (*Bishvili nivra ha'olam*).

Chapter 2

1. Genesis: Translation and Commentary (Kindle Locations 904-909). W. W. Norton & Company.
2. *Ecclesiastes Rabbah* 7:13.
3. Jerusalem Talmud, end of tractate *Kiddushin*.
4. Raheel Mushtag et al., "Relationship Between Loneliness, Psychiatric Disorders and Physical Health? A Review on the Psychological Aspects of Loneliness," *Journal of Clinical and Diagnostic Research* 8 no. 9, (September 2014), https://www.ncbi.nlm.nih.gov/pmc/articles/PMC4225959/.
5. Dale Archer, M.D., "Loneliness and Death," *Psychology Today*, April 23, 2015.
6. Jonathan Sacks, "Regular worship is the mortar of the Big Society," *The Office of Rabbi Sacks*, November 6, 2010.
7. Martin Buber, *Meetings,* edited with an introduction by Maurice Friedman. La Salle, Ill.: Open Court Publishing Company, 1973.
8. Jack Doyle, *Daily Mail*, "The rise and rise of the boomerang generation," July 14, 2014.
9. Nahum Rabinovich, *The Edah Journal* 3:1, 2003.

Chapter 3

1. According to one imaginative Midrash (ancient rabbinic commentaries on and stories about the Torah), the snake pushed Eve against the tree and when she saw nothing bad ensued, she concluded everything that Adam told her about the tree was inaccurate. *Genesis Rabbah* 19:3.
2. Talmud *Sanhedrin* 29a.
3. Having often been misquoted, I know how destructive it can be. To cite one example, the *New York Times*, in an article about me, wrote "Prager suggested" words I never said. Proofs that I never said the words attributed to me were that the *Times* wrote "suggested," not "said" or "wrote," and that the words were not placed within quotation marks. That was how the writer was able to attribute to me an extreme point of view I never expressed. Then other news sources throughout America wrote that I *said*—not merely "suggested"—those words; and they did place the words within quotation marks. But they were quoting the *New York Times*, not me—and every reader understandably assumed it was a direct quote from me. I explain this in detail in "How the Mainstream Media Operate," RealClearPolitics, August 23, 2017.

4. See, for example, Gangestad, S. W., Simpson, J. A., Cousins, A. J., Garver-Apgar, C. E., & Christensen, P. N. (2004), "Women's preferences for male behavioral displays change across the menstrual cycle," *Psychological Science*, 15, 203–206. Cited in Gwendolyn Seidman, Ph.D., "Why Some of Us Seek Dominant Partners," *Psychology Today*, May 8, 2015.

5. "Study confirms that women tend to do more housework than their male partners, irrespective of their age, income or own workloads," *Science Daily*, September 26, 2017. The lead author was Rebecca Horne of the University of Alberta in Canada; "Working women 'still do housework,'" *Daily Mail*, March 3, 2018.

6. Hamilton, whose commentary I obviously hold in high esteem, has a different read: "Far from being a reign of co-equals over the remainder of God's creation, the relationship now becomes a fierce dispute, with each party trying to rule the other. The two who once reigned as one attempt to rule each other."

Chapter 4

1. Personal correspondence from Leeor Gottlieb.

2. See Dennis Prager and Joseph Telushkin, *Why the Jews: The Reason for Antisemitism, the Most Accurate Predictor of Human Evil*, Simon & Schuster, 2003. The same has held true for attitudes toward America. Those who have hated America and resented its achievements have generally failed to produce decent and affluent societies. On the other hand, those who have not resented, but adopted, American values such as liberty, free markets, and limited government have vastly improved their societies.

3. For further exploration of this topic, see the chapter "Fun vs. Happiness" in Dennis Prager, *Happiness Is a Serious Problem*, HarperCollins, 1998, William Morrow paperback, 1999.

4. Talmud Mishnah *Sanhedrin* 4:5.

5. Alan Dershowitz, *Taking the Stand: My Life in the Law*, p. 426.

6. I thank Joel Alperson for this insight.

7. Brian Resnick, "The scientific mystery of why humans love music," *Vox*, February 4, 2016. https://www.vox.com/science-and-health/2016/2/4/10915492/why-do-we-like-music.

8. Nicholas Wade, "We Got Rhythm; the Mystery Is How and Why," *New York Times*, September 16, 2003. https://www.nytimes.com/2003/09/16/science/we-got-rhythm-the-mystery-is-how-and-why.html.

Chapter 5

1. Jerusalem Talmud, *Nedarim* 9:4.
2. Talmud Mishnah *Sanhedrin* 4:5.
3. Hugh Ross, *Why the Universe Is the Way It Is*, Baker Publishing, 2008.

Chapter 6

1. Genesis Rabbah 9:7.
2. Talmud Mishna Ethics of the Fathers 3:15.
3. Talmud Bava Mezia 84a; Gittin 47a.
4. Talmud Sanhedrin 108a.
5. I thank Joel Alperson for this insight.
6. Bruce K. Waltke, *Genesis: A Commentary*, Zondervan, 2016.
7. Robert Proctor, *The Nazi War on Cancer*, Princeton University Press, 1997.

Chapter 8

1. The debate may be viewed at https://www.prageru.com/videos/dennis-prager-uc-berkeley. My question about man being basically good is near the end.
2. The Carter Center, "Equitable Globalization?" March 1, 2005.
3. The U.S. Department of State, cited in *The Weekly Standard*, January 15, 2014.
4. James Q. Wilson, *The Moral Sense*, Free Press, 1993.

Chapter 9

1. Joseph Albo, *Sefer Ha-Ikkarim*, volume 3, chapter 15.
2. Jacob Milgrom, "The Biblical Diet Laws as an Ethical System, *Interpretation*, July 1963.
3. I wrote the word "premeditated" because the Torah states the death penalty for homicide is to be invoked only in the case of premeditated murder—see, for example, Exodus 21:13.
4. Talmud Mishna *Makkot* 1:10.
5. Talmud Mishna *Makkot* 1:10.

Chapter 10

1. "In addition to the intentional sum of 'seventy,' the narrator shows a preference for "seven" and its multiples. Japheth has seven sons and seven grandsons. Ham has seven descendants of Cush (10: 6–7 and seven of Mizraim (excluding the Philistines) (10: 13). Counting Cainan (see below), fourteen distinct names are given in the lineage from Shem to Eber. The last of the elect ancestors before the line of Shem is divided between Eber's sons, Peleg and Joktan. This number is contrived by throwing in the name of Japheth (10:21– 24). The number of Shem's named sons to Eber's two sons is also fourteen, again counting Cainan. The narrator gives fourteen names in the 'cul-de-sac' line of Shem, Joktan, and Jobab (10:26– 29). 'Sons of' [b'nei] occurs fourteen times, seven times in 10: 1–7, before Nimrod, and seven times in 10:20–32 (i.e., after the Hamitic lineage). Cassuto also notes, "if we add to these the other terms that are characteristic of a genealogy…and the forms of the verb *y lad* ['to bear'] we obtain twenty-eight—four times seven." By contrast, there are uniquely no sevens in the structuring of the Canaanite genealogy. The representation of the Canaanites in the Table of Nations stands apart by its asymmetry to match their chaos"; Bruce K. Waltke, *Genesis: A Commentary*, Zondervan, 2001.

2. Robert Alter, *Genesis: Translation and Commentary*, W. W. Norton & Company, 1996.

Chapter 11

1. In 1987, a photograph by the American artist and photographer Andres Serrano showing a crucifix submerged in a jar of the artist's urine (titled Piss Christ) was an award-winning work of "art" shown in museums and galleries throughout America. In 2011, a German sculpture depicting a lifelike policewoman squatting and urinating—even the puddle is sculpted—received an award from a prestigious German foundation, the Leinemann Foundation for Fine Art. In 2013, the Orange County Museum of Art in California placed a huge twenty-eight-foot sculpture of a dog outside the museum, where it periodically "urinates" a yellow fluid onto a museum wall. In 2016, one of the most prestigious art museums in the world, the Guggenheim in New York, featured a pure gold, working toilet bowl that visitors to the museum were invited to use. The name of the exhibit was "America"—so one could literally relieve oneself on America. In 2018, the Museum Boijmans van Beuningen in Rotterdam, the Netherlands, featured an exhibit of "giant turds." This "artwork" was seriously covered by the *New York Times* in an article titled, "In This Exhibition, You Walk Through Excrement." An excerpt: "There were

four giant turds inside the 16,000 square feet of museum space. One mammoth piece of feces was reminiscent of a long, winding steel sculpture by Richard Serra. One was a brown spiral. Another resembled an enormous chocolate chip. Yet another featured intertwined layers with a gap in between that I could have crawled through, if I had been brave enough. All four sculptures of fecal matter sat on elegant Persian rugs, like welcome-home gifts left by a huge, vengeful dog" (*New York Times*, June 7, 2018).

2. P.D. Miller, "Eridu, Dunnu and Babel: A Study in Comparative Mythology," *Hebrew Annual Review* 9 [1985].

3. https://www.afpnet.org/files/ContentDocuments/Charitable%2520Giving%2520by%2520Type%2520of%2520Community%2520-%2520Comparing%2520Donation%2520Patterns%2520of%2520Rural%2520and%2520Urban%2520Donors.pdf.

4. The American Founder, Thomas Jefferson, shared the Torah's suspicion of cities. "Jefferson," Rutgers University Professor Leonardo Vazquez wrote, "was of one mind about cities: he hated them.... Though Jefferson partied in Paris and had a hand in shaping Washington D.C., he thought cities were dens of corruption and inequity that would spoil the young American republic."

Chapter 12

1. "The famous painting in the tomb of Khnum-hotep III at Beni Hasan, about 150 miles north of Cairo, from the time of Sesostris II (1897–1878 B.C.), shows the arrival of thirty-seven Asiatics, men, women, and children, in Egypt" (Hamilton).

2. The Rackman essay is contained in Milton Himmelfarb, ed., *The Condition of Jewish Belief*, Macmillan 1966.

Chapter 15

1. See the discussion concerning Western intellectuals in Exodus.

2. K. A. Kitchen, *Ancient Orient and Old Testament*, Tyndale Press, 1966.

3. W. F. Albright, "Abram the Hebrew: A New Archaeological Interpretation," *Bulletin of the American Schools of Oriental Research* 163 (1961). Cited by Hamilton.

Chapter 17

1. In the words written to me from Dr. Jeremiah Unterman, formerly Adjunct Professor of Bible at Yeshiva University, and author of numerous books and articles on the Bible:

   "No one knows for sure what the original meaning of that appellation [Shaddai] for God is. There are a few candidates:

   "A. It relates to *sadeh*—that is, "field"—perhaps uncultivated fields, i.e., wilderness.

   "B. It relates to Akkadian *shadu*—"mountain," i.e. a reference to "holy or divine mountain."

   "C. It relates to *shaddad*—"destroy," compare Isaiah 13:6 and Joel 1:15! The word might originally have referred to strength; the Arabic *shaddid* means "strong." That, in turn, may have resulted in the common translation in the Septuagint (which influenced the English)—"God Almighty."

   "D. It relates to *shadayim* [Hebrew for "breasts"] which represents fertility, i.e., the God of Fertility (with a decidedly female nuance/metaphor).

   "E. There's an opinion that the word has a northern origin because there's a tel in Syria that means, "the city of two breasts"—presumably a reference to two hills.

   "F. There's a rabbinic midrash that divides the word into *sheh-dai*, i.e., "it is enough/sufficient." That is, "God (El) is the Sufficient One." That translation "the Sufficient One" appears in the Septuagint to Ruth 1:20, 21."

2. As there were approximately four and a half million Jews right before the destruction of the Second Temple in the year 70, without expulsion from their land and persecution, Jews would number in the hundreds of millions today, not a mere thirteen million. The leading Jewish historian of the twentieth century, Salo Baron, professor of history at Columbia University from 1930 to 1963, estimated ten percent of the Roman Empire were Jews. (See also "Study Traces Worldwide Jewish Population From Exodus to Modern Age," *Haaretz*, April 29, 2005.)

3. Michael Milgraum, "Trauma, Anger and Confronting God," February 25, 2012, http://www.aish.com/sp/ph/Trauma_Anger_and_Confronting_God.html.

4. *Pediatrics*, August, 2012.

5. Nicholas Bakalar, "Circumcision May Not Reduce Sensitivity of Penis," *New York Times*, April 19, 2016.

6. Kisumu, Kenya, Krieger JN, Mehta SD, Bailey RC, Agot K, Ndinya-Achola JO, Parker C, Moses S, "Adult male circumcision: Effects on sexual function and sexual satisfaction," *Journal of Sexual Medicine*, November 2008.

7. Midrash *Tanhuma B, Lekh Lekha* 40.

Chapter 18

1. Talmud *Bava Mezia* 87a.
2. Ernest van den Haag, *The Jewish Mystique*, Stein & Day, 1977.
3. Edward M. Flannery, "The Greatest Hatred in Human History," *New York Times*, November 30, 1974.
4. Sir William Blackstone, *Commentaries on the Laws of England*, Clarendon Press Oxford, 1765.

Chapter 19

1. Jung Chang, *Wild Swans: Three Daughters of China*, Simon & Schuster, 1991.
2. Every word or group of words in the Torah has a corresponding musical notation known as "trope." This indicates how the word should be chanted when the Torah is publicly read. As the trope is ancient, it can be a great help in understanding the intent of various words in the Torah. The notation for the Hebrew word for "delayed" (*vayitma'ma*) here is the longest musical note (*shalshelet*) in the entire trope and is rarely used. Its repeated tone suggests how many times Lot dawdled before leaving Sodom. (For another example and a fuller explanation of *shalshelet*, see the commentary on Genesis 39:8.)
3. Christine Hayes, *Introduction to the Bible*, Yale University Press, 2012.

Chapter 20

1. Voltaire, *God and Human Beings*, 1769.
2. Cited in David Dalin ed., *American Jews and the Separationist Faith*, Ethics & Public Policy Center, 1993.

Chapter 22

1. The binding of Isaac for sacrifice (the *akedah*) comes right after the story of the banishment of Hagar and Ishmael to show that now Sarah, like Hagar, will learn what it is like to almost lose a child. In keeping with the pattern of "that which goes around comes around" that pervades Genesis, Abraham nearly caused the death of the child of Sarah just as Sarah nearly caused the death of Hagar's child (Genesis 21:9-16). It is true

God had instructed Abraham to listen to Sarah about what to do with Hagar—because God knew things would turn out well for Hagar and Ishmael. But that still does not entirely absolve Sarah of her ill treatment of Hagar and Ishmael. Unlike God, she did not know things would turn out well.

2. See, for example, Owen Jarus, "25 Cultures That Practiced Human Sacrifice," *Live Science*, June 16, 2017.

3. "The priest quickly sliced into the captive's torso and removed his still-beating heart. That sacrifice, one among thousands performed in the sacred city of Tenochtitlan [a city-state in what is now the center of Mexico City], would feed the gods and ensure the continued existence of the world. Death, however, was just the start of the victim's role in the sacrificial ritual, key to the spiritual world of the Mexican people in the 14th to the 16th centuries. Priests carried the body to another ritual space, where they laid it face-up. Armed with years of practice, detailed anatomical knowledge, and obsidian blades sharper than today's surgical steel, they made an incision in the thin space between two vertebrae in the neck, expertly decapitating the body. Using their sharp blades, the priests deftly cut away the skin and muscles of the face, reducing it to a skull. . . . For the Aztecs—the larger cultural group to which the Mexicans belonged—those skulls were the seeds that would ensure the continued existence of humanity." (Lizzie Wade, "Feeding the gods: Hundreds of skulls reveal massive scale of human sacrifice in Aztec capital," *Science Magazine*, June 21, 2018.)

4. Charles Q. Choi, "Ancient Human Sacrifice Victims Faced Slavery Before Death, *Live Science*, June 16, 2017. Choi is a science writer for *Scientific American*, the *New York Times*, *Science*, and elsewhere.

5. Fredrick Ngugi, "Why the Horrible Tradition of Human Sacrifice in Africa Needs To Stop," *Face2Face Africa*, January 13, 2017. Kiran Moodley, "Human sacrifice in Uganda: 'They target children; they catch them when they walk to school or go to fetch water,'" *Independent*, June 15, 2015. Saralyn Salisbury, "The Practice of Ritual Killings and Human Sacrifice in Africa," *Human Rights Brief*, September 6, 2012.

6. G. Coats, "Abraham's Sacrifice of Faith: A Form-Critical Study of Genesis 22," Int 27 (1973) 397.

Chapter 23

1. In Hebrew, the word translated here as "to bewail," literally means "to cry over." This verse has strongly influenced Jewish life. Based on it, one goal of the eulogy delivered at a Jewish funeral, in addition to enumerating the good traits of the deceased, is to move the listeners to tears.

Chapter 24

1. The link is through the Latin word *testis* ("witness").

Chapter 26

1. Rathenau to Hans Breisig, 1919; cited in Joseph Baron, ed., *A Treasury of Jewish Quotations*, Jason Aronson, 1977.
2. John O. Koehler, *Stasi: The Untold Story of the East German Secret Police*, Westview Press, 2000.
3. George Gilder, *The Israel Test*, Richard Vigilante Books, 2009. See the Gilder video, "The Israel Test," at www.prageru.com.

Chapter 28

1. The Hebrew word for "you shall spread out" (*ufaratzta*) was turned by Rabbi Menachem Mendel Schneerson, the Lubavitcher Rebbe, into a theme song for the movement known as Chabad, which has as its purpose proselytization of Judaism to fellow Jews. The movement has lived this verse, "You shall spread out to the west and to the east, to the north and to the south." There are now "Chabad Houses" in all fifty American states and in over one hundred countries around the globe.
2. Ethics of the Fathers 4:2.
3. There is a Jewish exception to the rule of not making deals with God. To encourage people to give charity, Jewish law permits making conditional vows such as "I will donate [state the amount] to charity if such-and-such happens." Rabbi Moses Isserles (sixteenth century), the Ramah, explains: "If a person says, 'If so-and-so, who is deathly ill, will be cured…I will donate [a specified amount] to charity,' but then the sick person dies, the person is not obliged to fulfill his vow because it was clearly conditional" (Shulchan Arukh, Yoreh Deah 220:15). Otherwise, Jewish law prohibits setting conditions for one's observance. Thus, for example, it is forbidden to say, "I'll observe the Sabbath if I become rich," since Jews are obliged to observe the Sabbath whether they are poor or rich. That Jewish law allows conditional vows concerning charity underscores how eager the rabbis were to encourage charitable giving.

Chapter 29

1. See J. A. Diamond, "The deception of Jacob: a new perspective on an ancient solution to the problem," *Vetus Testamentum* (1984) 211–13; and C. Carmichael, *Women, Law and the Genesis Traditions*, University of Edinburgh, 1979, p. 99 n. 22. These sources are cited by Hamilton.
2. Richard Crossman, ed., *The God That Failed*, Scribner, 1941.

Chapter 30

1. Jayaram V., "Children in Hinduism," http://www.hinduwebsite.com/hinduism/h_children.asp.
2. Talmud Nedarim 64b.
3. For a thoughtful discussion of the childless issue within Judaism and Jewish life, see Elliot Jager, *The Pater: My Father, My Judaism, My Childlessness*, Toby Press, 2015.
4. The name of Israel's Holocaust Museum, Yad Vashem, is taken from this verse in Isaiah.
5. Nehama Leibowitz, *New Studies in Genesis*, World Zionist Organization, 1981.
6. Jon Meacham, *American Lion: Andrew Jackson in the White House*, Random House, 2008.
7. For another example of the use of *shachav*, see Genesis 35:22, which, literally translated, describes Reuben's "laying Bilhah," his father's concubine—and contrast it with the language of Genesis 2:24, which lyrically depicts lovemaking.

Chapter 31

1. The summary is taken from the *New York Times*, October 24, 2016.

Chapter 32

1. In Milton Himmelfarb, ed., *The Condition of Jewish Belief*, Macmillan, 1966.

Chapter 33

1. Jon Levenson in *The Jewish Study Bible*, Oxford University Press, 2003.

Chapter 34

1. Alter notes "'lay with' is more brutal in the Hebrew" than in the English because it is not followed by the preposition 'with' (as, for example, in Rachel's words to Leah in 30:15, [Jacob] shall lie with you tonight"), but by a direct object. So, the text literally reads "he laid her...."

2. Talmud *Kiddushin* 41a.

3. Avraham ibn Shushan, *Ha-Millon Ha-Chadash (Hebrew), volume 2*, 865.

Chapter 36

1. See Rashi's commentary in Talmud *Sanhedrin* 99b.

Chapter 37

1. Talmud *Shabbat* 10b.

2. Talmud *Brachot* 55a.

Chapter 38

1. The Rabbis of the Talmud (*Pesachim* 50a) found Judah's marrying a Canaanite particularly problematic since he is so important an ancestor of the Jewish people. They therefore translated "Canaanite" as "merchant," which is the way the word is used in Isaiah 23:8. They may be right. But the Torah always means "Canaanite" when it uses the term, and that is what the Torah most likely means here.

2. In the Talmud *Niddah* 13a, Rabbi Yochanan states, "Whoever discharges semen for naught [masturbates] is liable to death [at the hands of Heaven], for it is stated [in the Torah in Genesis 38:10]: 'What he did was displeasing to the Lord, and He took his life also.'" And the classic 19th century code of Jewish law, *Kitzur Shulchan Aruch* (by Rabbi Shlomo Ganzfried), ruled that "It is forbidden to discharge semen in vain. This sin is more severe than any of the other prohibitions in the Torah."

   The Catholic Church's catechism states: "Both the Magisterium of the Church, in the course of a constant tradition, and the moral sense of the faithful have been in no doubt and have firmly maintained that masturbation is an intrinsically and gravely disordered action."

Within Protestant Christianity there are varied views. I will cite two contemporary evangelical Christian theologians.

Jason DeRocuhie, a professor of Old Testament and Biblical Theology at the Bethlehem College and Seminary (Minneapolis, Minnesota): "God purposed that all righteous forms of sexual expression be for the marriage bed. Masturbation removes sexual expression from its only God-intended context" (*If Your Right Hand Causes You to Sin: Ten Biblical Reflections on Masturbation*, desiringGod website).

Dr. James Dobson, a child psychologist and Christian theologian with a large following among American evangelicals: "The Bible says nothing about masturbation, so we don't really know what God thinks about it. My opinion is that He doesn't make a big issue of it" (*Preparing for Adolescence*, Regal, 1989).

3. Edward Lipinski, "Cult Prostitution in Ancient Israel?" *Biblical Archaeology Review*, January/February 2014, https://members.bib-arch.org/biblical-archaeology-review/40/1/10.

Chapter 39

1. "Zionism versus Bolshevism," *Illustrated Sunday Herald*, February 8, 1920. Cited in Andrew Roberts, *Churchill: Walking with Destiny*, Penguin Random House, 2018. In the same article, Churchill also noted (as I have in this commentary), the malevolent role a number of Jews were then playing (through leadership and support of Bolshevism):

    "And it may well be that this same astounding race may at the present time be in the actual process of producing another system of morals and philosophy, as malevolent as Christianity was benevolent, which, if not arrested, would shatter irretrievably all that Christianity has rendered possible. It would almost seem as if the gospel of Christ and the gospel of Antichrist [anti-West, anti-Christian, anti-Jewish Bolshevism] were destined to originate among the same people; and that this mystic and mysterious race had been chosen for the supreme manifestations, both of the divine and the diabolical."

    As I write in the commentary to Genesis 26:4: "Jews have disproportionately founded, led, or been involved in utopian causes such as Marxism and socialism. They have been influenced, often not consciously, by the Bible and Judaism's universal mission. However, nearly all of these Jews dropped commitment to God and Torah and often wound up doing more harm than good for both humanity and the Jews. *Jewish idealism without*

God, Torah, and Israel (the three components of Judaism) has often been destructive, sometimes murderously so." (Italics added.)

Chapter 40

1. "The first grinding stone, called a quern, was invented in Egypt, and the first grain was crushed" (encyclopedia.com).
2. See, for example, Talmud *Brachot* 55b.

Chapter 41

1. Josephus, *Antiquities* II, 6.1.
2. The British Psychological Society summarized its findings concerning Recovered Memory (*The Psychologist*, June 2006) this way:
"We believe:
– that what appear to be newly remembered (i.e. recovered) memories of past trauma are sometimes accurate, sometimes inaccurate, and sometimes a mixture of accuracy and inaccuracy;
– that much of what is recalled cannot be confirmed or disconfirmed;
– that, because of these two beliefs, reports of past trauma based on such recovered memories are not reliable enough to be the sole basis for legal decisions."
3. I owe this insight to Sean McConnell, the engineer of my radio show.

Chapter 42

1. Maimonides, *Mishneh Torah,* "Laws of Repentance" 2:1.

Chapter 43

1. W. Lee Humphreys, *Joseph and His Family: A Literary Study*, University of South Carolina Press, 1988. Cited by Hamilton.

Chapter 44

1. W. W. Hallo and W. K. Simpson, *The Ancient Near East: A History*, Harcourt, Brace, Jovanovich, 1971. Cited by Hamilton.
2. Talmud *Brachot* 34b.

Chapter 45

1. That is, at least, the common paraphrase. The precise quote from Mark Twain (from *Following the Equator: A Journey Around the World*, Chapter XV) is "Truth is stranger than fiction, but it is because Fiction is obliged to stick to possibilities; Truth isn't."
2. Dale DeBakcsy, "Do we have free will? The atheist case for determinism," *New Humanist*, June 23, 2015.
3. Pharaoh's invitation to Jacob and his family in verses 16-20 to move to Goshen duplicates (with some variations) Joseph's invitation in verses 9-15 to his family to move to Goshen. Because of the variations, scholars using the Documentary Hypothesis ("Source Criticism") to attribute Joseph's invitation to Source "E" and Pharaoh's invitation to Source "J." But Robert Alter, a secular biblical scholar, writes: "The obtuseness of conventional source criticism [The Documentary Hypothesis] is nowhere better illustrated than in its attributing to a duplication of sources this brilliantly effective repetition so obviously justified by the dramatic and psychological situation." Robert Alter, *Art of Biblical Narrative*, Basic Books, 1981.

Chapter 46

1. Roy F. Baumeister, Brad J. Bushman, and W. Keith Campbell, "Self-Esteem, Narcissism, and Aggression: Does Violence Result from Low Self-Esteem or From Threatened Egoism?" *Current Directions in Psychological Science*, Journal of the Association for Psychological Science, Volume 9, Number 1, February 2000.
2. "Belief in Hell Predicts a Country's Crime Rates More Accurately Than Other Social or Economic Factors," *Medical Daily*, June 19, 2012.
3. "Different views of God may influence academic cheating," University of Oregon, Media Relations, April 20, 2011.

4.   Exodus 24:1 and 9; Numbers 11:16, 24, and 25; Judges 1:7, 8:30, and 9:2; 1 Samuel 6:9; and 2 Kings 10:6.

Chapter 49

1.   Talmud *Eruvin* 65b.

Chapter 50

1.   Quote taken from E. I. Lowenthal, *The Joseph Narrative in Genesis*, Ktav, 1973.
2.   This is the position of the Talmud Yevamot 65b.
3.   Victor Hamilton: "If one examines the life span of the three patriarchs in Gen. 12–50, the years of the patriarchs are formed as square numbers that constitute a succession. Thus the following pattern emerges:

> Abraham: $175 = 7 \times 5^2$
> Isaac: $180 = 5 \times 6^2$
> Jacob: $147 = 3 \times 7^2$

"Gevirtz has carried this observation one step further by noting that Joseph's 110 years are the sum of these consecutive square numbers ($110 = 5^2 + 6^2 + 7^2$). He also notes that the first man in Genesis, Adam, has a life span of 930 years ($= 30^2 + 30$), and the last man in Genesis, Joseph, has a life span of 110 years ($= 10^2 + 10$).

"This numerical pattern may be extended as follows:

> Abraham: $175 = 7 \times 5^2$
> Isaac: $180 = 5 \times 6^2$
> Jacob: $147 = 3 \times 7^2$
> Joseph: $110 = 1 \times 5^2 + 6^2 + 7^2$.

"That is, Joseph is the successor in the pattern 7–5–3–1, and the sum of his predecessors ($5^2 + 6^2 + 7^2$). In this way, Joseph is linked intimately with his family line. He is certainly no marginal figure, and he comes close to being considered a fourth patriarch. That Joseph's life span of 110 years reflects the ideal length of life by Egyptian standards is not an attempt by the author to give the Joseph story an Egyptian flavor. Rather, it appears that the narrator is suggesting that Joseph symbolically brings to a conclusion the patriarchal narratives. "It is hardly likely that the above data may be explained as simple coincidence...."